D0082996

A Logical Approach
to Expert Systems
and Natural Language
Processing

Knowledge Systems and Prolog

A Logical Approach
to Expert Systems
and Natural Language
Processing

Knowledge Systems and Prolog

Adrian Walker (Editor)
Michael McCord
John F. Sowa
Walter G. Wilson

IBM T. J. Watson Research Center

ADDISON-WESLEY PUBLISHING COMPANY, INC.
Reading, Massachusetts • Menlo Park, California • Don Mills, Ontario
Wokingham, England • Amsterdam • Sydney • Singapore • Tokyo
Madrid • Bogotá • Santiago • San Juan

Library of Congress Cataloging-in-Publication Data

Knowledge systems and prolog.

   Bibliography: p.
   Includes index.
   1. Expert systems (Computer science)   2. Prolog
(Computer program language)   I. Walker, Adrian.
QA76.76.E95K58   1987   006.3'3   86-22126
ISBN 0-201-09044-9

Reprinted with corrections March 1987.

Reproduced by Addison-Wesley from camera-ready copy supplied by the authors.

ISBN 0-201-09044-9
   CDEFGHIJ-MA-8987

Preface

This book is about knowledge systems. It is about how to design them, how to use them, and how to program them in a language called Prolog. A knowledge system is a computer program that solves, or helps to solve, problems that would otherwise have to be handled by a human expert alone. A knowledge system may be

- an expert system,
- a program that understands English (or another natural language),
- or a combination of the two.

In addition it may make good use of a database management system to store parts of its knowledge.

Knowledge systems are used to give advice and to solve problems in many areas, such as business, science, technology, and law. The knowledge systems described in this book have been developed at IBM, and have been used for experiments in several subjects, including manufacturing planning, communication network management, evaluation of the ease of use of software packages, and machine translation from one natural language to another.

Prolog is a programming language based on logical reasoning. As such, it draws strength from the principles of mathematical logic—principles that were developed well before the invention of the computer. Each of us can reason, using knowledge in order to produce advice on several subjects, and each of us can communicate in English or another natural language. Prolog is a very useful programming language in which to write down our methods of reasoning and of using English, so that they can be used by a computer. Prolog forms the basis for a major national research effort in Japan, and it is increasingly used worldwide as a very high level programming language, for work in artificial intelligence in general, and for knowledge systems in particular. The Prolog programming

techniques in this book are drawn from existing knowledge systems, from classes
the authors have taught at IBM over a number of years, and from experience
with several programming projects including large system performance analysis,
analysis of assembler programs, and Programmable Logic Array simulation.
The programming examples are in IBM Prolog, which has built-in links to other
software, such as relational database management systems. It is available as
VM/Prolog (for the VM operating system) and as MVS/Prolog (for the MVS
operating system). This version of Prolog was developed at the Paris Scientific
Center of IBM.

The book has several levels of information. It contains

- an introduction to knowledge systems,

- sections about how to set up and use knowledge systems,

- introductory and advanced sections about how to program in Prolog, and

- some summaries of advanced research.

This is an unusual span of topics and levels in one book. It is made possible, and
we think useful, by a unifying theme—the ability of people and of computer
programs to reason with everyday logic. Prolog is based on logic, and it provides
a clear, almost common sense view of the subject.

In keeping with the span of topics and levels, this book can be read in several
ways, with several purposes in mind.

- Because the book is partly about codifying the kinds of knowledge that all of
  us have, it should be of interest to readers who would like to get a feel for
  how their own areas of expertise could be represented in a knowledge system.

- Because the book also goes into depth in how to program in Prolog, it can be
  read as a university text in Prolog programming, with applications to
  knowledge systems and with pointers for research. In a practical course, it
  can be used directly with IBM Prolog. For a course that emphasizes
  principles, there is material on the logical basis for the semantics of Prolog
  programs. Because the book describes many interesting aspects of expert
  systems and natural language processing, it can be useful in university
  courses on artificial intelligence, and in courses for Linguists and
  Psychologists who are interested in computational experiments in their
  fields.

- For readers who already know one or more programming languages, this
  book can be used as an introduction to Prolog that will take them rapidly
  beyond the introductory level, and that provides interesting examples of
  knowledge systems. For those who are already Prolog programmers, the
  book describes IBM Prolog—its syntax, and its rich set of built-in predicates
  for direct support of many common programming practices.

Four different chapter sequences are suggested.

- For readers who are interested mainly in the possible uses of *expert systems*, the suggested sequence is

  - Chapter 1,
  - then Sections 4.2.1, 4.2.2, 4.2.4, 4.3.1,
  - with more detail drawn from Chapters 2 and 3, plus the remainder of Chapter 4 as needed.
  - The only prerequisite for this sequence is a liking for computing and for reasoning logically.

- For readers who are interested mainly in *natural language processing* the suggested sequence is

  - Chapters 1, 2 and 5,
  - with additional material drawn from Chapter 3 as needed.
  - Again, the only prerequisite for this sequence is a liking for computing and for reasoning logically.

- For readers who are interested first in *programming in Prolog*, and second in the uses of expert systems or in natural language processing, the suggested sequence is

  - Chapters 1 and 2,
  - Chapter 3 as far as page 166,
  - Appendix A on how to use IBM Prolog,
  - the rest of Chapter 3, then Chapters 4 and 5.
  - For this sequence, some background in logic, or in programming, or in discrete mathematics will be a help, although the book is self-contained. It will also be useful to have available a computer with IBM Prolog installed.

- For readers who are interested first in the *logical fundamentals* of our approach to knowledge systems and Prolog, the suggested sequence is

  - Chapters 1 and 2,
  - Appendix B on the logical basis for Prolog and Syllog,
  - then Chapters 3, 4, and 5.
  - For this sequence, some background in logic, or in discrete mathematics will be a help, although again the book is self-contained.

There are exercises at the ends of Chapters 2, 3, 4 and 5. The exercises are discussed—and complete solutions are given for some of them—in the text.

Chapter 1, *Knowledge Systems: Principles and Practice*, discusses the importance of knowledge systems. It gives a view of what a knowledge system is and what it should be able to do. We look at the evolution of knowledge systems and their supporting software technology, and we describe the role of logic and of the Prolog language in this evolution. Examples are given to show that logic provides a good common notation for knowledge representation, and we describe some of the trends that will make it easier to transfer knowledge.

Chapter 2, *A Prolog to Prolog*, describes Prolog as a programming language based on symbolic logic. It shows how to write simple Prolog programs and run them on a terminal, and gives many examples of Prolog programs. We look at the declarative and procedural styles and interpretations of Prolog programs. We introduce Prolog data structures and Prolog's all-important generalized pattern match mechanism, which is called *unification*.

Chapter 3, *Programming Techniques in Prolog*, describes some more advanced programming methods. We show the importance of declarative style in writing Prolog programs. We look at this style of writing in Prolog as a distillation of good software engineering practices. We describe some advanced data structures and the relation of data structures to the control and use of recursion. Meta-level programming in Prolog is introduced, and we describe some techniques for supporting large knowledge bases.

Chapter 4, *Expert Systems in Prolog,* looks at some specific expert systems; how they are used, how they acquire and assimilate knowledge, and how their underlying inference mechanisms are programmed. We look at ways of using Prolog to reason with diverse representations of knowledge. We describe exact and judgmental reasoning for expert systems, the importance of explanations, and methods of producing helpful explanations.

Chapter 5, *Natural Language Processing in Prolog,* looks at the techniques that can be used to support English dialogue with a knowledge system. We look at the process of translating an English sentence into a special Logical Form Language, so that we can reason directly about the meaning of the sentence. The translation process uses a dictionary, a grammar of English, and a way of transforming the structure of a sentence into a logical form. A technique for representing large lexicons is described. A grammar is used to show the process of extracting an underlying structure from an English sentence. Then we show how to find meaning in the structure by translating it into a logical form.

Chapter 6 contains our *Conclusions*—the book discusses significant aspects of artificial intelligence, logic, and programming. The methods used in the book are based on computational logic, which acts as a bridge between the empirical aspects of knowledge systems and the formal foundations of reasoning in logic. Logic programming, in the form of Prolog, makes it possible to cover an unusually wide range of topics, and to do so in the practical sense that we show how to program much of what we discuss.

There are two appendices. Appendix A, *How to Use IBM Prolog* describes the use of Prolog at a terminal, including techniques for metainterpretation, for holding different programs in one Prolog workspace, and for input and output using files. Appendix B, *Logical Basis for Prolog and Syllog*, outlines a basis in mathematical logic for the meaning of Prolog programs, including a special treatment of negation in Prolog.

It is a pleasure to acknowledge that many conversations with colleagues have helped to shape the material in this book. We would like to thank Andre Algrain, Arendse Bernth, Joan Dunkin, Se June Hong, Ann Gruhn, Doug Lorch, Peter Marusek, Alexa McCray, Gustaf Neumann, Fernando Pereira, J. Alan Robinson, Bill Santos, Ehud Shapiro, Oded Shmueli, Doug Teeple, Daphne Tzoar, Maarten van Emden, Jean Voldman, Barbara Walker, and Wlodzimierz Zadrozny. We would particularly like to thank Professors Jacques Cohen (Brandeis University), Edward L. Fisher (North Carolina State University), Frank Kriwaczek (Imperial College, London) and Michael Lebowitz (Columbia University) for their incisive reviews of an early version of this book. Special thanks go to John Prager for meticulous reading of a final draft, and to Reed Hyde for material on MVS/Prolog. Chapter 1 and Section 4.2.2 are based on material that has appeared in the IBM Journal of Research and Development and we would like to thank the journal for permission to use that material here. We are most grateful to IBM for the support we have received for our research in knowledge systems and Prolog, and for the resources that IBM has kindly provided for the preparation of this book. Finally, we thank the people at Addison-Wesley for being so well organized and for their good advice.

Michael McCord, Adrian Walker, Walter G. Wilson
IBM T. J. Watson Research Center

John F. Sowa
IBM Systems Research Institute

Yorktown Heights, N.Y.

Contents

Chapter 5.
Natural Language Processing in Prolog   291

1
Knowledge Systems: Principles and Practice

Adrian Walker

"The object of reasoning is to find out, from the consideration of what we already know, something else which we do not know."

Charles Sanders Peirce, *Fixation of Belief*.

As noted in the Preface, a knowledge system is an expert system, or a program that understands a natural language such as English; it may also be some combination of the two, and it may make good use of a database management system.

The rate of publication of papers about knowledge systems is now higher than ever before. There are survey articles in computer science journals, in popular computing and scientific journals, and in the general press. The volume of research publication is also unusually high. Expert systems have so far proved their worth in structure elucidation in chemistry, in helping to find mineral deposits, in helping technicians in hospitals, in suggesting maintenance procedures for locomotives, and in many specialties for which we do not have enough human experts. The commercial potential of the subject is being recognized.

In a period of such intensive activity, it can be healthy to step back from the day to day excitement of new uses of knowledge systems, new research results, product announcements, and the formation of new companies in the area of knowledge systems. This chapter describes some of the interplay between principles and practice in knowledge systems; we argue that it is very fruitful to combine principles and practice closely, and that logic programming (in particular Prolog) is a strong candidate for bridging the traditional gap between the two. We set out a particular view of where work on expert systems and natural language processing has come from, what is being done now, and of some trends for the future. Because of the scope of the subject, our view necessarily focuses on just some of the trends and achievements.

What is a knowledge system, an expert system, a natural language understanding program? The name expert system has been applied to many diverse programs. So in the next section we describe the properties that we think such a system should have. Section 1.2 sketches some central issues in expert systems from a historical point of view. In Section 1.3 we outline the role of Prolog and logic programming in expert systems. In Section 1.4 we note that an expert system is only as good as the knowledge it contains, and we describe some methods of knowledge representation. Section 1.5 outlines some of the methods used in getting a computer to understand a natural language such as English. Then in Section 1.6 we describe some trends in knowledge acquisition. Section 1.7 is a summary.

1.1 WHAT IS A KNOWLEDGE SYSTEM?

Every program contains knowledge about some problem. A payroll program, for example, has knowledge about pay rates, deductions, and tax schedules. It also includes "common sense" knowledge about business practices and the number of hours in a week or days in a month. What makes knowledge systems different from conventional programs is that they represent the knowledge in a higher-level form. Instead of encoding knowledge in low-level statements, they store it in a *knowledge base* of rules and facts that stay close to the way people think about a problem. This book presents the two major kinds of knowledge systems:

- Expert systems: problem-solving systems that reach expert or at least highly competent levels of performance.
- Natural language systems: systems that converse with people in their native languages at a level that approaches the generality and flexibility of ordinary discourse.

Besides introducing these subjects, the book goes on to present detailed methods for designing and implementing such systems in Prolog, and for using them when they are completed.

What distinguishes an expert system from a conventional program is not just its expertise, but the way that the expertise is stored and processed. A payroll program, for example, certainly has more expertise about tax rates and deductions than most people, but it applies the expertise in a rigid, inflexible way. Furthermore, it cannot explain its knowledge or answer questions about its use: an employee who believes that the wrong tax rate was applied cannot ask the payroll program why it made a certain deduction. An expert system behaves more like an intelligent assistant. It can apply its knowledge in flexible ways to novel kinds of problems. Whenever it reaches a conclusion, the user can ask how that conclusion was reached and what rules were used to deduce it.

Since knowledge about any subject is constantly growing and changing, an expert system should be flexible in integrating new knowledge incrementally into the knowledge base. Indeed, the expert system should help the designer to translate knowledge into rules and facts. We would also like it to display its knowledge in a form that is easy for us to read. If we are to take actions that can have serious consequences in the real world, based on advice given by an expert system, then we would like the system to provide explanations of its advice (Michie 1982). Because the expert knowledge that people have is often incomplete and only partly understood, we would like an expert system to be able to reason with judgmental or inexact knowledge. This knowledge may be *declarative* (about the nature of a task), *procedural* (about ways of doing the task efficiently), or both.

Although all expert systems encode their knowledge in a more accessible form than conventional programs, many of them have complex notations that can only be used by a trained computer scientist. There are two complementary methods of making it easier to put in knowledge and to get advice:

■ make the notation closer to English (or another natural language)
■ make the system able to work effectively when given only *declarative* knowledge about the nature of a task.

Generally, we can make a system easier to use by improving its ability to handle English, by making it so that the knowledge we give it can be more declarative, or by doing both. We can choose how far we go along the path to full English. In this book we shall show a limited approach in Chapter 4, and a full English approach in Chapter 5.

In an approach described in Chapter 4, we work with *sentence forms* on the screen of a computer terminal. Sentence forms consist of any words in English (or any other natural language) together with variables that can be filled in by other words. We give meaning to the sentence forms by using them to write rules containing our knowledge about a subject. The system remembers the sentences that we type in. When we want to ask a question, the sentences the system knows about are presented as a grouped menu, with the sentences that are most important shown in the first group. We pick one sentence; then we optionally modify some of the variables to make the sentence correspond to our question. (If we want to be able to ask the same question using two different sentences, then we must tell the system that the two sentences mean the same thing.) This approach has the disadvantage that it is somewhat restricted. It has the advantage that it works with any natural language or jargon, and that there is no need to construct a dictionary or a grammar beforehand—we simply type in the knowledge and use it. Chapter 4 describes a knowledge base about manufacturing planning that is built in this way.

In Chapter 5 we show how to develop a parser and a semantic interpreter that come to grips with the full richness of natural language. Natural languages allow people to express information in different forms to emphasize different points or just to allow some stylistic variation. All of the following requests, for example, ask for the same information:

```
What is Sam's age?
How old is Sam?
Please print Sam's age.
I would like to know how old Sam is.
```

A general language handler can parse each sentence to determine its syntax and then build up an internal logical form that describes the meaning. Appropriate rules of inference can relate the different logical forms. They would show, for example, that age is a measure of the degree of oldness. Chapter 5 presents a general method for mapping natural language into a logical form and handling problems of this sort. The methods of Chapter 5 are of value not only for creating natural language interfaces to expert systems, but also for other natural language applications, such as machine translation (McCord 1986).

We mentioned that if a system is to be easy to use, it should cope with sentences that are easy to read, or that are in full English. There is another dimension to ease of use. We also want a system to reason with *declarative* knowledge, so that rather than telling it *how* to do a task, we can just tell it *what* the task is. This means that, internally, the system must be able to derive enough *procedural* knowledge to execute the declarative knowledge both correctly and efficiently. We can choose how far we go along the path to direct use of declarative knowledge. This is discussed in Chapter 4 and in Appendix B.

In summary, a full-scale knowledge system should be able to do the following tasks:

- Solve or help to solve important problems that would otherwise require the services of a human expert.

- Integrate new knowledge incrementally into the knowledge base.

- Help the designer to elicit, organize, and transfer knowledge.

- Display knowledge in a form that is easy for people to read.

- Provide explanations of its advice.

- Reason with judgmental or inexact knowledge about the nature of a task or methods of doing it efficiently.

- Reason with declarative knowledge.

- Support a readable and natural interface.

Some of these features may be missing in one system or another, but they can serve as criteria that measure the sophistication of a knowledge system. They also serve to outline, in a general way, many of the research goals in the field. To support these features, knowledge systems typically have the following components:

- A knowledge base encoded in the form of rules and facts,

- An inference engine for reasoning with the rules and facts,
- An explanation generator for explaining a line of reasoning,
- Methods for acquiring new knowledge and encoding it in the knowledge base,
- A dialogue handler that may range in complexity from a menu to a full natural language processor.

This book presents techniques for using Prolog to support all of these components. We also give examples of how to use knowledge systems that have been built from such components.

1.2 FROM GENERAL TO SPECIFIC, AND BACK AGAIN

In this section we sketch some central issues in work on expert systems over the last three decades, and we outline how the issues are currently treated. At a meeting in 1956 at Dartmouth College, John McCarthy (now of Stanford University) coined the term "artificial intelligence." At the same meeting a system called the Logic Theorist was discussed, (see Newell, Shaw and Simon 1963). It proved theorems in logic and may be thought of as the first, or at least one of the first, expert systems. It seems useful to outline the subsequent evolution of expert systems in the United States in terms of a *thesis,* an *antithesis*, and a *synthesis*. We shall then look at the corresponding evolution outside the USA.

The *thesis* states that general methods of expert problem solving can be found, and that these can be made computational and can be applied to many different problems. This approach is represented by the Logic Theorist (mentioned above), the General Problem Solver described in Newell and Simon (1963), and by early work in automatic theorem proving, notably that of Green (1969). Implicit in the thesis is the concept that the *procedural* aspect of how to solve a problem is independent of the task at hand. The idea is that we should just be able to *declare* what the task is, and the problem solving procedure should then do it. While this thesis works well in principle, the early implementation efforts were very inefficient in practice. One apparent source of difficulty is that there is no obvious place, within the framework prescribed by the thesis, to put specialized procedural knowledge about how to do each task efficiently. In the absence of this knowledge, the problem solver searches for answers along many blind alleys before succeeding.

This difficulty led Edward Feigenbaum of Stanford University to advocate an *antithesis*. The antithesis states that, rather than looking for generality, we should set out empirically to capture human knowledge and procedures for specific tasks; see Feigenbaum and McCorduck (1983) for a recent summary of this view. Essentially, we should be willing to write a new program for each task. This technique led to the first practical expert systems. For example, the DENDRAL program of Buchanan and Feigenbaum (1978) is a "smart assistant" for a chemist concerned with structure elucidation in organic chemistry. The Meta-DENDRAL program (described in the same paper) is a knowledge acquisition program for DENDRAL. The antithesis approach, and its reduction to practice, has clearly been responsible for the present commercial interest in expert systems. However, the approach is intellectually labor intensive, so far as the acquisition of knowledge is concerned. It is usual for a *knowledge engineer* to study the task at hand, specify appropriate inference engines, and then work with both the task experts and with programmers to construct a system. Since the conceptual levels dealt with by the task experts and the programmers are usually far apart, success can depend on the skill of the knowledge engineer. Often the experts, knowledge engineer, and programmers must invest years of work in building a useful expert system. Moreover, with the notable exception of DENDRAL, the systems so constructed have not by and large contributed much to our knowledge of the principles of expert systems.

Thus we have a *thesis*, that general problem solvers are desirable, and an *antithesis*, that the best practical approach is to build specific systems for specific tasks. The *synthesis* of these two approaches essentially takes the middle ground. The idea is that many tasks have requirements in common, and that these requirements can be met by an expert system *shell*, to which we add knowledge about particular tasks. Typical shells, such as EMycin, described by Buchanan and Shortliffe (1984), and OPS5 (see Forgy 1981, Brownston et al. 1985), each cover a range of tasks, but no one shell covers them all. There are variations on this synthesis, one of which is to provide a *tool kit* containing many of the methods used in the various expert system shells. The ESE system (Hirsch et al. 1985, 1986), KEE (Fikes and Kehler 1985) and LOOPS (Stefik et al 1983) systems can be thought of as tool kits of this kind. Since even a tool kit may not support all of the expert systems that we may wish to build, it appears important that such kits be packaged as *open systems*, in the sense that the underlying programming language is accessible. It should be easy to write new tools and to link them with the ones provided.

When we described the thesis about generality, we noted that there was no place in the general framework for procedural knowledge about how to do a specific task efficiently. So it is natural to ask how the synthesis avoids the efficiency problems that led to the suspension of the thesis. There seem to be several reasons why individual expert system shells are efficient enough to be useful. First, individual shells do not try to cover such a broad class of problems as the thesis methods, so each shell can be designed to be efficient for the class of problems for which it is intended. Second, the processing speed provided by the underlying hardware has increased significantly since the time the thesis was first proposed, although not enough for direct support of the thesis. Third, although we like to keep the knowledge about a task as declarative as possible, in practice we often program some efficiency know-how into it. However, this last step tends to make the knowledge harder to examine and change. It is usually better to put as much of the procedural knowledge as possible in the inference engine.

In its most general form the thesis calls for more computational power than current hardware can supply, but it allows us in principle just to specify a task to be done, so that we do not have to give a procedure for how to do the task. Thus the thesis is computation intensive. As we mentioned the antithesis, on the other hand, is intellectual-labor intensive. Task experts, knowledge engineers, and artificial intelligence programmers have in some cases spent years building a single specialized system. The synthesis, taking the middle ground, tends to reduce the amount of intellectual work in constructing a system, and tends to result in a system that is reasonably efficient on current computers. Work on computer-assisted acquisition of knowledge, which we describe in Section 1.6 and in Chapter 4, shows some promise of further reducing the intellectual work needed to build a system, without increasing the computer power needed to run the system after it has been built. Interestingly, the more ambitious knowledge acquisition methods call for very large amounts of computing. Often this is worthwhile: we may be willing to compute for days or weeks to build a system, although we often expect fast response from the system once it has been built.

So far, we have outlined some central trends in expert systems research and practice in the USA since the late 1950s in terms of a thesis, an antithesis, and a synthesis. The thesis was based on mathematical logic, while the antithesis and synthesis dispensed with the logical approach on the grounds of efficiency. Most of the experimental work in all three phases has been done in the language Lisp, invented by John McCarthy at about the start of the thesis period (see McCarthy et al. 1962), and elaborated through many different versions since. Interestingly, although Lisp is designed for symbol manipulation, it is a *functional* rather than a *relational* (logical) language; various operations for logic, such as unification and search, must be programmed in Lisp when needed.

Outside of the USA, there was a thesis stage concerned with automatic theorem proving, but there was generally much less of the antithesis-inspired activity in building individual systems. Around the mid 1970s, the synthesis happened in the USA; several expert system shells with good but not completely general coverage appeared on the scene. In the meantime research elsewhere also led to some new logical techniques for expert systems, and we discuss these next.

1.3 PROLOG AND LOGIC PROGRAMMING

At about the same time that the synthesis made itself known in the USA, a new language called Prolog was designed in Europe (Kowalski 1974, Roussel 1975, Pereira et al. 1978). Although Prolog was first implemented mainly to support natural language processing (Colmerauer 1978) it works essentially as an efficiently executable part of mathematical logic, hence it is interesting for many subjects. By 1981, Prolog was adopted by the Japanese as the basis of their Fifth Generation Project, (ICOT 1981). The technical aims of this 10-year project include fundamental work on both software and hardware for advanced knowledge bases. In 1984, at the end of the first phase of the project, substantial progress was reported on a Prolog-based workstation, a database machine, studies of parallel machines to support Prolog, and in some experimental expert systems (ICOT 1984).

Prolog has a certain hybrid vigor in that it contains some declarative features from computational mathematical logic (Robinson 1965, 1979) and some procedural aspects from conventional programming. Thus it is called a Logic *Programming* language, and, like the expert system shells and tool kits, it occupies the middle ground between our general thesis and specific antithesis. It is worth emphasizing that many people who work on knowledge systems and Prolog consider that, while Prolog represents a great step forward, there is even more to be gained from logic programming in general. Several major research projects around the world are currently devoted to designs for the next family of logic programming languages.

Prolog is somewhat weighted toward the thesis idea and toward generality. Many of the mechanisms one needs for an expert system shell are in the language, yet the language has very few features in the conventional sense. (For example, Prolog has a generalized logical pattern match called *unification* but it is built-in, and one usually does not see it or call it explicitly when writing a program.) Perhaps because of the lack of conventional features, Prolog has a very elegant and practical semantics that seems to be the key to much of its appeal. For example, it is possible to say what a well written Prolog program should compute, independent of any particular interpreter or compiler, and it is possible to say this precisely without getting into undue complexities. One analytical tool for doing this is model theory in logic (van Emden and Kowalski 1976, Apt and van Emden 1982, Apt et al. 1986). Model theory turns out, in many examples, to be quite close to the intuition that most people have about what a program should do. As a very simple example, the Prolog program

```
route(X,Z) <- road(X,Z).
route(X,Z) <- road(X,Y) & route(Y,Z).
road(b,c).   road(c,d).   road(d,e).
```

says that there is a route from X to Z if either there is a road from X to Z, or if there is both a road from X to Y and a route from Y to Z. It also says that there are roads from b to c, c to d, and d to e. The following is a model of the program:

```
road(b,c).    road(c,d).    road(d,e).
route(b,c).   route(c,d).   route(d,e).
route(b,d).   route(c,e).   route(b,e).
```

To say that this is a model of the program means that every relevant instance of each rule in the program evaluates to *true* in the model. It is also just the collection of common sense consequences of the rules and facts in the program.

Because of its relation to mathematical logic, Prolog has a theoretical basis (Lassez et al. 1983, Jaffar et al 1983, and Lloyd 1984), as well as a body of associated practical experience. In fact, the theory and practice can be made to mesh quite well, (Brough and Walker 1984, Apt et al. 1986), and can usefully be extended to include relational databases.

One consequence of the simple meaning of Prolog is that it works very well as its own metalanguage. That is, it is rather easy to describe the meaning of Prolog in Prolog. While a Prolog interpreter written in a conventional language may consist of upwards of 10,000 printed symbols, an interpreter for most of Prolog can be written in Prolog in about 100 symbols (less than half a printed page). This may seem to be just an academic curiosity, until we realize that many inference engines for expert systems are somewhat similar to the Prolog inference engine. For example, by making relatively minor changes to a Prolog interpreter in Prolog, we get the core of the EMycin expert system shell; by making some other changes, we get rules by which each object belonging to some class inherits the general properties of the class unless otherwise stated. We pay an efficiency price for this conceptual elegance, since the inference engines that we build in this way are generally slower than if they had been written directly. However, when supported by a fast computer, the performance is adequate for many tasks, the flexibility advantages are overwhelming, and it is possible to compile some aspects of the inference engine if necessary, (Walker 1982, Neumann 1986). The inference engine consists of Prolog rules that function as metainformation; they are rules about how to use the rules for particular tasks. If we have procedural information about how to do a range of tasks efficiently (e.g, always use a relevant fact before trying a rule) then we can encode this in the metarules that define the inference engine. Thus in the metalanguage approach to expert systems in Prolog, there is a natural place for procedural knowledge, and the task knowledge can remain largely declarative. If our target is high performance on small machines, then we can first make a metalanguage prototype of the inference engine on a large machine and then rewrite or compile it as necessary.

We mentioned that Prolog is a simple language with few features. In fact, the main part of Prolog lacks many of the standard constructs of other programming languages. For example, destructive assignment (as in X:=5) is rarely used in Prolog, whereas modification of a working memory is a central feature of OPS5. This tends to guide the programmer away from machine-level state-transition programming and toward a more declarative style. Simultaneously, it appears to make Prolog more suitable for implementation on parallel hardware. Such hardware now seems to be promising for the support of some of the more ambitious tasks, such as real time control, that are proposed for expert systems. Some expert systems for real-time control can be built by very efficient programming on a sequential machine (Griesmer et al. 1984), while others appear to need more; the kind of underlying performance that is expected from parallel machines.

So far, we have sketched some of the issues in expert systems over the last three decades, both inside and outside the USA, in terms of a *thesis* about generality, an *antithesis* about specialization and efficiency, and a *synthesis* containing a partial return to generality. We have touched on a spectrum of activities from general to specific, and from theoretical to empirical. An expert system is only as good as the declarative and procedural knowledge that it contains, and as its ability to communicate with us. In the next sections, we look at knowledge representation, English language processing, and knowledge acquisition.

1.4 KNOWLEDGE REPRESENTATION

In order to use knowledge in a machine, we must first choose a way of representing it. We need a notation that supports what we expect an expert system to do. The notation should make it easy for us to add and change knowledge, should be easy for us to read, and should support generation of explanations. In addition, the notation should suggest ways in which it will be used and should allow us to write down different methods of use. The notation should also encourage us to separate declarative knowledge (what a problem is about) from procedural knowledge (how to solve the problem), yet it should support efficient problem solving. So we can use these criteria to estimate how useful conventional programming is for expert systems, and to compare the various knowledge representations that are used for expert systems. When we write a program in a conventional language, we are writing down knowledge about how to do a task. When we load the program into a computer, the computer could be said to acquire knowledge. However, it may be quite hard to add to the knowledge or to change it. It can also be hard for a person other than the author to read and understand the program, and it is rare for ordinary programs to provide explanations of what they do. On the plus side, ordinary programming notation does suggest how one should use it, since the meaning of a program can (in principle) be worked out in terms of how it changes the state of the computer on which it runs. Yet, most conventional programming languages encourage us to mix declarative and procedural knowledge so much that it can be difficult to separate the two. On the plus side again, the knowledge can often be used very efficiently.

The kind of task for which we build an expert system is, almost by definition, complicated. When we describe a task in English, we usually keep the description to a readable length by relying on knowledge that the writer and the reader already have in common. If the task is simple, it is usually feasible to write a suitable program from the description— although there may be many different programs that fit the description. However, if the task is complicated and specialized we cannot rely so much on shared knowledge. An English description of readable length is no longer enough, while if we make the description long and pedantic we get lost in the details. So there are several notations for knowledge that stand somewhere between English and programs. They are useful to the extent that we can use them to write down knowledge in a form that both people (who need not be programmers) and computers can use.

Some of our methods for representing knowledge for expert systems make use of the notion of a *hierarchy* in which lower items are normally assumed to have some of the properties of higher items. For example, if a manager in a company is interested in expert systems, then we assume that the people who work in her group have the same interest, unless we are told that one of them specializes in hardware. Some notations for knowledge are often used without explicit reference to a hierarchy, for example, *rules* and *nets*. Others, such as *frames* and *objects*, are centered around the hierarchical notion. Although the various notations have been designed separately and have been used for many different purposes, each one can usefully be written down in logic.

Knowledge is represented as *rules* for expert systems shells such as EMycin (Buchanan and Shortliffe 1984), and Syllog (Walker 1984). For example, an EMycin-style rule reads

```
if 'plant is wilting' and
      not 'leaves have yellow spots'
                then 'there is not enough water' : 60.
```

The number 60 indicates that we have 60% confidence in the rule and is used in a numerical form of judgmental reasoning. A Syllog rule reads

```
site eg_number has eg_type rock in suitable form
eg_group fossils have been found at site eg_number
eg_group fossils are characteristic of the eg_p period
there are known reserves in eg_type rock from the eg_p period
-----------------------------------------------------------
some evidence for oil at site eg_number
```

Here, the conclusion below the line is established if all of the premises above the line are true. The `eg_` items are variables that make the rule general.

In EMycin, judgmental reasoning proceeds by chaining rules together to form deductions, and by using a built-in algorithm to combine the numerical confidences at each step in the chain. So it is a design assumption that there should be some way of assigning confidence numbers to rules so that the built-in algorithm will assign reasonable confidences to the answers that the system produces. The algorithm is a part of the EMycin shell, and most of its operation is hidden from the user. In writing a knowledge base it is not always easy to assign suitable numbers to rules, perhaps because one cannot easily tell without experimentation just what their effect will be on the answer confidences.

In Syllog, there is no built-in algorithm for judgmental reasoning. When needed, judgments are written and used explicitly (and usually symbolically) rather than implicitly and numerically in the EMycin style. For example, the phrases *suitable form* and *some evidence* in the Syllog rule above carry judgment. If we carry the judgmental reasoning explicitly in this way, we are not forced to assume that there is a uniform method (e.g, Bayesian) for weighing evidence; the way in which evidence is weighed may be quite different from rule to rule. Although the lack of a built-in algorithm for combining numerical confidences appears at first sight to be a disadvantage, it seems very natural in practice to use judgmental English phrases in the syllogisms, and to show in explanations how the judgments are combined at each step.

For the Prospector system (Duda, Gaschnig and Hart 1979), knowledge is written down as a *net* with nodes and arcs. The nodes represent geological evidence or hypotheses, and the arcs represent causal linkages between the nodes.

We can think of part of a net as represented inside the computer by logical facts, such as

```
arc(favorable_level_of_erosion,
    favorable_environment, 5700, 0.0001)

arc(preintrusive_throughgoing_fault_system,
    favorable_environment, 5, 0.7)
```

This describes two arcs in a net. The first arc is from a node called "favorable level of erosion" to one called "favorable environment," and it bears numbers for judgmental reasoning. The second arc is similar, and both arcs can provide evidence to support the conclusion "favorable environment."

We can think of a *frame* (Minsky 1975) as something like a form that we can fill in, which may have a place in a hierarchy of forms. For example, a form about a kind of house might be filled in like this:

```
house has
     street_name : main
     number_of_bathrooms : 2
     wall_color : white
```

Then we might fill in a form about a more particular kind of house like this,

```
type_A_house has
     number_of_bedrooms : 8
```

and about an individual house like this,

```
house1 has
     street_name : delaware
     wall_color : green
```

Now, given that house1 is a type A house, and that a type A house is a kind of house, we can reason that house1 has 8 bedrooms and 2 bathrooms, and that, exceptionally, its walls are green rather than white. The notation is a succinct one for describing many houses, provided that the houses can be grouped according to common features.

An *object* can be thought of as a process or an agent that receives a message, changes its internal state, and sends out a message (Hewitt 1977). An object can also be used as a template to generate other objects with similar properties. Objects form an intuitively appealing way of representing knowledge in situations where there are many agents (say, people and computers) that work together on a task. In fact, there is a language called Smalltalk (Goldberg and Robson 1983) that is based on objects. In our frames example, we looked at the description of a house, and if we did not find a property there, we looked at the descriptions of the kind of house. Similarly, if an object receives a message it may handle it according to its own procedure, or it may look among more generic objects for a suitable procedure. For example, Shapiro and Takeuchi (1983) use logic to describe a screen-management program for a computer terminal. Windows on the screen correspond to objects that can send messages to one another; a window with a caption is a special case of a window, which in turn is a special case of a rectangular area of the screen.

We have seen that symbolic knowledge can be represented in several ways, including *rules* or *nets,* in *frames,* or as *objects,* and that logic provides a natural common notation. Many kinds of knowledge that are largely symbolic contain a few numbers, as in our examples above. Sometimes it is useful to express knowledge, particularly knowledge about how to search a space of possible actions for the best action to take, almost purely numerically (Pearl 1984). In the numeric case logic is also a strong candidate notation. However, numeric knowledge is traditionally written down as functions rather than as logical relations—that is, there is an implied direction of computation from input numbers to an output number. Writing the same knowledge in logic allows us, in principle, to also specify the output and generate the corresponding sets of inputs. This generalization is very powerful since it allows a program written for one purpose to be used for several purposes, and it often works directly in Prolog for the symbolic case. However, in the numeric case Prolog must usually be supported by extra knowledge about how to solve equations. Thus the ability to treat symbolic knowledge declaratively is to a certain extent built into Prolog, while the ability to treat numeric knowledge declaratively must, in most cases, be added by extra programming, see e.g Bundy and Welham (1981).

We have looked at some of the useful ways of representing knowledge in a computer, and we have seen that logic is a useful common notation. We have mostly used English-like notations for the logic. It would be good to be able to ask a knowledge system for advice, in unrestricted English, and to get the answers, also in English.

1.5 GETTING THE COMPUTER TO UNDERSTAND ENGLISH

Ideally we would like to be able to communicate with a knowledge system much as we do with a person. We would like to put in new knowledge in English (or in our preferred natural language), to ask questions in English, and to get answers in English. This section outlines some of the issues that arise in getting a computer to usefully understand English, while Chapter 5 describes some current techniques and research. There are many possible different sentences in ordinary English. A sentence may be ambiguous in a given situation, as in

```
Which gate for the Chicago plane?
```

The question could be about an arriving or a departing plane. A sentence may mean different things in different situations

```
Where is the salt?
```

This question could be asked at table, or in connection with spreading salt on icy roads. Although people can deal with this diversity, most knowledge systems, and most natural language components of such systems, are written for use on specific topics. Even when a single topic is chosen, much of the diversity remains. Current systems usually deal with the diversity by processing a sentence in English in the following steps:

A. Break up the sentence into a list of words.

B. Look up each word in a dictionary, finding out for example whether it is a noun or a verb, and what inflection it has.

C. Use a grammar of English, to find one or more *parses* of the sentence. A *parse* is a grouping of words into phrases, and of phrases into a sentence. An ambiguous sentence usually has more than one parse.

D. Map the parse or parses into the internal language of the knowledge system. (In many systems, this internal language is logic.)

E. Process the internal form of the sentence, perhaps using some kind of logical deduction. If the sentence is a question, an answer is produced.

F. If an answer is produced it is in the internal language of the system; do steps D, C, B, and A (each in reverse) to translate the internal form into English.

Step A is easy in written English (and in most natural languages) since we just have to find the blanks between the words. In Step B, there may be several ways of finding a word in the dictionary, but Step C may eliminate some of the possibilities. Similarly, Step C may produce many different parses, not all of which have sensible meanings in the internal language of the system. For conceptual clarity the programs for Steps B, C, and D are usually distinct rather than intermixed. However if they are run separately they may take a lot of computer time, since a step may produce many alternatives that are rejected by the next step. So for efficiency reasons it can be very useful to run the steps cooperatively. Thus B may produce a few word forms, which are checked by C, which produces a partial parse, which is checked by D; if D indicates that the partial parse cannot be completed to form anything with a meaning, then C tries to produce a different partial parse; if C cannot produce one, then B is asked to look up the words in a different way in the dictionary. The Steps B, C and D thus negotiate to make sure that they agree as they go along, rather than waiting for an earlier step to complete the whole sentence first.

An early and justifiably famous system was able to hold conversations at the keyboard by using only Step A, plus simplified forms of the Steps E and F which worked directly with English words. The system was called Eliza, and was written by Weizenbaum (1966). It worked essentially by recognizing certain keywords and discarding the rest of a sentence. There were several occasions on which people typing at keyboards actually thought that they were exchanging messages with a person rather than with the Eliza program, so although the system is simple, it performed rather well. However Weizenbaum, the author of the program, has protested vigorously against thoughts of using such "keyword" programs in real life (Weizenbaum 1976). Although they appear to "understand," the appearance is deceptive. As a simplified example, an elementary keyword program might miss the difference between the question

Have the brakes been checked

and

The brakes have been checked

by paying attention only to the words brakes and checked. A parser (Step C) typically detects that a question is a transposed version of a statement.

Historically, the next systems used Steps A, B and C. In Step C, a grammar of English specifies the legal sentences. The grammar is used to assign structure to a legal sentence, and to reject ungrammatical sentences. The program that uses a grammar to do this is called a *parser*. A parser can use one of several *control strategies*, the most usual of which are *top down* (in which a tree structure representing a parse is built from the root of the tree toward the words of the sentence at the "leaves"), and *bottom up* (in which the parse tree is built from the words at the leaves toward the root that represents the whole sentence). We note in passing that parse trees (unlike natural ones) are usually drawn with their roots at the top, see e.g page 34. Interestingly, a simple system that does top down parsing can be written in Prolog without writing a parser—it is enough to write down the grammar rules and to execute them directly using Prolog's top down inference method. However, the grammar rules need to carry variables that keep track of the extent to which the sentence has been parsed, and it is possible to insert these variables automatically into the rules. As we mentioned, the original motive for the development of Prolog was for natural language processing, (Colmerauer 1975). Since then, several logical approaches to parsing have been proposed and developed. Kowalski (1975) showed that a graphical proof procedure could parse a sentence, using a mixture of top down and bottom up control. Pereira and Warren (1980) used their logic-based *Definite Clause Grammars* in a system that answers questions about world geography. The development of logic grammars has continued with the *Modular Logic Grammars* of McCord, described in Chapter 5.

So far we have spoken about using just Steps A, B and C. To some extent the parse tree of a sentence indicates its intended meaning. For example, if we look for a moment at arithmetic instead of English then the "sentence" 1 + 2 * 3 can be parsed as 1 + (2 * 3) or as (1 + 2) * 3. In the first case the meaning is 7, in the second case 9. However, the parse tree of an English sentence does not show the meaning this clearly, and Step D is needed to translate it into a logical form. In fact, there may be more than one logical form for a given parse of a sentence. This question is explored in detail in Chapter 5.

If a question is put to a knowledge base, then the Steps A - D can translate the question into an internal logical form. Step E can then deduce an answer, also in logical form. As we indicated, the final Step F translates the answer into English, and conceptually F consists of the Steps D, C, B and A in reverse. Since Prolog programs can be written to be reversible, there is some potential for actually using the same programs for input and output. However, in practice it is sometimes easier to write efficient programs if the input and output phases are handled separately.

So far, we have spoken about translating an English sentence into a logical form, processing it deductively, and possibly getting an answer that is translated back into English. There are more general ways of using English. For example a sentence may be part of a story. If we are halfway through the story, then the earlier sentences have set up a *state of affairs* in which the current sentence is to be interpreted. Just as a predicate can be used to define a relation between people (as in `father_of(fred,mary)`), a sentence can be regarded as a relation between states of affairs. For example state S1 might have Fred in San Francisco and Mary in Toronto, state S2 might have them both in Toronto, and the sentence

    `Fred went to see Mary`

is then a relation between S1 and S2.

So suppose we want to write a system that will follow a story and answer questions about it afterwards. Then it seems promising to have the system regard each sentence as a relation between states of affairs. It is clear also that when a person reads a simple story (say about going to a restaurant), there is an expected sequence of states: being outside, being inside, sitting at a table, holding a menu, and so on. Schank has suggested that a sequence of states should be represented as a *script*, and that a story should be understood by matching its sentences to relations between states, such as the physical transfer of a person from one place to another, see for example Schank and Riesbeck (1981).

In this brief sketch, we have seen that most programs that deal with English sentences do so in steps. A sentence is broken up into words; the words are looked up in a dictionary; the dictionary entries are grouped in a parse tree so that part of the meaning of the sentence appears; the parse tree is translated into a logical form to get the rest of the meaning; and then the logical form is used to deduce what should be done about the sentence. For example, if the sentence is a question, the deduction finds an answer. To deal with narrative and dialogue we need to represent general knowledge, and to reason with it. Researchers are looking into various methods for this, including the idea of regarding a sentence as a relation between states.

1.6 SOME TRENDS IN KNOWLEDGE ACQUISITION

As we mentioned, our general name for an expert system or a natural language understanding program is "knowledge system." It is clear that such a system is useful only insofar as it contains knowledge. For a person it is an open question as to how much knowledge is innate and how much is acquired. For a computer, however, the answer is clear. All knowledge must be acquired, since nothing significant is built-in during manufacture. If we think for a moment about human learning, it is clearly difficult for a person to acquire a full slate of common sense and specialized knowledge; it takes about a quarter of a lifetime, and this fact may influence our research approaches to machine learning (Simon 1983). We can calculate that, roughly speaking, a person may be able to change the information in his or her brain at a rate (in bits per second) that is at least comparable to, and may be much greater than the rate at which the fastest current computer can change its information. So, if the human potential is in fact used for learning, and if artificial methods are no faster than the natural ones, we may expect general knowledge acquisition to be very difficult for computers. It could require substantially faster computers than we now possess.

However, it already seems clear that we can write useful knowledge acquisition programs that can help us to build expert systems. We can set up some useful forms of machine learning, although what is currently practical falls far short of the kinds of learning that people can do. Once we have chosen to represent knowledge so that it is easy to examine and change, we can set up several methods by which a machine can acquire it. It is useful to group the methods like this:

- Learning by being told,
- Learning by induction from examples, and
- Learning by observation and discovery.

In the following subsections we look at each of these methods of knowledge acquisition.

1.6.1 Learning by Being Told

This is the simplest form of knowledge acquisition, and it can be surprisingly useful. We simply tell the system facts and rules about the task at hand. For example, in the expert system shell called Syllog, which we describe in Chapter 4, we can add syllogisms that contain knowledge about a particular subject, such as airline reservations or manufacturing planning. We can easily examine the knowledge, and when the system answers a question, it can also provide an explanation of its answer. The implemented Syllog system does partial checking of the incoming knowledge. Checking can also be done in EMycin-style systems that use numbers for judgmental reasoning (Suwa et al. 1984). We can make learning by being told more helpful, and thus hopefully use up less of the time of a human expert, by having an expert system assist in pinpointing faulty or missing rules. This process has been called "interactive transfer of expertise" (Davis 1984). Once a faulty rule has been found, it can be specialized (e.g, by adding a premise) or generalized. If a rule is missing, it can be very useful if the system can suggest what kind of premises and conclusions should be added. Shapiro (1983) describes some methodical techniques for computer-assisted debugging of Prolog programs that essentially interview a person at the terminal to find out, by example, what he or she has in mind. Notably, Shapiro's techniques are not only implemented as a program but also have a clear theory to back them up. The techniques extend to inductive inference of programs from examples, as discussed in Section 1.6.2, "Learning by Induction from Examples."

In principle we would like an expert system to check what it is told thoroughly. Basically there are three things that can happen when we present a system with a new item of knowledge (Bowen and Kowalski 1982):

(a) The new item is already deducible from the current knowledge. Efficiency issues aside, we may set up the system to reject the item, with a suitable message to the user.

(b) The new item is inconsistent with the current knowledge. Either the item is to be rejected, or the knowledge is to be changed before the item is accepted. Rejection is straightforward. Alternatively we can set up the system to automatically add the item as an exception to the knowledge, or to hold a dialogue about what action to take with person providing the knowledge.

(c) The new item is neither deducible from the current knowledge, nor inconsistent with it. The item is added to the knowledge. However, there may now be redundancies, e.g if we have added a general rule that covers a number of facts. So we may wish to edit these out of the new knowledge.

We have spoken so far about adding an item to a knowledge base. In relational database systems (Codd 1971), items are also deleted, and this presents some additional theoretical and practical problems. Indeed, Kowalski and Sergot (1985) propose that, rather than deleting an item, one can add to the knowledge base the fact that the item ceased to be true at some point in time. This is intuitively appealing, perhaps because people do not automatically forget past facts or knowledge. It also has far reaching consequences for database normalization theory. However, in practice it needs very large archival memories, and it may have to be combined with some measures to limit the amount of knowledge that is stored.

Steps (a)-(c) above can be written as a logic program that assimilates new information into a knowledge base. The declarative version of the program is short and clear, about a page of Prolog, and it works well for small knowledge bases. However, it is not efficient in general for large knowledge bases. There are some techniques available for writing a longer, more procedural logic program that is more efficient (Walker and Salveter 1981). However, for certain knowledge bases some of the checking that the program does is inherently slow, even on a fast computer.

In this situation the natural choice is to do only partial checking, or (equivalently) to run the full checking program with a resource bound on Steps

(a) and (b), and to do Step (c) if the resources are used up. This can result in an inconsistent knowledge base. In principle, any answer to any question can be obtained from a logic knowledge base that is inconsistent. Fortunately, most logic programming interpreters and compilers, including the Prolog and Syllog inference engines, impose relevance conditions that prevent a local inconsistency from causing a global one.

So there is really a continuum here. Some knowledge systems provide no checking of the incoming knowledge at all, placing the entire burden on the users. Some, such as Syllog, do some checking, thus moving part of the burden from users to the machine. In future, additional machine speed, as well as more efficient methods, should allow us to increase the amount of checking that is done by the machine. We mentioned that even with a consistent knowledge base it is important that a system be able to explain the answers that it gives to questions. In the absence of full checking, explanations also give us a way of verifying the knowledge while a system is being built and when a system is in use.

1.6.2 Learning by Induction from Examples

It is now generally accepted that people often have expertise that they find difficult to write down explicitly. A person may be very good at a task, but may find it difficult to tell someone else, or an expert system shell, how to do the task. One reason for making the language of a system shell declarative and as English-like as possible, and for providing explanations, is that some experts may actually experiment directly with the shell and thus may be able to make their implicit knowledge explicit. On the other hand, an expert can usually provide a wealth of examples about how to do a task for which we would like to build a knowledge base. A particular experimental study by Michalski and Chilausky (1980) found that a knowledge base induced automatically from examples of expert behavior gave better advice than one that was built by being *told* by the expert. In general, the difficulty is to make the leap from examples containing some underlying pattern to general rules that summarize the examples and are capable of dealing with new examples that have not been seen before. Logically, this is not a deduction (given K, and that K implies E, conclude E), but an induction (given E, find a *suitable* K such that K implies E). Here, the examples are represented by E, and the knowledge base that is to be found is K.

In thinking about criteria for *suitable* knowledge bases K, we can immediately rule out two particular inductive inferences from the examples E. A case that is much simpler than a real knowledge induction problem helps to illustrate this. Suppose we are given as examples E just the numbers

     1 4 9 16 25 36 49 64

and we are asked for a K which generalizes this. Most people would say

K consists of the squares of the integers.

Intuitively, this is suitable. However, it is much easier to recognize suitability on particular cases than to capture it as a general concept. At least we can avoid two kinds of induction that are almost always unsuitable. The first is that K is just E; i.e the induced knowledge base is just a look-up table of the examples that have been seen. This is unsatisfactory because we usually want a knowledge base that is smaller than the examples from which it was induced, and because no new examples can be handled. (In our simple case above, K would not imply 81.) The second inductive inference is that K is a most general possible knowledge base that implies E; that is, it implies everything in the domain from which E is a sample. (In our simple case, K would consist of all of the integers.) Although such a knowledge base can often be summarized in a form that is much smaller than the examples, it tends to be vacuous, in the sense that it indicates that anything is possible.

Shapiro (1983) shows how to induce Prolog programs automatically from examples of their desired behavior. There can be many programs that cover a set of examples, but which one to choose is not the only concern. The number of examples needed to produce a program and the computer time needed for the induction process must also be weighed. Shapiro gives an induction algorithm that can be used with different search strategies. In one case a strategy that needs many examples yields a short program, while a strategy that sometimes needs fewer examples can (with an adverse ordering of the examples) yield an arbitrarily long program. Kitakami et al. (1984) describe a way of combining knowledge acquisition by being told with the inductive approach of Shapiro.

Several criteria have been used to strike a balance between small, overly general inductions on the one hand, and large, overly specific ones on the other hand. In the Ockham system of Walker (1977), a Bayesian measure was used to steer a search through a space of causal graphs. Quinlan (1983) introduces a system in which a decision tree is induced from examples, and different trees are ranked by the amount of information that is gained from the questions asked. Relational databases can be compressed, as described by Walker (1980), by replacing several entries by the name of a class to which they belong. For example, "cat" and "dog" could be replaced by "mammal." However, they could also be replaced by "pet." The resulting compressed databases are inductive generalizations, and their succinctness can be compared by running the compression backward and seeing how close we get to the original database. The version space technique of Mitchell (1975, 1978) provides a compact representation for all of the inductive hypotheses that are compatible with a collection of examples and nonexamples of a concept. The idea is to store the most general hypotheses that do not imply any nonexample, and the most specific hypotheses that do not exclude any example. The admissible hypotheses then lie in a "version space," that is partially ordered by generality, between these extremes. If a balance criterion is added, then the hypotheses that satisfy it can be found from the version space.

We noted in Section 5 that there are many different representations of knowledge, but that logic is a useful common notation. As we have seen, there are many different criteria for judging the quality of an inductive inference. It appears that further empirical work is needed to relate these criteria and to try to find some useful common ground among them.

1.6.3 Learning by Observation and Discovery

So far, we have looked at learning by being told and at learning by induction from examples, both of which are techniques for acquiring knowledge for subsequent use in an expert system. In this section, we look at the extent to which a system can be said to discover new knowledge. In learning by being told, the system is given facts plus general rules about how to use the facts, which together amount to a knowledge base K that implies the advice that we wish it to give. Generally, K is very much smaller than an explicit listing of the advice.

In learning by induction from examples, the knowledge acquisition part of the system is given a collection of examples of good and bad advice (so labeled) from which it should induce a knowledge base K that implies the good advice, refrains from implying the bad advice, and gives correct advice on examples that are not in the original collection. In order to do this, the knowledge acquisition engine needs a guidance criterion (let us call it G) to choose a *good* knowledge base K that implies sensible consequences.

For learning by discovery, we equip the knowledge acquisition system with a minimal initial knowledge base k, some operators O for adding information to k, and some guidance G about what operators to apply in what circumstances. We then let the acquisition system run, applying O to k, guided by G. If we have chosen k, O and G well, the system will discover a larger knowledge base K containing some conjectures that can turn out to be useful. For example, in the AM system of Lenat (1983) k consists of some simple nonnumerical knowledge about mathematical sets, O contains some operators such as

```
if f(x,y) is a function in the knowledge base, then
add to the knowledge base the function g(z) = f(z,z)
```

and the guidance G is a prioritized agenda.

Equipped in this way, the AM system produced a K containing, among other conjectures (not all of which were interesting) de Morgan's laws and the unique factorization theorem, although nothing resembling either of these was present in k, O or G. In fact, it also made some interesting numerical conjectures that were unknown to Lenat at the time he wrote AM. Unfortunately, when the program moved away from the symbolic domain with which it had been primed, and into the numeric domain, it made many uninteresting conjectures as well.

Lenat then observed that, since the program could make interesting conjectures in a domain such as mathematics, it should also be able to discover useful new guidance heuristics G. This led Lenat to formulate metaheuristics— heuristics about how to find heuristics—such as

if a heuristic is occasionally useful but usually bad,
then add specializations of the heuristic

and even to have the system apply this heuristic to itself.

In learning by being told, the expertise given to the system usually contains rules that are general in the sense that they contain variables. In learning by induction from examples, the knowledge acquisition part of a system will often generalize the examples it is given by replacing constants with variables (perhaps with range restrictions). A notable feature of learning by discovery is that variables ranging over function or predicate names are often used; that is, viewed as logic, the process is second order. For example, Lenat's operator that specializes $f(x,y)$ to $f(z,z)$ is intended to apply to *any* function of two variables; if f is plus then g is twice, if f is times then g is square, and so on. Another study, by Emde et al (1983), describes a program that discovers the geographical concept of an equator. The program is primed with some geographical facts and also with some second order logical knowledge. McCarthy (1980) gives a second order logic technique, called circumscription, that can be used to discover some general properties of a situation. Thus while our first two kinds of learning can often be stated in first order logic, guidance for some kinds of discovery appears to be naturally expressed in second order logic. Since we have little experience so far in practical computing with second order logic, it seems likely that metalanguage techniques in first order logic (Bowen and Kowalski 1982) will be used for learning by discovery.

1.7 SUMMARY

We have described some principles of knowledge systems, and some links with logic and with the Prolog language.

Behind early work in the field, there was a *thesis* that general problem solving engines could be built, and that it would suffice to add declarative knowledge about a task to an engine to get an expert system. However, the thesis did not have a niche for procedural knowledge about how to do a task efficiently. Consequently, the thesis led to very slow computation on early machines and still cannot be supported directly on current computers.

There followed the Feigenbaum *antithesis* that we should collect declarative and procedural knowledge for a specific task and be willing to write a new expert system for each task. The antithesis has the first practical expert systems to its credit and has been mainly responsible for the current commercial interest in expert systems. However, the antithesis approach is intellectually labor intensive for task experts and for knowledge engineers whose job it is to collect and codify the expertise.

As computer power increased, a practical *synthesis* of the two earlier approaches appeared. The common elements needed to support various ranges of expert system tasks are collected into expert system shells. These shells each cover a range of tasks efficiently, but no one shell is as general as the extreme form of the original thesis. Together, the shells support a wide range of tasks, so they can be collected together into tool kits for building expert systems. Some of the shells and most tool kits must still be primed by knowledge engineers, but the time taken to build an expert system is much reduced.

The original thesis had a strong flavor of mathematical logic to it. About the time of the expert system shell synthesis, the Prolog language for logic programming appeared. (The Prolog language is described in Chapter 2.) Prolog can be viewed as a restricted form of logic for which there are efficient interpreter/compilers. It appears to be very suitable for implementation on parallel machines. Although it is a language, Prolog is at a conceptual level much closer to a shell or a tool kit than to a conventional programming language. Prolog is almost feature-free, but an important technique called metalanguage programming allows us to tailor expert system shells (see Chapters 3 and 4.) This technique provides separate niches for procedural and declarative knowledge, and the separation further eases the knowledge engineering task. Because of the connection with logic, Prolog allows us to apply theory to the actual practice of building and using expert systems.

Even with the separation of declarative and procedural knowledge, it is clear that more can be done to ease the transfer of knowledge from human experts to expert systems. A good choice of knowledge representation is important, and, now that it can be supported efficiently enough, logic seems to be a highest level common notation for the representations in current use. An expert system can acquire knowledge by being told (in which case we like it to help us by checking the consistency of what we say), by induction from examples, or by semi-autonomous learning from observation and discovery. A problem with induction from examples is that we sometimes cannot get explanations automatically from an induced expert system. Learning by being told or by induction from examples is mainly a first order logic activity, while discovery is sometimes guided by statements in second order logic. However, metalanguage techniques allow us to handle some second order logic at the first order level.

As knowledge systems become more useful, it may be good to keep in mind that there are several levels of detail at which they can be built. At the least detailed level, we supply simple rules and facts that describe English (or other natural language) abstractions that people use to make decisions. As we go further into detail, we may wish to simulate certain theories about our own cognitive processes (e.g by using situation-action rules) or we may wish to approximately simulate some aspect of the real world (e.g a mechanical device that an expert system is to diagnose). At the limits of feasible detail we may actually simulate events in our brains at the level of individual neurons, or the detailed functioning of a mechanical device that we wish to diagnose. We have achieved most of our expert system successes so far with very little detail. It is a fascinating question whether this trend will continue, or whether we shall find it more useful to be more detailed in future.

The economically successful expert systems so far have each addressed a specialized task, such as finding mineral deposits. It is worth noting that most human experts specialize too, in professions such as geology. However, each human expert also has common sense knowledge about the world in general and knows how to consult experts in subjects other than his or her own. While we each find it easy to do common sense reasoning, no one so far has produced an account of *how* we do so (or even of the declarative knowledge we might be using) that is sufficient for us to write a "common sense expert system." We can speculate that, as in the case of specialized expert systems, good progress will be made where there is an interplay between theory (influenced by logic) and specific empirical work in building prototype common sense systems.

We are now ready to look at knowledge systems in more detail:

- For readers who are interested mainly in the possible uses of *expert systems*, the suggested reading sequence is

    - Sections 4.2.1, 4.2.2, 4.2.4, 4.3.1,
    - with more detail drawn from Chapters 2 and 3, plus the remainder of Chapter 4 as needed.

- For readers who are interested mainly in *natural language processing* the suggested reading sequence is

    - Chapters 2 and 5,
    - with additional material drawn from Chapter 3 as needed.

- For readers who are interested first in *programming in Prolog*, and second in the uses of expert systems or in natural language processing, the suggested sequence is

    - Chapter 2,
    - Chapter 3 as far as page 166,
    - Appendix A on how to use IBM Prolog,
    - the rest of Chapter 3, then Chapters 4 and 5.

- For readers who are interested first in the *logical fundamentals* of our approach to knowledge systems and Prolog, the suggested reading sequence is

    - Chapter 2,
    - Appendix B on the logical basis for Prolog and Syllog,
    - then Chapters 3, 4 and 5.

2
A Prolog to Prolog

John F. Sowa

"The very first lesson that we have a right to demand that logic shall teach us is how to make our ideas clear; and a most important one it is, depreciated only by minds who stand in need of it. To know what we think, to be masters of our own meaning, will make a solid foundation for great and weighty thought."

Charles Sanders Peirce, *How to Make Our Ideas Clear*.

This chapter is a problem-oriented tutorial on Prolog. It covers all of the major features of the language by means of examples. Chapter 3 will take a more systematic look at many of the same features and present them from a more analytic perspective. To understand Prolog, the reader should study both of these chapters and work the exercises and examples at the terminal. Reading alone is sufficient for an overview, but practice at the terminal is essential for understanding.

2.1 FEATURES OF PROLOG

Programming languages designed by committees typically start with enormous collections of "features." Other languages, like Basic and Lisp, started with simple forms, but they have grown to a point where they look like languages designed by committees. Prolog's strength is not derived from a laundry list of features, but from its underlying structure based on logic. Some features have been added to Prolog for interfaces with the operating system, but the logical core is complete enough for a universal computing system. This section presents a quick overview of Prolog structures. Later sections will explore these structures with more detailed examples.

2.1.1 Nonprocedural Programming

Prolog has procedural and nonprocedural aspects. Instead of writing a procedure with an explicit sequence of steps, a Prolog programmer writes a declarative set of rules and facts that state relationships. Because of its declarative style, conventional flowcharts and coding techniques cannot be used with Prolog. Yet Prolog rules are executed by an underlying *inference engine*, which does impose an order of execution. Because of that implicit ordering, Prolog rules also have a procedural interpretation. Unlike the linear flow through conventional procedures, Prolog rules are executed by *backtrack search*. This method is very powerful for many problems in artificial intelligence, but it requires that programmers learn a new way of thinking.

Ten-year-old children have found Prolog an easy language to learn. But professional programmers with many years of experience often find it puzzling and confusing. What is puzzling about Prolog is its simplicity. It does not have the most frequently used features of the common procedural languages:

- Assignment statements,
- Go-to statements,
- If-then-else statements, and
- Do-loops, for-loops, and while-loops.

Without these features, standard flowcharts cannot be translated into Prolog. After many years of structured programming, people have learned to replace go-to statements with loops and if-then-else statements. But Prolog does not have those statements either. The most surprising feature of Prolog, however, is the absence of an assignment statement. Without it, there is no way to change the value of a variable. In Prolog, it is possible to write X:=X+1, but the result is always *false*, since there is no value of X that could ever be equal to X+1. Before using Prolog effectively, a programmer has to forget all the old procedural habits and learn a new declarative way of thinking.

After programmers recover from the initial shock of learning what Prolog does not have, they can begin to appreciate the features that it does have:

- Predicates that express relationships between entities,
- A method of defining predicates by asserting rules and facts,
- A method of asking questions or starting computations by issuing goals,
- A backtracking search procedure for evaluating goals,
- Data structures that can simulate Pascal-like records or Lisp-like lists,
- A pattern matcher that builds and analyzes the data structures, and
- A set of built-in predicates for arithmetic, input/output, and system services.

These features provide a language that is universal in the sense that it can simulate a Turing machine—the most general digital computing device known. In principle, Prolog can compute anything that can be computed in any other programming language. But the way that it is done in Prolog is totally different from conventional languages. For complex problem solving, the Prolog approach is typically the most convenient.

2.1.2 Facts and Predicates

In Prolog, a fact is a statement that some entity has a particular property or that some relationship holds between two or more entities. Facts are expressed by applying a *predicate* to a list of *arguments*. For example, human(socrates) is a Prolog fact: the predicate is named human, and the argument is the constant socrates. This fact corresponds to the English sentence "Socrates is human." Following are other examples of facts stated in Prolog notation:

```
odd(5).
married(zeus, hera).
supply(acme, toothbrush, 100, 'July 14, 1986').
```

(Here, the single quotes around 'July 14, 1986' say that this is a string in IBM Prolog.) The fact odd(5) states that 5 is an odd number. The second fact says that Zeus and Hera are married; and the third says that Acme supplied 100 toothbrushes on July 14, 1986.

A constant or a predicate name can be chosen in many ways. The fact qz3x(gglfn5) is handled by the Prolog system in the same way as human(socrates). For readability, however, the names should reflect the intention of the human programmer. Following are common naming conventions:

- A predicate with one argument, in the form p(A), usually means that the entity A has property or attribute p. The fact dog(snoopy) means "Snoopy is a dog."

- A predicate with two arguments, in the form r(A,B), typically means that A stands in relation r to B. The fact child(sam,mary) means "Sam is a child of Mary."

- For a predicate that does some computation, the input arguments are usually placed first, and the results are put at the end: sum(3,5,8) means "The sum of 3 and 5 is 8."

- For a predicate that takes many arguments, the more important arguments are put first, and the less important ones later. For the fact "Acme supplied 100 toothbrushes on July 14, 1986," the most important argument is probably the supplier, next the type of item, next the quantity, and finally the date. Therefore one would write

```
supply(acme, toothbrush, 100, 'July 14, 1986')
```

Although these conventions are commonly followed, they do not always apply. Some predicates, like `married(A,B)`, are symmetric, and either argument could be written first. For many computational predicates, any argument may be treated as the output and the other arguments as input: `sum(X,5,8)` computes a number X, which when added to 5 produces 8; in this case, the first argument X may be considered the output. The flexibility in treating any argument as either input or output makes many Prolog predicates *reversible*. This property will be used in a number of examples throughout this book.

2.1.3 Variables and Rules

Words that start with an uppercase letter are treated as variables, and words that start with a lowercase letter are constants. A sequence of characters that starts with an uppercase letter or contains blanks and punctuation may be treated as a string constant by enclosing it in single quotes (`'July 14, 1986'` is a string constant) or as an atom constant by enclosing it in double quotes (`"July 14, 1986"` is an atom constant). If an atom starts with a letter and contains no blanks or special characters, then the quotes are not needed. Besides variables like X or T1 that begin with an uppercase letter, Prolog also supports *anonymous variables* represented by just an asterisk `*`. The asterisk is truly variable because it can have a different value every time it appears. For example, `p(*,*)` permits any values to occur in the two different argument places, such as `p(3,99)` or `p(socrates,7)`; but `p(X,X)` requires that both arguments be the same, such as `p(3,3)` or `p(socrates,socrates)`. An anonymous variable may be used anywhere that a named variable can occur; but each time it occurs, its previous value is ignored. For that reason, anonymous variables are primarily used as place holders when their values are not needed in future references.

Predicates may be defined in two ways: by a complete list of all the facts in which they occur; or by general rules that determine their truth or falsity. As an example, all family relationships are determined by lists of facts for three basic predicates: `child(C,P)` means that C is a child of P; `male(M)` means that M is male; `female(F)` means that F is female; and `married(X,Y)` means that X is married to Y. Following are examples of facts for the `child` predicate:

```
child(oidipous,iokaste).
child(oidipous,laios).
child(antigone,iokaste).
child(antigone,oidipous).
child(eteokles,iokaste).
child(eteokles,oidipous).
child(polyneikes,iokaste).
child(polyneikes,oidipous).
```

Following are some facts that define the `male` and `female` predicates:

```
male(laios).        male(oidipous).
male(eteokles).     male(polyneikes).
female(iokaste).    female(antigone).
```

The married predicate is symmetric: if X is married to Y, then Y is married to X. Therefore two facts must be stated for each marriage; one for each ordering of the arguments.

```
married(laios,iokaste).
married(iokaste,laios).
married(oidipous,iokaste).
married(iokaste,oidipous).
```

With these four predicates defined by lists of facts, all other family relations can be defined by rules. The easiest to define is parent, which is the converse of child:

```
parent(P,C) <- child(C,P).
```

In this rule, which is an example of a *conditional*, the arrow <- may be read as the English word *if*. Translated into English, the rule says that P is a parent of C if C is a child of P. Unlike standard logic, which has implications pointing to the right, the conclusion in Prolog is written on the left. This way of writing Prolog rules makes it easier for a person to find the rules that define a predicate: when a predicate appears on the right side (the *body* of a rule), it is being used or *called*; but when it appears on the left side (the *head* of a rule), it is being defined. By scanning down the left margin of a listing, the Prolog programmer can quickly find all the rules that define a given predicate.

The predicates father and mother require a conjunction of two conditions: M is the mother of C if C is a child of M and M is female. Likewise, F is the father of C if C is a child of F and F is male.

```
mother(M,C) <- child(C,M) & female(M).
father(F,C) <- child(C,F) & male(F).
```

The symbol & is the Boolean operator for conjunction; it may be read as the English word *and*. The reader should practice translating these rules into English sentences: the term mother(M,C) is read as "M is a mother of C"; the arrow is read "if"; and the & symbol is read "and." In the first rule above, C occurs twice. If C has a value, then both occurrences have the same value. However, there is no coupling to the C in the second rule. Thus the *scope* of a variable in Prolog is just the rule in which the variable occurs; variables with the same name in different rules are treated as different variables.

The next more complicated predicate is sibling: X is a sibling of Y if X is a child of some P, Y is a child of the same P, and X and Y are not the same person.

```
sibling(X,Y) <- child(X,P) & child(Y,P) & ¬(X=Y).
```

The symbol = represents a built-in predicate that tests for equality; it could be written in the basic notation as =(X,Y), but it is more readable in the *infix form* X=Y. The symbol ¬ represents negation. Both of the symbols = and ¬ have some subtle properties that will be discussed in more detail later.

Rules may be defined in terms of predicates that are themselves defined by rules. The predicates sister and brother, for example, can be defined in terms of sibling:

```
sister(S,X) <- sibling(S,X) & female(S).
brother(B,X) <- sibling(B,X) & male(B).
```

A *recursive rule* is one that defines a predicate in terms of itself. An example is descendant: D is a descendant of A if either D is a child of A or D is a child of a person P who is a descendant of A.

```
descendant(D,A) <- child(D,A)
                 | child(D,P) & descendant(P,A).
```

This rule introduces the symbol | for the Boolean disjunction or *or* operator. The & operator has higher precedence (tighter binding) than the | operator.

Strictly speaking, the | operator is not needed in Prolog, since every use of | can be eliminated by writing extra rules. The predicate descendant, for example, can be defined by two separate rules. The first says that D is a descendant of A if D is a child of A; the second says that D is a descendant of A if D is a child of P and P is a descendant of A:

```
descendant(D,A) <- child(D,A).
descendant(D,A) <- child(D,P) & descendant(P,A).
```

Both of these ways of defining descendant are about equally readable and equally efficient. There is not much reason for choosing one or the other. In some cases, however, the | operator can improve efficiency. Consider the definition of uncle. U is an uncle of N under either of the following two conditions:

- By blood, N is a child of P, who is a sibling of U, and U is male;
- By marriage, N is a child of P, who is a sibling of a person Q, who is married to U, and U is male.

That pair of conditions can be mapped into two Prolog rules:

```
uncle(U,N) <- child(N,P) & sibling(P,U) & male(U).
uncle(U,N) <- child(N,P) & sibling(P,Q) &
        married(Q,U) & male(U).
```

Since both of these rules have similar beginnings and endings, the | operator could be used to combine them in a single rule with the common parts factored out. But in the case of an uncle by blood, an extra equality Q=U must be added to show that the sibling Q and the uncle U are the same person.

```
uncle(U,N) <- child(N,P) & sibling(P,Q)
          & (Q=U | married(Q,U)) & male(U).
```

To understand this rule, read it as an English sentence: U is an uncle of N if N is a child of P, P is a sibling of Q, either Q is equal to U or Q is married to U, and U is male. Parentheses are needed around the phrase (Q=U | married(Q,U)) since | does not bind as tightly as &. This phrase in the factored form of the rule illustrates an interesting property of family trees: two people who are married to each other have equal status in defining relationships like *aunt* and *uncle*. This property holds for the English kinship terms, but it is not true of the kinship terms in many other languages and cultures.

All of the rules discussed so far are conditionals. *Unconditional rules* look like facts, but they contain variables. For example, the predicate related might be defined by the following English statements:

- Every person is related to himself or herself.

- X and Y are related if they are married to each other.

- X and Y are related if X is a child of some Z who is related to Y or Y is a child of some Z who is related to X.

Those three English sentences map into the following Prolog rules:

```
related(X,X).
related(X,Y) <- married(X,Y).
related(X,Y) <- child(X,Z) & related(Z,Y)
             | child(Y,Z) & related(Z,X).
```

The first of these three rules is unconditional. The other two are conditional. The third rule also happens to be recursive. The predicate related, as defined by these rules, has some interesting properties: any two people who have a common ancestor are related; aunts and uncles by marriage are related to their nieces and nephews; and if X is related to Y, then Y is related to X.

2.1.4 Goals

Facts and rules reside in a Prolog *workspace*, but no action takes place until a *goal* is entered. A simple goal looks like a fact or an unconditional rule. The difference lies in its use. For example, human(socrates) could be added to the workspace as a fact. But it could also be entered as a goal to ask the question "Is Socrates human?" The same character string may be interpreted as either a fact or a goal:

- Since facts and rules are normally loaded from a file, the input human(socrates) from a file is interpreted as a fact to be asserted (added to the workspace).

- Since goals are commonly entered from the terminal, the input human(socrates) from the terminal is interpreted as a goal that asks a question.

These are the defaults in many versions of Prolog. With extra symbols in front of the string, the defaults may be overridden to assert a fact at the terminal or enter a goal from a file. In IBM Prolog, an arrow `<-` must be added in front of a goal in a file, and a period must be added in front of an assertion at the terminal.

Goals may also contain variables. The goal `human(X)` asks the system to find some human and *bind* its value to the variable X. Suppose the following facts had been asserted:

```
human(socrates).   human(cicero).   human(voltaire).
greek(socrates).   roman(cicero).   french(voltaire).
```

When the goal `human(X)` was entered, the system would look for the first fact that matched the goal, in this case `human(socrates)`, and bind the value `socrates` to the variable X. The other possible values `cicero` and `voltaire` would be ignored, unless for some reason the system had to *backtrack* to find another value.

To show why the system might backtrack, consider the compound goal `(human(X) & roman(X))`. As before, the system first binds the value `socrates` to X. Next, it tries to match the subgoal `roman(socrates)` to some fact in the workspace. Unfortunately, no fact matches. Therefore the system backtracks to the previous goal `human(X)`; it *unbinds* the old value of X and binds the next value `cicero`. With this new value, the subgoal `roman(cicero)` matches one of the facts. Therefore the goal succeeds, and the final value of X is `cicero`. Goals may be grouped in three categories, according to their use:

- *Verifier goals* ask whether a certain predicate is true.

- *Finder goals* ask for values to be bound to one or more variables.

- *Doer goals* ask the system to perform some operation.

A verifier is like a yes–no question that asks whether a particular relationship is true or false. Verifiers have no unbound variables: `child(sam,mary)` asks whether Sam is a child of Mary; it succeeds if true and fails if false. A finder is like a *who* or *what* question in English. It asks the system to find a value for one or more unbound variables. The goal `child(X,mary)` asks who is a child of Mary; the answer is bound to the variable X. A doer goal is not used to ask a question, but to cause some side effect. It may invoke subgoals that are finders or verifiers, but it also invokes subgoals that may change the workspace or perform some input/output. Since doers have side effects, they are not part of pure Prolog.

To determine whether a goal is a finder or a verifier, the values of the variables at the moment the goal is invoked must be considered. For example, the goal `(human(X) & roman(X))` has two subgoals, each with a single variable X. The first subgoal to be issued is `human(X)`; this is a finder goal that seeks a value for X. Once X has been bound to a value, such as `socrates`, the next subgoal is issued as the verifier goal `roman(socrates)`. Verifier goals cannot change a value of a variable. Instead, they may cause a failure to occur that causes Prolog to backtrack to a previous finder goal to seek a different value. In this case, the finder goal human(X) is issued once more to find a different value for X.

In pure Prolog, the order in which subgoals are issued has no effect on the final answer. The goal (roman(X) & human(X)) would find the same answer X=cicero. In this order, roman(X) is the finder goal, and human(X) is the verifier. Although the same answer is computed, this goal executes a few microseconds faster, since the finder roman(X) finds the correct answer on the first try, and no backtracking is necessary. But before considering performance, the main concern is to write rules that are logically correct. The last section of this chapter discusses methods of reordering rules to improve performance.

2.1.5 Prolog Structures

Facts, goals, and rules are special cases of Prolog *clauses*. The most general clause is a statement of the form,

$$head \; <\!\!- \; body.$$

The head must be a single *predication* (a predicate symbol followed by a list of arguments). The body may be either one predication or a combination of predications separated by & for *and* and | for *or*. The negation symbol ¬ may also be placed in the body of a clause. Either the head or the body of a clause may be missing. A clause with no head is a goal; a clause with no body is called a *unit clause*, since it only has one predication. A conditional rule has both a head and a body. Unit clauses are either facts or unconditional rules.

Prolog is a relational programming language, unlike Lisp, which is a functional programming language. In Lisp, as in most languages, functions take input arguments and compute results. In Prolog, however, only predicates (also known as relations) compute results. To see the difference, consider the arithmetic expression that would be written (A+B)/(A-B) in Fortran, Pascal, PL/I, or Ada. In Lisp, it would be written,

    (QUOTIENT (PLUS A B) (DIFFERENCE A B)).

Here PLUS and DIFFERENCE are functions that take the values of A and B as input and compute results that serve as input to the QUOTIENT function. In Prolog, that expression could be evaluated by a series of predicates:

    sum(A,B,T1) & diff(A,B,T2) & quot(T1,T2,T3).

Here Prolog uses temporary variables T1 and T2 to hold the results of sum and diff. Then quot takes those values and computes a new value for the temporary variable T3. For doing arithmetic, this notation is more awkward than Lisp.

In IBM Prolog (and in many other Prolog implementations) the := symbol is defined as an operator for evaluating *infix notation* like the following:

```
X := (A+B)/(A-B).
```

In this form, `:=` is the predicate that triggers the evaluation. Other operators, such as `+` and `-`, form data structures that are evaluated by the rules for `:=`. Note the difference: in most programming languages, the `+` and `-` operators themselves compute a result; in Prolog, however, the `+` and `-` operators simply form data structures that are evaluated by the rules for `:=`. For the programmer who is writing arithmetic expressions, the difference can often be ignored.

Although Prolog does not use functions to compute values, it supports them as a notation for building data structures. They are treated as undefined symbols that are carried around inside the arguments of predicates. A *term* is a function symbol called an *identifier* followed by a list of *arguments*:

```
human(socrates)    f(g(Abc,2),100)    +(5,+(3,4))
```

The arguments may be constants, variables, or other functions applied to their arguments. Functions applied to arguments form trees, which may themselves consist of functions applied to other arguments. The term

```
s(np(cats),vp(v(like),np(mice)))
```

represents the tree

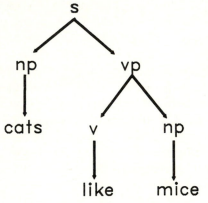

Trees like this can represent the parsed form of an English sentence. Other trees can represent the *records* in programming languages like Pascal. Following is a definition for a Pascal record of type `person`:

```
type person = record
              name: string;
              address: string;
              date_of_birth: array[1..3] of integer;
              sex: boolean
          end
```

The `person` record has four subfields: `name`, `address`, `date_of_birth`, and `sex`. In Prolog, the equivalent data would be stored as a tree constructed from functions and their arguments. To emphasize the similarity with Pascal, the subparts may be written on separate lines:

```
person(
    name(N),
    address(A),
    date_of_birth(D.M.Y),
    sex(S))
```

In the default notation, the function identifier is written first, followed by the arguments in parentheses. But Prolog also supports *infix notation* like A+B, *suffix notation* like N!, and *prefix notation* like -X, where the parentheses may be omitted. A function or predicate that is written in one of these forms is called an *operator*, but its effect is exactly the same as the default form. In fact, the internal representations of A+B+C and +(+(A,B),C) are identical.

The data structure for person includes one of the most important infix operators in Prolog, the *dot operator* illustrated in the form (D.M.Y). This operator, which may also be written in prefix form as,

```
.(D,.(M,Y))
```

connects pairs of items to form binary trees. When used repeatedly, it forms arbitrarily complex list structures. Techniques for using it in list processing will be discussed later.

2.1.6 Built-in Predicates

In pure Prolog, every predicate is defined by a list of rules and facts. In principle, pure Prolog is rich enough to define all computable functions without any built-in predicates at all. But in practice, built-in predicates are needed for three purposes: improved performance for arithmetic and string handling; ease of programming for certain kinds of operations; and access to external facilities, such as input/output services and the operating system.

In the family database, the primitive predicates are defined by lists of facts. Numeric valued predicates could also be defined by lists of facts, but it is more common to state a general rule that computes their values upon request. Consider the predicate factorial(N,X), whose second argument X is the factorial of the first argument N. It could be defined by the following list:

```
factorial(0,1).            factorial(1,1).
factorial(2,2).            factorial(3,6).
factorial(4,24).           factorial(5,120).
factorial(6,720).          factorial(7,5040).
factorial(8,40320).
```

This list only defines factorial for the inputs 0 to 8; it is undefined for all other inputs. A more complete way of defining it is to state one fact that gives the value of `factorial` for input 0 and then to give a *recursive rule* that computes the result for all inputs greater than 0:

```
factorial(0,1).
factorial(N,X) <- (M := N - 1) & factorial(M,Y) &
    (X := N * Y).
```

The general rule states that the factorial of N is X if the difference of N and 1 is M and the factorial of M is Y and the product of N and Y is X. This is an example of a *recursive rule* that calls itself repeatedly. To compute the factorial of 1, for example, it computes the difference of 1 and 1, which is 0. Then it calls itself to find the factorial of 0, which is given by the first fact as 1. Finally, it computes the product of N (which is 1) times Y (which has just been found to be 1) to generate the result X (which is also 1). For each nonnegative integer N, the `factorial` predicate is invoked N+1 times.

The above definition works for nonnegative integers. But if the first argument ever happened to be negative, the recursive rule would keep calling itself indefinitely. Eventually, the system would run out of space and print an error message, `STACK OVERFLOW`. To avoid that error, an extra rule may be inserted to trap negative inputs:

```
factorial(0,1).
factorial(N,X) <- lt(N,0) &
    write('Negative input to factorial').
factorial(N,X) <- (M := N - 1) & factorial(M,Y) &
    (X := N * Y).
```

As before, the fact `factorial(0,1)` matches goals where the first argument is 0. The next rule matches all other goals. The predicate `lt(N,0)` succeeds for values of N less than 0. If N happens to be less than 0, the rule calls the `write` predicate to print out the message "Negative input to factorial." After the call to `write`, the rule is finished, and the last rule is never invoked. This rule is also invoked for positive values of N, but `lt(N,0)` fails. Therefore the system stops executing the second rule. Instead, it invokes the last rule to compute `factorial` recursively.

Besides computational predicates for arithmetic and string handling, Prolog also has a set of *nonlogical predicates*. Unlike the computational predicates, which might be defined by logical rules, the nonlogical predicates perform services that cannot be specified in pure logic. There are three basic kinds of nonlogical predicates:

- *Execution control predicates* change the way Prolog executes rules. These have a number of complex properties that will be discussed later.

- *Workspace predicates* change the Prolog workspace itself. They may add and delete rules and facts, turn on tracing and debugging, or reset certain global parameters.

- *System predicates* interact with the operating system to do input and output or to execute some external system command.

Whereas predicates defined by pure Prolog can never change anything but data passed as arguments, the nonlogical predicates have *side effects*: they can change hidden data or structures that are not specified in the arguments. In the case of input/output, the side effects may occur on paper or display screens that are far removed from the computer itself.

2.1.7 The Inference Engine

Logic was designed for stating timeless truths. It is purely declarative, and has no procedural facilities at all. Prolog, however, makes logic executable: declaratively, predicates are either true or false; procedurally, goals either succeed or fail. The procedural effect results from the combination of logic with a special program called an *inference engine*. This program provides the sequencing that causes rules and facts to be invoked when needed. As an example, consider the following rule and fact:

```
mortal(X) <- human(X).
human(socrates).
```

Declaratively, the rule says that X is mortal if X is human; the fact states that Socrates is human. To show the procedural effect, suppose that Prolog were given the goal mortal(Z). This goal is matched to the left side of the rule, causing the two variables X and Z to be *bound* to each other. The system then issues the body of the rule, human(X), as a subgoal to be satisfied. This goal matches the fact human(socrates). Therefore the goal is satisfied by binding the value socrates to the variable X. Since the variables Z and X are cross-bound to each other, Z is also bound to the value socrates. Prolog finally responds to the original goal by typing the output,

```
<- mortal(socrates).
```

The Prolog inference engine has two basic procedures: a *goal processor* and a *rule processor*. In an interpreter, there will be actual code that performs each of these functions. A highly optimized compiler, however, may take shortcuts so that the two tasks are inextricably intertwined. But to simplify the discussion, assume an interpreted version of Prolog. A compiled version will have the same effect, even if it simplifies or eliminates some of the intermediate steps.

The goal processor and the rule processor call each other recursively: in executing a goal, the goal processor must invoke rules; in executing a rule, the rule processor issues the body of the rule as a new subgoal. Both processors use a pushdown stack of *choice points* to which backtracking returns in case of a failure. Whenever the goal processor reports a failure, the calling program (which could be either the goal processor or the rule processor) takes the most recent choice point from the stack and resumes execution. If a failure occurs when no choice points are left, the failure is reported to the user sitting at the terminal. The stack of choice points is saved even when the original goal succeeds. If the user types a semicolon, the Prolog inference engine resumes execution from the most recent choice point.

The goal processor is the first to be invoked when the user enters a new goal. If the goal is a simple one like `mortal(socrates)`, it immediately calls the rule processor to find some rule with a matching head. But in searching a database for Greek goddesses, the user might type a complex goal like `(greek(X) & female(X) & ¬mortal(X))`. Before calling the rule processor, the goal processor must break down such complex goals into simple ones, each with a single predicate. Let G be the current goal:

- If G is a conjunction (P & Q), first process P; if P succeeds, then process Q. If Q fails, check whether P left any choice points on the backtracking stack. If so, backtrack to the last choice point left by P. G succeeds only if both subgoals succeed (possibly after some backtracking from Q back to P).

- If G is a disjunction (P | Q), first process P and place a choice point on the backtracking stack that points to Q. If P succeeds, then G succeeds, and Q is left as a choice point that might be tried later if something else happens to fail. If P fails, then Q is removed from the backtracking stack and processed. G succeeds if either P or Q succeeds.

- If G is a negation ¬P, then P is issued as the next subgoal. If P succeeds, G fails. If P fails, G succeeds.

- If G is a simple goal, then call the rule processor to handle it. If the rule processor reports success, then G succeeds; otherwise, G fails.

The goal processor may call itself recursively many times when processing a complex goal. For the goal of finding Greek goddesses, it processes the first subgoal `greek(X)` and returns with some value for X, such as `socrates`. Then it issues the next subgoal `female(socrates)`. Since this subgoal fails, the processor backtracks to `greek(X)` to find another value for X. If it returns with X=hera, the next subgoal `female(hera)` is processed. Since that succeeds, it next tries `¬mortal(hera)`. To process the negation, the goal processor calls itself recursively to process `mortal(hera)`. Since this subgoal fails, the negation succeeds. Finally all of the conjuncts have succeeded, and the goal processor returns successfully with X=hera. Now if the user at the terminal types a semicolon, the inference engine resumes execution from the most recent choice point to find another Greek female immortal.

The rule processor is called from the goal processor, but it may in turn call the goal processor. It is invoked with a simple goal such as `mortal(X)`. It then searches the list of rules and facts to find one with a matching head. Let G be the current goal with a predicate named N.

- Match G to the head of each rule for N until one is found whose head matches. If no match is found, return with failure. If a match is found, place a pointer to the remaining list for N on the backtracking stack and continue processing the rule that matched.

- If the matching rule is an unconditional rule or fact, there is no body to execute. Therefore the rule processor can immediately return with success.

- If the matching rule is conditional, call the goal processor to execute the body (right hand side) of the rule. If the goal processor returns with success; then return with success for G. If the goal processor fails on the current rule, then take the list of remaining rules for N from the backtracking stack and continue searching for another one that matches G.

- When all rules for N have been tried without success, return with failure.

In short, rules are tried in the order in which they are entered (typed or read into a workspace). The body of a rule is executed just as if it had been a goal typed at the terminal. When the current rule fails, the rule processor abandons it and tries the next rule with the same predicate name.

2.2 PURE PROLOG

All versions of Prolog share a common core called pure Prolog. This core is directly derived from symbolic logic and supports the great bulk of all Prolog programming. Although features outside the core are needed for input/output and system interfaces, the pure Prolog subset determines the spirit of the language. This section illustrates Prolog programming style with emphasis on the pure Prolog core.

2.2.1 Solving Problems Stated in English

Translating Prolog into English is relatively straightforward. But translating any natural language into any formal language is much more difficult. Chapter 5 presents formal rules for automatically mapping English into a logical form. This section presents more informal methods of analyzing a problem statement and mapping it into Prolog. Following are some rules of thumb for doing that mapping:

- Proper names like "Bill" or "Socrates" map into constants: `bill`, `socrates`; unnamed individuals must be assigned unique identifiers, such as `i1, i2, i3`.

- Common nouns like "cat" or "table" map into one-place predicates: `cat(X), table(X)`.

- Adjectives like "red" or "heavy" map into one-place predicates: `red(X), heavy(X)`.

- Intransitive verbs like "walk" or "sleep" map into one-place predicates: `walk(X), sleep(X)`.

- Transitive verbs like "see" or "carry" map into two-place predicates: `see(X,Y), carry(X,Y)`.

- Bitransitive verbs like "give" or "tell" (which take both a direct and an indirect object) map into three-place predicates: `give(X,Y,Z)`, `tell(X,Y,Z)`.

- The main verb usually maps into the conclusion of a rule (the head) and other words map into the conditions (the body).

- The verb "be" in its various forms usually does not map into a predicate: the following noun, adjective, or participle tends to become the main predicate.

- The verb "have" sometimes indicates possession, but more often it indicates a relation between two nouns that depends on the context.

These nine rules cover a useful subset of English. But they are only a rough approximation. There are many fine points of language that they do not cover. Some of these points will be discussed later. But to show their applicability, consider Exercise 2 at the end of this chapter:

> Washable allergenic things are washed. Nonwashable allergenic things are vacuumed. Everything that is gray and fuzzy is allergenic. Shirts, socks, pajamas, dogs, and llamas are washable. Lamps, sofas, cats, and computers are nonwashable. Following are my gray, fuzzy possessions: my pajamas, my sofa, my cat Thothmes, and my llama Millicent.

In the first sentence, the adjectives "washable" and "allergenic" map into the predicates `washable(X)` and `allergenic(X)`. The common noun "thing" maps into the predicate `thing(X)`. But what about the verb "are washed"? The active verb form "wash" is transitive, but the passive form is consistently used in this problem without any indication of the one who does the washing. Since the subject is omitted, a one-place passive form `washed(X)` may be used. Given these predicates, the next step is to identify the condition and conclusion of the rule. The conclusion is `washed(X)`. The condition under which X is washed is that it must be a washable allergenic thing. Therefore the Prolog rule becomes

    `washed(X) <- washable(X) & allergenic(X) & thing(X).`

This rule may be read "X is washed if X is a washable allergenic thing," which is Prolog's closest approximation to "Washable allergenic things are washed." By the same kind of analysis, the second sentence becomes,

    `vacuumed(X) <-`
        `nonwashable(X) & allergenic(X) & thing(X).`

Note the separate predicate `nonwashable(X)` instead of `¬washable(X)`. This separate predicate is needed since a later rule uses `nonwashable` in the conclusion, and Prolog normally uses negations only in the condition or body of a rule. The third sentence has a different syntactic form, but it also maps into a similar Prolog rule:

    `allergenic(X) <- gray(X) & fuzzy(X) & thing(X).`

The next sentence implies that X is washable if X is a shirt, a sock, a pajama, a dog, or a llama:

```
washable(X) <- shirt(X) | sock(X) | pajama(X) |
               dog(X) | llama(X).
```

Similarly, the sentence after that becomes,

```
nonwashable(X) <- lamp(X) | sofa(X) | cat(X) |
                  computer(X).
```

The last sentence introduces some complexities: "Following are my gray, fuzzy possessions: my pajamas, my sofa, my cat Thothmes, and my llama Millicent." The word "following" can be ignored; it is not about the subject matter itself, but about the form of the statement. The word "my" introduces a new individual, me, who possesses several things. The common noun "possession" does not map into a one-place predicate, since it is actually derived from a transitive verb "possess." The other common nouns map into one-place predicates, and the proper names "Thothmes" and "Millicent" map into the constants thothmes and millicent. But this sentence also mentions two other individuals, my pajamas and my sofa, which do not have names. In order to record facts about these things, they must be identified by constants; since they are not named, unique identifiers such as pj1 for my pajamas and sf1 for my sofa may be introduced. With these predicates and constants, this sentence maps into a series of facts with five individual constants: pj1, sf1, thothmes, millicent, and me. In standard logic, a single formula could assert that I possess pj1 and pj1 is a gray fuzzy pajama:

```
possess(me,pj1) & pajama(pj1) &
    gray(pj1) & fuzzy(pj1).
```

But since Prolog facts may contain only one predication, that information must be split into four simple facts (which may be written on a single line). The last sentence of Exercise 2 therefore maps into the following collection of facts:

```
possess(me,pj1). pajama(pj1). gray(pj1). fuzzy(pj1).
possess(me,sf1). sofa(sf1).   gray(sf1). fuzzy(sf1).
possess(me,thothmes). cat(thothmes). gray(thothmes).
    fuzzy(thothmes).
possess(me,millicent). llama(millicent).
    gray(millicent). fuzzy(millicent).
```

These Prolog rules, when asserted in a single workspace, represent a complete translation of Exercise 2 into Prolog. Unfortunately, there is something missing: the English statement never said how the noun "thing" is related to the other nouns like "cat" or "sofa." Another rule must be added to say that X is a thing if X is a shirt or sock or whatever:

```
thing(X) <- shirt(X) | sock(X) | pajama(X) | dog(X)
          | llama(X) | lamp(X) | sofa(X) | cat(X)
          | computer(X).
```

Every time a new type of entity is introduced, this rule must be augmented with another disjunction. A simpler and more general solution is to say that everything is a thing. That can be stated in one very short unconditional rule:

```
thing(X).
```

This rule always succeeds for any value of X.

Suppose all those rules have been typed into the file washable prolog. Then the following is a transcript of a Prolog session at the terminal. The first step is to invoke the consult predicate that reads the file and adds all the rules to the current workspace.

```
consult(washable).
10MS SUCCESS
 <- consult(washable).
```

(Here, what we type at the terminal is in this typeface, while the answers from the machine are in this typeface.) The first line is the goal that calls consult. The second line is a response that shows the goal took 10 milliseconds on an IBM 3081 computer to complete successfully. The third line is an *echo* that repeats the goal that was entered, but with variables replaced with the computed values (in this case, there were no variables). The next goal typed at the terminal asks what is washed; Prolog responds with pj1 substituted for X:

```
washed(X).
OMS SUCCESS
 <- washed(pj1).
```

Note the time of 0 ms. Nothing actually takes zero time to compute, but anything less than half a millisecond is rounded down to 0. After a goal succeeds, typing a semicolon forces the system to backtrack and find another solution. The next thing that is washed turns out to be millicent:

```
;
OMS SUCCESS
 <- washed(millicent).
```

Typing another semicolon shows that there are no further solutions:

```
;
OMS FAIL
```

Next are the goals that determine what is vacuumed. In this case, the answers are sf1 and thothmes:

```
vacuumed(X).
OMS SUCCESS
```

```
    <- vacuumed(sf1).
  ;
OMS SUCCESS
    <- vacuumed(thothmes).
  ;
OMS FAIL
```

Prolog does have other methods for computing all possible solutions without requiring the user to type a semicolon for each one. These methods will be discussed in Section 2.3.2. IBM Prolog also has *pragmas* that change the input and output formats; they can be used to suppress the echo and the information about execution time. These are useful features that are discussed in Appendix A. They improve the human factors of the system, but they do not illustrate any fundamental principles about Prolog or logic programming.

2.2.2 Subtle Properties of English

Natural languages are highly systematic structures, but the system is not always marked by obvious syntactic features. For that reason, superficial patterns are often misleading. In fact, one of the pioneers of computer science, Edsger Dijkstra, said that a solid understanding of one's native language is one of the most important requirements for success in programming. As an example of a common misunderstanding, consider the sentences "Sam likes Jane" and "Cats like fish." After learning that the first sentence maps into the Prolog fact `like(sam,jane)`, many beginners translate the second sentence into the fact `like(cats,fish)`. But the rules of thumb in the previous section suggest that common nouns should map into predicates. Therefore "Cats like fish" maps into the following rule:

```
    like(C,F) <- cat(C) & fish(F).
```

This rule says that C likes F if C is a cat and F is a fish. The reason for this difference is that a proper name normally designates a unique individual within a given context. Therefore the fact `like(sam,jane)` is an unconditional assertion. If there happened to be many people named Sam and Jane, further conditions would be needed to specify the context more narrowly. The following rule, for example, says that X likes Y if X is named `sam`, Y is named `jane`, X lives at 23 Main Street, and Y lives at 19 Blossom Lane:

```
    like(X,Y) <- named(X,sam) & named(Y,jane)
              & live(X,'23 Main St.')
              & live(Y,'19 Blossom Lane').
```

The general principle that each individual must be identified by a unique constant is always true. But when names are not unique, that constant must be something more specific, such as a social security number. Except in unusual circumstances, common nouns apply to multiple individuals. Therefore they typically map into predicates rather than constants.

The rule that common nouns map into predicates is generally true, but they may map into predicates with more than one argument. Consider the sentences "My cat is my friend" and "Friends like each other." The word "friend" does not indicate the type of individual in the same way as "human" or "cat"; instead, it shows the *role* that some person (or cat) plays with respect to another. In general, nouns that specify the type of individual designate *natural types*, which correspond to predicates with a single argument; nouns that specify a role that the individual plays designate *role types*, which correspond to predicates with more than one argument. Examples of natural types include human, cat, dog, beagle, tree, table, house, and number. Examples of role types include father, sister, lawyer, employee, pet, possession, home, and quotient. Note the distinction: Sam may be a human by nature, but a father by virtue of a certain relationship to someone else; Thothmes is a cat by nature, but a pet in relation to some person; 4 is a number by itself, but a quotient as a result of 20 divided by 5. For further discussion of these types, see the book by Sowa (1984).

To represent the noun "friend," two arguments are needed on the predicate: the first indicates the person who is the friend, and the second indicates the other person involved. Since friendships are normally reciprocal, two facts are needed to make the predicate symmetric. The sentence "My cat is my friend" maps into the following facts:

```
friend(me,thothmes).  friend(thothmes,me).
```

The sentence "Friends like each other" uses the phrase "each other" to abbreviate two statements: X likes Y if X is a friend of Y; and Y likes X if X is a friend of Y.

```
like(X,Y) <- friend(X,Y).
like(Y,X) <- friend(X,Y).
```

Actually, only one of these rules would be needed if the system guaranteed that the friend predicate were always symmetric. English also uses other words like "respectively" or "reciprocally" to indicate relationships that Prolog would represent with variables.

The sentence "My cat eats everything he likes" raises some interesting issues. In mapping it into Prolog, the main verb becomes the conclusion and the other parts are the conditions. If the cat is the same one mentioned in Exercise 2, the rule becomes,

```
eat(thothmes,X) <- like(thothmes,X).
```

When this rule is added to the previous rules, it leads to the conclusion that Thothmes eats me. One way to limit his appetite is to amend the specification to say "My cat eats X if he likes X and X is not a friend of his":

```
eat(thothmes,X) <- like(thothmes,X)
                  & ¬friend(X,thothmes).
```

This rule seems reasonable, since it would allow Thothmes to make friends with Tweety without eating him while still eating other birds.

Exercise 4 (page 100) can now be solved with the techniques discussed so far. Some of the sentences are fairly complex. For example, the sentence "Any man who likes a woman who likes him is happy" maps into the following rule:

```
happy(M) <-
    man(M) & woman(W) & like(M,W) & like(W,M).
```

The sentence "Bertha likes any man who likes her" causes trouble for about 50% of the people who translate it into Prolog. Those who translate it into the following rule are lucky:

```
like(bertha,M) <- man(M) & like(M,bertha).
```

The unfortunate ones map it into the following rule:

```
like(bertha,M) <- like(M,bertha) & man(M).
```

Both of these rules are recursive. But the first one checks whether M is a man before calling itself, and the second one calls itself recursively before checking M. In the first case, man(M) is a finder goal that determines some value for M. When the rule calls itself, it issues one of the subgoals

```
like(norbert,bertha)
like(pierre,bertha)
like(bruno,bertha)
```

The second rule, however, calls itself immediately. It gets into a recursive loop where it keeps issuing the same subgoal like(bertha,bertha). In general, a recursive rule that calls itself before making any change to its arguments will loop indefinitely (or until storage is exhausted). See page 422 for a keyboard command to terminate a loop.

In looking for some way to make everybody happy in Exercise 4, think of reasonable principles in English before writing them in Prolog. One reasonable principle is "Any man who is not rich likes any woman who is rich." In fact, this principle makes many people happy for many different reasons. With the goal happy(X), for example, Prolog would keep finding the same names again and again. The reason for the duplicate answers is that backtracking forces the system to examine all possible paths. If it finds that someone is happy for two or more reasons, that person will be listed once for each reason. The set_of predicate discussed later would find all solutions and eliminate duplicates.

Exercise 5 introduces a new issue: the distinction between individuals and types. That problem arises in many guises, as in the following faulty syllogism:

```
             Clyde is an elephant.
             Elephant is a species.
             ----------------------
Therefore    Clyde is a species.
```

A naive mapping of that syllogism into Prolog would lead to exactly the same fallacy:

```
isa(clyde,elephant).
isa(elephant,species).
isa(X,Z) <- isa(X,Y) & isa(Y,Z).
```

Given these two facts and rule, Prolog would conclude that the goal isa(clyde,species) is satisfied. The problem here is a nondistributed middle term: the word "elephant" is being used in two different ways. The first sentence says that the individual Clyde is of type elephant, and the second says that "elephant" is the name of a species. No conclusion is possible when the middle term of a syllogism is used in two different ways.

Talking about types in Prolog requires a change of notation. Normally, one would assert the fact elephant(clyde) where the individual maps into a constant clyde, and the type maps into the predicate elephant(X). To talk about types as individuals, however, requires types to be represented as constants. Then a new, more general predicate type(X,T) is needed to assert that individual X has type T. The premises about Clyde and elephants would map into the following Prolog facts:

```
type(clyde,elephant).
named(es1,elephant).   type(es1,species).
```

The first line says that clyde is of type elephant. The second line says that there exists some entity identified as es1, which has the name elephant and the type species. This analysis blocks erroneous inferences about Clyde's being a species, but it allows more abstract reasoning about types.

In Exercise 5, the main statements are about types. If Sam likes all kinds of sports, he undoubtedly likes all the subtypes, such as football or boxing, but he might be bored with a particular game or match. The problem also involves other complexities, such as unstated assumptions about the relationship between competing in a sport and playing the sport. There are two approaches to issues as complex as these: adopt a general set of predicates for talking about individuals, types, and subtypes; or simplify the English statements in a way that captures the main points with a minimum of abstraction. Simplifying assumptions may be necessary to solve a particular problem, but they may not generalize to other problems.

Another issue that arises in mapping English to a formal notation is that adjectives may have complex interactions with the nouns they modify. In particular, degree adjectives like "big" and "small" are relative to a standard determined by the noun: a big mouse is much smaller than a small elephant. By blindly mapping adjectives and common nouns into one-place predicates, one system made a serious blunder. It mapped the sentence "Sam is a good musician" into two Prolog facts:

```
good(sam).  musician(sam).
```

Then it mapped the sentence "Sam is a bad cook" into the following facts:

```
bad(sam).  cook(sam).
```

From these four facts, it answered "yes" to all of the following questions: Is Sam a good cook? Is Sam a bad musician? Is Sam a good bad musician cook? The error here results from the fact that "cook" and "musician" do not designate natural types, but role types. Adjectives like "good" and "bad" do not apply to Sam as a person, but to his role as cook or musician. The mapping into Prolog (or any other logical form) must recognize the roles and the ways of qualifying them.

Besides these complexities, natural languages pose many philosophical problems, especially in talk about knowledge and belief, hopes and fears, intentions and expectations, tenses and modalities. Many of these problems are still unsolved in their full generality; but for many of them, the Prolog programmer can adopt a special-case solution that is adequate for the task at hand. Fortunately, many practical problems lie within the subset that Prolog can easily represent. But the problem solver (and poser) should recognize the areas where difficulties can be expected.

2.2.3 Representing Quantifiers

Standard logic has two basic quantifiers: the *universal quantifier* (∀ X), read "for all X," and the *existential quantifier* (∃ X), read "there exists an X." Prolog does not use explicit quantifier symbols like ∀ and ∃. Instead, all variables in a Prolog clause are assumed to be universally quantified. For example, the rule

```
thing(X).
```

from page 42 could be read "for all X, X is a thing." Because of this convention, universal quantifiers in logic are easy to map into Prolog. Existential quantifiers, however, require some care. There are three ways to handle them:

- Use names or other unique identifiers to represent entities bound by an existential quantifier that does not follow any universal quantifiers.

- Introduce special function symbols for existential quantifiers that follow one or more universal quantifiers.

- Observe that any variable that occurs in a negative context (such as the condition part of a rule) has the effect of being existentially quantified.

Some examples may help to clarify these three principles. With an existential quantifier, the sentence, "I own a fuzzy gray sofa," could be represented,

```
(∃ X) (own(me,X) & fuzzy(X) & gray(X) & sofa(X)).
```

In this formula, the sofa has no name. Instead, it is introduced by the quantifier (∃ X) to indicate "there exists an X." Without the quantifier, the sofa must be identified by some constant, such as sf1, which was suggested in Section 2.2.1. Since Prolog facts have only a single predication, the formula must also be broken up into four separate facts. It therefore becomes,

```
own(me,sf1).  fuzzy(sf1).  gray(sf1).  sofa(sf1).
```

When an existential quantifier follows a universal quantifier, it must be represented by a function symbol. As an example, consider the sentence, "Every person has a mother." That may be paraphrased, "For every P, there exists an M such that M is a mother of P if P is a person." If Prolog had quantifiers, that sentence could be written,

```
(∀ P) (∃ M) mother(M,P) <- person(P).
```

In standard Prolog, the universal quantifier (∀ P) would be dropped. But the existential quantifier (∃ M) cannot be replaced with a unique identifier such as m1. Otherwise, the resulting Prolog rule would express something quite unintended:

```
mother(m1,P) <- person(P).
```

This rule says that m1 is a mother of P if P is a person. In other words, m1 is a universal mother of everyone. Since the existential quantifier (∃ M) follows a universal quantifier (∀ P) the variable M depends on P. That dependency can be shown with a special function, say mom(P):

```
mother(mom(P),P) <- person(P).
```

This rule may be read, "For all P, mom(P) is a mother of P if P is a person." The function mom(P) shows the dependency on P. Such functions are called *Skolem functions* in honor of the Norwegian mathematician Thoralf Skolem, who introduced them as a technique for eliminating quantifiers. This method of replacing quantifiers with function symbols is sometimes called *skolemizing*.

As a more complex example, take the sentence, "Every chicken coop has a chicken that is pecked by every other chicken in the coop." The first part of this sentence, "Every chicken coop has a chicken," has the same structure as "Every person has a mother," but the extra clause at the end makes it more complex. To map it into Prolog, first select predicates coop(X) and chicken(X) for the coop and the chicken, a predicate peck(X,Y) for the verb "peck," and a predicate loc(X,Y) for location "in." According to the rules of Section 2.2.1, the verb "has" typically indicates a highly context-dependent predicate. In this context, it represents the location loc(X,Y). Since the English sentence implies a universal quantifier ranging over chicken coops followed by an existential quantifier ranging over chickens, there must be a special function, say loser(X), which designates the poor chicken that is pecked by every other one in coop X. The English sentence has three implications: the loser of the coop is a chicken; it is located in the coop; and it is pecked by every other chicken located in the coop. Since Prolog rules have only one conclusion each, that sentence must be mapped into three separate rules:

```
chicken(loser(X)) <- coop(X).
loc(loser(X),X) <- coop(X).
peck(Y,loser(X)) <- coop(X) & chicken(Y)
      & loc(Y,X) & ¬(Y = loser(X)).
```

These three rules may be read "The loser of X is a chicken if X is a coop; the loser of X is located in X if X is a coop; and Y pecks the loser of X if X is a coop, Y is a chicken, Y is located in X, and Y is not the same as the loser of X."

The third method of handling existential quantifiers results from the way quantifiers interact with negation. In standard logic:

```
(∀ X) ¬P(X)     is identical to     ¬(∃ X) P(X).
(∃ X) ¬P(X)     is identical to     ¬(∀ X) P(X).
```

The first rule says that for all X, P is false if and only if it is false that there exists an X for which P is true. The second rule says that there exists an X for which P is false if and only if it is false that for all X, P is true. These two rules can be summarized in the following principle: when a quantifier moves in or out of a context governed by a negation, ∀ becomes and ∃ becomes ∀. In applying this principle to Prolog, note that the standard logic conditional "P if Q" is equivalent to "P or not Q." Similarly, the Prolog <- operator contains an implicit negation that governs the condition or body of a rule. As an example, consider the following definition of `mother_in_law` with the universal quantifiers shown explicitly:

```
(∀ M) (∀ X) (∀ Y)
    mother_in_law(M,X) <- mother(M,Y) & married(X,Y).
```

The quantifiers (∀ M) and (∀ X) govern variables that occur in both the condition and the conclusion of the rule. But the variable Y occurs only after the arrow. Therefore it is possible to move (∀ Y) into the condition. But when it moves into the negative context, it becomes (∃ Y):

```
(∀ M) (∀ X) mother_in_law(M,X) <- (∃ Y) mother(M,Y)
        & married(X,Y).
```

This may be read, "For all M and X, M is a mother in law of X if there exists a Y where M is a mother of Y and X is married to Y." Although Prolog does not use explicit quantifier symbols, variables that occur only after the arrow have this existential effect.

Since variables that occur only in the condition part of a Prolog rule are effectively governed by an existential quantifier, a problem occurs in expressing conditions that contain universal quantifiers. Consider the sentence, "Every mother whose children are all above average is a super mom." The following rule does not accurately represent the meaning:

```
supermom(M) <- mother(M,C) & above_avg(C).
```

This rule may be read, "M is a super mom if there exists a C where M is a mother of C and C is above average." Notice that C is effectively bound by an existential quantifier, since it occurs only in the condition. Therefore the rule does not exclude the possibility that other children of M may be below average. To exclude those cases, some negations are needed:

```
supermom(M) <- mother(M,C) &
    ¬(mother(M,D) & ¬above_avg(D)).
```

Note that D occurs within a negative context nested inside another negative context (the condition). Therefore the quantifier that governs D flips from ∀ when it is in front of the formula to ∃ when it moves after the arrow and back to ∀ when it goes into the nested negative context. Therefore this rule may be read, "M is a supermom if there exists a C where M is a mother of C and it is false that for all D where M is a mother of D, D is not above average." This contorted way of expressing universal quantifiers by double negations is also required in certain database query languages.

In order to express quantifiers in a more natural way, McCord introduces the notion of *focalizers* in Chapter 5. He uses the focalizer all(P,Q) to express the statement that in every case where P is true, Q is also true. Using the focalizer all, the definition of supermom becomes somewhat simpler and more readable:

```
supermom(M) <- mother(M,C)
            & all(mother(M,D), above_avg(D)).
```

This rule may be read, "M is a supermom if there exists a C where M is a mother of C and for all cases where M is a mother of D, D is above average." The focalizer all is defined by the following rule:

```
all(P,Q) <- ¬(P & ¬Q).
```

In this rule, P and Q are *metavariables*, which match arbitrary predications or combinations of predications. The body of the rule invokes P and Q as goals to be proved. This rule says that all(P,Q) succeeds if it is false that there is ever a case when P succeeds and Q does not succeed. Metavariables are discussed in more detail in Chapter 3, and focalizers are discussed in Chapter 5.

2.2.4 Choosing a Data Structure

Before writing rules to define predicates, a Prolog programmer must decide what data structures the rules will process. The choice of structure has a major effect on the way rules are written and the efficiency of their execution. As an example, consider Exercise 6 at the end of this chapter:

> A farmer has a wolf, a goat, and a cabbage (a very large one). He wants to get all three of them plus himself across a river, but his boat is only large enough to hold one item plus himself. How can he cross the river without leaving the wolf alone with the goat or the goat alone with the cabbage?

This is a typical state-transition problem where the starting state has all four items (plus the boat) on one side, and the goal state has everything on the other side. In between are various intermediate states where some things are on one side and some things are on the other side.

In the farmer problem, the state of the system is defined by the position of each of the four items: farmer, wolf, goat, and cabbage. (The boat, the fifth item, can be ignored, since it must always be on the same side as the farmer.) There are two major choices of data structures for this problem:

- A structure with four variables: each variable represents the location of one item (farmer, wolf, goat, or cabbage).

- A pair of two sets: all items on the first side in one set; and all items on the second side in the other set.

This description has three words that indicate data structures: "structure," "pair," and "set." Before writing rules for this problem, the programmer must decide how to map these data structures into Prolog terms.

A structure of four variables can be represented as a Prolog function symbol applied to four arguments. A suitable function is `loc(F,W,G,C)`. The variable F represents the location of the farmer, W the wolf, G the goat, and C the cabbage. To be more explicit, each variable could be labeled with the name of the item:

    `loc(farmer(F),wolf(W),goat(G),cabbage(C))`

This data structure is analogous to the record structures used in many programming languages, such as Pascal. The similarity is more striking when each subpart in the Prolog structure is written on a separate line:

Prolog Structure	Pascal Record

`loc`
   `(farmer(F),`
    `wolf(W),`
    `goat(G),`
    `cabbage(C))`
	`type loc = record`
	       `farmer: string,`
	       `wolf: string,`
	       `goat: string,`
	       `cabbage: string`
	   `end`

The Prolog structure has a function named `loc` applied to four arguments. Each argument is itself a function applied to one argument, which is a variable whose value is to be computed. In the Pascal structure on the right, `loc` is the name of a record type that has four fields; each field can hold a single character string that represents the location of the corresponding item. Although the syntax is quite different, the two structures serve the same purpose. This comparison illustrates a basic point about Prolog: functional forms are used to build data structures, not to do computations; they should be compared to data structures in other languages. Predicates do the actual computations in Prolog; they should be compared to procedures in other languages.

Given the simpler data structure `loc(F,W,G,C)`, the next task is to define a predicate `move(Current,Next)` that determines a possible move from the state `Current` to the state `Next`. The first rule that defines move says that the farmer can move by himself from location F to F2, leaving the other items unchanged, provided that the new location F2 is opposite F and the resulting state is safe:

```
move(loc(F,W,G,C), loc(F2,W,G,C)) <- opp(F,F2)
    & safe(loc(F2,W,G,C)).
```

This rule illustrates a powerful feature of Prolog: in most languages, the head of a procedure lists variable names for the parameters, and the body of the procedure uses operators that extract substructures from the input variables. Then it uses other operators to assemble the output. In Prolog, however, the extraction and assembly can be done automatically by pattern matching with structures in the head of a rule. The above rule could be written in a style similar to more conventional languages by using the = operator to take apart the structure Current and assemble the new structure Next:

```
move(Current,Next) <-
    Current=loc(F,W,G,C) & opp(F,F2) &
    Next=loc(F2,W,G,C) & safe(Next).
```

In this version, the subgoal Current=loc(F,W,G,C) causes subparts of the structure Current to be matched to the variables F, W, G, and C. But the original version of the rule does that same pattern matching before execution of the rule even starts. It is usually simpler and more efficient to do as much of the pattern matching as possible in the head of a rule instead of in the body.

There are three other kinds of moves: the farmer takes the wolf across, the goat across, or the cabbage across. The corresponding rules are similar to the previous rule, but with one other item moving with the farmer:

```
move(loc(F,F,G,C), loc(F2,F2,G,C)) <- opp(F,F2)
    & safe(loc(F2,F2,G,C)).
move(loc(F,W,F,C), loc(F2,W,F2,C)) <- opp(F,F2)
    & safe(loc(F2,W,F2,C)).
move(loc(F,W,G,F), loc(F2,W,G,F2)) <- opp(F,F2)
    & safe(loc(F2,W,G,F2)).
```

The predicate opp can be defined by two facts to say that east is opposite west, and west is opposite east:

```
opp(east,west).    opp(west,east).
```

In determining whether a state is safe, the critical item is the goat, which can either eat the cabbage or be eaten by the wolf. The next two rules say that a state is safe if either the farmer is on the same side as the goat or everything else is on the opposite side from the goat:

```
safe(loc(F,W,F,C)).
safe(loc(F,F,G,F)) <- opp(F,G).
```

Given these rules, the farmer problem is completely defined. The only thing that is needed is a general search procedure that tries to find a path of safe states from the start to the goal:

```
Start state:     loc(west,west,west,west)
Goal state:      loc(east,east,east,east)
```

Suitable search procedures are defined on page 80.

The other choice of data structure is a pair of sets. To represent pairs, Prolog uses a dot (or period) between two items. The pair `abc.def` consists of the atom `abc` followed by the atom `def`. Pairs of numbers must have blanks around the dot: `(3 . 14159)` is a pair of two integers, but `3.14159` is a single floating-point number. Pairs can include other pairs: `(a.b).(c.d)` is a pair of two pairs. The dot operator is *right associative*: the structure `a.b.c.d` is exactly equivalent to `(a.(b.(c.d)))`. And pairs can freely mix various data structures, such as numbers, character strings, functional forms, other pairs, and even variables. The following are sample Prolog structures:

```
a.X.c.(Y.Z).'My Old Kentucky Home'. 7037 .xyz

farmer(north).wolf(south).goat(drowned).cabbage(eaten)

f(g(X),39).h(ABC).z(smith).order('One dozen eggs')
```

Sets are commonly used in logic and mathematics, but very few programming languages support them directly. Instead, most languages provide some kind of ordered list or vector. To represent a true set, the ordering must be ignored. In Prolog, lists are represented as a sequence of items connected with dots followed by the atom `nil`:

```
a.b.c.d.e.f.g.h.nil
```

The atom `nil` has two purposes in Prolog: it is the name of the empty list, and it serves to mark the end of longer lists. However, there is nothing magic about this atom; the atom `end` could have been used instead, but `nil` is the traditional name of the empty list in other languages, such as Lisp. Most implementations of Prolog also provide a *bracket notation* for lists that omits the final `nil` (although `nil` is still present in the underlying representation).

```
[a,b,c,d,e,f,g,h]
```

The dot and the bracket notations are exactly equivalent. The dot form is closer to the internal representation, and the bracket form is a permissible alternative. Following are some examples of lists in both the dot form and the bracket form:

```
nil                       []
abc.nil                   [abc]
nil.nil                   [[]]
abc.def.ghi.nil           [abc,def,ghi]
nil.nil.nil.nil           [[],[],[]]
(abc.nil).(def.nil).nil   [[abc],[def]]
((abc.nil).nil).nil       [[[abc]]]
```

For representing constants, the bracket form tends to be shorter, since it does not require a terminal nil. For combinations of variables, however, the dot form tends to be shorter. Since the dot form shows more clearly how Prolog processes lists, this book will primarily use the dot form in the examples. IBM Prolog, however, supports both forms.

Given this notation for pairs and lists, consider the second option for representing states in the farmer problem: a pair of lists, with all items on the first side of the river in the first list and all items on the other side in the second list. Following are the starting state, one of the intermediate states, and the goal state for this option:

```
(farmer.wolf.goat.cabbage.nil) . nil
(wolf.cabbage.nil) . (farmer.goat.nil)
nil . (farmer.wolf.goat.cabbage.nil)
```

Remember that these lists are actually supposed to be sets. Therefore the order must be ignored. But ignoring order is not easy, since all possible permutations must be treated as equivalent. Extra processing is needed to compare two lists or to search for a particular element.

With the first data structure, the move predicate accesses each item by a direct pattern match. With the second data structure, however, it must call another predicate to search for each item. The predicate pick(X,L1,L2), which will be defined later, picks one element X from list L1 and puts all of the remaining elements in list L2. If X does not occur in L1, the predicate fails. Given that predicate, the first rule for move can be written:

```
move(S.G, S2.G2) <- pick(farmer,S,S2) & (G2=farmer.G)
    & safe(S2.G2).
```

In this rule, S.G represents a state where S is the list of items on the starting side of the river, and G is the list of items of items on the goal side. The next state is the pair of lists S2.G2. To generate the new state, the subgoal pick(farmer,S,S2) takes the farmer out of the list S and leaves the remaining items in S2. Then the next subgoal (G2=farmer.G) puts the farmer in front of the list G to form G2. Finally, the predicate safe checks the new state S2.G2. Actually, this rule is not complete, since it does not allow the farmer to move back from the goal side to the starting side. Another option is necessary to allow the farmer to move both ways:

```
move(S.G, S2.G2) <-
    (pick(farmer,S,S2) & (G2=farmer.G) |
     pick(farmer,G,G2) & (S2=farmer.S)) &
    safe(S2.G2).
```

With the pair of lists, the rules for safe are also more complex. The rule that a state is safe if the farmer and the goat are on the same side becomes the following:

```
safe(S.G) <- member(farmer,S) & member(goat,S)
            | member(farmer,G) & member(goat,G).
```

This rule uses the predicate member(X,L) to check whether X is a member of the list L; member is also defined later (it is actually the same as the pick predicate without the third argument). As an exercise, the reader should practice writing the other rules for move and safe, using this data structure instead of the first one.

As these examples show, fixed-length structures are easy to access by direct pattern matching. Variable-length lists require more searching with predicates like member or pick. This principle is true of almost all programming languages: if some item is in a known position, it is easier to access than when it must be found by searching through a list. Although lists require some searching to find an element, they are essential for structures that are constantly growing and shrinking. In choosing a data structure, the first question to ask is whether the number of items is fixed or changing:

■   If the number of items cannot change by the very nature of the problem, choose a fixed data structure, such as a pair X.Y, a triple X.Y.Z, or a functional form loc(F,W,G,C).

■   If the number of items may change or their location in the structure is unknown, use a list (which is a structure of dotted pairs terminated by nil).

At this point, the reader should turn to Exercises 7 through 10, which are state-transition problems similar to the farmer problem. In Exercise 7 with the two water jugs, the amount of water is variable, but the number of jugs is fixed. Therefore a good representation for the state is a pair of numbers that show the amount of water in each jug. The starting state is (5 . 0), and the goal state is (* . 1), where the anonymous variable * shows that any amount of water in Jug A is permissible in a goal state. One of the rules for defining the move predicate is the following:

```
move(A.B, A2.B2) <- gt(A,0) & lt(B,2)
      & Total := A + B
      & ( ge(Total,2) & (A2 := Total - 2) & B2=2
        | lt(Total,2) & A2=0 & B2=Total).
```

This rule defines the conditions for pouring water from Jug A to Jug B. The pair A.B is the amount of water in each jug in the current state, and A2.B2 is the amount in the next state. The condition part of the rule says that Jug A must not be empty, gt(A,0), and Jug B must not be filled to the brim, lt(B,2). Then the rule computes the total amount of water in the system, Total. The last two lines consider the cases where the total amount is greater than or equal to the capacity of Jug B, ge(Total,2); or where it is less than the capacity of Jug B, lt(Total,2). If the total is greater than or equal to 2, Jug A receives the total minus 2, and Jug B is filled to its capacity 2. If the total is less than 2, Jug A becomes empty, A2=0; and Jug B has everything, B=Total.

The previous rule also illustrates two operators = and :=. The = operator *unifies* two things (variables or constants or structures) to make them equal; it fails if they cannot be unified. But the := operator evaluates the expression on the right before unifying it to the variable or constant on the left. In A2=0, the variable A2 becomes 0. In (Total := A + B), the expression (A + B) is evaluated before the result is unified with the variable Total. By contrast, (Total = A + B) without the colon would do no evaluation; it would simply bind the unevaluated expression (A + B) to Total. The process of unification is described in more detail in the next section.

In Exercise 8 with missionaries and cannibals, the identities of the individuals are irrelevant; only the number of each kind is significant. The position of the boat is now important, since the missionaries and the cannibals can both operate it. Therefore a fixed-length structure of five variables could represent the state. One possibility is B.M.C.M2.C2, where B is the position of the boat, M and C are the numbers of missionaries and cannibals on the starting side, and M2 and C2 are the numbers on the goal side. The atom nil could be tacked to the end of this structure, to form the list B.M.C.M2.C2.nil. However, nil is not needed, since the structure has a fixed number of items that will be accessed by a pattern match, not by searching with predicates like member or pick.

In Exercise 9 with the monkey and bananas, the state could be represented by a fixed-length structure with three variables. One possibility is the triple M.B.P, where M is the monkey's location, B is the box's location, and P is the monkey's posture (standing, on box, or reaching). The following rule says that if the monkey is standing next to the box, it can push the box somewhere else:

```
move(M.M.standing, N.N.standing) <-
    member(N,a.b.c.d.m.nil) & ¬(M=N).
```

The condition that the monkey is next to the box is that the monkey's location M is the same as the box's location. The member predicate is used here as a finder goal to pick some value for N out of the list of possible locations, a.b.c.d.m.nil. Then the test ¬(M=N) verifies that the new location N is not the same as the old location M. Note that the predicate member can be used either as a finder goal or as a verifier goal. Negated predicates, however, can only be used as verifiers.

2.2.5 Unification: Binding Values to Variables

Variables in Prolog are bound to values during pattern matching. The algorithm that binds values to variables is called *unification*. Special cases of unification have been used in all of the examples given so far: whenever a goal is matched to the head of a rule or fact, the arguments in the goal are unified with the arguments in the head. For example, if the goal is human(X), the variable X is unified or bound to some constant such as socrates. If the goal already has a constant, such as human(cicero), unification consists of checking whether the two constants are identical. Unlike conventional assignments, the binding performed during pattern matching is only tentative. If the value bound to X happens to cause some conflict in a later subgoal, the system *backtracks* and undoes the tentative binding. Then some other match may bind a new value to X.

Variables other than * must have the same value at every occurrence within a clause; but they may have different values in different clauses. In other words, the *scope* of a variable name extends for just a single clause (rule, goal, or fact). The next two rules both have the same internal form:

```
sibling(X,Y) <- child(X,Z) & child(Y,Z) & ne(X,Y).
sibling(C1,C2) <- child(C1,Parent) & child(C2,Parent)
                  & ne(C1,C2).
```

Internally, the system numbers the variables that occur in each clause. On output, it prints the first variable in a clause as V1, the second one as V2, and so forth.

In simple pattern matching, one pattern is made up of constants (character strings or integers) and the other is a mixture of constants and variables. The unification algorithm in Prolog is more general: it allows both patterns to contain unbound variables, and it tries to find values for the variables that will make both patterns the same. For example, if g(7,X,Y) is unified with g(Z,W,22), the value 7 is bound to Z, 22 is bound to Y, and X and W are *cross-bound* to each other. Two variables that are cross-bound do not immediately acquire a value, but if any value is later bound to one of them, the other gets exactly the same value. Unification can cause some complex substitutions. For example, f(g(X),X) matches f(Y,g(3)) with X bound to g(3) and Y bound to g(g(3)). The unification process is most easily seen when the functions are drawn in tree form:

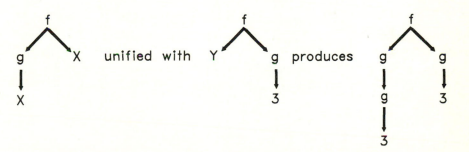

Unification starts by matching the heads of each tree. Since f=f, it continues by matching the left sides of the trees, making Y equal g(X). Then it matches the right sides, making X equal g(3) and thereby causing Y to become g(g(3)). When the final tree is rewritten in linear form, the result is f(g(g(3)),g(3)).

In the above example, unifying two data structures produced a structure that was bigger than either of the starting structures. The two occurrences of the variable X caused the structure to grow by multiple substitutions. With repeated substitution, it is even possible to produce infinite data structures. One way is to assert the rule,

    p(X,X).

and then issue the goal p(Y,f(Y)). In trying to satisfy the goal, Prolog attempts to find some binding for the variable Y that will unify both arguments of p. Therefore it tries to substitute f(Y) for Y in the first argument. To be consistent, it must make the second argument f(f(Y)). But then it goes back to substitute f(f(Y)) for Y in the first argument and thereby makes the second argument f(f(f(Y))), and so on. Some versions of Prolog get hung up in a loop with such goals. The version described in this book, however, can represent *infinite terms*, with pointers that point back to a higher node. For the above goal, the system produces the answer f(@(1)) to indicate an infinite tree with a loop of length 1 (shown by @(1)). The resulting structure does not actually occupy an infinite amount of storage. It simply contains a pointer that cycles back to a higher node. For most common applications, infinite terms are not needed, but the ability to create them keeps Prolog from getting hung up in a loop.

The unification operator = tries to unify its left- and right-hand arguments. If they are unifiable, it succeeds; otherwise, it fails. Since unification is one of the fundamental processes performed by the underlying inference engine, it could be defined by a single rule:

    X = X.

This rule succeeds if the built-in pattern matcher can unify both arguments; otherwise, it fails. Because the = operator is so useful, IBM Prolog provides it as a built-in predicate.

The = operator can be used either to test for equality or to force two terms to become equal. If X were an unbound variable, either goal X=5 or 5=X would bind the value 5 to X. But if X has a previous value, then the same goal tests whether that value is 5. For unbound X, it has the effect of an assignment; otherwise, it has the effect of a comparison. The evaluation operator := has the same effect as the unification operator in the form X:=5. But consider the next two goals:

    X = 4 + 5.
    X := 4 + 5.

With =, the unevaluated expression (4 + 5) is bound to X. But with :=, the result 9 is bound to X. Whenever evaluation is required, the := operator must be used. When a simple unification is required, = should be used.

Unification is a general tree-matching process. The most commonly used operator for building trees in Prolog is the dot operator, used in forming lists. Suppose the pattern of variables A.B.C.D.E were unified with the following list:

apples.peaches.pumpkin.pie.nil

Then the pattern match would succeed with the result, A=apples, B=peaches, C=pumpkin, D=pie, and E=nil. If the pattern had more than five variables, the pattern match would fail. But if the pattern had less than five variables, the pattern match would still succeed. For example, the single variable A by itself could match the entire list. But what about a pair of variables, say A.B? To see how patterns of variables match a list, draw the list as a tree. Since the dot is a *right-associative operator*, the fully parenthesized form of the fruit list would be

apples.(peaches.(pumpkin.(pie.nil))).

Following are the tree forms for the pair A.B and the entire fruit list:

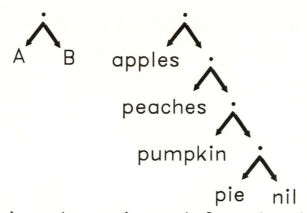

Here A matches apples, and B matches the entire sublist peaches.pumpkin.pie.nil. When a dotted pair of variables, like A.B, matches a simple list, the first one matches a single element, called the *head* of the list; the second one matches an entire sublist, called the *tail*. If there are more than two variables, each variable but the last matches a single element, and the last variable matches everything that is left over. If the pattern X.Y.Z were matched to the fruit list, the result would be X=apples, Y=peaches, and Z=pumpkin.pie.nil.

When parentheses are used for grouping, any element could itself be a complex subtree. In the list (a.b.nil).(c.d.nil).(e.f.nil).nil, the head is the list a.b.nil, and the tail is a list of two elements, each of which is itself a list of two elements: (c.d.nil).(e.f.nil).nil.

Instead of the dot notation, the fruit list could also be written in bracket notation as [apples,peaches,pumpkin,pie]. To represent patterns of variables, the exclamation point ! separates the variables that match single elements at the beginning from the variable that matches the tail. The pair A.B is equivalent to the bracket form [A!B], and the pattern X.Y.Z is equivalent to [X,Y!Z]. Note that for patterns of variables, the dot notation is shorter than the bracket notation.

Ordinary Prolog lists branch to the right because the dot operator is right associative. By means of the special predicate op, new operators can be defined to form different kinds of structures. The dot, for example, is defined by the assertion

    op(".",rl,100).

The second argument r l says that it is right-to-left associative, and the third argument defines its precedence as 100 (which gives it tighter binding than the Boolean operators and most of the common predicates). It is possible to declare some other symbol, such as ?, as a kind of list-forming operator that would be left-to-right associative:

    op("?",lr,100).

Then the structure a?b?c?d would be equivalent to the fully parenthesized form ((a?b)?c)?d. Note the difference between the tree for this structure and the tree for the dotted form a.b.c.d:

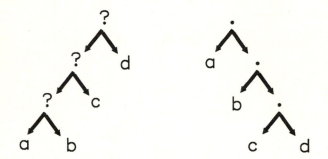

With the left associative ? operator, the rightmost value d is closest to the top of the tree. With the right associative . operator, the leftmost value a is closest to the top. For the pair A?B, the variable A would match the entire subtree a?b?c, and B would match the single element d. Either the dot or the question mark could be used as a basis for list processing, but the right associative dot is the more traditional.

In list processing, the most common operations are to extract the head or the tail of an input list. Lisp, for example, has two *selector functions* called CAR and CDR to perform those operations. Instead of using special functions, Prolog performs those extractions by pattern matching with a pair H.T where H matches the head and T matches the tail. Pattern matching normally takes place while unifying arguments when a rule is invoked. Sometimes it is more convenient to use the = operator in the body of a rule. Consider the following goal:

    L=(H.T).

This goal might be used in three ways: If H and T were unbound variables, it would split the list L in two parts, binding the head to H and the tail to T. If only L were an unbound variable, the same goal would construct a new list L from a head H and a tail T. Finally, if all variables L, H, and T were bound, it would simply check for equality.

One of the strengths of Prolog is its ability to express its own definition. It is not difficult to describe the unification process in Prolog itself. However, most applications of unification can be understood just by drawing trees and doing repeated substitutions.

2.2.6 List-Handling Predicates

Predicates that process lists are usually defined by recursive rules. Their definitions typically require two rules. The first rule processes the empty list, and the second rule processes any list longer than nil. Following is the general scheme:

- If the list is nil, return the value expected for nil.

- Otherwise, split the list into its head and tail, process the head, call the predicate recursively to process the tail, and combine the result of processing the head with the results of processing the tail.

As an example of this scheme, the predicate total(L,T) computes the total T of a list of numbers L:

```
total(nil,0).
total(Head.Tail,T) <- total(Tail,Subtotal)
     & T := Head + Subtotal.
```

In this case, the expected result for nil is 0. For any longer list, the pattern Head.Tail splits the input list with Head matching the first element, and Tail matching all the rest. The recursive call to total computes the subtotal, which is added to the head to form the total T. Note that this computation will always terminate because each recursive call processes a sublist that is shorter than the previous list.

The predicate length(L,N), which computes the number of elements N in the list L, is slightly simpler than total since it only counts elements instead of adding them.

```
length(nil,0).
length(Head.Tail,N) <- length(Tail,M) & (N := M + 1).
```

The first fact says that the length of the empty list is 0. The second rule says that the length of any list Head.Tail is one more than the length of Tail.

The predicate member(X,L), which checks whether X is a member of the list L, does not exactly fit the general scheme since it does not specify a rule or fact to deal with nil:

```
member(X,X.Tail).
member(X,Head.Tail) <- member(X,Tail).
```

The first rule says that X is a member of a list if it is the head. The second rule says that X is a member of a list if it is a member of the tail of the list. If the list were originally empty (represented by the symbol nil), both of the patterns that contain dots, X.Tail and Head.Tail, would fail to match. Therefore both rules would fail. That is exactly what should happen, since by definition, nothing is ever a member of the empty list.

The predicate pick(X,L1,L2), which picks an element X out of the list L1 and puts the remainder in L2, behaves like member with an extra argument:

```
pick(X,X.Tail,Tail).
pick(X,Head.Tail,Head.Rem) <- pick(X,Tail,Rem).
```

The first rule says that if X occurs at the head of a list, the remainder is the tail. The second rule says that X can be removed from a list by picking it out of the tail; the remainder Head.Rem is the old head combined with the remainder Rem of picking X out of the tail. If the list were originally empty, both rules would fail to match, as indeed they should.

Many predicates process two input lists L1 and L2 to generate an output list L3. There are three basic ways of combining the elements of L1 and L2 to generate the elements of L3. Each method is recursive, but they differ in the ways they treat their input and output arguments.

- *Element-by-element*: Each step combines the head of L1 with the head of L2 to form the head of L3. Then the predicate calls itself recursively to process the tails. The predicate listadd is an example of this method.

- *Appending*: Each step processes the head of L1 to form the head of the output L3. When L1 is finally reduced to nil, the second argument L2 is processed to form the tail of L3. The predicate append is the primary example of this method.

- *Reversing*: Each step processes the head of L1 to form the head of L2. When L1 has been reduced to nil, the second argument L2 has the results built up in reverse order. Then the whole list L2 is transferred unchanged to L3 to be passed back as the result. The three-argument form of reverse, given at the end of this section, is an example of this method.

These three methods are language-independent techniques for handling lists. Variations of them are used in Lisp and in pointer-based languages like Pascal and PL/I. Recognizing them as distinct approaches helps to explain why different rules handle their arguments in different ways.

As an example of the first approach, consider the predicate listadd, which does an element-by-element add of L1 to L2 to generate L3. It is defined by the following rules:

```
listadd(nil,nil,nil).
listadd(H1.T1,H2.T2,H3.T3) <-
    (H3 := H1 + H2) & listadd(T1,T2,T3).
```

If both of the input lists have been reduced to nil, the result (the third argument) is also nil. The second rule takes care of the general case: it splits the first list into a head and a tail (H1.T1); splits the second list into (H2.T2);

and generates the result (H3.T3) by adding the two heads and calling itself recursively to add the two tails.

With the element-by-element approach, a problem would occur if one input were shorter than the other. Therefore two starting rules may be used to say what to do if either one input or the other is reduced to nil:

```
listadd(nil,L,L).
listadd(L,nil,L).
listadd(H1.T1,H2.T2,H3.T3) <-
     (H3 := H1 + H2) & listadd(T1,T2,T3).
```

The first rule says that if the first list is nil, the result (the third argument) is the second list unchanged. Then the next rule says that if the second list is nil, the result is the first list. The last rule is the same as before.

Concatenating two lists is not as simple as concatenating two character strings. The reason why lists are more difficult to handle is that they are actually trees, not flat structures like strings and vectors. For flat structures, the position of the end can be computed from the length. For trees, however, a program must scan to the end, looking for the marker nil. As an example, consider the two lists X=a.b.nil and Y=c.d.nil. The result Z should be a.b.c.d.nil. But simply writing the pair X.Y produces a very different structure (a.b.nil).(c.d.nil). The difference is most obvious when the structures are drawn as trees:

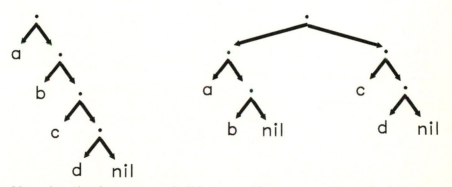

Note that the dot operator builds a new binary tree with each of the previous trees as branches. A full concatenation (typically called append) must scan through the first tree to find the ending nil and replace it with the second tree. That scanning process takes place while concatenating lists in any language. In pointer-based languages like Pascal and PL/I, that scanning would be done by a while-loop that continues until a null pointer is found. In Lisp and Prolog, the scanning is done by recursive calls that continue until the first argument is reduced to nil.

Given input lists L1 and L2, each recursive call to the append predicate moves the head of L1 to the head of the output list L3. When L1 has been reduced to nil, the second input L2 is passed to the output L3 unchanged. Then as each recursive call returns, the final result is built up as the third argument. Although this process sounds complicated in English, it is much shorter in Prolog:

```
append(nil,L,L).
append(Head.Tail,L,Head.T2) <- append(Tail,L,T2).
```

The first rule says that appending `nil` to any L leaves L unchanged. The second rule says that appending a list of the form `Head.Tail` to L yields `Head.T2` if `Tail` appended to L yields `T2`.

To show how Prolog processes these rules, the `trace` predicate may be used to turn on tracing of all calls and exits. To trace the `append` predicate, type the following goal:

```
trace(append(*,*,*)).
```

This goal turns on tracing for the `append` predicate; the three asterisks represent the three argument places of `append`. After tracing has been turned on, the goal

```
append(a.b.nil, c.d.nil, L)
```

generates output in the following form:

```
1 : call ==> append(a.b.nil, c.d.nil, *) .
  2 : call ==> append(b.nil, c.d.nil, *) .
    3 : call ==> append(nil, c.d.nil, *) .
    3 : exit ==> append(nil, c.d.nil, c.d.nil) .
  2 : exit ==> append(b.nil, c.d.nil, b.c.d.nil) .
1 : exit ==> append(a.b.nil, c.d.nil, a.b.c.d.nil) .
```

The numbers on the left indicate the nesting level of calls; indentation makes the nesting more visible. The first call has the original inputs. The second line shows the next recursive call, where the tail of the original list `b.nil` is now being appended to the second list. By the third call, the first argument has been reduced to `nil`. Therefore this call matches the first rule for `append`, which forces the third argument to be equal to the second. At each exit from the recursion, the value of `Head` at that level is tacked onto the front of the list returned from the previous level. At the end, the third argument contains the final result.

The techniques for handling lists in Prolog are similar to the Lisp techniques for equivalent operations. They also have strong similarities to the techniques used in pointer-based languages like Pascal or PL/I. The best way to become familiar with them is to practice them with various kinds of lists. Try tracing `append` on different combinations of lists: a one element list `a.nil` with an empty list; longer lists, such as `a.b.c.nil` and `x.y.z.nil`; and lists with complicated sublists, `((a.b.nil).c.nil).(x.nil).nil`. Study the output to see which rule is being invoked at each step and which substructure is being matched to each variable in the rule.

Tracing shows how the recursive process works. But the best way to understand a recursive rule is to ignore all of the calling and returning, which can become extremely confusing in complex cases. Instead, recursive rules should be analyzed by the process of *mathematical induction*:

- First show that the rule works for the starting case, such as the empty list nil.

- Then *assume* that it works for any list of length N and show that it must therefore work for any list of length N+1.

To apply these principles to append, note that the first rule gives the correct result of appending nil to any list. Then if the first argument is of length N+1, *assume* that the recursive call correctly computes the result T2 of appending Tail (which is of length N) to L. If that assumption is correct, then Head.T2 must be the result of appending a list of length N+1. The principle of mathematical induction guarantees that such assumptions are always safe. Therefore the details of how the recursion actually takes place can always be ignored. Programmers who think recursively just "assume away" all of the messy details.

As another example, consider a predicate to reverse a list. In this case, the simplest predicate to define is not the most efficient. But it is interesting to see why it is not efficient and to see how it could be improved. The next two rules define the simple version of reverse:

```
reverse(nil, nil).
reverse(Head.Tail, R) <-  reverse(Tail, RT)
      & append(RT, Head.nil, R).
```

The first rule says that the reversal of nil is nil. Then the second rule says that to compute the reverse of a list Head.Tail, first reverse the tail to form RT; then append RT in front of the head. This predicate will work correctly, but it runs in time proportional to the square of the number of elements in the list. The number of calls to reverse itself is just proportional to the length N. But the number of calls to append is proportional to the square of N, since append calls itself many times for each call to reverse.

A slightly more complex version of reverse uses an extra variable as intermediate storage. Each time it calls itself recursively, it builds up a reversed list in the second argument, which is finally returned as the answer in the third argument:

```
reverse(nil, Answer, Answer).
reverse(Head.Tail, Int, Answer) <-
      reverse(Tail, Head.Int, Answer).
```

The first rule says that when recursion finally reduces the first argument to nil, the second argument should be returned as the answer. The second rule splits the head from the first argument, and tacks it on the front of the list Int, which is building up the intermediate result in reversed form. At each recursive call, the third argument is carried along unchanged. When the recursion hits bottom, the list in second position is moved to the answer. Following is a trace of reverse for the goal reverse(a.b.c.d.nil, nil, *):

```
  1 : call ==> reverse(a.b.c.d.nil, nil,*) .
    2 : call ==> reverse(b.c.d.nil, a.nil, *) .
      3 : call ==> reverse(c.d.nil, b.a.nil, *) .
        4 : call ==> reverse(d.nil, c.b.a.nil, *) .
          5 : call ==> reverse(nil, d.c.b.a.nil, *) .
          5 : exit ==> reverse(nil, d.c.b.a.nil,
                                d.c.b.a.nil) .
        4 : exit ==> reverse(d.nil, c.b.a.nil,
                              d.c.b.a.nil) .
      3 : exit ==> reverse(c.d.nil, b.a.nil,
                            d.c.b.a.nil) .
    2 : exit ==> reverse(b.c.d.nil, a.nil,
                          d.c.b.a.nil) .
  1 : exit ==> reverse(a.b.c.d.nil, nil,
                        d.c.b.a.nil) .
```

Notice how each level of recursion picks the head off the first argument and tacks it on to the front of the second argument. When the first argument becomes nil, the second argument is transferred totally over to the third argument. That result is finally passed back as the answer. On an IBM 3081, the first version of reverse took 17 milliseconds to reverse a list of 52 elements, but the second version took less than one millisecond.

Since the three-argument form of reverse uses the middle argument only for intermediate storage, it would be convenient to have a two-argument version that omits the middle argument. Since Prolog allows the same predicate name to be used with different numbers of arguments, a two-argument version could be defined that calls the three-argument version:

```
reverse(L1,L2) <- reverse(L1,nil,L2).
```

This version is simpler to use, since the programmer does not have to specify the second argument.

2.2.7 Reversible Predicates

The list handling predicates in the previous section perform the same tasks as similar predicates in Lisp. But an amazing property of Prolog that is not true of Lisp (or of any other common programming language) is that these predicates are reversible. Although they were defined by taking the first argument as input and the second (or third) argument as output, any argument could in fact be used as either input or output. The only predicate in the previous section that is not reversible is total, because the sum (T := Head + Subtotal) loses information.

Although the built-in arithmetic predicates are nonlogical, they are partially reversible: sum(X,3,8) works backwards to compute the value X=5. But they do not have the full reversibility of the logical predicates. For example, the goal sum(X,X,8) is satisfied by X=4, but the sum predicate prints an error message if two of its arguments are unbound variables. In contrast, the append predicate is fully reversible. The following goal, for example, will compute the value L=a.b.c.nil:

> append(L, L, a.b.c.a.b.c.nil).

This reversibility is more than an intellectual curiosity. It is an efficient way to check whether a list splits into two identical halves. Following are a variety of goals that run append backwards to compute something useful:

- Given lists L1 and L2, check whether L1 is equal to the beginning of L2. If so, bind the remaining part of L2 to the variable Rem:

  > append(L1,Rem,L2).

- Given lists L1 and L2, check whether L1 is equal to the end of L2. If so, bind the front part of L2 to the variable Front:

  > append(Front,L1,L2).

- Find all possible ways of splitting a list L into two parts Front and Rem, ranging from Front=nil and Rem=L up to Front=L and Rem=nil. The following goal produces a different split each time backtracking reaches it:

  > append(Front,Rem,L).

To see how this process works, trace the append predicate, and try running examples of these goals at the terminal. Programmers who are familiar with conventional languages find it hard to believe that these predicates can actually run backwards. The only way to be convinced is to run one example after another. Study how the rules are invoked, and what data structures each variable matches.

The member predicate is also reversible. As a verifier goal, member(c,a.b.c.d.e.nil) succeeds, because c is a member of the second argument. As a finder goal, member(X,a.b.c.d.e.nil) has five possible choices for binding the variable X to some element of the list. When first called, it finds X=a. If a does not satisfy later subgoals in the computation, the system backtracks to member, which picks the next element b. Each time backtracking reaches it, member picks a different element of the list. If all possible choices fail, member also fails. As an example, consider the following goal:

> member(N, 1 . 2 . 3 . 4 . 5 . 6 . nil) & rem(N,2,0).

First, member succeeds with N=1. Then the remainder predicate rem checks whether N divided by 2 leaves a remainder of 0. Since that is false, backtracking returns control to member, which selects the next value N=2; then that value succeeds and the goal terminates. If the goal were retried, say with a semicolon

from the terminal, the system would backtrack to find the next successful value
N=4, and another retry would give N=6.

The most interesting way to use member is with an unbound variable in the
second argument, as in the following goal:

    member(fish,L).

This goal generates possible list forms that contain fish. It first succeeds with
L=fish.V1.   Here, V1 represents the arbitrary tail of some list.   If
backtracking returns to this goal, it will succeed again, but with
L=V1.fish.V2; the variable V1 is an undefined head, fish is in the second
position, and the variable V2 the undefined tail. Subsequent retries of this goal
succeed with L equal to V1.V2.fish.V3, then V1.V2.V3.fish.V4, and so
forth.

The length predicate is also reversible.   The normal way to call it is with a
known list in the first argument, such as length(a.b.c.nil,N).   Here the
value 3 is computed for N.   But if the first argument is unknown, as in the goal
length(L,3), the predicate computes a list of three unbound variables
V1.V2.V3.nil.   A structure of unbound variables can be used as a template of
"slots" to be filled later.   Consider the following goal:

    length(L,6)
    & member(a,L) & member(b,L) & member(c,L)
    & reverse(L,L).

First   length   creates   a   list   L   of   six   unbound   variables
V1.V2.V3.V4.V5.V6.nil. Then the three calls to member insert a, b, and
c into the first three slots of L to form a.b.c.V1.V2.V3.nil. Finally, the
reverse predicate forces L to become a.b.c.c.b.a.nil. If a semicolon
were entered to force the system to backtrack several times, the member
predicates would insert their values in different slots to form other permutations,
such as c.a.b.b.a.c.nil.

Patterns of unbound variables can support the various forms of *frames*,
scripts, or *schemata* used in artificial intelligence systems. The member
predicate provides a way of filling slots in the frames. Exercise 16 on marching
bands illustrates patterns of unbound variables and the use of member to fill
slots:

> Four bands, each from a different side of town, marched in a parade. Each
> band played only one piece, and no two bands played the same piece. From
> the following clues, determine the order in which the bands marched and the
> pieces they played.
>
> 1.   The band from the north side was at the head of the parade.
>
> 2.   "American Patrol" was the second piece played.
>
> 3.   The band from the east or west side played "Yankee Doodle."
>
> 4.   The last band played "When the Saints Go Marching in," just behind the
>   band from the west side.

5. The bands that played "American Patrol" and "Stars and Stripes Forever" are from opposite sides of town.

The information for each band can be represented by a triple (Order.Side.Piece). Here Order is the order of marching (1, 2, 3, 4); Side is the side of town; and Piece is the piece played. The solution to the problem can be computed as a list of such triples. The next rule computes that list L:

```
bands(L) <- L=((1 .*.*).(2 .*.*).(3 .*.*).(4 .*.*).nil)
    & member(1 .north.*, L)
    & member(2 .*.'American Patrol', L)
    & member(*.S1.'Yankee Doodle', L)
    & (S1=east | S1=west)
    & member(4 .*.'When the Saints Go Marching in', L)
    & member(3 .west.*, L)
    & member(*.S2.'American Patrol', L)
    & member(*.S3.'Stars and Stripes Forever', L)
    & opp(S2,S3)
    & member(*.north.*, L) & member(*.south.*, L)
    & member(*.east.*, L) & member(*.west.*, L).
```

In the first line, the variable L is bound to a list of four triples. Each triple has the value of Order filled in, and the other values are left as unbound variables. Each of the subsequent lines of the rule maps one of the English statements into Prolog. The predicate member(1 .north.*, L) forces the triple (1 .north.*) to be unified with some triple in the list L; it thereby forces the triple for order 1 to have the value north for its side of town. The third line forces the triple for order 2 to have the value 'American Patrol' for Piece. The next line implies that the triple with Piece='Yankee Doodle' has a side S1, which is either east or west. The next two lines imply that the triple with Order=4 has the piece 'When the Saints Go Marching in', and the one just before it has Side=west. The next two lines imply that the triple with Piece='American Patrol' is from side S2, which is opposite the side S3 for 'Stars and Stripes Forever'. The last two lines ensure that each side of town occurs in some triple. When the goal bands(L) is invoked, the following list of triples is generated for L:

```
(1 . north . 'Stars and Stripes Forever') .
(2 . south . 'American Patrol') .
(3 . west . 'Yankee Doodle') .
(4 . east . 'When the Saints Go Marching in') . nil
```

This problem is typical of a wide variety of puzzles that combine many scattered pieces of information. But the technique has practical applications to situations beyond puzzles. For example, when a computer hardware failure occurs, system directories may be left in a chaotic state; to recover the data and reconstruct the previous state, the system may have to assemble such scattered information. Exercise 17 on allocating offices is similar. The solution is a list of triples (D.N.F) where D is the department identifier, N is the number of offices required, and F is the floor number. The following list L combines the known values with slots to be filled:

L = (m43 . 9 . F) . (m77 . 11 . F) . (j39 . 9 . *)...

The constraint that departments m43 and m77 must be on the same floor is enforced by having the same variable F in both of their triples. Unconstrained triples have * for the floor. The problem can be solved by a recursive predicate allocate(L,Available), where L is the above list, and Available gives the number of rooms on each floor. At each recursive call, allocate assigns the department at the head of L to one of the floors and decrements the availability list by the number of offices assigned. In this example, the predicate allocate is used in a partially reversible way: some of the slots in L are initialized before calling allocate, and others are filled during execution.

Although predicates in pure Prolog tend to be reversible, there are some pitfalls that may cause problems. Consider again the definition of length:

```
length(nil,0).
length(Head.Tail,N) <- length(Tail,M) & (N := M + 1).
```

With the rules in this order, the predicate is reversible. But if they were interchanged, the length predicate would no longer be reversible. It would run correctly when the first argument is defined, but it would get into a recursive loop if the first argument were an unbound variable. Many of the list-handling predicates are reversible when the terminating rule (what to do with nil) is stated first, but they may get into a loop when that rule is stated at the end. In pure Prolog, the order of the rules can never affect the computed result (if one is found), but it may determine whether a computation terminates. If more than one answer is possible, the order of the rules may also determine which answer is computed first.

For some problems, reversibility is a curiosity that has no practical applications. For others, however, a predicate can often be easier to define in one direction than the other. Then it can be run backwards to compute the inverse. Maarten Van Emden has given a clever example of reversible predicates for solving the game of Mastermind. In that game, one player has a secret code consisting of some list of colors and the other player tries to discover the code by giving various test probes; the first player then responds with a score consisting of the number of colors in the probe that match exactly in color and position, and the number that match in color but not in position. To compute the score, van Emden defined a scoring predicate mm(Code,Probe,Score), where Score is computed when Code and Probe were given. But then the same predicate could be run backwards to break the code. The following goal

mm(Code,red.blue.black.white.nil,1 . 2).

determines a value for Code that gives the score (1 . 2) with the given probe. A version of Van Emden's code is also printed in the collection by Coelho et al. (1980).

2.3 PROCEDURAL PROLOG

Programming style in Prolog is strongly influenced by the pure Prolog subset. In fact, all of the examples so far have used only this subset, except for comparison predicates like ge and arithmetic operators like (X := A + B). But to make Prolog run on conventional computers, the underlying inference engine imposes a strict order of execution. For purely declarative rules, that order can often be ignored. For complex applications, however, that order can have a major effect on performance. A Prolog programmer should write declarative rules, but should also be aware of the way those rules are executed by the inference engine.

2.3.1 Backtracking and Cuts

Two features distinguish Prolog from conventional programming languages: the unification algorithm for pattern matching, and the backtracking algorithm for executing rules. Backtracking can be viewed as a generalization of ordinary procedure calls. It allows rules that have been called and exited to be reactivated at some later time. The following diagram illustrates the flow through a conventional procedure:

$$\text{Call} \longrightarrow \boxed{\text{Conventional Procedure}} \longrightarrow \text{Exit}$$

The arrows in this diagram indicate flow in only one direction. The procedure is activated by a call and terminated by an exit. After it exits, there is no way that it can be reactivated except by another call. Many systems allow programs to be interrupted. Then the system saves the state of the current activation, performs some higher priority task, and reactivates the suspended procedure. But one thing that conventional systems never do is to reactivate a procedure that has already run to completion and exited normally.

In Prolog, the rules and facts that define a predicate behave like a procedure. They can be called by a goal and can exit successfully like a conventional procedure. But backtracking adds another way of exiting and another way of reentering. The next diagram shows the flow through the Prolog clauses that define some predicate:

The top line shows the ordinary flow through a rule that terminates successfully. But if a goal fails, control does not pass to the next goal to the right. Instead, the goal terminates by failure, and the previous goal on the left is reactivated by a redo. To illustrate the possible entries and exits, consider the following two rules that define the predicate p:

```
p(X) <- q(X) & r(X) & s(X) & t(X).
p(X) <- u(X) & v(X).
```

The first rule is called when the head p matches some goal. Then the predicates in its body are called from left to right. If they all succeed, the clause is exited in the normal way. Suppose, however, that predicate s happened to fail. Then control does not pass to t, but to the redo entry for r. Another choice is taken for r, and s is called again. If s fails once more, control passes back to r. If no more options are available for r, then r also fails and control passes back to a choice point for q. If all choices for q fail, then the whole rule fails and control passes to the second rule that defines p. If the second rule fails, then the original goal that called p also fails.

Each option in a rule creates a *choice point*, a point where control returns when a rule is reentered by a redo. There are two ways of specifying options: multiple rules (or facts) with the same head predicate or the | operator in the body of some rule. The more basic way is by multiple rules, since every use of the | operator can be replaced by multiple rules. The following rule, for example,

```
a <- b & (c | d) & e.
```

is equivalent to the pair of rules

```
a <- b & c & e.
a <- b & d & e.
```

Although the | operator can always be eliminated, it may simplify the statement of the rules. In some cases, it can also improve their execution speed. In the pair of rules above, for example, the predicate b must be executed a second time if c fails. If b had side effects such as input/output, the final results might be different.

In the basic Prolog inference method, choice points result from multiple rules. The | operator behaves as though it were defined by the following two rules:

```
(P | Q) <- P.
(P | Q) <- Q.
```

The first rule says that to execute a goal of the form (P | Q), first do P. If P succeeds, then (P | Q) succeeds without any need to try Q. But if P fails (or some later failure forces a redo), then go to the second rule, which tries Q. In these rules, P and Q are *metavariables*, whose values are predicates rather than ordinary data structures. These rules are sufficient as long as there are no complications introduced by cuts. In order to handle those complications, IBM Prolog provides | as a built-in operator.

Sometimes the choice points may not be obvious because they are buried in the rules for some other predicate. The next rule, for example, has no explicit choice points:

```
woman(W) <- human(W) & female(W).
```

Although there are no alternatives in this rule, the predicate human may be defined by a long list of facts in the workspace. If the goal is woman(X), the first value found by the finder goal human(W) might be W=socrates. Since female(socrates) fails, the system backtracks to the redo point for human to find W=cicero. Since female(cicero) also fails, it keeps trying until it finds some value for W that makes both predicates true.

In some cases, backtracking can be a highly efficient way of searching. In other cases, it may cause a great deal of overhead. Prolog provides a way of controlling the search process by means of a built-in operator called *cut*, written /. The cut operator commits Prolog to the current path in the search process by throwing away choice points. Thus it cuts out the remaining part of the search space that would otherwise result from the open choice points. However, a careless use of cuts can destroy the logical integrity of the computation. Consider the following example:

```
woman(W) <- human(W) & / & female(W).
human(mary).
human(george).
female(mary).
```

Here, the goal woman(X) succeeds with X=mary. But consider the next example:

```
woman(W) <- human(W) & / & female(W).
human(george).
human(mary).
female(mary).
```

Now human(W) finds W=george. Then the cut throws away the choice point leading to human(mary). But now female(george) fails. Since the choice point is gone, the system cannot redo the human predicate to find another value for W. Therefore the entire rule fails. As this example shows, cuts can destroy the declarative reading of a program. Following are three reasons for using cuts:

- If a goal is known to have at most one solution, a cut following the goal may prevent unnecessary backtracking.

- Doer goals that have side effects (such as input/output) may cause erroneous results if executed more than once; a cut can prevent them from being repeated by backtracking.

- When an error occurs in a deeply nested computation, a cut may be necessary as part of the recovery process.

To illustrate backtracking, the count predicate keeps incrementing its argument each time backtracking returns to it:

```
count(0).
count(I) <- count(J) & (I := J + 1).
```

The first line starts the count at 0. Then the recursive rule adds 1 to the value computed by the previous call. To see how it works, type the following goal at the terminal:

    count(I) & write(I) & fail.

At the first call, count(I) matches the first rule with I=0. Then the write predicate prints 0 at the terminal. The fail predicate takes no arguments and always fails when it is called. The failure causes backtracking to go to the second rule, which calls count to compute J=0. Then I=1, and write prints 1 at the terminal. The predicate fail forces backtracking to return to the subgoal count(J), which computes J=1, whereupon I=2. As a result, the system keeps printing the integers from 0 up to the point where the user causes an interrupt. (This can be done by typing sp.)

   To keep counting from going on forever, some limit N is necessary. But a cut is also needed to keep backtracking from redoing the previous rules. The two-argument version of count calls the one-argument version to do the counting, but it uses the second argument as a limit:

    count(I,N) <- count(I) & (gt(I,N) & / & fail | true).

As long as I is less than or equal to N, the second option in this rule calls the predicate true, which always succeeds. As soon as I becomes greater than N, the cut is executed to prevent backtracking from redoing the one-argument count goal. Then fail causes a failure that stops the process. Because of the limit, the following goal only prints the integers up to 5:

    count(I,5) & write(I) & fail.

   Cuts in Prolog are like go-to statements in conventional languages: they are very powerful, but they may destroy the structure of the program and make it difficult to read and maintain. The best way to use cuts is to define better structured operators in terms of them. Then use those operators instead of the more primitive cuts. Two operators defined in terms of cuts are the negation ¬ and the if-then operator ->. Following is a definition of negation:

    ¬P <- P & / & fail.
    ¬P.

The first rule says that to prove ¬P, first try P. If P succeeds, do the cut that throws away the choice point to the second rule. Then the goal fail forces a failure. Since the pointer to the second rule is gone, there is nothing else to do, and the original goal ¬P fails. Therefore ¬P fails if P succeeds. On the other hand, if P fails, the choice point for the second rule is still available. The second rule does nothing and always succeeds. Therefore ¬P succeeds if P fails. In IBM Prolog, the ¬ operator is built-in, and it does some additional checking to handle cases where the goal P itself does cuts that may affect the success or failure of ¬P.

The if-then operator is represented by a right pointing arrow. The combination (P -> Q; R) may be read "If P then Q else R." It has the following definition:

```
(P -> Q; R) <- P & / & Q.
(P -> Q; R) <- R.
```

If P succeeds, the cut throws away the choice point for the second rule. Then Q is executed; Q may succeed or fail, but backtracking will never cause R to be executed after P has succeeded. On the other hand, if P fails, the second rule is performed to execute R. As with the definition of ¬, the system actually does more checking than this definition shows in order to handle cases where P itself contains cuts.

Logically, the if-then operator is not necessary, since it could be simulated with a construction of the form (P & Q | ¬P & R). However, this form is less efficient, since it executes P twice. It could also give different results if P had side effects. As an example of the use of if-then, consider the notin predicate, which is the negation of member:

```
notin(X,L) <- ¬member(X,L).
```

This rule says that X is not in the list L if it is false that X is a member of L. With the cut operator, it is possible to give a more basic definition of notin:

```
notin(X,nil).
notin(X,X.Tail) <- / & fail.
notin(X,Head.Tail) <- notin(X,Tail).
```

The first rule says that for any X, X is not in the empty list. The second rule says that if X matches the head of the list, discard the choice point and force an immediate failure. Then the third rule says that if X is not equal to Head (since the choice point must not have been discarded), check whether X is not in Tail. Using the if-then operator leads to a clearer definition:

```
notin(X,nil).
notin(X,Head.Tail) <-
    (X=Head -> fail; notin(X,Tail)).
```

The second rule says that if X equals the head, then fail; else check whether X is not in the tail.

Repeated if-then operators can be used to simulate a case statement in other languages. For example, the following rule determines pet sizes:

```
pet_size(P,S) <- (P=mouse    -> S=small;
                  P=cat       -> S=normal;
                  P=dog       -> S=normal;
                  P=horse     -> S=big;
                  P=elephant -> S=enormous;
                              S=unknown).
```

This predicate, however, can be defined much more simply by just a list of facts:

```
pet_size(mouse, small).
pet_size(cat, normal).
pet_size(dog, normal).
pet_size(horse, big).
pet_size(elephant, enormous).
pet_size(*, unknown).
```

The case construction may be useful when the test predicate is complex, but as this example illustrates, Prolog does an implicit case check in deciding which rule to invoke. That implicit check is usually more efficient than a case check inside the body of a rule. However, the case construction might be useful to avoid problems with backtracking. Suppose, for example, that P=dog, but the predicate were followed by some other goal that might fail. In that case, backtracking might lead to pet_size(*,unknown), which would give the size unknown for the dog. To avoid that backtracking, cuts could be added to all the clauses but the last:

```
pet_size(mouse, small) <- /.
pet_size(cat, normal) <- /.
pet_size(dog, normal) <- /.
pet_size(horse, big) <- /.
pet_size(elephant, enormous) <- /.
pet_size(*, unknown).
```

Each of the conditions has just a single cut. That cut has no effect on the success or failure of the clause in which it occurs, but it prevents backtracking from leading to later clauses. However, this proliferation of cuts is not desirable. They should be avoided by using the if-then operator if backtracking might cause a problem.

2.3.2 Saving Computed Values

Unification binds values to variables, but backtracking unbinds the old values before finding new ones. The automatic backtracking, which can be powerful for certain operations, sometimes erases results that are needed later. There are two basic ways of preserving a result to keep it from being erased by backtracking:

- Cause some nonlogical side effect that backtracking cannot erase.
- Use the compute or set_of predicates, which accumulate a list of results.

To illustrate a side effect for preserving intermediate results, consider the Fibonacci series 0, 1, 1, 2, 3, 5, 8, ..., where each number is the sum of the previous two. Following is a recursive predicate for computing the Nth number in the series:

```
fib(0,0).
fib(1,1).
fib(N,X) <-  N1 := N - 1  &  N2 := N - 2
             &  fib(N1,X1)  &  fib(N2,X2)
             &  X := X1 + X2.
```

The first two facts state the starting values for the series. Then the general rule computes X by calling itself recursively to compute the values for (N - 1) and (N - 2). Since each call to the general rule for fib makes two recursive calls, the amount of computation increases rapidly. In fact, it increases as the Fibonacci series itself: for N=30, X=832040. In principle, the value of X for N=30 should take only 29 additions; to make 832040 recursive calls is an enormous amount of overhead. One way to improve performance is to add an extra argument to fib that saves the previous value (see Exercise 19). Another way is to use the built-in addax predicate to assert a new fact:

```
fib(0,0).
fib(1,1).
fib(N,X) <-  N1 := N - 1  &  N2 := N - 2
             &  fib(N1,X1)  &  fib(N2,X2)
             &  X := X1 + X2
             &  addax(fib(N,X),1).
```

The last line of this rule adds the new fact fib(N,X) to the workspace. The second argument of addax is used here to specify that the new fact should be placed in position 1 of the clauses for the predicate fib. Without that argument, the new fact would be placed *after* all of the other clauses, and the recursive rule would still be invoked.

To compute fib(16, 987), the first version took 55 milliseconds on an IBM 3081, but the version with addax took less than a millisecond. The version with addax took 3 milliseconds to compute fib(46, 1836311903), which is the largest value of fib that can be computed with 32-bit integers. With infinite storage, the original version of fib might have taken 28 hours to compute this value; in fact, it ran out of stack space for N=17. To compute fib for larger inputs, it is necessary to switch to floating point beyond N=46. That switch can be accomplished by adding one extra fact to the definition of fib:

```
fib(46, 1836311903.0).
```

This fact should be inserted just before the general rule for fib. Since the second argument has a decimal point, it forces all computations for N>46 to use floating point arithmetic. With this additional fact, fib can compute all values up to N=364 before causing an overflow.

For computing Fibonacci numbers, a version of fib with three arguments can run in linear time without using addax. In fact, the three-argument version takes 8 milliseconds for N=364, while the addax version takes 24 milliseconds. However, once all the values have been asserted by means of addax, the answer to each future question is found by simply looking it up; this takes one millisecond or less. This technique is useful for mixing computation with table look-up. For more complicated problems, there may be no simple linear algorithm, and `addax` can be valuable for avoiding duplicate computations. Game playing programs, for example, frequently reach the same positions through multiple paths. They can often run much faster if they save each position that has been evaluated. This is a typical tradeoff of space versus time: chess programs on large machines save previous values, but programs on small machines do not have the space.

The `addax` predicate has a variety of uses. For example, the predicate `married` is supposed to be symmetric. But it may happen that one fact `married(zeus,hera)`, but not the converse `married(hera,zeus)`, has been asserted. The following goal searches for all nonsymmetric pairs and asserts the missing fact:

```
married(X,Y) & ¬married(Y,X) &
addax(married(Y,X)) & fail.
```

The first subgoal `married(X,Y)` serves as a finder goal to retrieve some married pair. If the converse has also been asserted, the goal `¬married(Y,X)` fails and forces backtracking to find another pair. If the converse has not been asserted, `addax` asserts it, and `fail` forces backtracking to find the next married pair. The process continues until all married pairs have been checked.

Side effects can also accumulate a list or set of results that are generated by some goal. Suppose, for example, that one wanted to find all pairs of siblings in the family database. The goal `sibling(X,Y)` would find the first pair; then a semicolon from the terminal would find the second pair. For each pair, a semicolon would be necessary to force the inference engine to backtrack and find another pair. Another way to force backtracking is to use the built-in `fail` predicate, as in the following goal:

```
sibling(X,Y) & write(X.Y) & fail.
```

First, `sibling` finds one pair of siblings, and `write` prints out that pair. Then `fail` forces backtracking to the most recent choice point. Since there are no choices for `write`, backtracking continues to the redo entry for `sibling` and searches through the list of facts for `child` to find another pair who have a common parent. Then `write` prints out that pair, and `fail` forces another backtrack. When all pairs of siblings have been printed out, the goal fails.

Since `sibling` is a symmetric predicate, all pairs are printed twice, once for `sam.mary` and again for `mary.sam`. The extra pair can be suppressed by using the less-than predicate, which forces them to appear in alphabetical order:

```
sibling(X,Y) & lt(X,Y) & write(X.Y) & fail.
```

Since `lt(mary,sam)` is true, that pair is printed, but the pair `sam.mary` is rejected.

Even with the `lt` predicate, there may still be duplicate data. If Sam and Mary have only one common parent, they are printed only once in the form `mary.sam`. But if they have two common parents, backtracking finds both parents and prints the same pair twice. The `set_of` predicate avoids that problem. It accumulates a list of results, sorts them, and removes duplicates. Although the `set_of` predicate is difficult to define in pure Prolog, many versions of Prolog support it directly. IBM Prolog has a general built-in predicate, `compute`, which supports `set_of` as a special case:

```
set_of(V,G,L) <- compute(set,V,G,nil,L).
set_of(V,G,nil).
```

(This is a simple definition of `set_of`—it should not be used in programs that will backtrack into it.) The first argument of `compute` is either `list` for a list of all values in the order they were found or `set` for a list of values sorted in alphabetical order with duplicates removed. The fourth argument of `compute` is `nil` for this special case; Chapter 5 (page 300) describes a more general use of `compute` with a list of variables in that position. The variables V, G, and L are the ones needed for `set_of`: V is a single variable or a structure of variables whose values are to be found; G is some finder goal that finds values for the variables in V; and L is a list of all instances of V for which G succeeds. To find all pairs of siblings in the database, issue the following goal:

```
set_of(X.Y, sibling(X,Y) & lt(X,Y), L).
```

The first argument is the pair X.Y whose values are sought; the second argument is the finder goal `sibling(X,Y) & lt(X,Y)`; and the third argument is the list L, accumulated from all pairs X.Y that make the second argument succeed.

Readers who are familiar with relational databases should note that the `set_of` predicate is strongly reminiscent of database query languages. The three variables V, G, and L in `set_of` correspond exactly to the three parts of a database query:

- V: A pattern of fields in some database relations whose values are to be found.

- G: Some condition or logical combination of conditions that must hold between those values.

- L: The place to send the results, which may be the terminal, a file, or some intermediate storage area.

This similarity should not be surprising, since both Prolog and relational database theory are based on symbolic logic. In fact, database relations correspond to Prolog predicates that are defined solely by lists of facts. The main difference is that database relations typically contain large volumes of data that are stored on external disks, whereas Prolog predicates are held in main storage. Virtual relations or "views" in database theory correspond to Prolog predicates that are defined by rules.

2.3.3 Searching a State Space

Planning, problem solving, and game playing techniques in artificial intelligence are commonly cast as searches through a *state space*. Each state in the problem is represented as a data structure, permissible moves between states are defined by purely declarative rules, and the search procedure is defined by a problem-independent set of rules. Exercises 6 through 10 at the end of this chapter can all be handled by state-space searches:

■   For the farmer, wolf, goat, and cabbage problem, the state is represented as the structure loc(F,W,G,C), which shows the locations of each of the four critical items. Rules for the possible moves are described starting on page 52.

■   For the water jug problem, the state is a pair of numbers (A.B) representing the amounts of water in each jug. Possible moves are described on page 55.

■   For the missionary and cannibal problem, the state is a five-tuple B.M.C.M2.C2, as described on page 56.

■   For the monkey and bananas problem, the state is a triple M.B.P, as described on page 56.

For each of these problems (and many more like them), problem-dependent information is embodied in a predicate move(Current,Next), which specifies possible moves from a current state to a next state. The search procedure uses this predicate as a finder goal that finds a new state Next when given a state Current. The task is to find a sequence of safe, permissible states from the start to the goal. Ideally, the procedure should minimize the amount of computing time needed to find the solution.

The simplest search procedure to implement in Prolog is a depth first, backtracking search that takes advantage of the built-in mechanisms. The predicate

    depth_first(Goal, History, Answer)

is a recursive procedure with two inputs, Goal and History, and an output Answer that represents the solution. The variable Goal contains a single state; History is a list of states that have already been traversed, with the current state at the head; and Answer is a list of states from start to goal. The search can be defined by two rules:

    depth_first(Goal, Goal.*, Goal.nil).
    depth_first(Goal, Current.Past, Current.Future) <-
        move(Current,Next) &
        ¬member(Next,Past) &
        depth_first(Goal, Next.Current.Past, Future).

The first rule says that if the goal state is identical to the current state (the head of the history list), then the problem is solved: the answer is just a list of one

state (Goal.nil). The second rule uses the pattern Current.Past to split
the history list into the Current state and a list Past of previous states. The
third argument Current.Future returns the answer as a list with the current
state at the head followed by the future list to be computed. In the body of the
rule, the goal move takes one step from Current to another state Next. Then
the test ¬member(Next,Past) checks the history list Past to make sure that
Next has not already been visited. Finally, depth_first calls itself
recursively to compute Future with the state Next at the head of the history
list.

   If the farmer is crossing from the west side of the river to the east, the goal is
loc(east,east,east,east), and the initial history list has the single
starting state, loc(west,west,west,west). The following goal triggers the
computation:

```
depth_first(loc(east,east,east,east),
            loc(west,west,west,west).nil, Answer).
```

For this goal, the depth first search computes the following answer list. The first
state is the start, and the last state is the goal; each intermediate state shows one
step along the way.

```
loc(west,west,west,west) . loc(east,west,east,west) .
loc(west,west,east,west) . loc(east,east,east,west) .
loc(west,east,west,west) . loc(east,east,west,east) .
loc(west,east,west,east) . loc(east,east,east,east) .
nil
```

As this list shows, the first step moved the farmer and the goat from west to east;
then the farmer returned by himself. The eighth state is the goal. This list
shows only the successful moves from start to goal. A trace of the move
predicate would show a number of false steps that caused one of the later
predicates to fail: either the Next state failed the ¬member check, or it led to a
dead end from which depth_first could not find a solution. The reader
should try this example at the terminal, tracing one predicate at a time:
depth_first, move, or member. Tracing all three predicates simultaneously
would tend to obscure the process with a large volume of output.

   A depth first search maintains a single history list at all times. When one
branch of the search reaches a dead end, backtracking automatically prunes the
tree up to an active choice point. When the system resumes the search from that
point, the history list grows along the new path. Automatic pruning minimizes
the amount of storage space required. Storage efficiency is one of the major
strengths of a depth first search. One of its weaknesses, however, is that the path
it finds may not be the shortest: since it pursues each branch as far as it can
before trying any other, it may find a lengthy solution along one branch when
some other branch might have been much shorter. In some cases, it may even
continue forever in a fruitless search when a neighboring branch had a short path
to the solution.

A breadth first search keeps track of all possible paths instead of just the current history list. As its second argument, the predicate `breadth_first` maintains a list of histories, each of which is a list of states. It is defined by two rules, which are slightly more complex than the depth first search. The first rule (see below) is the stopping rule that checks whether the goal has been reached. It is more complex than the stopping rule for the depth first search for two reasons:

1. Since `Histories` is a list of lists, the test for the goal state must use the `member` predicate to scan through the list.

2. Whereas the depth first rules built up the answer list in the correct order, this rule must reverse the history list selected by `member`. (Note that the depth first rules use the appending technique for building up the answer list; compare them to the rules for `append` on page 64.)

```
breadth_first(Goal, Histories, Answer) <-
    member(Goal.Past, Histories) &
    reverse(Goal.Past, Answer).

breadth_first(Goal, Histories, Answer) <-
    Histories=(*.*) &
    set_of(Next.Current.Past,
            member(Current.Past, Histories) &
            move(Current,Next) & ¬member(Next,Past),
                                New_history_list) &
    remove_duplicate_head(New_history_list,
                            Clean_list) &
    breadth_first(Goal, Clean_list, Answer).
```

The second rule uses the `set_of` predicate to find the set of all paths that extend the search one step farther. The subgoal `Histories=(*.*)` merely checks that the list is not `nil`; this test causes a slight improvement in performance, but it is not essential, since the `member` predicate would fail if `Histories` were `nil`. After that check, `set_of` finds the set of all lists of the form `Next.Current.Past` where `Current.Past` is one of the history lists, there is a permissible move from `Current` to `Next`, and `Next` is not a member of the list `Past`. All such lists are accumulated as a list of lists in `New_history_list`. Since the same state can often be reached by multiple paths, the predicate `remove_duplicate_head` removes all redundant paths in the history list. This check makes a major improvement in performance, but it makes it impossible to use this predicate to find more than one solution. Finally, `breadth_first` calls itself recursively to continue the search for another step.

The predicate that removes duplicate heads from a list of lists depends on the fact that `set_of` produces a sorted list. Therefore all duplicates can be removed in a single sweep that compares the heads of adjacent sublists.

```
remove_duplicate_head(F.S.Tail,Clean) <-
   ((F=(Head.*) & S=(Head.*)) ->
         remove_duplicate_head(F.Tail,Clean);
         (remove_duplicate_head(S.Tail,L) &
          Clean=(F.L))).
remove_duplicate_head(F.nil,F.nil).
remove_duplicate_head(nil,nil).
```

The variables F and S match the first and second lists in a list of lists. If both F
and S have the same head, the S list is discarded; and the rule calls itself to
remove duplicates from the list F.Tail. If they have different heads, it saves
both F and S and calls itself to remove duplicates from the list S.Tail.

Since the breadth first search extends all paths one step at a time, it is
guaranteed to find a shortest solution. But since it preserves all paths (or at least
all nonredundant paths), it uses up more storage space. Many implementations
of Prolog (including IBM Prolog) use *structure sharing* to save space: when the
system builds a new list, it moves pointers whenever possible instead of copying
the lists. With such systems, the depth_first predicate will use the minimum
amount of storage that is logically necessary to do the search. Although
Histories appears to be a list of lists, it is actually stored as a tree where
common sublists are shared. In particular, the starting state, which is the root of
the tree, is common to all of the sublists.

2.3.4 Input/Output

Except for differences in syntax, the pure Prolog subset is essentially the same in
all versions of Prolog. But the built-in predicates, especially the ones for
input/output, diverge from one version to another. This section will use the I/O
facilities of IBM Prolog. The principles are similar for other versions, but the
details may differ.

The following predicate, called farmer, uses IBM Prolog input and output
to provide a user interface for the Farmer program. It prompts the user for the
starting side, and it formats the output nicely.

```
farmer <-  prst(
'Please enter the starting side for all items.')
  & nl
  & prst('Type "east"  or  "west".')
  & nl & readat(S) & opp(S,G)
  & depth_first(loc(G,G,G,G), loc(S,S,S,S).nil,
                                        Answer)
  & system('clear') & nl
  & prst('Stages in transit:') & nl
  & prtans(Answer).
```

The farmer rule uses the following predicate

```
prtans(nil) <- nl &
 prst('Everybody''s safely across.') & nl .
prtans(loc(F,W,G,C).Tail) <-
   nl & prst('Farmer on the '||F)
 & nl & prst('Wolf on the '||W)
 & nl & prst('Goat on the '||G)
 & nl & prst('Cabbage on the '||C)
 & nl & prtans(Tail).
```

Whereas write has no choice point, read can be used with or without a choice point. For example, to read a file of Prolog terms and display it on the screen, we can do either display1(File) or display2(File), as defined in:

```
display1(File) <- open(File, input) &
    read_show1(File) & close(File).

read_show1(File) <-
    read_no_choice(Term, File) & write(Term) &
    read_show1(File).
read_show1(File).

read_no_choice(Term, File) <- read(Term, File, 1).

display2(File) <- open(File, input) &
    read_show2(File) & close(File).

read_show2(File) <-
    read_choice(Term, File) & write(Term) & fail.
read_show2(File).

read_choice(Term, File) <- read(Term, File, 3).

open(File, input) <-
 dcio(File, input, file, File, prolog, a, f, 80) & /.

close(File) <- dcio(File, close).
```

The predicate read_show1(File) works by calling itself recursively until there are no more terms to be read from the file, while read_show2(File) works by backtracking to a read with a choice point until the last term is read from the file. dcio is a general purpose predicate for dealing with files (see Appendix A for more details).

A common technique is to write a processing loop that does the following: write a prompt (such as tellme:); read an input; if the input is the word quit, exit from the loop; otherwise, process the input and repeat. The following rule does just that:

```
loop <- write('tellme:') & read(Input) &
        (Input=quit | process(Input) & loop).
```

In this case, `read` does not need to have a choice point. If `Input=quit`, the first option does nothing and the rule succeeds. Otherwise, the second option passes `Input` to the predicate `process`. When `process` finishes, `loop` executes the rule again.

We note that if we quit from the loop above we are still in the Prolog interpreter, and we can then set other goals. There is a built-in predicate called `fin` which has the effect of taking us out of the Prolog interpreter. It can be used like this:

```
loop <- write('tellme:') & read(Input) &
        (Input=quit & fin | process(Input) & loop).
```

Now a `quit` answer given to the program causes us to leave Prolog.

Our examples of looping using built-in predicates are quite procedural. While we prefer declarative programming where possible, a few fragments that can only be read procedurally do little harm, so long as they are small. In Chapter 3, we return to this subject, and look at ways of keeping the procedural fragments small and easy to understand.

2.3.5 String Handling

In IBM Prolog, strings can be concatenated using the `||` operator, and they can be converted to and from lists using the built-in `st_to_li` predicate. Concatenation of strings can be combined with arithmetic by using the `:=` operator, as in

```
X := 'The elapsed time is '||((T+30)/60)||' minutes.'
```

Other transformations on strings are usually done by using `st_to_li` to convert to list form. The lists are transformed, element-by-element if necessary, and the result is changed back to a string, also by using `st_to_li`. For example the goal `st_to_li('abc',*)` gives the answer

```
st_to_li('abc', a.b.c.nil)
```

and so does the goal `st_to_li(*,a.b.c.nil)`.

Another common example of string handling is to group a string of characters into a list of words or tokens. The predicate

```
tokenize(Input,Tokens)
```

takes a string of characters `Input`, and generates a list of words `Tokens`. As examples of how tokenize should work, consider the next five goals:

```
tokenize('Now is the time.', T1).
tokenize('Now    is the    time.    ', T2).
tokenize('abc123', T3).
tokenize('a(1,2,3)', T4).
tokenize('        ', T5).
```

Since extra blanks are ignored, both T1 and T2 should be the list

'Now' . 'is' . 'the' . 'time' . "." . nil

T3 should be the list of one word 'abc123'.nil, but T4 should be the list

'a' . "(" . '1' . "," . '2' . "," . '3' . ")" . nil

Since a blank string has no tokens, T5 should be nil. Following are the rules
for tokenize:

```
tokenize(String,Tokens) <- st_to_li(String,List) &
    tokenize1(List,Tokens,nil).

tokenize1(L1,Word.Tokens,L3) <-
    token(L1,Word,L2) & /
    & tokenize1(L2,Tokens,L3).
tokenize1(*,nil,*).
```

The first rule for tokenize1 assumes that token will take the list L1, put the
first token in the variable Word, and leave everything following Word in the list
L2. Then tokenize1 calls itself recursively to tokenize L2 into the list
Tokens with the remainder in L3. The cut / in the first rule for tokenize1
prevents unnecessary backtracking if some rule that calls tokenize happens to
fail. If the first rule fails to find a word, the second rule gives nil as the list of
tokens.

Various languages assume different rules for tokenizing. A common
convention is that a token is either an alphanumeric string or a single nonblank
character that is neither a digit nor a letter.

```
token(" ".L1,Word,L2) <- / & token(L1,Word,L2).
token(C.L1,Word,L2) <- (letter(C) | digit(C)) & /
    & alphanum(L1,Chars,L2) & st_to_li(Word,C.Chars).
token(C.L,C,L).
```

The first rule matches any input list starting with a blank; it just ignores the
blank and calls itself recursively to process everything after the blank. The
second rule looks for either a letter or a digit as the first character; it calls
alphanum to put the following alphanumeric characters in Chars; then it calls
string to convert the list C.Chars into the string Word. If the first character
is anything other than a letter, digit, or blank, the third rule treats it as a
single-character word. The cuts in the first two rules prevent backtracking from
reaching the third rule inadvertently. If a string is nil or all blank, the token
predicate fails.

The predicate `alphanum(L1,Chars,L2)` takes a list of alphanumeric characters from the beginning of `L1`, puts them in `Chars`, and leaves the remainder of `L1` as the list `L2`:

```
alphanum(C.L1,C.Chars,L2) <-
    (letter(C) | digit(C)) & / &
    alphanum(L1,Chars,L2).
alphanum(L,nil,L).
```

The first of these rules takes an alphanumeric character `C` from the head of a list and calls itself recursively. The second rule leaves `nil` as the list of characters if the head of the list is not alphanumeric. The remainder `L2` may contain letters or digits, but its head cannot be alphanumeric.

The standard `read` predicate reads terms that obey the Prolog syntax. To read an arbitrary character string, the `readch` predicate must be used to read one character at a time. The `readlist` predicate invokes `readch` repeatedly to read an entire list:

```
readlist(C.L) <- readch(C) &
    (readempty & / & L=nil | readlist(L)).
```

The `readempty` predicate followed by cut stops recursion if the end of an input line has been reached. Otherwise, `readlist` calls itself recursively to continue reading characters.

The `readtokens` predicate invokes `readlist` to read a list of characters and `tokenize1` to group that list into a list of words:

```
readtokens(Tokens) <-
    readlist(L) & / & tokenize1(L,Tokens,nil).
```

This rule uses the cut to prevent backtracking from deleting characters from the end of `L`. All the examples in this section make liberal use of cuts because tokenizing is a deterministic process that has no need of backtracking, but a later parsing stage may require a considerable amount of backtracking.

2.3.6 Changing Syntax

The default notation of a predicate followed by a list of arguments is not always the most readable. Fortunately, the Prolog syntax is easily extensible. That is, new operators can easily be defined. In the fact `likes(sam,mary)`, the first argument is usually considered the subject, and the second one the object. But the *infix form*, `sam likes mary`, takes advantage of English word order to make the relationship obvious. Infix notation sometimes coincides with English, but it is not true English. It is simply a syntactic variant of the standard Prolog notation.

Infix notation depends on the `op` predicate, which defines the syntax of new operators. It has three arguments:

```
op(Symbol,Assoc,Prec)
```

where Symbol is an atom that represents the operator, Assoc is its associativity, and Prec is its precedence. For example, before we can write sam likes mary instead of likes(sam,mary), we must declare likes to be an operator by saying op("likes",rl,50). Here, rl stands for right to left associativity. (In IBM Prolog double quotes normally enclose an atom, while single quotes signal a string. If an atom contains no special characters then the double quotes are optional.) For operators with equal precedence, associativity determines whether the operators group to the right or to the left (see the examples on page 60). The second argument of the op predicate must be one of four possible strings: lr defines a left-associative infix operator, rl defines a right-associative infix operator, prefix defines a prefix operator, and suffix defines a suffix operator.

The op predicate may appear in goals and facts like any other predicate. Unlike other predicates, however, op has the side effect of changing the way Prolog parses inputs. Following are the declarations for some of the built-in operators:

```
op(".",rl,100).
op("<-",prefix,10).
op(&,rl,30).
op(|,rl,20).
op("¬",prefix,40).
```

A higher precedence means tighter binding. Since <- has precedence 10, | has precedence 20, and & has precedence 30, the expression p<-a&b|c&d has exactly the same effect as p<-((a&b)|(c&d)). For user-defined predicates that represent English verbs, a precedence of 50 is appropriate. That makes them tighter binding than the logical operators, but less tight than the list-forming dot operator. Therefore with precedence 50 for verbs, the following expressions would have the expected parsing:

```
fred likes cabbage & barbara likes hamburgers.
fred eats nuts.dates.figs.nil.
```

If the likes operator had a precedence less than 30 and the eats operator had a precedence greater than 100, Prolog would parse the above expressions as though they had been parenthesized as,

```
fred likes (cabbage & barbara) likes hamburgers.
(fred eats nuts).dates.figs.nil.
```

Most English verbs are right-associative. Therefore the expression,

```
walter says mary thinks sue believes fred eats cabbage
```

is parsed in the following way:

```
walter says (
    mary thinks (sue believes (fred eats cabbage))).
```

If the verbs had been left-associative, the following, erroneous parsing would be found:

```
(((walter says mary)
     thinks sue) believes fred) eats cabbage.
```

Prefix operators normally group to the right, and suffix operators group to the left. An operator symbol can have different precedence in its infix, prefix, and suffix forms.

An important use for infix notation is to express the arithmetic operators in a more readable form. In IBM Prolog, we can write arithmetic expressions such as

```
X := -(4+5)/(7-(2*2)) .
```

which binds X to -3. This is made possible via built-in definitions for the operators := for assignment, + for plus, / for division, - for minus, and * for multiplication. The corresponding operator precedences are

```
op(":=",lr,50)
op("+",lr,60)
op("/",lr,100)
op("-",lr,60)
op("-",prefix,120)
op("*",lr,100)
```

Although we have called := an assignment operator, it differs from assignment in conventional languages, in that it produces a binding that can be undone later. The symbol /( ), with zero or one argument, has a special meaning in Prolog. It is the cut operator, that changes control flow. But with two arguments, it is an infix operator for division.

2.4 PERFORMANCE AND OPTIMIZATION

Prolog can be a highly efficient language when its features are used to their best advantage. But the powerful backtracking facilities can lead to a combinatorial explosion when they are not used properly. This section discusses ways of avoiding inefficiencies and improving performance. There are two basic ways of improving performance: finding a better algorithm, and reordering the search.

2.4.1 Choosing an Algorithm

The choice of algorithm is the most important factor in determining performance. A microprocessor running an efficient algorithm can outperform a supercomputer running an inefficient one. As an example, consider the problem of sorting a list in alphabetical order. Three different algorithms might be considered:

- A permutation sort that tries all possible permutations of a list in order to find one that is ordered.

- A bubble sort that interchanges pairs of elements until the result is sorted.

- A version of Hoare's Quicksort (Hoare 1962) which partitions the list into smaller parts, each of which can be sorted more quickly.

Although Quicksort is the most practical, the other sorts are interesting to examine, since they illustrate important Prolog techniques. Even if the techniques are inefficient for sorting, they may still be highly useful for other kinds of processing.

The first step in writing the permutation sort is to define the `permute` predicate for permuting a list. With the `pick` predicate defined on page 62, `permute` can be defined in two lines:

```
permute(nil,nil).
permute(L,H.T) <- pick(H,L,Rem) & permute(Rem,T).
```

The first line says that the only permutation of the empty list `nil` is `nil` itself. The second line says that any other list L can be permuted by picking an arbitrary element H from L as the new head and permuting the remainder Rem to form the new tail T. As an example, consider the following goal:

```
permute(a.b.c.nil,P).
```

At the first call to `permute`, `pick` selects the first element H=a, and the remainder Rem is `b.c.nil`. Then the first call to permute Rem leaves the result T=`b.c.nil`. Therefore the first permutation is the identity: P=`a.b.c.nil`. Each time bactracking returns to the `pick` predicate, a different element is selected. The second permutation is `a.c.b.nil`, and so on up to the sixth permutation `c.b.a.nil`. Then asking for another permutation causes a failure. To see how the permutations are generated, the reader should type these goals at the terminal, tracing both the `pick` and `permute` predicates.

To sort a list L1, find another list L2 that is an ordered permutation of L1. The following rule defines `psort` in exactly that way:

```
psort(L1,L2) <- permute(L1,L2) & ordered(L2).
```

If L1 is already ordered, `permute` leaves it unchanged at the first call, and `ordered` verifies that it is correctly sorted. But if `ordered` fails, backtracking keeps returning to `permute` to run through all possible permutations until an ordered one is found. The predicate `ordered` is defined by one recursive rule together with unconditional rules to handle `nil` or a one-element list:

```
ordered(A.B.Tail) <- le(A,B) & ordered(B.Tail).
ordered(A.nil).
ordered(nil).
```

The `ordered` predicate is deterministic: it does no backtracking and takes N calls to check that a list of length N is ordered. But the number of permutations increases as the factorial of N. To sort a list of two or three elements, psort is fast. It is also fast if the original list is already ordered. But to sort the 26 letters of the alphabet from typewriter order (q.w.e.r.t.y...) to alphabetical order would take more than a trillion centuries on an IBM 3081.

The psort predicate is an example of the *generate and test* method of problem solving: it generates a trial solution and calls ordered to test it. If ordered fails, backtracking goes back to generate another. There are two ways of improving a generate and test approach:

- *Heuristics*: Use knowledge about the problem to guide the choice of trials and avoid those that have no chance of succeeding.

- *Divide and conquer*: Split the problem into multiple subproblems, each of which is easier to solve; then combine the partial results to produce the final result.

Instead of trying all possible permutations, heuristics could guide the sort program by only selecting ones that make some "improvement"; i.e each new trial must be slightly better ordered than the previous one. A divide and conquer approach would split the list in two parts, sort those, and combine the results.

The bubble sort calls the predicate bubble to improve each pass through the list. Although a bubble sort is not usually considered a heuristic program, it illustrates the use of knowledge about the solution to improve performance. The predicate bsort calls bubble to generate an improved permutation:

```
bsort(L,L) <- ordered(L).
bsort(L1,L2) <- bubble(L1,L) & bsort(L,L2).
```

Instead of using backtracking to generate each permutation, bsort calls itself recursively. The reason it does not use backtracking is that each call needs the previous result to generate an improved permutation. Backtracking is good when the previous result is not needed, but it throws away information that algorithms like this may need. The bubble predicate checks pairs of adjacent elements and interchanges them if they are out of order. After each pass by bubble, the list is better sorted than before.

```
bubble(A.B.Tail, L) <-
    (le(A,B) -> (bubble(B.Tail,T) & L=A.T);
                (bubble(A.Tail,T) & L=B.T)).
bubble(A.nil, A.nil).
bubble(nil,nil).
```

The recursive rule checks whether A and B are in order. If so, it calls itself to check B.Tail; if not, it makes B the new head and calls itself to check A.Tail.

The time for the bubble sort increases as the square of the length N. For the list of 26 letters in QWERTY order, bsort takes 15 milliseconds. Yet the predicate qsort is even faster: it takes only 3 milliseconds for the same list, and its computing time increases as $N*log(N)$. The qsort algorithm is a version of divide and conquer, called Quicksort by its originator, Anthony Hoare. It uses a predicate `partition(M,L,L1,L2)` to split a list L into two parts L1 and L2. M is an arbitrary element of L; for best performance, it should be near the midpoint, but any element of L is acceptable. After partitioning, every element of L1 is less than or equal to M and every element of L2 is greater than M.:

```
partition(M,H.L,H.L1,L2) <-
    le(H,M) & partition(M,L,L1,L2).
partition(M,H.L,L1,H.L2) <-
    gt(H,M) & partition(M,L,L1,L2).
partition(*,nil,nil,nil).
```

The first two rules compare M to H, the head of the list. Depending on the comparison, they put H in front of L1 or L2. The third line takes care of `nil`.

The `qsort` predicate keeps calling `partition` to split the input list into smaller and smaller sublists. Then it calls itself to sort the sublists and calls `append` to combine the results:

```
qsort(nil,nil).
qsort(M.L,S) <- partition(M,L,L1,L2) &
    qsort(L1,S1) & qsort(L2,S2) &
    append(S1,M.S2,S).
```

The recursive rule takes the head of the input list M as the partitioning element. Then all the elements no larger than M go to L1, and the others go to L2. Finally, `append` combines the sorted sublists S1 and S2 with M in the middle. The choice of partitioning element M can have a major impact on performance. For relatively random lists, choosing the head is generally good. But if the input list is almost sorted, the head is the worst choice. If the 26 letters were already in alphabetical order, `qsort` would take 10 milliseconds, but `bsort` and even `psort` would only take 1 millisecond. Variations of `qsort` that take one of the later elements as the partitioning element are often preferred.

Sort programs rarely sort simple lists of numbers or character strings. Usually, they sort larger records or structures where one part is the key and the rest is some data associated with the key. In Prolog, such structures can be represented as lists with the head element as the key.

Note that the only places at which the above `qsort-partition` program deals with items that cannot be structures are `le(X,M)` and `gt(X,M)`. To handle structures, it is enough to replace these with, say, `new_le(X,M)` and `new_gt(X,M)`. As long as we provide appropriate rules for these new predicate names, the program will sort lists of any kind of data structure. For our proposed `Key.Data` structure, we need

```
new_le(K1.*,K2.*) <- le(K1,K2).
new_gt(K1.*,K2.*) <- gt(K1,K2).
```

Suppose we make these changes, and then give the goal

```
qsort((4 .door).(2 .shoe).(3 .tree).(1 .bun).nil,S).
```

Then S gets the value

```
(1 .bun).(2 .shoe).(3 .tree).(4 .door).nil.
```

For this example, the key is a number, and the associated data is a single word. The program would work just as well with data of varying length, such as:

```
(4 .door.knob.lock.key).
    (2 .shoe.sock).(3 .tree.leaf).(1 .bun).nil.
```

In rearranging the lists, structure sharing versions of Prolog move pointers rather than the actual data. Therefore qsort takes a similar amount of execution time for lists with one word of data per key as for lists with hundreds of data items per key.

2.4.2 Generate and Test

In a large class of artificial intelligence problems, values must be assigned to a number of variables to meet certain constraints. Simple examples are the *cryptarithmetic problems* that assign digits to letters to satisfy equations like SEND+MORE=MONEY or DONALD+GERALD=ROBERT. A database query system must search a database to find a combination of values that satisfies certain conditions. More complex examples include expert systems for design. The R1 computer configurator, for example, assigns values to about 1,000 different variables in determining a complete system configuration (McDermott 1982).

A common approach to solving such problems is *generate and test*: pick some value for each design variable, then test to see if that combination of values satisfies the constraints. If so, the problem is solved. If not, pick a new set of values, and try again. The psort program on page 90 is a particularly simple example of this.

This method is the epitome of the fixed-control approach: it fits all problems; all constraints may be stated in pure logic; and the control is clearly separated from the logic. Its only drawback is inefficiency: for the R1 computer configurator, there are about 1,000 variables to be defined with an average of 3 possible values for each one. The number of combinations to be tested is 3^{1000} — an array of supercomputers calculating since the beginning of the universe could not finish this computation.

To reduce the combinatorial explosion, R1 uses flexible control. The knowledge engineer explicitly adds control information that determines the order of assigning values and testing constraints. With such ordering, R1 can reduce the exponential term to a nearly linear one. As a result, it finds a satisfactory assignment of values to the 1,000 variables in about two minutes of CPU time. The efficiency of R1 is a strong argument for a judicious blending of logic and control. Yet it does not show whether the blend should be determined by a person or by an optimizing compiler.

To illustrate the issues, consider a simple cryptarithmetic problem with 8 variables — in this case, the puzzle SEND+MORE=MONEY. Each letter represents a single digit; no digit is repeated; and the initial digits S and M must be positive. (See Raphael (1976) for an analysis of the problem BEST+MADE=MASER, which is the same problem with some variables renamed.) Newell and Simon (1972) extensively studied protocols of human problem solvers who addressed such puzzles. As a result, they recommended production systems as a model of human performance. The OPS5 production system used to implement R1 (Forgy 1981) is a direct descendant of their original proposals. This section, however, argues that a conscious imitation of human approaches is unnecessary; an optimal blend of logic and control can be determined by an analysis of the problem structure itself. We can determine a good sequence of execution from the declarative information that defines the problem.

For the sample problem, the declarative information is derived from the statement SEND+MORE=MONEY. Let C1 represent a carry from the units position; C2, a carry from the tens position; C3, a carry from the hundreds position; and C4, a carry from the thousands position. Then the puzzle determines five constraint equations:

$$
\begin{aligned}
D + E &= Y + 10*C1 \\
N + R + C1 &= E + 10*C2 \\
E + O + C2 &= N + 10*C3 \\
S + M + C3 &= O + 10*C4 \\
C4 &= M
\end{aligned}
$$

The carries C1, C2, C3, and C4 are restricted to be 0 or 1, with possible repetitions; the other variables are restricted to 0, 1, 2, 3, 4, 5, 6, 7, 8, 9 with no repetitions; and the leading digits must be positive: S>0 and M>0.

To solve the problem in Prolog, the first step is to define a nondeterministic predicate pick(X,L,REM) for picking an arbitrary element X out of a list L and putting all the remaining elements of L in the third argument REM. As we saw in on page 62 the predicate is defined by the following two rules in Prolog:

```
pick(X,X.TL,TL).
pick(X,HD.TL,HD.REM) <- pick(X,TL,REM).
```

Given the pick predicate, the following Prolog rule defines the solve predicate for the puzzle. This predicate has 3 arguments, each of which is a list of variables connected by dots. As the rule is executed, each variable is bound to an integer. At the end, S.E.N.D becomes the list 9.5.6.7; M.O.R.E becomes 1.0.8.5; and MONEY becomes 1.0.6.5.2. (Writing strictly in IBM Prolog, the first list is 9 .5 .6 .7, and so on. A space is needed to distinguish the list of two numbers 9 .5 from the real number 9.5. In a list, a space after a dot is optional.)

```
solve(S.E.N.D, M.O.R.E, M.O.N.E.Y) <-
  pick(M, 0 . 1 . 2 . 3 . 4 . 5 . 6 . 7 . 8 . 9 . nil,R9)
    & pick(S, R9, R8)
    & pick(O, R8, R7) & pick(E, R7, R6) & pick(N, R6, R5)
    & pick(R, R5, R4) & pick(D, R4, R3) & pick(Y, R3, R2)
```

```
& gt(M, 0) & (C4=0 | C4=1) & M=C4 & gt(S, 0)
& (C3=0 | C3=1)
& O   :=   S + M + C3 - 10*C4
& (C2=0 | C2=1)
& N   :=   E + O + C2 - 10*C3
& (C1=0 | C1=1)
& R   :=   10*C2 + E - N - C1
& Y   :=   D + E - 10*C1.
```

This rule first picks a value for M from the 10 digits 0 through 9 and puts the remaining 9 digits in R9. Then it picks a value for S from R9 and puts the remaining 8 digits in R8. After it has picked a value for each of the variables, it begins testing the constraints to see if the choice of values constitutes a valid solution to the puzzle.

As the body of the solve rule is executed, the first choice of values is M=0, S=1, O=2, E=3, N=4, R=5, D=6, and Y=7. When the constraint M>0 is tested, a failure occurs, and the system backs up to the most recent choice point — in this case, the predicate, pick(Y,R3,R2). It then picks the new value Y=8 and tests the constraints once more. Again the test M>0 causes a failure, and the system backs up to try Y=9. At the next failure, it tries D=7 and Y=6. It continues exhaustively testing all 181,440 combinations of values for variables other than M before it finally backs up to try M=1. After more brute-force searching, it eventually finds the correct combination M=1, S=9, O=0, E=5, N=6, R=8, D=7, and Y=2.

This routine takes about 22 seconds of CPU time on an IBM 3081. Although 22 seconds does not sound like a long time, it represents about about 160 million instructions. Most of those instructions were wasted because this program explores thousands of irrelevant combinations.

2.4.3 Reordering the Generate and Test

The ideal shape for a search tree is a straight line that leads directly to a solution. The search tree that corresponds to the above program is a bush with 1,814,400 short branches, of which only one is correct. For the SEND+MORE=MONEY problem, there is no way to convert the search tree into the ideal, but it is possible to prune most of the unnecessary branches and make it more tree-like than bush-like. The optimization follows two general principles:

- Prune branches on the search tree as early as possible.
- Reduce the number of new branches that are allowed to sprout.

These principles give a graphic image of the approach, but they are not detailed enough to implement in an optimizing compiler. For generate-and-test problems, however, they map into the following more detailed principles:

■ Whenever all the variables in a constraint have values, that constraint should be tested before any new values are picked for other variables.

■ If every constraint has one or more unbound variables, select the constraint that has the smallest choice space and pick some value for each of its unbound variables.

To define the size of a *choice space*, let $X1$, $X2$, ..., Xn be the unbound variables in a constraint whose values cannot be computed from any other variables in that constraint. Then let choice(Xi) be the number of possible values that Xi can assume. The size of the choice space is defined as the product choice($X1$)*...*choice(Xn). This method is a common technique in artificial intelligence. It has been described by Kowalski (1979) for optimizing logic programs and implemented by Warren (1981).

To illustrate these rules, apply them systematically to optimize the SEND+MORE=MONEY problem. Of the five constraint equations, the one with the fewest choices is C4=M. Since M is determined by the value of C4, the choice space is limited to the two possible values of C4. The further constraint M>0 eliminates the value 0 and completely determines the values M=1 and C4=1. The rule for solve can therefore begin without any nondeterminism:

```
M=1 & C4=1
& R9=(0 . 2 . 3 . 4 . 5 . 6 . 7 . 8 . 9 . nil)
```

When C4 and M have values, the next most restricted constraint is S+M+C3=O+10*C4. In this equation, the three variables S, O, and C3 are without values; a choice for any two of them determines the third. Since C3 is limited to 0 or 1 and S is restricted by the further constraint that S>0, the choice space is 2 times 8, or 16. All·the other equations have a choice space of 112 or more. The procedure should next pick a value for S, test S>0, pick a value for C3, compute the value of O from the choices for S and C3, and check whether the computed value for O is one of the possible values left to be assigned. In Prolog, that sequence becomes

```
pick(S, R9, R8)
& gt(S, 0) & (C3=0 | C3=1)
& 0   :=   S + M + C3 - 10*C4
& pick(O, R8, R7)
```

After these choices have been made, the next most restricted constraint is E+O+C2=N+10*C3, which has unbound variables E, N, and C2. There are two choices for C2, and seven for E and N. Since E and N have the same choice space, either one can be picked first to determine a value for the other. Choosing E gives

```
pick(E, R7, R6) & (C2=0 | C2=1)
& N   :=   E + O + C2 - 10*C3
& pick(N, R6, R5)
```

Now the most restricted constraint is N+R+C1=E+10*C2. Only R and C1 are unbound variables, and picking 0 or 1 for C1 determines R:

```
(C1=0 | C1=1)
& R   :=   10*C2 + E - N - C1
& pick(R, R5, R4)
```

Finally, the last constraint to be tested is D+E=Y+10*C1, in which only D and Y are left unbound. Picking a value for either one determines the other. The end of the solve rule is therefore

```
pick(D, R4, R3)
& Y   :=   D + E - 10*C1
& pick(Y, R3, R2).
```

Putting the pieces together produces the following Prolog rule. Except for the first line of the body, which simplifies parts of the previous rule, the rest of the rule is just a reordering of the previous one. The improvement in performance, however, is dramatic: it finds the correct solution in only 0.008 seconds — over 2700 times faster.

```
solve(S.E.N.D, M.O.R.E, M.O.N.E.Y) <-
    M=1 & C4=1
    & R9=(0 . 2 . 3 . 4 . 5 . 6 . 7 . 8 . 9 . nil)
    & pick(S, R9, R8)
    & gt(S, 0) & (C3=0 | C3=1)
    & 0   :=   S + M + C3 - 10*C4
    & pick(0, R8, R7)
    & pick(E, R7, R6) & (C2=0 | C2=1)
    & N   :=   E + 0 + C2 - 10*C3
    & pick(N, R6, R5)
    & (C1=0 | C1=1)
    & R   :=   10*C2 + E - N - C1
    & pick(R, R5, R4)
    & pick(D, R4, R3)
    & Y   :=   D + E - 10*C1
    & pick(Y, R3, R2).
```

2.4.4 Observations on the Method

The improved program is still a form of generate and test, but a more distributed form. Instead of having a single block that generates all combinations followed by another block that tests all constraints, it repeatedly generates a few combinations and immediately tests them. The generate block in the first program had a single choice space of 1,814,400 combinations. The improved program has a sequence of five generate blocks with choice spaces of 1, 16, 14, 2, and 4 options each. The product of all these options is 1792 possible combinations. For the worst case, when all options have to be tested before a solution is found, the improvement is 1,814,400/1792 for a factor of 1012.5. The observed improvement in execution time, however, was a factor of 2700.

Reordering the sequence of generating and testing improves performance in three ways:

1. Dependencies in the constraints allow certain values to be computed deterministically from the values already bound to other variables. In this example, the choice spaces for M, O, N, R, and Y were narrowed down to 1.

2. Some constraints, such as M>0 and S>0, do not determine a unique value, but they at least reduce the size of the choice spaces.

3. Other constraints serve as filters that break up the monolithic generate block into a sequence of smaller generate blocks — in this example, five blocks.

With weak constraints that are almost always true, the filtering effect is of little value. The ideal case occurs when the constraints that separate the generate blocks filter out all but one combination. With ideal filtering, the large problem breaks down into separable subproblems with no possibility of backtracking from a later block to an earlier one. If the SEND+MORE=MONEY problem were completely separable, the choice space for the reordered program would be the sum 1+16+14+2+4 or 37 instead of 1792. In fact the constraints were doing useful, but not ideal filtering.

Unfortunately, not all problems can be optimized. The problem of assigning values to variables to meet certain constraints is equivalent to a kind of satisfiability problem, for which only the only known algorithms take up time that increases exponentially with the size of the problem. In the general case, no optimizer — human or machine — can derive a program that avoids the combinatorial explosion. Such cases arise when every constraint requires values for all variables before it can be evaluated. Then reordering does not help.

Fortunately, the constraints for many practical problems involve small subsets of the variables. The generate block can then be partitioned into a separate block for each subset. An ideal partitioning should have a large number of subblocks with just a few variables in each one. The partitioning is improved further when the constraints are so strong that they filter out all but a single option in the passage from one block to the next. With such strong filtering, the total number of combinations that have to be tested is the sum of the choice spaces in each subblock rather than their product.

EXERCISES

These exercises illustrate a wide variety of Prolog programming techniques. Many of them are discussed in detail or even completely solved in the text; following those exercises are references to the pages where the discussion starts.

1. Build a database of facts about family relationships. You may choose your own family, the family of gods and goddesses in Greek mythology, or any other family about which you can find sufficient data. Define four

predicates by lists of facts: `child(C,P)` means that C is a child of P; `married(A,B)` means that A is married to B; `male(X)` means that X is male; and `female(X)` means that X is female.

a. Define predicates for various family relationships, including mother, father, sibling, brother, sister, uncle, great-grandfather, and mother in law.

b. Define a predicate `cousin(X,Y,N)`, which means that X and Y are N-th level cousins; i.e, N=1 for first cousins, 2 for second cousins, etc.

c. Use Prolog to determine whether there is evidence of immorality in the family history. (As the U.S. Supreme Court has declared, morality is defined by the standards of the community. If the family is rather proper or the community is rather lax, this question may have a null answer.)

(Partial solution, page 28)

2. Translate the following sentences into Prolog: "Washable allergenic things are washed. Nonwashable allergenic things are vacuumed. Everything that is gray and fuzzy is allergenic. Shirts, socks, pajamas, dogs, and llamas are washable. Lamps, sofas, cats, and computers are nonwashable. Following are my gray, fuzzy possessions: my pajamas, my sofa, my cat Thothmes, and my llama Millicent." Use Prolog to determine which of my possessions are washed and which are vacuumed. (Complete solution, page 40)

3. Translate the following sentences into Prolog: "Tweety is a bird. Goldie is a fish. Squiggly is a worm. Birds like worms. Cats like fish. Cats like birds. Friends like each other. My cat is my friend. My cat eats everything he likes."

a. Use Prolog to determine what my cat eats.

b. Is that answer reasonable? If not, check whether the difficulty lies in the original English specifications or in your translation from English into Prolog.

c. If the problem lies in the specifications, revise them, translate the revised form into Prolog, and ask the question again.

(Hints, page 43)

4. Translate the following sentences into Prolog: "Ursula is pretty. Norbert is rich and handsome. Bertha is rich and strong. Pierre is strong and handsome. Bruno is kind and strong. All men like pretty women. All rich men are happy. Any man who likes a woman who likes him is happy. Any woman who likes a man who likes her is happy. Bertha likes any man who likes her. Ursula likes any man who likes her provided that he is either rich and kind or handsome and strong."

a. Use Prolog to find out who is happy.

b. For this problem, think of a reasonable rule to add that will make everybody happy.

c.   For the new version, find all cases of mutual affection (two people who like each other), divided affections (one person likes two or more people), and rivalries (two or more people like the same person).

(Hints, page 45)

5.   Translate the following English sentences into Prolog: "Sam likes all kinds of sports. Football, swimming, and boxing are sports. Any physical activity that involves competition between people is a sport. Bill and Mary compete in bilboquet. Bob competes with Bill in yobizumo. Tom plays all the sports that Bill plays."

a.   List some sports that Sam likes.

b.   List some sports that Tom plays.

c.   Is there sufficient information to determine which sports Sam plays?

Note: Like most specifications, this problem statement leaves out a number of assumptions that are supposed to be "common sense." State the implicit assumptions that are necessary to solve the problem, and write Prolog rules for them. (Discussion, page 46)

6.   A farmer has a wolf, a goat, and a cabbage (a very large one). He wants to get all three of them plus himself across a river, but his boat is only large enough to hold one item plus himself. How can he cross the river without leaving the wolf alone with the goat or the goat alone with the cabbage? (Complete solution, page 52 and page 80)

7.   Water jug A has a capacity of 5 liters, and water jug B has a capacity of 2 liters. Assume the following constraints: initially, A is filled and B is empty; the jugs are irregularly shaped, so that it is not possible to measure any intermediate amount; either jug may be poured into the other or down the drain, but no new water can be added. By what sequence of pouring, can exactly 1 liter of water be left in jug B? (Hints, page 55 and page 80)

8.   Three missionaries and three cannibals want to cross a river, but their boat is only large enough to hold two persons at one time. How can they all get across? Assume the constraint that the number of cannibals can never be greater than the number of missionaries on either side of the river at any one time. (Hints, page 56 and page 80)

9.   A room has four corners (A, B, C, D) and a middle (M). A monkey is standing at A, a box is at C, nothing is at B or D, and a bunch of bananas are hanging high above M. Assume that the monkey can perform the following actions:

a.   If standing at any location, move somewhere else.

b.   If standing next to the box, push it somewhere else.

c.   If standing next to the box, get on the box.

d.   If on the box, get off the box.

e.   If on the box under the bananas, reach for the bananas.

By what sequence of moves can the monkey reach the bananas from the starting state? (Hints, page 56 and page 80)

10. The nickel and dime game uses two kinds of coins (say, nickels and dimes). In the starting state, all the coins are lined up with the nickels on the left, the dimes on the right, and an empty space between them. For example, with two nickels and two dimes, the starting state would be n.n.'_'.d.d.nil. The goal state has all the dimes on the left and all the nickels on the right: d.d.'_'.n.n.nil. There are four possible moves: slide a nickel into an empty space on the right; slide a dime left; hop a nickel over another coin into an empty space on the right; or hop a dime over another coin into an empty space on the left.

   a. Try playing the game with coins to get some feeling for the techniques involved.

   b. Write rules that define the possible moves, and execute them with depth first, breadth first, and best-first (according to some evaluation of a move) search strategies. Compare the results and execution times of the different strategies.

   c. Generalize the rules to allow any number of nickels and dimes (not necessarily equal numbers of each).

   d. Write a user interface that asks for the number of each kind of coin and prints a nicely formatted trace of the steps from start to goal.

11. Let X and Y be lists of numbers. If the two lists are not of the same length, treat the shorter one as if it were padded with zeroes to match the length of the longer. Write Prolog rules to define the following predicates:

   a. listadd(X,Y,Z) adds the i-th element of X to the i-th element of Y to form the i-th element of Z.

   b. innerprod(X,Y,Z) computes the inner product of the lists X and Y: the i-th element of X is multiplied by the i-th element of Y, and the sum of the products is bound to Z.

   c. element(X,I,Z) extracts the i-th element of the list X and binds it to Z.

   After writing rules to compute these predicates with the input and output variables indicated, check whether the definitions are reversible (with inputs and outputs exchanged). If they are not reversible, either rewrite the rules to make them reversible or explain why such a rewrite is not possible or practical. (Partial solution, page 62)

12. Define a predicate take(N,L,L1,L2) that takes the first N elements from a list L, puts them in L1, and leaves the remaining elements in L2. If N=0, then L1=nil, and L2=L. If L has fewer than N elements, the predicate should fail. How reversible is take? Which arguments may be undefined upon a call to this predicate?

13. The predicate pick(X,L1,L2) defined on page 62 picks an element X out of list L1 and leaves the remainder in list L2. Generalize that predicate for picking N items out of one of several bins: pick(N,B,L1,L2), where N is the number of items to be picked, B is a number that identifies the bin, L1 is a list of nonnegative integers giving the number of items in each bin, and L2 is derived from L1 by subtracting N from position B (the result may become zero, but not negative). Assume that N and L1 are given in advance, but that B and L2 may be unbound variables whose values are to be found. (Note: only two rules are needed to define this predicate; it may be used in allocating offices in Exercise 17.)

14. Define a predicate weave(L1,L2,L3) that interleaves alternate elements of lists L1 and L2 to form the list L3. Check that it has the following properties:

    a. If L1=a.b.c.nil and L2=x.y.z.nil, then the result is L3=a.x.b.y.c.z.nil.

    b. If either input is shorter than the other, the tail of the longer input is passed to L3 unchanged.

    c. The rules are reversible: if L3=a.b.c.d.e.f.nil, then L1=a.c.e.nil and L2=b.d.f.nil.

    The definition requires two unconditional rules and one conditional rule. The conditional rule should call itself recursively, but it does not need to call any other predicate.

15. For any positive integer N, the *hailstone function* is easy to define: if N is even, its value is N/2; if N is odd, its value is $3*N+1$. But the values of this function rise and fall in a complex, unpredictable way that has fascinated mathematicians. The following Prolog rule computes the value X for any input N:

        hailstone(N,X) <-
            (rem(N,2,0) -> X := N/2; X := 3*N + 1).

    For any N≥1, the *hailstone path* is defined as the list of integers starting at N and ending at 1, where the predicate hailstone(I,J) must be true of any adjacent integers I and J in the path. (If N=1, the hailstone path is just the list 1.nil.) Write Prolog rules to define the following predicates:

    a. hpath(N,P), where P is the hailstone path for N.

    b. hlimit(N,Max,Length), where Max is the largest integer in the hailstone path for N and Length is the number of integers in the path from N to 1.

    c. hlong(N,M), where M is the integer between 1 and N that has the longest hailstone path (if multiple integers have equally long paths, let M be the smallest).

    For further discussion of this function, see Hayes (1984).

16. Four bands, each from a different side of town, marched in a parade. Each band played only one piece, and no two bands played the same piece. From the following clues, determine the order in which the bands marched and the pieces they played.

    a. The band from the north side was at the head of the parade.

    b. "American Patrol" was the second piece played.

    c. The band from the east or west side played "Yankee Doodle."

    d. The last band played "When the Saints Go Marching in," just behind the band from the west side.

    e. The bands that played "American Patrol" and "Stars and Stripes Forever" are from opposite sides of town.

(Complete solution, page 68)

17. A company is moving into three floors of a new building. Each floor has 40 offices. Following are the office requirements for each department that is moving in: Department m43 needs 9 offices; d48, 6 offices; m77, 11 offices; m54, 13 offices; j39, 9 offices; j76, 12 offices; m20, 11 offices; j92, 11 offices; j83, 7 offices; j64, 10 offices; m06, 11 offices; and j48, 10 offices. All the offices for a given department must be on the same floor. Furthermore, the following pairs of departments that work closely together must also be on the same floor: m43 and m77; d48 and m54; and j92 and j83.

    a. The solution could be computed as a list L of triples (D.N.F), where D is the department identifier, N is the number of offices needed, and F is the floor allocated to D. Initially, D and N are constants, but F is to be determined.

    b. Define a predicate allocate(L,Available), where L is the list of triples for each department and Available gives the number of available offices on each floor. Using the version of pick defined for Exercise 13, the allocate predicate requires only one recursive rule plus an unconditional rule that does nothing when L=nil.

    c. Then call allocate(L, 40 . 40 . 40 . nil) to solve the problem.

(Problem suggested by Karen Roberts of IBM; discussion, page 69.)

18. Study the rep predicate as defined by the following rule:

```
rep(X,N,L) <- length(L,N) & append(X.nil,L1,L)
        & append(L2,X.nil,L) & L1=L2.
```

For inputs X and N, give a simple English description of the result L. Define Prolog rules for rep that do not call any other predicates, but compute exactly the same result. Compare the execution times of the two versions for several values of N.

19. The Fibonacci series starts with 0 and 1. Each subsequent number is the sum of the previous two: 0, 1, 1, 2, 3, 5, 8, 13, 21, etc. Define a recursive

rule that computes the N-th number in the series (starting with the facts
fib(0,0) and fib(1,1)).

a. Note how the execution time increases with N. Why?

b. Use addax to improve performance.

c. Define a new version of fib with three arguments instead of two that
    runs in linear time.

(Partial solution, page 76)

20. Build a database of geographical information. Start by listing facts for the
    following five predicates: ocean(X) means X is an ocean; country(X)
    means X is a country; continent(X) means X is a continent;
    borders(X,Y) means X borders Y, where X and Y are either countries or
    oceans; and loc(X,Y) means X is located in Y, where X is a country and Y
    is a continent. You do not have to type all possible information about every
    country in the world, but include enough data to provide non-null answers to
    the following questions.

    a. What European countries border an ocean?

    b. What oceans border some Asian country, but do not border an African
        country?

    c. Find all pairs of countries located in different continents that border a
        common ocean.

    d. Find all pairs of countries A and B, where A and B have a common
        border, A borders one ocean, B borders another ocean, and A and B do
        not border the same ocean.

21. Generate possible hybrids between animals. Hybrids are not determined
    genetically, but by an overlap of two or more letters at the end of one
    animal's name with the beginning of another animal's name. Define a
    predicate that prints a listing of hybrids in the following form: Cross a tiger
    with a gerbil to get a tigerbil. Cross a kangaroo with a rooster to get a
    kangarooster.   Cross   a   hippopotamus   with   a   mussel   to   get   a
    hippopotamussel.

22. Write   Prolog   rules   to   solve   the   cryptarithmetic   problem
    DONALD+GERALD=ROBERT. Order the search to optimize performance.
    (See pages 94 and 97 for two solutions to a similar problem.)

23. Build a database of information about courses at some school. First enter
    data to define the predicate course(N,P,C,M), where N is the course
    number, P is a list of zero or more course numbers that are prerequisites for
    N, C is the number of credits for N, and M is a list of meetings for N. Assume
    that meetings are represented by two letters and a number: tu9 means
    Tuesday at 9 am, and mo15 means Monday at 3 pm; a course that meets for
    two consecutive hours might have the meeting list we16.we17.nil. Let S
    be a list of course numbers in some student's proposed schedule. Write
    Prolog rules to define the following predicates:

- The predicate `conflicts(S,L)` should determine a list L of courses in S that have a common meeting. If there are no conflicts, L should be `nil`.

- The predicate `credits(S,C)` should compute the total number of credits C for all the courses in S.

24. Add student information to the course database described in the previous exercise: the predicate `student(N,Name,T,S)` gives the student number N, name Name, transcript T, and current schedule S. The transcript should be a list of pairs `(N1.G1).(N2.G2)...nil` where each Ni is the number of a course that the student has taken and Gi is the grade that the student received in that course. Assume that valid grades are the letters a, b, c, d, f, i (incomplete), and p (passed by advance placement or in an ungraded course). Write Prolog rules to define the following predicates:

    - Let `gpa(N,A)` compute the grade-point average A for all courses in the transcript for student N. Assume 4 points for an a; 3 for a b; 2 for a c; 1 for a d; and 0 for an f. Ignore courses with grades of p or i. Weight the average by the number of credits for each course. If a student's transcript has no graded courses, let A be `nil`. (Either use floating point arithmetic or scale the integers by 100.)

    - Let `checkprereq(N,S,M)` compute a list of courses M with missing prerequisites in the schedule S for student N: either some prerequisite for the course is not in the student's transcript or the grade for the prerequisite is d, f, or i.

    - Let `ranking(R)` compute a list R of student numbers ordered by descending grade-point averages.

25. Let `schedule(N,Min,Max,Pref,S)` determine a new schedule for student N chosen from the list of preferences in Pref where Min and Max are two numbers. The schedule S should meet the following constraints:

    - No conflicts: `conflicts(S,nil)`.

    - If `credits(S,C)`, then $Min \leq C$ and $C \leq Max$.

    - Meets prerequisites: `checkprereq(N,S,nil)`.

    - Assuming that Pref is ordered in descending order of preferences, `schedule` should select more preferred courses before less preferred ones.

    - Find S with the constraint that the student's adviser has said that all courses in the list Req must be taken. Do not write any new rules. Just use the `schedule` predicate together with the `append`, `member`, and `set_of` predicates defined in the text.

26. The dot operator in Prolog builds binary trees. The trees may be straight, right-branching ones like `a.b.c.d`; straight, left-branching ones like `((a.b).c).d`; or kinky ones like `(a.b).(c.d)`. Write Prolog rules for

the following predicates. For these rules, do not assume that lists end in
nil; if nil does occur, treat it like any other atom.

- Let flatten(T,F) take an arbitrary tree T and create a straight,
  right-branching tree with exactly the same leaves in exactly the same
  order.

- Let kinky(F,K) take a flat tree F and create another tree K with the
  same leaves in the same order as F, but possibly with a more complex
  branching structure. For any flat tree F

      kinky(F,K) & flatten(K,G)

  should leave G identical to F.

- Check that the goal

      (kinky(a.b.c.d.e,K) & write(K) & fail)

  prints all possible binary trees with five leaves (there should be 14 of
  them).

- Is the definition of kinky reversible (i.e, is it possible to define
  flatten by the following rule)?

      flatten(T,F) <- kinky(F,T).

  Define a reversible form of kinky that would work if either argument
  were an unbound variable and the other were a list of constants.

27. Define rules to do symbolic differentiation of algebraic expressions. Assume
    that expressions are written in an infix form like (2*x + 3*a*y) or
    sin(a*x). The derivatives of these expressions with respect to x should be
    2 and a*cos(a*x), respectively. (Note that variables in these expressions
    are expressed by constants x and y instead of Prolog variables X and Y.)
    The solution should specify rules for two predicates: d(U,X,V) means that
    the derivative of U with respect to X is V, and s(U,V) means that V is the
    simplified form of U. Without simplification, the derivative of x*x is
    1*x+x*1; but with it, the derivative becomes the more standard 2*x.
    Following are the first four rules for the predicate d:

    ```
    d(X,X,1).
    d(U,X,0) <- atom(U) & ne(U,X).
    d(U+V,X,W) <- d(U,X,DU) & d(V,X,DV) & s(DU+DV,W).
    d(U*V,X,W) <-
          d(U,X,DU) & d(V,X,DV) & s(DU*V+U*DV,W).
    ```

The rules for simplifying expressions must deal with many special cases for
adding 0 or multiplying by 1. Following are the first two rules for the s
predicate: the stopping rule which says that atomic expressions (integers
and strings) cannot be simplified further; the second rule simplifies
expressions where the main operator is + :

```
s(X,X) <- atomic(X).
s(U+V,W) <- s(U,SU) & s(V,SV)
     & ((numb(SU) & numb(SV)) -> W:=SU+SV;
          SU=0                 -> W=SV;
          SV=0                 -> W=SU;
          SV=-T                -> s(SU-T,W);
          SU=SV                -> s(2*SU,W);
          ((A*T=SU | T*A=SU)
           & (B*T=SV | T*B=SV)) -> s((A+B)*T,W);
          (A*SU=SV | SU*A=SV)  -> s((A+1)*SU,W);
          (A*SV=SU | SV*A=SU)  -> s((A+1)*SV,W);
          W=SU+SV).
```

Write one rule for the d predicate and the s predicate for each function or operator that can occur in an expression. (Note the use of W:=SU+SV to evaluate the expression if the values are numbers, as opposed to W=SU+SV, which binds the unevaluated expression to W.)

28. The following rules define two different sort predicates:

```
sort1(L,A.B.Tail) <-
     pick(A,L,Rem) & sort1(Rem,B.Tail) & le(A,B).
sort1(A.nil,A.nil).
sort1(nil,nil).

sort2(L,A.B.Tail) <-
     pick(A,L,R) & pick(B,R,R2) & le(A,B)
     & sort2(B.R2,B.Tail).
sort2(A.nil,A.nil).
sort2(nil,nil).
```

Read the discussion of sorting in Section 2.4.1 and study these two predicates.

a. Use mathematical induction to prove that both of these predicates are correct. (Assume that the pick predicate defined on page 62 works correctly.)

b. Which of them is more efficient?

c. How do their performances vary with the length of the list?

d. Is either one fast enough to be useful for any practical problem?

3

Programming Techniques in Prolog

Walter G. Wilson

> "The productions of the mind and hand seem very numerous in books and manufactures. But all this variety lies in an exquisite subtlety and derivations from a few things already known, not in the number of axioms."
>
> Francis Bacon, *Novum Organum.*

This chapter has two parts. The first part talks about the usefulness of Prolog's declarative reading and identifies some pragmatic concerns that sometimes make it difficult to maintain this good programming practice in writing Prolog programs. The second part gives specific techniques and examples that illustrate how to get Prolog to do specific tasks. These include searching graphs, handling cyclic terms, alpha-beta pruning of game trees, and writing metainterpreters.

As we have mentioned, the power of Prolog as a programming language comes from several of its properties. A Prolog program has a declarative and a procedural reading. Unification, Prolog's bidirectional pattern matcher, covers many of the kinds of matching needed in artificial intelligence. The core of the Prolog language is surprisingly simple, yet the built-in inference method can easily be extended. Prolog programs tend to be much shorter than their equivalents in other languages.

Nevertheless, it is possible to write bad Prolog programs. This chapter describes some guidelines for good programming style. Some of the guidelines (e.g top down development, meaningful names) are the same as for other languages. However, since Prolog captures a part of logic, and programs can be thought of as declarative specifications, some of our guidelines do not apply in other languages. For example, we often try to write as declaratively as we can, rather than spelling out procedural steps.

3.1 HOW TO STRUCTURE PROLOG PROGRAMS

As stated in Chapter 2, a logic program can be interpreted as a collection of statements about which predicates hold true in a particular problem domain. So it is useful to think of a Prolog program as a relation, or as a predicate that holds, among its arguments. The predicate is usually best defined top down. That is, we first say

> This predicate is true for these items *if*
>
> these other predicates are true.

Then do we the same for the other predicates referenced, and so on. At each step there are many ways to proceed. The next section outlines the logic program development process. Then Section 3.1.2 emphasizes the importance of the declarative style of logic programs. Different ways of representing data are described in Section 3.1.3, "Data Representation," and the effect of data structure on program structure and verification is described in Section 3.1.4, "Structuring and Verifying Recursive Programs." Section 3.1.5, "Control Structures" presents the programming side of logic programming by showing how to realize various control structures.

3.1.1 Logic Programming Development Process

The first step in writing a program in Prolog is to find out what the program should do. This is not an idle remark. It seems so basic, yet some people do not take the trouble to do this before plunging ahead and writing a program in *any* language. When writing Prolog, this step can be very helpful.

It can be useful to discuss the task with someone familiar with it, or to think it through carefully, and then to follow these steps.

1. List all the different types of objects relevant to the task.

2. Name all the significant ways the types are related.

3. Define these relations in English (or another natural language).

4. Decide on a representation for the object types.

5. Restate the relations as Prolog rules, writing "top down."

6. Verify logical correctness of the rules.

7. Add side effect rules.

8. Polish up items such as operator precedence and user interface.

9. Look for inefficiencies in the declarative program, and reprogram or add control as needed.

It is natural to cycle through these steps in top down stages. Eventually, different portions of a program will be in different parts of this cycle simultaneously. With more than one person working on a project, it may be a good idea to formalize the stages, so everyone will know what is going on.

The initial informal description will leave out references to important objects; it will stop at concepts that seem obvious, but which must be defined for the machine. As with any programming task, the better the library of concepts we have on hand, the less work is needed.

The predicates and object types will become our vocabulary for describing problems to the machine. Just as with a human conversation, the more shared concepts and language we have, the easier it is to communicate precisely. In doing the steps 1 to 9 above, it is a good idea to follow these guidelines.

- Keep each individual definition simple.

- Make it modular. Smaller, self-contained pieces are easier to write, fix, and in general deal with, than are large intricate pieces with lots of interrelations. This follows from a general observation about the complexity of writing a program. If we have to worry about the relation of each piece with every other piece, then the conceptual complexity increases exponentially with the number of pieces. However, if the interdependency of the pieces can be localized to "modules" that interact in fixed form, then the complexity can be held to an overall linear increase. Programs do not have to get very large for that to be really good news.

- Write in "pure" Prolog, without using addax or delax, as far as possible. Essentially, this will mean passing data as parameters to predicates, rather than having one predicate addax data for another predicate to check. When it seems essential to use addax and delax, try to modularize the use.

- Use self-documenting names for predicates and variables. In Prolog, the scope of a variable name is just the one rule in which it occurs. So it is a good idea to give each variable a name that reflects the type of item it represents. This makes predicates vastly more readable. In different rules, we give the variables for the same type of item the same name.

3.1.2 Declarative Style

It is often possible to restrict the occurrence of the more procedural features of Prolog to a few well isolated places in a program. This makes a program readable as a set of "declarative truths" about a problem. Each rule can be read simply as a declaration that a certain relationship holds among some objects if some conditions are met. The set of rules is intended to express true relationships existing in the problem domain being programmed. This declarative reading does not hold if *side effects* are used in the logic program.

For our purposes, a side effect is an action, caused by part of a program, that would not automatically be undone by backtracking. In Prolog, there are three kinds of predicates that have side effects.

- System predicates, specifically input and output (`read, write`). These have several different forms, and we discuss them below.

- Workspace modification (`addax,delax`). There are also several variations here. Our discussion begins on page 117.

- Execution control (`cut, label, retry`...). There are just a few variations here. This discussion begins on page 123 and wraps up the section on declarative style.

Next we take a closer look at the special uses and problems of each of these kinds of predicates.

System Predicates for Input and Output

The first major type of side effect we look at is caused by reading and writing to files and to the terminal for interactive applications. Prolog programs do not execute "in a vacuum," with no other programs on the machine. Rather, they are imbedded in an operating system and a set of existing programs that provide a number of services. One of the most important of these services is file creation and maintenance. Prolog programs may be written to get and store data using the system's file services. This is so much a part of conventional languages that trying to avoid it may seem strange and awkward.

What could possibly be wrong with a simple `read` or `write` statement? After all, every language must include some interface to the outside world. A program must be able to communicate with people, machines, and other programs. The problem is that we would like to be able to read programs declaratively as far as possible. This means that we should be able to change the order of the rules in a program, and of the goals in the right side of a rule, and still have the same program (although the efficiency might be different). However, it is easy to see that when side effects are included this is not the case. For example in

```
g1<-human(X) & write(X).
g2<-write(X) & human(X).
human(george).
```

the goals g1 and g2 behave quite differently.

It is possible in principle to do input and output declaratively, rather than by side effect. We can consider output as simply a monitor on terms as they are built up by unification, and input as the unification of a term with an external process. Such an approach confines the procedural aspects of communication to a well defined interface outside the body of the Prolog program; the program can then be declarative.

To see how far we can carry this principle into practice, consider for what we primarily use `read` and `write`:

- Reading data formatted as standard Prolog terms,
- Reading and writing "foreign" data not in Prolog format,
- Communicating with the user of the program in interactive applications.

Next we look at some examples of good versus bad programming style for each of these purposes.

Data intended for use by a Prolog program is often formatted as standard Prolog terms. We may want to read a term, do some processing, then read another term, and so on. See Section 2.3.4, and Appendix A for precise details on how to use the built-in `read` and `write` routines. For the purposes of this section we assume that a term can be read from an open file just by saying `read(Term, Filename)`.

The declarative reading of a Prolog program does not extend easily to cover writing data to a file or reading data from a file. Once a collection of data is represented as facts in the Prolog workspace, it has a declarative reading, but it is hard to separate file input and output from procedural notions. Yet it is sometimes be necessary to store parts of an executing Prolog program (typically a large collection of facts) in a disk file, or in the SQL/DS database management system, and to access them as needed.

In this situation, we can keep most of the declarativeness of a program by isolating the side effects of the `read` or `write` to a single *representative predicate*, which reflects the meaning of the data. The following example illustrates the case for `read`.

Suppose we want to write a program that will send letters to customers of a corporation about the appropriate products appearing in the new catalog. This can be done declaratively or procedurally, but consider the difference in readability. First we give a program fragment in the procedural style:

```
read(X,file1) & read(T,file2) & process(X,T)...
```

which says "read some value X from `file1`, then read T from `file2`, then process X and T." Contrast that with the declarative style:

```
...customer(Name) & catalog_item(Item) &
   interested_in(Name,Item) &
   letter(Name,Item) ...
```

which says "We have a customer Name *and* a catalog Item *and* the customer Name is interested in Item *and* there is a letter to customer Name about that Item." Because meaningful names have been chosen, this fragment documents what it is meant to do. The procedural definitions have been isolated to specific representative predicates. For example, `catalog_item` may simply read the next term.

An extra benefit of localizing the read is the opportunity for improved performance. Most Prolog implementations provide some sort of keyed access to clauses in the workspace, but few provide this sort of efficient retrieval for terms in files.   By isolating the necessary read and write statements to the representative predicates, we can implement an efficient storage management scheme for secondary storage if needed. If interested_in(Name, Item) came from a file, we would not want to search the entire file every time we wanted to see if a certain customer is interested in a specific item.   At a minimum we would want to maintain an index based on the customer name.

File access differs from calling a predicate.   In Prolog, every call to a predicate is considered a new event. Solutions provided to previous calls to the same predicate do not influence the solutions provided to a new call. Backtracking into a call provides the next solution for that call.   This is not usually the way that files are managed. IBM Prolog maintains an indication of what is the next record in a file. Any read request from any procedure gets the next record.   To reflect proper behavior accurately as a Prolog procedure, representative predicates should maintain the appropriate record number each time they are re-entered by backtracking to provide another solution.

When data are not in Prolog term format, we can use IBM Prolog's character stream readch, readli, readat, and prst built-in procedures to read and write this "foreign" data.   These procedures handle a conceptual "stream" of characters coming in from some source (or being sent to a destination).   However, in many cases it is convenient to think of related data being read in together, in a larger structure called a "record." For example, an editor program might present one line of text as a single record.   A good technique here is to write a predicate that reads (or writes) one complete item from (or to) the file. These predicates translate between the foreign data format and Prolog term format.   They should be used from then on like the other input/output routines ... carefully!

The predicates can be implemented by specifying a grammar of what is to be read. As a simple example, suppose the input record consists of a name, some blanks, and a telephone number of the form 123-4567. The predicate

        name(Name,TelephoneNumber,File)

is called whenever the next name and number are to be read from the File. The definition of the predicate acts as a mapping between standard Prolog form and the form of the foreign data.

```
name(Name,TelephoneNumber,File) <-
    get_next_record(File,Record) &
    parse_record(Record,
               name(Name,TelephoneNumber)).
```

```
parse_record(Record,name(Name,TelephoneNumber)) <-
    parse_name(Name,Record,Rest_of_record) &
    parse_blanks(*,Rest_of_record,
            Last_of_record) &
    parse_telephone(TelephoneNumber,
            Last_of_record,*).

parse_name(Name,Record,Rest_of_record) <-
    parse_token(Name,Record,Rest_of_record).

parse_blanks(*, ' '.Record,Rest_of_record) <-
    parse_blanks(*,Record,Rest_of_record).
parse_blanks(*,A.Record,A.Record) <-
    ¬blank(A).

parse_telephone(Exchange-Extension, Record, *) <-
    parse_number(Exchange,
            Record, '-'.Rest_of_Record) &
    parse_number(Extension, Rest_of_record, *).
```

See Chapter 5 for a more complete discussion of parsing in Prolog.

Logic programs communicate with the user of interactive applications in two ways. The ways are dual in that the person and the program switch roles. The person may ask a question (or give a command), and get an answer from the program. Or, the program may ask a question, and get an answer from the person. These two modes can be interleaved to create a dialogue.

Here, as usual, the explicit side effects of reading from and writing to the terminal (or other device) should be isolated from the main part of the program, which should be kept declarative.

We start by defining the topmost predicate of the program in the abstract. All information required from the user and all responses given back have their place as arguments of the predicate:

```
some_predicate(Input_needed, Output_produced)
```

This can then be surrounded by two calls: one to get the input, and one to display the output:

```
get_input(I) & some_predicate(I,O) & write_output(O)
```

With this technique we are not worried about the nondeterministic effects of Prolog, which can often produce odd and unexpected dialogue. Backtracking can be isolated in the "logic" part, and side effects can be isolated in the "programming" part. All neat and tidy.

Asking the user for information can be handled neatly with the "Query-the-User" method introduced by Marek Sergot (1982). During the course of executing a Prolog program, a goal may fail. Then, the user can be asked to supply values for the unbound variables in the goal, which make the goal true. The user can supply them, or reply "none."

The value of this technique lies in the fact that the failing predicate has a declarative reading. Input values are supplied by unification. This can be done as follows.

Consider the following goal and predicate definition.

```
...& user(Name) &...

user(Name) <-
    write('What is your first name, please?') &
    read(Name).
```

In the goal, the user(Name) entry has a nice declarative meaning. Only in the definition of user does side effect dialogue occur.

As is often the case, especially with logic programs, good style opens the door to many unforeseen advantages. Localizing the user dialogue gives us a convenient place to check the validity of a user's answers. The predicate (in our example, user) still retains its declarative meaning. Local checks can verify that the predicate does not succeed until the requirements are met.

In our example, the name must satisfy some conditions defined in the predicate verify. Note that the use of read, write, and / is localized to these procedures.

```
user(Name) <-
    write('What is your first name, please?') &
    read_verify(Name).

read_verify(Name) <- read(Name) &
    verify(Name) & /.

read_verify(Name) <- write('Not verified') &
    user(Name).
```

The effect of the goal user(Name) is to ask for a name, read in what is typed, and verify it. If verification fails, then "Not verified" is printed, and the user is asked again. Here we used the deterministic form of read, so that backtracking from verify will not cause the system to wait for input without telling the user. (IBM Prolog also has a nondeterministic form of read, which causes it to be re-executed on backtracking).

This is an example of the use of a nice property of Prolog. If the predicate specified by a rule is too general, it may be made more specific by simply adding more conditions. Instead of "user(Name) is something read from the terminal," the condition is added that "user(Name) is something read from the terminal that passes the verify conditions."

Another serendipitous advantage of this technique is that it allows us to localize a second type of side effect— modifying the database. This is discussed more in the section on workspace modification below.

We discussed some advantages of adopting a "Query-the-User" method for interaction with a person, even if the implementation we are using does not provide this automatically. There are some variations and extensions of the basic concept that need to be mentioned.

Asking the user redundant questions must be controlled. Since the user is acting the role of a Prolog program in providing a set of answers, the program can keep asking for different solutions every time backtracking occurs. The user eventually replies "No more solutions," or its equivalent. In many cases the program author knows in advance that there is only one answer to the question. In this case it makes good sense to constrain the Query-the-User code to fail on backtracking into the queried predicate, as we did in `user(Name)`.

The basic concept can be generalized. Perhaps we want to ask the user before trying to prove something, rather than afterwards. Or perhaps we want to look for the data in a certain file if it is not already in storage. This basic technique in conjunction with those discussed in the next section goes a long way toward isolating side effects, leaving our main logic program pure and clean.

Since the user and the program act in dual roles, it is natural to ask what is the dual of Query-the-User. It is *Inform the User*. Simply stated, we must inform the user whenever a predicate has been proved. To keep the dialogue from being just an overwhelming swamp of program trace information, the author or user should be able to declare which predicates are of interest. Special steps are needed to avoid repeating the question in Query-the-User while the program is investigating different paths in its search for a proof. This unwanted sensitivity to the procedural characteristics of the program can be avoided in Inform the User. Simply inform the user after the entire proof has been established. This can result in very nicely organized output, and makes a natural explanation of why a program computed what it did. We shall discuss this further in Sections 3.2.1, "Meta-level Programming," 4.2, "Syllog—an Expert and Data System Shell" (page 248), and 4.4, "Generating Useful Explanations."

Workspace Modification

The second main type of side effect to consider after input and output is workspace modification. A logic program consists of a sequence of rules. These rules are loaded into a *workspace*. Rules that exist only in a file and have not yet been loaded into the workspace cannot directly affect program execution. Prolog does not and cannot see them as part of the program. Prolog only "knows" what is in the workspace, nothing more, nothing less. The built-in predicates `addax` and `delax` directly modify what is in the workspace. Since every clause in the workspace is part of the program as Prolog sees it, using these workspace modification predicates within a program amounts to writing a self-modifying program. Programs of this type are notoriously difficult to understand and debug. Therefore they should be avoided.

A rule may or may not have conditions that must be satisfied before it is true. Rules without conditions (e.g, facts), are frequently referred to as "data," especially if they have no variables in them. However, we should remember that they are part of the logic program, with the same status as the rules that have conditions. A clause does not cease being a clause simply because it does not call other procedures. So, changing the facts in a Prolog program is program modification.

However, controlled use of workspace modification is sometimes useful. This is because logic programs lack the concept of "global" variables. The scope of a variable is only within the rule in which it occurs. On page 111 we urged that all data and results be passed as parameters. Now, however, we describe some disciplined techniques that maintain a declarative reading, yet handle the cases where direct `addax` and `delax` are most tempting.

Many programmers tend to feel that it is useful to change the facts in a Prolog program while the program is running. After all, it is like changing some data in a relational database. But what would they say to someone who suggested that one piece of an assembly language program should overwrite the section just about to be executed? This is clearly a dangerous practice, and can make assembly programs almost impossible to maintain. Any advantages gained by increased speed or code compaction is quickly overshadowed by the difficulty of maintaining and extending the program.

Updating the Prolog rule set during execution is this same nasty device again, only this time it is easier to do. Do it once, and there goes the declarative meaning of your program. Do it twice, and the maintainability of your program is open to question. Besides losing the declarative reading, frequent use of `addax` and `delax` can also make a program very slow. Of course, there are some programs that may legitimately modify other programs. Editors, debuggers, and various other programming assistant programs are good examples.

Let us look at some cases where it is tempting to change the database, see the arguments against them, and propose a few alternatives. The primary motivations for explicit database update are:

- A certain value is only needed several calls later,
- A problem involves context and implicit assumptions,
- The problem involves database interactions, and
- Bottom up or some other inference method is needed.

In developing a program in the top down fashion encouraged by the nature of the Prolog language, it is frequently discovered that a certain value is not needed in the immediately called predicate P, but will be needed later on in a predicate called during the course of proving P. This may be true for the *procedural program*, but for the *declarative logic* it is definitely not true. A predicate either does or does not express a relation involving a certain value. If it does, then the value must be mentioned in the predicate, regardless of the predicate's eventual definition.

If we find ourselves asserting a value to be picked up later, rather than passing arguments to procedures, we can think about restructuring our predicates so that they are "wider." That is, we put another argument in the procedure to hold the needed value. We also redefine the clauses of a procedure to include a goal that refers to the value, instead of burying it as a subgoal to be called later. The notion of *sequentiality* should progress across a procedure's goals, not down into successive nested levels. For example, it is better to write

    `...p(X) & q(X,Y)...`

than

    `...p(X) & addax(note(X)) & q(Y) &...`

where

    `q(Y) <- note(X) &...`

The following diagram shows the two methods of passing information—as procedure arguments or asserted values.

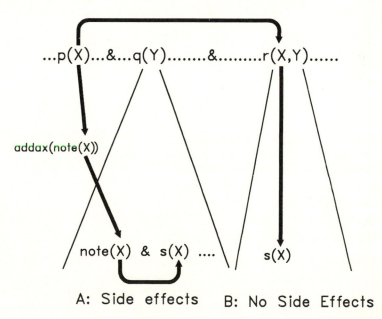

A: Side effects   B: No Side Effects

    In the discussion of user interaction on page 115, we saw a way to control the use of `read/write` side effects, and how not to annoy the user when backtracking. However, we did nothing to keep from asking a second time for information we had already been told. We could try passing around to every predicate a list of what input has been acquired so far. But this would not be enough to avoid repeating the question upon backtracking, because in that case the passed list is reset to the value it had when first called. That is the nature of backtracking. This is one of the rare occasions for using `addax`.

So, to avoid asking a user the same question twice, we can reluctantly use the technique A above. However, we should still be careful to isolate the side effect from the declarative part of the program, as follows:

```
user(Name) <- known(user(Name)) & /.
user(Name) <-
    write('What is your first name, please?') &
    read_verify(Name) &
    addax(known(user(Name))).
```

In this example, only the first call to the subgoal user(Name) will cause the user to be asked a question. Subsequent calls to the subgoal will retrieve the remembered value. The goal user(Name) can be used declaratively in several clauses. Each use is independent of checks for whether the information is known. Those checks are localized to the user(Name) procedure itself.

This process can be generalized as a special note routine:

```
user(Name) <- note(user(Name)).

note(Fact) <- special_token_unique_to_note(Fact) & /.
note(Fact) <-
    prompt_message_for(Fact, Message, Reply, Checks) &
    write_out(Message) &
    read_in(Reply) &
    Checks &
    addax(special_token_unique_to_note(Fact)).

prompt_message_for(user(Name),
        'What is your first name, please?',
        Name, verify(Name)).

write_out(Message) <- .......

read_in(Value) <- read(Value).
```

Complex programs often depend on a particular context and embody implicit assumptions. This is really a variation on the first theme, that it is inconvenient to pass all parameters. It takes work to write programs that know about subtle variations on a problem. When the context or assumptions change, it is tempting to use explicit database update to communicate between subprocedures. As more and more of these changes occur, the program becomes increasingly difficult to understand declaratively. One is forced to rely on a procedural meaning that is made more tangled with each change. It is precisely in these larger, more complicated instances that the techniques in this chapter are most important.

Logic programs seem ideally suited to database applications. It is almost too easy to update the facts, and even the rules. Prolog provides a full and general relational model of data as described in Codd (1971). As we have mentioned,

Prolog predicates stand for relations. Codd's relational model of data consists of relations and operations on relations. A complete basis set of these operations is *union*, *set difference*, *Cartesian product* (a special kind of *join*), *project*, and *select*, see Ullman (1980). Each of these operations can also be written directly in Prolog, see e.g Walker (1981).

Present versions of Prolog do not directly support some of the features provided by practical systems for large databases. However, VM/Prolog can be coupled to the SQL/DS database management system, and MVS/Prolog can be coupled to the DB2 DBMS, via the `sql` built-in predicate. This is described in the VM/Prolog and MVS/Prolog manuals.

Besides these practical considerations about Prolog and relational databases, there is also a matter of principle to note. In Prolog, we like to use `addax` and `delax` as little as possible, in order to keep our programs declarative. On the other hand, much of the published work on relational databases is about how best to arrange things so that facts can be added and deleted. There are a few steps toward reconciling these opposing points of view, notably in Bowen and Kowalski (1982).

For some problems Prolog's built-in top down inference method may not be adequate and another method, such as bottom up inference, is preferable. Recall that Prolog programs may be viewed as a collection of logical axioms. If there are no ¬ signs in a program, the process by which Prolog answers a question corresponds to finding in ordinary logic a proof that the answer follows from the axioms. Any sound method of establishing such a proof is guaranteed to give only correct results (although a sound method may fail to give a result where one is expected, i.e a sound method may be incomplete).

The Prolog control component starts with the goal and applies a top down, left-to-right evaluation strategy. This has many advantages, including efficiency of implementation and ease of understanding. However, there are some situations in which Prolog's built-in control is unsuitable. For example the rule `married(X,Y)<-married(Y,X)` will not run correctly in Prolog. It is tempting to deal with such cases by using `addax` and `delax` in the program. However, it is much better to write an interpreter with a more suitable control strategy, such as one that evaluates such rules bottom up, rather than top down. Although this can be a formidable task in other languages, it is rather straightforward in Prolog, as we shall see in Section 3.2.1, "Meta-level Programming." Although the new interpreter may use `addax`, these instances are clearly separated from the program being interpreted, which keeps its declarative meaning. Whether using rules bottom up or top down, there is no worry over correctness once we have convinced ourselves that the rules we have written are in fact the ones we intended to write.

Here are some techniques for modifying the facts used by a Prolog program without obscuring the declarative reading too much. They involve defining and using the following data types.

■ Global variables,

■ Stacks, and

■   Property lists.

The procedures that define these data types explicitly record and erase values. Note that none of these data types are part of the Prolog language. Instead, they are programs and utilities that are written *in* Prolog. They provide a disciplined, higher level interface to the nonlogical Prolog primitives. They use so-called "global variables" as a means of keeping intermediate values that would otherwise be erased in the backtracking process. However, global variables should not be used very frequently. Their declarative meaning is not clear, nor is their use very efficient. A more efficient alternative in VM/Prolog is to use the Rexx interface to set and retrieve Rexx variables, see IBM (1985).

The global "variables" here are our own construct: they are not really Prolog variables in the usual sense. What we do is to relate a keyword (the "variable") with a value. For example, we can use the `global_value` predicate name to record this relationship, as in

```
global_value(Variable, Value).
```

The first argument need not be a constant; it can be a structured term. In that case, `global_value` relates two structures. A predicate, say `::=` can be defined to set the value.

```
A ::= B    <-
    try(delax(global_value(A, *))) &
    addax(global_value(A,B)).

try(X) <- X.
try(*).
```

The current value can be retrieved or tested by calling `global_value(A,B)`.

Stacks are another commonly used data type. The `global_value` technique described above can be used to simulate a stack, as follows.

```
push(Stack, Item) <-
    addax(global_value(Stack, Item), 0).

pop(Stack, Item) <-
    delax(global_value(Stack, Item)).
```

The predicates `push` and `pop` have their obvious meanings. The second argument of `addax` in IBM Prolog can be used to indicate where to add the clause in the list of existing clauses of the same name and number of arguments (arity). (The second argument can also be used to specify a clause name space, in which case the third argument can be used to indicate the position at which the clause is to be added.) A 0 in the second argument indicates that the clause should be added at the beginning. That way it is tried before any other clause.

Here we have used the idea of a stack to illustrate a way of using global values. However, it is often more elegant to stack and unstack items using pure

Prolog. A particularly simple method is to manipulate a list. For example, we can write the unconditional rule

```
stack(Top.Rest,Top,Rest)
```

Then the goal stack(b.c.d.nil,Top,Rest) binds Top to b and Rest to c.d.nil. This corresponds to "popping" the top element b off the stack, leaving c and d on the stack.

The property list is familiar to Lisp programmers. Recall our discussion on page 33 about functional and relational languages. Since Lisp is at heart a functional language, it has an extra feature, called the *property list* to try to handle relations. Essentially, for each Lisp identifier, there is a set of binary relations of the form *key.value*. Here are the Prolog equivalents of the Lisp putprop, getprop, and remprop functions. Getprop has been turned into a predicate in Prolog. Putprop and getprop are essentially the same predicate, but they have different side effects.

```
putprop(Identifier, Property, Value) <-
    addax(property(Identifier, Property, Value)).

getprop(Identifier, Property, Value) <-
    property(Identifier, Property, Value).

remprop(Identifier, Property) <-
    delax(property(Identifier, Property, Value)).
```

These predicates actually do more than their Lisp counterparts. The identifier, property, and value can all be general structures; in Lisp they are restricted to being identifiers. Getprop can be used in a relational sense. The goal getprop(X,Y,42) can be used to locate all identifiers that have a property whose value is 42. Prolog implementations that use an index to locate clauses containing specific constants will be generally as efficient as Lisp for this purpose.

Execution Control

The third major type of side effect after read/write and workspace modification, is execution control. The most common control predicate provided in Prolog implementations is called *cut*, and is denoted by an exclamation mark (!) or a slash (/). IBM Prolog provides this as well as several variations, such as cut(Label), retry(Label), and so on. Section 3.1.5, "Control Structures" discusses these in more detail. Here we give only a brief overview of cut and retry to illustrate the way different control methods can be categorized. (Recall that we introduced the use of the cut on page 73)

Cut, as we mentioned before, can be thought of as modifying the program, in that it (temporarily) bars the interpreter from using rules at earlier choice points. The effects of the cut can sometimes be quite hard to follow, which is another way of saying that it lacks a declarative meaning. Nevertheless, it is

useful. We note that a rule a<-b can normally be read as a if b. The cut is
often used to get the effect of a if and only if b. So here are some ways
to think of cut that make it more manageable.

We can view it as a short cut for specifying the else part of the preceding
goals. For example,

```
a(X) <- b(X) & / & c(X).
a(X) <- d(X).
```

is nearly just a short form of

```
a(X) <-  b(X) & c(X).
a(X) <- ¬b(X) & d(X).
```

The difference is that the second form allows backtracking into b(X) to try
other alternatives. In the first case the / eliminates all choice points in b.

We also use / when the terms in the heads of the clauses of a procedure are
used to distinguish cases, and there is a catchall final rule that unifies with
anything. In this case it is used immediately to the right of the implication
arrow, signifying that if this rule unifies, then no others are applicable.

```
a(g(...)) <- / &...
a(h(...)) <- / &...
a(*)       <- otherwise...
```

This can be generalized. When unification is not enough to determine cases,
then predicates are added to the left of the "cut" to distinguish between them:

```
a(X) <- case_1(X) & / &...
a(X) <- case_2(X) & / &...
a(X) <- case_3(X) & / &...
```

Besides the cut, we can also control execution with retry, which transfers
control to an earlier point specified by a label. Earlier behavior is simply
repeated unless it contained side effects. We can simulate iteration using
retry. The idea is

```
simulate_iterate <-
    label(come_back_here) &
    retrieve_state(State) &
    do_another_cycle(State, NewState) &
    store(NewState) &
    retry(come_back_here).
simulate_iterate <- write(done).
```

However, it is better style to write this without retry as

```
simulate_iterate <-
    retrieve_state(State) &
    do_another_cycle(State, NewState) &
    store(NewState) &
    simulate_iterate.
simulate_iterate <- write(done).
```

IBM Prolog recognizes the fact that the last predicate in a rule is a deterministic call of the first predicate, and it does not use up stack space for it. Thus the effect is very close to conventional iteration. This particular use of recursion to simulate iteration is known as *tail recursion optimization* or *last call optimization*.

3.1.3 Data Representation

This section takes look at how to choose a data representation, structure the program, and verify its logical correctness.

Choosing a Representation

Data structures can be represented in Prolog in two fundamentally different ways. One way is as a *structured term*, which can be passed as a data structure among procedures. The second way is as a *set of facts*. So the fundamental choice is between using data structures or predicates to represent items.

There are essentially three basic data types in logic programming languages: constants, variables, and structured terms. The word "term" by itself refers to any one of these. Sometimes the word "structure" is used to mean "structured term."

Function symbols are used to form structured terms. The function symbol is the name of the structure, and is followed by some number of arguments. Each argument may be any sort of term. This is analogous to record structures in other languages. The following are all terms:

- `f(1,2)`
- `f(g(X),h(Y))`
- `+(1,-(7,/(X,?(3))))`

Recall from page 87 that certain function symbols are also called *operators*. Prolog allows operators with only one argument to be defined as prefix or suffix; operators with two arguments may be defined as infix. If `"+"`, `"-"` and `"/"` are defined to be infix, and `"?"` is defined to be suffix, then the last term above can be written as `1 + 7 - X / 3?`. Unless we know the operator definitions, we do not know whether this last term represents `(1 + (7 - (X / (3?))))`, or `((1 + (7 - X) ) / 3)?`, or some other term.

In general it is convenient that Prolog does not print the fully parenthesized form of a structure containing operators—for example fully parenthesized lists make busy reading. However one must be aware of the type and precedence of each operator when programming, since Prolog manipulates the structure corresponding to the form with parentheses. For example if we make the operator definition op("?", lr, 100) then X ? Y unifies with a ? b ? c, and X is bound to a ? b, rather than just a. This happens because the lr definition of the operator means that a ? b ? c is actually shorthand for (a ? b) ? c.

The terms used to represent data are constants and structured terms. IBM Prolog subdivides the constants further into integers, floating-point numbers, strings and atoms. (A string is enclosed in single quotes 'thus', while an atom is signalled by double quotes "thus". If an atom contains no special characters it can be written without quotes.) Structured terms are subdivided into lists, trees, and graphs. It is convenient for us to separate graphs further into cyclic and acyclic graphs.

Constants are best used for names, single values, and very simple items. It is possible, although computationally expensive, to inspect the characters which make up a constant by using special type conversion routines such as IBM Prolog's st_to_at built-in predicate. It is best to think of constants as simply tokens which can be distinguished one from another, and not to rely on any internal property of an individual token. If all occurrences of one constant were replaced in all predicates with another unique constant, the programs should still work.

Lists are familiar items used extensively in symbolic programming. They are simple and convenient, and can be used for many different purposes. Because they are so common and useful, they are generally given special treatment in Prolog implementations. There are two interesting forms of a list — *simple lists* and *difference lists*. Simple lists were introduced in Section 2.2.6, "List-Handling Predicates." We shall discuss difference lists shortly (page 136), and we shall make extensive use of them in Chapter 5.

Trees are the general form of Prolog terms —see page 34. A list is really a special kind of binary tree. Trees can be thought of as records in the Pascal sense.

Acyclic Graphs are trees that may have some subtrees shared. It is possible to construct these in Prolog implementations that use *structure sharing*, as does IBM Prolog. We will not discuss the details of Prolog implementations. However, understanding a little bit of what is happening may help in writing more advanced Prolog programs. There are two main methods of implementing both interpreters and compilers for Prolog. One uses *structure sharing* and the other uses *structure copying*. In the structure sharing method, all structures appear only once, in the code area. Prolog execution builds up structures by a so called *molecule*, which consists of a pointer to a structure and an *environment*, which is a list of values of the variables occurring in the structure. Thus all terms constructed during program execution share the same structures in memory, which are never copied.

The structure copying method, on the other hand, creates new copies of referenced structures whenever a variable unifies with a structure. Variables are still references to structures, and whenever a variable is encountered its value is copied, but term copying stops. Thus terms are only partially copied. The advantage of this is that constructed terms can be represented by a single pointer, instead of a molecule. This has the potential for saving space, conserving registers, and decreasing the number of references. Thus shared structures still occur in structure-copying implementations, where copying is stopped by a variable reference, but not as frequently as in structure sharing implementations. Below is an example from a structure-sharing implementation.

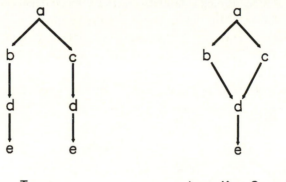

Tree   **Acyclic Graph**

When printed as terms, both these structures look the same:

```
a(b(d(e)), c(d(e)))
```

No Prolog program would be able to distinguish between these two terms.

Below are two programs that construct the above term. The first one constructs a tree, the second an acyclic graph.

```
construct_tree(a(b(X), c(Y)) ) <-
    construct_d1(X)&
    construct_d2(Y).
construct_d1(d(e)).               /* unique structures */
construct_d2(d(e)).

construct_graph(a(b(X),c(X)) ) <-
    construct_d(X).               /* shared structures */
construct_d(d(e)).
```

We can construct **Cyclic Graphs** (i.e graphs containing cycles) by using IBM Prolog's unification. We can think of a cyclic graph as representing an infinite tree. Two cyclic graphs unify if and only if their corresponding infinite trees unify. So there is no practical problem arising from allowing cyclic structures as terms. (As mentioned on page 58, we can make a simple cycle by unifying X with f(X).) We can also represent a cyclic graph as a collection of Prolog facts, one fact for each edge.

A disadvantage of representing data as structured terms is that as structures get large, finding things in them can get tedious. The programmer must write procedures to search the structures to find the desired items. An advantage is that logical variables in structures terms can be thought of as pointers to other structures. The programmer does not have to worry about whether an item is a variable that has been bound to a structure, or whether it is the structure itself. Prolog's pattern matching does this "dereferencing" automatically. This is one advantage of using terms to represent data.

On the other hand, when we choose to represent data not as structured terms but as collections of facts, Prolog's database-retrieval mechanisms can be used to do the searching for us. In this case, predicate names are used to relate *constants* only, not structures. A "pointer" to another datum is simply a constant used as a *key* or *index*. Although direct retrieval is easier, the programmer must dereference these "pointers."

As an example of these two contrasting representation styles, recall our parse tree from page 34 for the sentence "cats like mice":

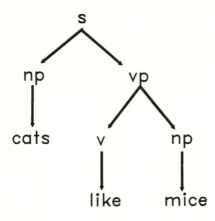

This can be represented as a structured term consisting of the single fact:

    sentence(s(np(cats),vp(v(like),np(mice)))).

Now suppose we want to find a transitive verb in such trees. We can do this by writing the unconditional rule:

    verb_in_sentence(s(*, vp(Verb, *)), Verb).

Then, the goal

    sentence(Tree) & verb_in_sentence(Tree, Verb) &...

binds Verb to v(like).

For large or variable length terms such as lists or trees, it is infeasible or impossible to give a retrieval procedure based on one matching step. Subprocedures are required to select and search substructures. In this case, verb_in_sentence can be defined by a rule such as

```
verb_in_sentence(S,Verb) <-
    verb_phrase_in_sentence(S,VP) &
    verb_in_verb_phrase(VP,V).
```

which requires two "selector predicates" to examine the structure. For larger structures, more explicit navigation may be required. All of this is more work for the programmer. It would be nice to let the Prolog processor itself keep track of data items, and access them as required. How can this be done?

We have so far represented our tree as a single fact containing several function symbols, such as np, vp, and s. We can use the Prolog database directly to store information as *facts*. Data structures are represented by using Prolog constants to say which facts are part of the same structure. In database terminology this is called a *normalized* representation. This structuring choice is analogous to choosing between a *hierarchical* or *relational* database. Each has advantages, and gives rise to its own set of problems. Prolog allows us to use both forms in one program, where appropriate.

There are many ways to do this. For example: Each node of a sentence structure is named by an integer S, or by a pair of integers S.N.   S is the number of the sentence of which the node is a part, and N represents the occurrence of a particular node type if there can be more than one. For example, suppose we call "cats like mice" sentence 1. Then we can represent it as the facts

```
s(1, np(1.1), vp(1)).
vp(1, v(1), np(1.2)).
v(1, like).
np(1.1, cats).
np(1.2,mice).
```

Since the sentence has two noun phrases, we had to number these specially. Finding the verb is now much easier, since the nodes of the tree are directly available. The numbers are keys that serve to identify the nodes uniquely. So we can say simply

```
verb_in_sentence(S,V) <- v(S,V).
```

This predicate says that verb_in_sentence is the same as v.

Structures represented as facts in the Prolog database can be retrieved simply by using Prolog rules. The drawback is that to change the structure we use addax and delax; we do not write declaratively. In addition to the side effect problems mentioned in the discussion starting on page 117, adding a fact to the database requires copying. Changing a large structure means doing a lot of copying, which can be computationally expensive.

The two methods of representing a tree give rise to different problems when we wish to transform a tree into another, related, tree. Tree transformation is useful in many different tasks, such as simplifying algebraic expressions and optimizing programs. For example, suppose we want to change a sentence such as "Cats like mice" to the past perfect form "Cats did like mice." That is, from the tree on the left, we want to build the tree on the right.

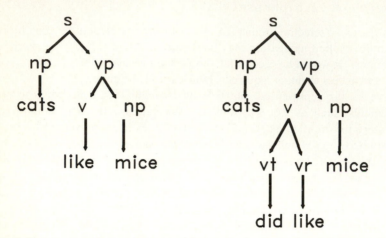

We define a procedure that relates the two. In English: "A simple sentence in present tense and its past perfect form have the same subject and object, the verb in the present tense is the verb root in the past perfect form, and the past perfect form has the tense marker d i d as part of its verb form."

When the tree is represented as a structured term, this can be written in Prolog as

```
present_past_perfect(s(NP1, vp(v(V), NP2)),
        s(NP1, vp(v(vt(did), vr(V)), NP2))).
```

which is a reversible predicate.

Transforming a sentence into the past perfect is more difficult when the data is represented in relational form.

```
present_past_perfect(S1,S2) <-
    new_number(S2) &
    copy_sentence(S1,S2) &
    delax(v(S2,V)) &
    addax(v(S2,vt(S2),vr(S2))) &
    addax(vt(S2, did)) &
    addax(vr(S2, V)).
```

Since it requires use of addax and delax, this procedure is not reversible. Most importantly, it is impossible to give the program its desired declarative reading.

We have seen how choosing whether to use structured terms or collections of facts to represent objects is a fundamental decision. Using structured terms allows more declarative procedures for transforming objects, but requires programming selector functions to navigate the structures. Using collections of facts allows more direct use of Prolog's database retrieval facilities, but transforming structures is more awkward. As a result, objects whose properties or relations do not change during a computation are generally represented as collections of facts. Otherwise, structured terms are generally used.

The next major activity in writing a logic program, after deciding on the representation of terms, is defining the structure of programs. We focus on the case where objects are represented by structured terms.

Recursively Defined Programs and Data Structures

After deciding to use structured terms rather than a collection of facts, the next step is to define the actual structure of the terms. This is a crucial step since the program structure will in large measure be defined by the data structures. There is no set of automatic rules we can follow to find the right data structure. That still requires thought, experimentation, and sometimes inspiration.

Terms are naturally recursive. Even the definition of what constitutes a structured term is recursive— a function symbol of arity N followed by N terms.

Objects frequently come in types, which may have subtypes, and so on. These types are reflected in the terms that represent the objects. Take, for example, the definition of a simple list. As we mentioned, a list is either

- Empty (represented by the constant of our choice, by convention "`nil`"), or
- A binary term (whose function symbol conveniently we may choose to be the infix operator "`.`") whose first argument is a *term*, and whose second argument is a *list*.

In Prolog's term notation, a list is either

- `nil`, or
- `Term.List`

Traditional languages have data structures such as records, arrays, trees, and lists. Records were introduced in Chapter 2 in the context of Pascal, a strongly typed language. on page 34 we looked at the following Pascal record and the corresponding Prolog data structure.

Pascal record:

```
type person = record
                name: string;
                address: string;
                date_of_birth: array-1..3- of integer;
                sex: boolean
            end
```

The Pascal programmer is allowed to define *new* types in terms of the old. Just as the built-in types of a language have predefined operators, the programmer can define certain operations on the new data types; these operations are then the only pieces of code that need information about how the types are defined in terms of other, lower-level types.

The Prolog structure corresponding to the above Pascal record is

Prolog structure:

```
person(
    name(N),
    address(A),
    date_of_birth(D,M,Y),
    sex(S)).
```

There is an important distinction between the Prolog and Pascal use of types. The Pascal type declaration tells the compiler what the data type looks like, whereas the Prolog form is an actual occurrence of an object. In Pascal, we must declare a variable to be of some type, then use the selectors to pick out fields. To say that the input argument X to a procedure P is of type person we write:

```
procedure p(X:person);
```

In Pascal, we refer to an actual occurrence in a later statement, such as

```
if  X.name = 'walter' then....
```

Prolog does not separate the declaration and the use of data types.

Prolog and Pascal differ in how subfields of records are located. Whereas Pascal has built-in selector functions, Prolog references are made by reproducing the "picture" of the Prolog term. Recall our verb_in_sentence example on page 128. Of course, arbitrary selector relations can be defined in Prolog as executable procedures. Note that unlike the Pascal selector functions they are relations and not functions. They may not be used in expressions, but they may be used as predicates in goals.

For example, expressions such as write(x.name) are valid Pascal constructs. The value of the selector function x.name is the name field of the record x. To get the corresponding effect in Prolog, we could use a temporary variable N whose value is passed to write

```
name_of(person(name(N),*,*,*), N).
```

The corresponding Prolog goal to write out the name field of a record of type person is

```
name_of(Person,Name) & write(Name).
```

Because Pascal data types are exhaustively declared, type agreement can be checked at compile time. This can detect errors before execution, but at the cost of some flexibility. One cannot write a generalized append in a strongly typed language, for example. One must have a different procedure for each type of list.

It is often useful to write a set of relations that define a particular data type. Only relations in this set deal with the internal representation of the data. Other relations are restricted to using these defining relations to manipulate objects of the given type. The internal representation of the objects is hidden from these other relations.

For example, we could provide definitions of the following set of procedures to define lists.

```
first(List,First).

rest(List,Rest)

empty(List).

append(List1,List2,List3).
```

To make these concrete, we can choose a representation, say, the standard dot notation for lists.

```
first(A.*, A).

rest(*.R,R).

empty(nil).

append(nil,B,B).
append(A.L, B, A.C) <- append(L, B, C).
```

Now suppose we find that we append long lists frequently. We shall look at how to do this efficiently, by changing representations, in a moment (page 136). Fortunately, Prolog allows us to swap representations just by changing the definitions of our four predicates; larger programs that use the predicates should mostly be able to run as is. They do not have to be extensively modified to use the new representation. The four new list predicates are

```
first((A.B) - *, A).

rest((*.B) - C, B - C).

empty(A - A) <- var(A).

append(A - B, B - C, A - C).
```

where "-" is a defined operator. Such collections of clauses can be thought of as a declaration of what a data type is and of how it is used computationally.

In traditional languages, *arrays* allow access to an element by an index (first, second, . . .). The advantage of arrays is that locating a particular element can be done rapidly by computing its address using the index of the element.

The underlying logical form of a Prolog term does not allow directly for array representation. The array is really a construct introduced into languages to reflect a particular low level machine-oriented capability, namely address arithmetic. Arrays have not been very important in most Prolog applications. Prolog programs usually need more flexible structures. Although arrays can be defined in the sense that an index can be used to locate an element, there is no guarantee that the representation of an array in Prolog provides fast access.

The Subtlety of Unification

Unification is the pattern matching technique used by Prolog. It was described in Chapter 2, and previous sections of this chapter assume a working knowledge of it. Since data structures are both inspected and constructed by unification, it is worthwhile to take a closer look at it at this time.

Unification was introduced by Robinson (1965) in the context of theorem proving. In essence, it tries to make two structures look the same by assigning values to unbound variables in the structures. This assignment is called a *substitution*. If T is a term containing a variable X, and F is a term, then the substitution T:X/F is the term derived from T by replacing with the term F all occurrences of X in T.   X/F is called the substitution of F for X. If S1 and S2 are substitutions not substituting for the same variables, then S = S1, S2 is a substitution.

A partial order may be placed on terms. A term T1 said to be *more general* than a term T2 if there is a substitution S such that T1:S = T2. This partial order can be extended to substitutions. A substitution S1 is more general than a substitution S2 if for all terms T the term T:S1 is more general than the term T:S2. If T1 and T2 are terms, then S is a *unifying substitution*, or *unifier*, if T1:S = T2:S; that is, the substitution S makes them look the same.

S is the *most general unifier* of terms T1 and T2 if S is at least as general as S1 whenever S1 is a unifier of T1 and T2. What this means in practice is that the variables in unified terms are not bound any more than is necessary to make them match.

There are three unifiers listed below in order of increasing generality. The last in the list is the most general unifier.

T1	T2	S	T1:S=T2:S
f(X)	f(g(Y))	X/g(h(a)),Y/h(a)	f(g(h(a)))
f(X)	f(g(Y))	X/g(h(Z)),Y/h(Z)	f(g(h(Z)))
f(X)	f(g(Y))	x/g(Z),Y/Z	f(g(Z))

As discussed on page 57 we can think of unification as the process of overlaying two trees. Wherever two nodes are overlaid, they must be the same, otherwise they *clash*. If one of the nodes that clash is a variable, then there is hope that unification can still proceed. We can assign the value of the other node to the variable, thus eliminating one clash. It only remains to be checked that nowhere else in the overlay is a term assigned to that same variable which will not unify with the term we just assigned. Dwork et al. (1984) discuss how this forces unification in general to be done sequentially, rather than in parallel.

There are four points about unification that are not always appreciated right away:

- Variable assignments can be made in both terms.

- A variable can be bound to two different terms, so long as the terms are unifiable. The variable ends up assigned to the unified term, of course.

- All occurrences of a variable in a rule refer to the same object. Binding any one of the occurrences binds all others.

- Unifying two variables makes them the same variable.

To see how variable assignments are made in both terms, consider the definition of append. When the head of the clause

```
append(Item.Rest, List, Item.Result) <-...
```

is to be matched with the goal

```
append(1.2.nil, 3.nil, Output)
```

1 is bound to Item, which occurs in two places in the head. This binds into the rule. However, Output is bound to the term 1.Result, where Result is computed later. This binds into the goal.

Variables occurring in the head that also occur in the body of a rule may be bound during execution of the body, rather than when the clause is invoked. Thus the origin of a value bound to a variable occurring in the head of a rule may be either the goal that invokes the clause or a subgoal in the body of the rule.

Graphically, this can be represented as follows. The arrows point from a term to the variable that gets bound to it. When the origin of a value is in the body of a rule, this is indicated by the phrase "in body."

```
        head                                  goal            body

    Item        <---------------------- 1
    Rest        <---------------------- 2 . nil
    Item.Rest      <----verified-----> 1 . 2 . nil
    List        <---------------------- 3.nil
    Item.Result ------------------> Output
    Result      <-------------------------------in body
```

If the goal were append(First, 3.nil, 1.2.3.nil) the bindings would be

```
          head                              goal              body

     Item      <-------------------- 1
     Rest      <----------------------------------in body
     Item.Rest -------------------> First
     List      <-------------------- 3 . nil
     Item.Result <----verified-----> 1 . 2 . 3 . nil
     Result     --------------------> 2 . 3 . nil
```

A variable can be bound to two different terms, as long as the terms are unifiable. Suppose the task is to construct a binary tree. Let Left(T) bind T to a term Left.*, where Left is a fully defined binary tree and let Right(T) do the corresponding task for the right tree. Ordinarily, we would think about defining the predicate tree(T) in the following way. (It is simplified to bring out the form, and is not a complete Prolog definition.) The English reading is

Left.Right is a properly constructed tree if

> Left is a properly constructed tree and
> Right is a properly constructed tree.

Expressed in Prolog notation this becomes

```
     tree(Left.Right) <- tree(Left) & tree(Right).
```

In this form, two substructures are computed and then explicitly put together. However, the following would also work. In this form, one structure is declared to have two properties, each of which takes care of constructing the appropriate part of the structure. The English reading is

T is a properly constructed tree if

> T has a properly constructed left subtree, and
> T has a properly constructed right subtree.

This is expressed in Prolog notation as

```
     tree(T) <- left(T) & right(T).
```

where

```
     left(L.*)  <- tree(L).
     right(*.R) <- tree(R).
```

The goal left(T) produces a term of the form L.*. The goal right(T) produces a term of the form *.R. When both of these structures are unified with the same variable T, the resulting value of T is L.R.

It is extremely important to note that *all occurrences of a variable in a rule refer to the same object*. One dramatic example is the *difference list*. This construct is List - Tail, where List is a dotted list in the usual sense, with the exception that it is not terminated by nil. Instead, its terminator is the variable Tail. (It does not have to be named Tail, of course, but it must occur both at the end of List and after the connecting "-" symbol.) For example, the list 1 . 2 . nil in difference list format is (1 . 2 . X) - X, which can be pictured like this:

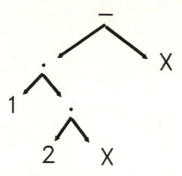

To add more items to the list after 2, it suffices to bind X. It is not necessary to sequence down the list 1 . 2 . X until the end is found, which is necessary with the definition of append for the customary list. A new variable can now represent the end of the new list. The definition of append for difference lists is quite simple.

    append(A - B, B - C, A - C).

is all there is to it. (However, this version of append is deterministic.) Suppose we call append((1 . X) - X, (2 . Y) - Y, L). Here is how the three terms will unify:

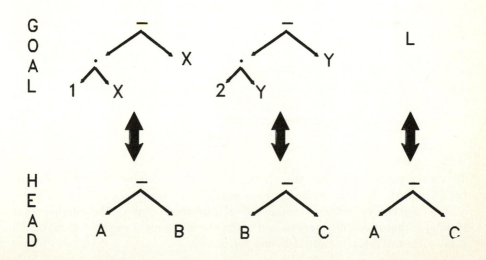

Resultant Bindings

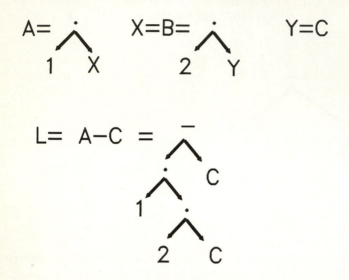

The difference list may be thought of in terms of an algebra of lists. In this algebra, every list is conceptually infinite to the right. Finite lists are represented by the difference between two infinite lists, which are identical except that one of them has the finite list tacked on front. The list (a.b.c) is the difference between an infinite list starting with (a.b.c.d.e.f...) and the infinite list starting at d (d.e.f...). Notationally

$$a.b.c \neq a.b.c.d.e.f.g... - d.e.f.g...$$

Of course, there are infinitely many such lists whose difference is exactly a.b.c.

In logic programming, variables stand for the set of all terms that may be substituted for them. As Prolog computation proceeds, terms become more specific as more constraints on acceptable values are added. This is nicely applied in thinking about difference lists. Since any two lists that differ by just the desired finite list may be used to represent the finite list, and we do not care which are chosen, we can use a Prolog variable to stand for all of them. We may also think about this variable as some specific but as yet unspecified continuation of the finite part of the list that has already been determined. This gives the following convenient (finite) representation:

$$a.b.c \doteq a.b.c.L - L$$

This algebra has some interesting properties, such as obeying an additive law of the form: A–C = A–B + B–C. However, it is not necessary to think in terms of this algebra in order to make use of difference lists. The fundamental technique that is usefully generalized is the use of a logical variable to make the same value available in more than one place.

This last example makes it important to realize that unifying two variables makes them the same variable. This can also be seen in the nonrecursive rule in the definition of `append` for standard lists.

```
append(nil,L,L).
```

When this is unified with the goal `append(nil,List2,Output)`, `List2`, `Output`, and `L` are all made the same thing. In this example, the effects are localized, but this effect can be propagated through any number of subpredicate calls. If the variable `Output` is not bound when the example goal is unified with the rule, but bound later, then the effect can propagate through the binding to `List2` to all other structures that may have been bound to `List2` anywhere along the way.

As we have mentioned, the logical variable can be thought of as a pointer or reference. A variable used in a Prolog goal or rule can be considered as naming a term. When two variables are unified, they name the same term—they become synonyms or aliases. When any alias is unified with a constant or structure term, then all aliases name that term. In languages other Prolog, a chain of pointers must be followed explicitly to find a value. In Prolog, dereferencing a variable is automatic. For example, the goal `X=Y & Y=Z & Z=3 & write(X)` prints a 3.

So when a term unifies with a variable, it in effect puts a pointer to the term in the variable. The difference from traditional languages is that this pointer in effect is put in all aliases. This way of thinking about variables may help us to understand how to use structures such as difference lists and infinite terms.

3.1.4 Structuring and Verifying Recursive Programs

Relations defined on lists tend to have the following recursive structure:

- What is true of the empty list.
- What is true of a list if *this* is true of an item and *that* is (recursively) true of a list.

In Prolog,

```
p(nil).
p(Item.List) <- q(Item) & p(List).
```

The same correspondence between data structure and program is seen for more complex terms. Take, for example, the relation between a binary tree and a list that says that both have identical node values, occurring in the same order. This relation will be used later in writing a program to sort lists. We write a node of an ordered binary tree as `node(Left, NodeValue, Right)`. Everything in the `Left` subtree comes before the `NodeValue`, and everything in the `Right` subtree comes after the `NodeValue`. The following are some

examples of these ordered trees. They all correspond to the ordered list
a.b.c.nil.

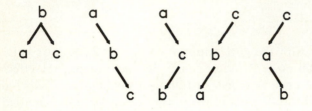

We can define data structures to represent ordered lists and trees, and specify
some of their properties as follows.

- The base cases

    - nil, for the empty tree. No element is out of order.
    - nil, for the empty list. No element is out of order.

- The structured cases

    - node(Left, NodeValue, Right) for nonempty trees. If X is in
      Left, then X<NodeValue, and if X is in Right, then X>NodeValue.
    - First.Rest for nonempty lists. If X is in Rest then X > First.

These definitions and their desired properties are simple to specify. In a moment
we shall define a predicate tree_list which succeeds when its first argument
is a binary tree, its second argument is a list, the tree and the list are both
ordered, and both contain the same elements.

   We shall see how the program structure follows these definitions. The more
complex structure is the tree. It has two subtrees and a node element. We would
expect the program to have two calls to recursive subroutines dealing with
subtrees, and a nonrecursive call dealing with the node element. There should
also be a subroutine call relating to the list. In this case, the call relating to the
node element and the list are combined into one, namely append.

```
tree_list(nil,nil).
tree_list(node(Left, NodeValue, Right), List) <-
    tree_list(Left, Left_list) &
    tree_list(Right, Right_list) &
    append(Left_list, NodeValue.Right_list, List).
```

As expected, the two subtrees each give rise to a recursive call to the predicate
tree_list, and the lists mentioned in these calls are related to the desired
result by the call to append. The non-recursive term NodeValue participates
in this call to append.

   So the primary recursion here is on the predicate tree_list. Append
brings the pieces all together by relating:

- Lists in the recursive calls to `tree_list`,
- The simple `NodeValue` for the tree in the head of the rule, and
- The `List` in the head of the rule.

`Append` (see page 64) will itself recurse on the structure of the list. This will happen in each subcall to `tree_list`. The entire program is multirecursive, and is a declarative specification of a relation between an ordered tree and a sorted list.

We have indicated how the structure of a Prolog program follows the structure of its data. Next we will discuss how verification of a program's correctness is related to its structure. Control structures other than recursion are discussed in Section 3.1.5, "Control Structures."

In a conventional programming language, a program can sometimes be usefully proved correct, in the sense that it behaves according to its specification. A well-written Prolog program can often be viewed as a declarative specification. In the next chapter, we discuss broadening the class of programs that can be read declaratively. In Appendix B we shall discuss the idea of a *model* of a program. Conceptually, a model is a hypothetical collection of facts consisting of all and only the true instances of a predicate. The collections are hypothetical since they sometimes consist of an infinite number of facts. Strictly speaking, proving a program correct means demonstrating that it would succeed for every item in the model, and fail in all those not in the model. However, if the program terminates and is efficient, there may be very little that really needs to be proved about it; the main task may be to be sure that we have really specified what we want. Sometimes, though, we transform our initial executable specification into a more efficient (but perhaps less clear) Prolog program (recall the change from `psort` to `qsort` in Chapter 2, pages 90 and 92). Then, we are interested in establishing that the second program really produces the same answers as the first, i.e, that the transformation step is correct.

There are two different things that we can establish to determine whether a Prolog program is correct:

- It does not compute any wrong answers, and
- It computes all the right answers.

We use a specification or a model to determine which are the right and wrong answers. Borrowing some terminology usually used to refer to proof procedures, we make these definitions:

A *soundness* proof shows that if a program gives an answer, then the answer is correct. A *completeness* proof tells us that the program in fact produces all of the correct answers.

The term *correctness* is often used just to refer to soundness. Here it implies both soundness and completeness. Correctness of a program depends on the fact that the Prolog language implements a particular proof strategy. The order of clauses and goals can affect a program's completeness.

In our `tree_list` example, we can specify that `tree_list(Tree, List)` is to be true whenever

1. `Tree` is an ordered binary tree with values on interior nodes as well as leaves, and
2. `List` is a sorted list, and
3. The items in `Tree` and in `List` are the same.

Recall from Chapter 2 that Prolog programs may be used to check that a condition is true of some terms, or to generate some terms as output when others are provided as input. Which terms are to be input and which output is not necessarily fixed. In this case, the procedure has two arguments, which gives us four cases: both arguments are input (checking), one argument is input and the other output (two cases), and both arguments are output. (There are actually more cases, since each argument could be a structure containing a mixture of variables and constants, but we shall just look at the four simple cases.) By including in the specification the intention of how the procedure is to be used, each of the four cases gives rise to a distinct correctness proof. Each of the four is oriented toward how the procedure is to be used.

If the procedure is to be used to check that two input terms stand in the specified relation, then 1 and 2 are assumed, and it remains to be proved that 3 therefore follows whenever the procedure succeeds. This is the first proof below. If the procedure is to be used only to produce a sorted list from an ordered tree, then we are interested in proving that if number 1 holds (the `Tree` is ordered...) then 2 and 3 follow. That is, the procedure produces an accurate list. This is the second proof below.

No proof is given for the remaining two simple cases. If the procedure is to be used only to produce an ordered tree from a list, then we are interested in proving that 1 and 3 follow whenever 2 is true. Lastly, if the procedure is to generate both arguments, then it must be proven that when the procedure succeeds, all three conditions hold. (The completeness of this last case is dependent on the completeness of the > and < relations.)

We will be content with reasoning that the present program is sound and complete with respect to the above English specification, which listed three requirements for `tree_list` to succeed. The program is wrong only if one of the three requirements is violated. Our argument follows the program structure. Where the program is recursive, the proof uses induction on the structure of the terms.

We want to show that if we pass an ordered tree and a sorted list (neither of which contain variables) to the program, and the program succeeds, then the tree and list have the same elements. We use proof by contradiction. Assume the input tree and list are ordered ground clauses, and the program succeeds in some case where the tree and the list do not have exactly the same elements.

If the program were not correct in this case (i.e, it succeeded when it should have failed), then there would have to be some item in the tree or the list that is not in the other term. The cases are

1. There is an item in the tree that is not in the list. The only two cases are for empty and nonempty trees.

   a. If the tree is empty, then it can contain no item not in the list.

   b. By induction on the maximum depth of the tree, there are no items in the subtrees that are not in their lists (left list and right list). Since `append` is correct (by assumption) and does not introduce any new items, the only item that can be in the tree that is not in the list is the root node. But it is added by `append`, so it is in the list.

   Since both of these contradict the assumption that there is an item in one term that is not in the other, the tree cannot have anything in it that is not in the list.

2. There is an item in the list that is not in the tree.

   a. If the list is empty, it can contain no item not in the tree.

   b. By induction on the maximum length of the list, there are no items introduced in the two sublists. Neither is a new item introduced by the append. Therefore the only new item must be the node. But that is the root of the tree. Therefore there cannot be an item in the list that is not in the tree.

Each case here gives rise to a contradiction. Since neither of these cases can happen, the items in the list are exactly the items in the tree, and our program is correct: if passed two input terms of the proper type, it succeeds if the terms have exactly the same node items. By proper type we mean that one is an ordered tree and the other a sorted list. If passed two incorrect ground terms, then the program would fail by violating one of the above cases.

The second proof to consider is where either `Tree` or `List` is an unbound variable and the other is ground. We can assume that the bound argument is ordered or sorted, as the case may be. We need to verify that the previously unbound variable gets bound to the proper structure. If the ordered tree is provided as input, then the sorted list is to be generated and vice versa. Once we show this, we know by the previous proof that the tree and list have the same elements. Therefore we need only to show that if we pass an ordered tree to the program and it succeeds, then the output is a sorted list.

The proof uses induction on the depth of the tree.

1. Suppose the tree is empty (`nil`). Then the list is also empty (`nil`), and is therefore sorted.

2. By induction on the size of the tree, `Right_list` and `Left_list` are sorted, with every element in `Left_list` less than every element in `Right_list`. Since append maintains the order of the lists (by assumption), then any item is out of order it must be `NodeValue`. But `NodeValue` is greater than every item in `Left_list`, and appears after every item in `Left_list`. It is also less than every item in `Right_list`, and appears before every item in `Right_list`. Therefore it cannot be out of order. Therefore there are no items out of order. Therefore the list is indeed sorted.

So the program correctly generates sorted lists from ordered trees. Generating a tree from a list is similar to the previous argument. The case where both arguments are variables does not succeed on any incorrect ground case, although it has partially specified solutions. Working through these two cases makes a good exercise.

As a further example of how recursive data structures affect the structure and verification of Prolog programs, we use the `tree_list` program from page 140 to sort a list. Recall that we defined an ordered binary tree to be a tree whose nodes look like either

- `nil`
- `node(Left,NodeValue,Right)`

where `Left` and `Right` are ordered binary trees. In addition, no node in `Left` has a value greater than `NodeValue`, and no node in `Right` has a value less than `NodeValue`. These same conditions apply recursively to the left and right subtrees. That makes the tree ordered. Here is an example of an ordered tree:

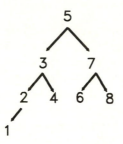

This tree contains the values 1 through 8. By traversing the tree in left-root-right order, the nodes can be read out in ascending sequence. Let us see informally why this is so. If the ordered tree is empty, then traversing the tree in left-root-right order produces nothing out of order. Assume that traversing an ordered tree in this fashion produces the values in proper sequence if the tree has maximum depth less than N. Assume the tree `node(Left, NodeValue, Right)` has maximum depth N. First traverse the `Left` subtree. This produces all its values in the proper sequence since `Left` has maximum depth less than N. Then produce `NodeValue`. This is still in proper sequence since `NodeValue` is greater than all values in `Left`. Then traverse `Right`. This produces its values in the proper sequence since `Right` has maximum depth less than N. No values are out of sequence since every value in `Right` is greater than `NodeValue` and all values in `Left`. We can define the relation `sort` between an ordered list, `List2`, and a permutation of it, `List1`, using these observations. Assume that `List1` contains the same elements as an ordered tree `Tree`, and that `List2` is the left-root-right traversal of `Tree`. Then `List2` is a sorted version of `List1`. A hidden assumption is that no element occurs twice.

To write the Prolog program, we express these conditions in infix notation:

```
op("contains_the_same_elements_as_ordered", rl, 145).
op("is_left_root_right_traversal_of", rl, 145).
op("is_the_same_as", rl, 145).
op("with_element", rl, 145).
op("added", suffix, 145).
```

The following single clause for sorted first establishes that Tree is an ordered tree having exactly the same elements as List1, and then declares that traversing Tree in the proper fashion will produce List2.

```
sorted(List1, List2) <-
    List1 contains_the_same_elements_as_ordered Tree &
    List2 is_left_root_right_traversal_of Tree.
```

The procedure for establishing the relationship between a list and an ordered tree has two clauses. The first clause relates empty trees and empty lists.

```
nil contains_the_same_elements_as_ordered nil.
```

The second clause relates a nonempty list to a tree by relating the tail of the list to an intermediate tree and then inserting the head.

```
(A.ListB)
  contains_the_same_elements_as_ordered Tree <-
    ListB
      contains_the_same_elements_as_ordered TreeB &
        Tree is_the_same_as TreeB with_element A added.
```

Inserting a node into a tree has three cases: where the tree is empty, where the inserted value is less than the value of the root, and where the inserted value is greater than the value of the root.

```
node(nil,A,nil)
    is_the_same_as nil with_element A added.


node(NewLeft, NodeValue, Right) is_the_same_as
        node(Left, NodeValue, Right)
        with_element A added
    <-
    A < NodeValue &
    NewLeft is_the_same_as Left with_element A added.


node(Left, NodeValue, NewRight) is_the_same_as
        node(Left, NodeValue, Right)
        with_element A added
    <-
    A > NodeValue &
    NewRight
      is_the_same_as Right with_element A added.
```

A previous example, `tree_list`, established that a tree and a list had the same elements, but did not ensure that the tree was ordered, so it could not be used to build an ordered tree. It can, however, be used to traverse the tree.

```
List is_left_root_right_traversal_of Tree <-
    tree_list(Tree, List).
```

Given this test data:

```
list1(5 . 3 . 7 . 2 . 4 . 6 . 8 . 1 .nil).

testsorted(L) <- sorted(L,L1) & write(L1).

testsorted <- list1(L) & testsorted(L).
```

Here is a sample of program execution:

```
testsorted.
(1 . 2 . 3 . 4 . 5 . 6 . 7 . 8 . nil) .

testsorted(4 .7 .22 .1 .3 .8 .nil).
(1 . 3 . 4 . 7 . 8 . 22 . nil) .
```

If the value of a node were a *key* for data to be stored, then we could simply change the representation to

```
node(Left, Value, Right, Data).
```

As these examples illustrate, the structure of a Prolog program follows its data structures. Informal verification of the program follows its structure. The declarative reading of Prolog programs makes this easier than in most other languages. However, logic programming also has a procedural aspect, which we emphasize in the next section.

3.1.5 Control Structures

The fundamental control construct in pure Prolog is *sequence*. Goals are tried in a "not" form left-to-right sequence; rules are tried in the order in which they appear in a program. A rule can be viewed as a sequence of predicate calls. A predicate can be viewed as a type of case statement, but one in which more than one case may apply. So the fundamental Prolog control structure is very simple. There are some extensions.

- Prolog does not have any way of directly expressing negative information, so a "not" form has been introduced.

- There is no direct way of affecting the rule selection strategy, so "cut" was introduced to eliminate rules from consideration. It also is used as an efficiency tool.

- As an additional temptation, "traditional" control constructs such as the do-loop can be programmed. Although their use may make one's first encounter with Prolog easier, they may actually hinder the transition to programming in logic.

We discuss five main classes of control facilities:

- The guard form,
- Traditional control constructs,
- The use of labels in Prolog,
- Remote cuts, and
- Using the Prolog *metavariable*. to pass a procedure call as an argument.

Because control issues necessarily go outside of the declarative aspect of logic programming, the topics discussed here do not all present a nice declarative reading. This is particularly true of the control constructs such as while P do Q, as well as all discussions of cut, labels, and so on.

The "Guard" Form

This form is one of the most common, after pure sequencing. It uses the cut. Each rule tests for a condition, discards other alternatives if this condition holds, and proceeds with the computation for this particular test. A special form of this was introduced in the discussion of cut on page 116. The general form is

```
case <- condition1 & / & action1.
case <- condition2 & / & action2.
```

In Prolog we often make some tests for a condition, discard other alternatives if the condition holds, and then cause the whole goal to fail. This is a round-about way of providing for negative information and we call it the "not form." Prolog normally only allows positive information to be added to the database. ("q is true if. . .." One cannot say "q is false if. . .," although as we shall see in a moment one can say "¬q is true if. . ..") In full first-order logic, on the other hand, we may be able to prove that something is true or that it is false, or there may simply be no proof either that it is true or that it is false.

It is possible to write a prover for full first order logic in Prolog, but what is usually done is simply to include a brief definition of a special kind of negation, called *negation as failure*. It was studied systematically by Clark (1978), and we describe a declarative theory for it in Appendix B. For many Prolog programs, it has the effect of causing Prolog to indicate that something is false if there is no proof that it is true. Note that this is rather different from a full logic system in which something may actually be proved to be false. Using negation as failure with Prolog is like saying "my Prolog program contains all of the knowledge needed to prove true anything that is true of a subject, so anything it cannot prove is false." The definition for negation is built into IBM Prolog. It behaves as if defined by just the two rules

```
¬P <- P & / & fail.
¬P.
```

Because of the cut symbol (/), there is no declarative reading. However, we can think of the rules as saying: ¬P is false if P succeeds, otherwise ¬P is true. In the body of the first rule, if P succeeds, then the cut commits the computation of ¬P to try to execute `fail`. On the other hand, if P fails in the first rule, control passes to the second rule, which says that ¬P succeeds.

We can also use pairs of rules of this form in a program. We call this the "not" form because the definition of "not" as negation-as-failure is the simplest case.

This form is used often when a computation has determined positively that the called predicate should fail: we discard remaining alternatives and then fail. It is possible to rephrase these constructs into ones that use ¬. There is a slight performance cost as an extra call is involved.

For example, should the Red Queen's gardeners paint a rose red? Only if it is not red, of course. Here is the form without ¬.

```
should_paint_rose(Rose) <- red(Rose) & / & fail.
should_paint_rose(Rose).
```

Here is the form with ¬. Note that it is a little simpler because work has been consigned to the ¬ procedure.

```
should_paint_rose(Rose) <- ¬red(Rose).
```

A simple transformation of the second program using ¬ produces the first program. Replace each call to a procedure by the procedure body, applying the unifying substitution. Where there are two clauses for a procedure, the replaced call gives rise to two replaced procedures. So replacing ¬red(Rose) with the body from the first clause for ¬ gives

```
should_paint_rose(Rose) <- red(Rose) & / & fail.
```

Replacing ¬red(Rose) by the empty body in the second clause for ¬ gives

```
should_paint_rose(Rose).
```

These two together make up the definition of `should_paint_rose`

The not form has one important characteristic to note: variables are not bound. This means that ¬p(X) will tell us that p(X) is false for any case the system can try; it will not tell us for which *particular* X it is that p is false. This fact can be annoying, but it can also be useful. Consider why X is not bound when ¬p(X) succeeds. This is because bindings are undone on failure, and the second rule for ¬ is the most general one there is.

The "not" form can be used frequently in place of an actual call to ¬P. However, we keep in mind that this is a performance optimization. An explicit ¬ is more readable.

Traditional Control Constructs

The `if A then B else C` construct is common in structured languages such as Pascal and PL/I. It is fairly straightforward to define a similar construct in Prolog. The syntax is slightly different, but the meaning is similar. Given proper operator declarations for `if`, `then`, and `else`, the definition can be easily stated:

```
(if A then B else C ) <-  A & / & B.
(if A then B else C ) <- C.
```

One thing to note is that the `/` eliminates all choice points in A.

Note the use of the not form. Converting to the explicit use of ¬ allows backtracking into A, at the cost of extra computation.

```
(if A then B else C ) <-  A & B.
(if A then B else C ) <-  ¬A & C.
```

IBM Prolog has predefined the operators `->` and `;` to be used in this fashion. `if A then B else C` is expressed as `A -> B ; C`.

Another construct in languages such as Pascal and PL/I is `While P do Q`. In these languages side effects, such as the explicit assignment of values to variables, are fundamental. If P is true, then Q must change the state, otherwise P never becomes false and the program stays in the loop forever. So what should be the logic equivalent? What is returned as the binding as soon as P fails? One suggestion is to use "global variables" with the `::=` construct as introduced on page 122. It is easiest to implement this using labels. Labels are discussed in more detail later, but this definition can be understood by thinking of `label(here)` as a conventional label, and `retry(here)` as a goto.

```
(while P do Q) <- label(here) &
    P & Q & retry(here).
(while P do Q).  /*after it is all over*/
```

A close relative is `forall P do Q:`.

```
(forall P do Q) <- P & one(Q) & fail.
(forall P do Q).  /*after it is all over*/
```

The predicate `one` is useful for eliminating backtracking.

```
one(Q) <- Q & /.
```

Pascal has a case statement similar to `C case L`. Here, C is a key whose value is used to select one of a set of alternatives. In our approximation, L is a list of pairs `(Key.Predicate)`, and C is a predicate that may be true for one or more of the `Key` values. With appropriate operator definitions, we can write this in Prolog as

```
c(Key) case ((Key.Predicate).*)    <-
    c(Key) &
    Predicate.
c(Key) case (*.List)  <-
    c(Key) case List.
```

This definition will return all cases upon backtracking, or fail if there are none. It is not really a useful definition, though. For one thing, the Pascal compiler can generate a branch table or some other fast branching mechanism for case statements. This is possible because the set of cases that can arise is defined beforehand, and the branching depends on simple characteristics of the keys such as type.

The Prolog version is more flexible in that the conditions can be more general predicates. However, it is not as efficient. The list of Key.Predicate pairs is searched linearly until one is found that satisfies the conditions. It is more efficient and more natural to make use of Prolog's built-in logic, which provides much more function than the case statement. Each case test can be given its own predicate name, and the list of Key.Predicate pairs simply added as rules for that predicate. Instead of calling c(abc) case Cases, the simpler goal c1(abc) is used, where c1 is defined with a set of clauses that look like

```
c1(Key)  <-  c(Key) & Predicate.
```

for each Key.Predicate pair in the original definition of case.

Most Prolog implementations, including IBM Prolog, index on the first argument of a predicate. In this case it is the input data Key. This allows the Prolog system we are using to access the clauses as efficiently as the corresponding Pascal case implementation. This is essentially a variation on the *guard form* discussed on page 147.

Labels

IBM Prolog has the concept of a *label*. In most languages labels are textual items. They are not executable, but rather, mark places in the text of the program. A Pascal statement can be given a label, that can then be used in control statements such as goto. The label indicates a place in the code generated for the Pascal program. Control may be moved to that spot so that the instructions being executed proceed from there. These instructions need not have been executed before.

In IBM Prolog, the label is not a textual item, but is a dynamically created marker that indicates a certain time in the history of a program's execution. A special marker is placed on Prolog's execution stack that is not reclaimed by "last-call" optimization. There is a built-in executable predicate label(L) that puts a marker on the execution stack when it is called. This label can be used by some execution control predicates, which include

- `query_1(Label)`
- `query_1(Label,N)`
- `retry(Label)`
- `fail(Label)`
- `cut(Label)`

Each invocation of a label is erased upon backtracking just as for other successful predicates. `label(L)` is deterministic. The actual label used can be any term.

A label is established by executing the built-in predicate `label(L)`. The built-in predicates `query_1(L)` and `query_1(L,N)` retrieve previously established labels. The unary case is deterministic. It only finds the first label. The binary case will find the Nth label that unifies with L. This is best explained by examples. Consider this clause, which puts the labels a and b on the stack in that order, then unifies L with a label on the stack.

```
test_label(L) <- label(a) & label(b) &
     query_1(L,*).
```

It gives the behavior:

```
test__label(L) & write(L) & fail.

b.
a.
FAIL
```

while on the other hand

```
test_label(L) <- label(a) & label(b) &
     query_1(L, 2).
```

gives this behavior:

```
test__label(L).

OMS SUCCESS
<- test_label(a).
```

This is the first time in this chapter that the actual form of the IBM Prolog response is given. The OMS SUCCESS message gives the execution time in milliseconds (in this case less than one) and then the initial call is repeated to the right of an arrow. Variables occurring in the initial call are replaced by their bound values, if any. In the following, we generally omit these messages when giving examples.

Note that the second label found is a, not b. That means that the labels are found by searching the execution stack *backwards* from the predicate `query_1`. This is the same for the other predicates that use labels. The most recent labels are found first.   Remember that `query_1(L,N)` will backtrack through preceding labels. `query_1(L)` is deterministic.

Labels may be structures, not just constants. They may include variables. In any of the control predicates that refer to labels, the goal label is unified with the labels on the stack.   This means that variables can be bound in both directions, and gives much more flexibility than in languages whose labels are limited to static constants that are lexically determined. Although one cannot jump to an arbitrary place in the program, this makes sense from a logical point of view. All the permitted operations that use labels refer to the proof being established by the program. They may reset the proof to an earlier point, discard alternatives, and so on. If the programmer wishes to dynamically compute code to be executed, then the logical variable must be used:

> `. . . decide_on(Goal) & Goal & ...`

This discussion concentrates on the use of labels.

Here are some examples that illustrate how labels are created. Each consists of one clause, followed by a listing of it in execution. In the first example, L is bound to b. On backtracking it gets bound to a.

> `test1(L) <- label(a) & label(b) & query_1(L,*).`

In the following example the semicolon invokes backtracking to produce the next solution.   User input is in this typeface, and machine output is in `computer typeface`.

> ```
> test1(*).
> 
> OMS SUCCESS
>  <- test1(b) .
> ;
> OMS SUCCESS
>  <- test1(a) .
> ;
> OMS FAIL
> ```

In this example L remains a variable, although X and L are unified.

> ```
> test2(L) <- label(X) & query_1(L).
> test2(*).
> 
> OMS SUCCESS
>  <- test2(V1) .
> ;
> OMS FAIL
> ```

In the next example, the variable L gets bound to a.

> `test3(L) <- label(L) & query_1(a) .`

test3(L).

```
OMS SUCCESS
 <- test3(a) .
```

This example puts the label X on the stack, followed by the label a. The first query_1(X) unifies X with the most recent label a. The stack now has two labels a, since X was put on the stack as a variable, and subsequently bound to a:

```
test4(L) <- label(X) & label(a) &
     query_1(X) & query_1(L,2).
```

test4(L).

```
OMS SUCCESS
 <- test4(a) .
```

As we saw on page 149, retry(Label) is similar to goto in procedural languages, in that execution continues at the point of the label. However, there are some crucial differences:

- The execution environment is restored to what it was when a preceding goal was called, and the goal is "retried." Execution cannot jump *forward* to a future point.

- Since Prolog has no "global" state, the status is restored to what it was at the time the label was established. Thus execution will repeat itself exactly as before, unless some side effect has changed things. For example, an addax may have changed a procedure that is used between the label and the retry. Without such a side effect, execution will endlessly repeat the cycle.

Here are some examples that demonstrate how retry(L) works. In the first example, there should be an unending loop that keeps writing the atom here.

```
testretry1   <-
     label(here) &
     write(here) &
     retry(here).
```

In this example, sp is a VM/Prolog immediate command that halts execution.

testretry.

```
here .
here .
here .
```

```
 . . .
sp
* evaluation ended by user *
11MS ERROR
```

The next example is the same, except the `retry(here)` is conditional. If `stop_retry` succeeds, then the `retry` is not done. If `stop_retry` fails, then the Prolog database is modified so that it will subsequently succeed, and the `retry` is performed.

```
testretry2   <-
     label(here) &
     write(here) &
     conditional_retry.

conditional_retry <-
     stop_retry | addax(stop_retry) & retry(here).
```

This should give us two occurrences of `here` written to the terminal. Depending on the setting of `pragma(noax,*)`, IBM Prolog optionally writes a message to the terminal whenever a goal is called for which there exist no clauses at all with same name and arity.

```
testretry2.

here .
* no rules can be applied to stop_retry() *
conditional_retry() <-
    stop_retry() | addax(stop_retry) & retry(here) .
here .
1MS SUCCESS
 <- testretry2() .
```

Remote Cuts

The cut `/` is available in most Prolog implementations. It is a means of pruning the and/or tree that represents a Prolog program's execution. It discards alternatives. IBM Prolog's remote cut, `cut(Label)`, also discards alternatives. However, it discards more than just the remaining alternatives for the clause in which it occurs. It has two effects:

1. `cut(L)` discards all alternatives (choice points) that exist between the execution of the remote cut and the first label that unifies with L. Since labels themselves are choice points, any labels that are on the stack between the target label and the `cut` also disappear.

2. All alternatives for the clause in which the `label(L)` was executed are discarded. It is as if a `/` occurred where `label(L)` is.

Here are some examples to illustrate the behavior of remote cuts. Suppose that these two facts for a and the one unconditional rule for b were in the database.

```
a(1).   a(2).   b(X).
```

Here is a program that has no cut.

```
test_no_cut(X) <- label(a) & a(X) & b(X).
test_no_cut(3).
```

When executing, it returns three values.

     test__no__cut(L) & write(L) & fail.

```
1 .
2 .
3 .
1MS FAIL
```

If we change the rule for b to include a remote cut to the label a, we see that only one intermediate value for a(X) is found. The second alternative for a(X) has been eliminated by the cut, as well as the second alternative for test_cut.

```
test_cut(X) <- label(a) & a(X) & b(X).
test_cut(3).

b(X) <- cut(a) .
```

We see that this is indeed the case.

     test__cut(X) & write(X) & fail.

```
1 .
OMS FAIL
```

In IBM Prolog, we can also `fail` to a remote label. Assuming that `label(L)` has been established, `fail(L)` is equivalent to `cut(L) & fail`.

Metavariables

Prolog has a very powerful construct called the *metavariable*. In effect, a program can construct a goal, which can then be called. There is an important difference between a goal or procedure and a term. Terms are data structures that get passed among procedures. Goals are procedure calls. The syntax of a term and a goal are the same, but Prolog treats them differently.

The built-in predicate `=..` allows a term to be constructed from a list consisting of a function symbol and arguments. For example

```
f(a,b) =.. (f.a.b.nil)

f(g(X),X) =.. (f.g(X).X.nil)
```

This is reversible, so that =.. can be used to take apart structures as well as construct them. When used with metavariables, it can construct goals to be executed or clauses to be addaxed.

A metavariable is a Prolog variable that can be executed as if it were a goal. There is a built-in IBM Prolog routine call(*) that is used to execute the variable. Addax automatically turns variables occurring in the body of clauses as a subgoal into the appropriate call. Thus if we assert a clause whose body includes the goal ...p(X) & Y & q(X) ..., then the actual stored body is ...p(X) & call(Y) & q(X)....

The following examples demonstrate how metavariables and =.. work. Here are the procedures.

```
testvar1(X) <- X.
testvar2(X) <- (G =.. X) & G.
a(1). a(2).
```

When executing, they give the following behavior. First we will pass a goal to testvar1, which will be executed. The results will be written out, and backtracking will be forced by fail to get all solutions. Passing a(X) we expect X to be bound first to 1 and then to 2.

testvar1(a(X)) & write(X) & fail.

```
1 .
2 .
1MS FAIL
```

The procedure testvar2 takes a list as an argument, and constructs a goal from it, which is then executed. If we pass a.X.nil then we should get the same behavior as in the previous example.

testvar2(a.X.nil) & write(X) & fail.

```
1 .
2 .
1MS FAIL
```

If we pass a.2 .nil, then we would expect to get only one solution.

testvar2(a.2 .nil).

```
OMS SUCCESS
  <- testvar2(a . 2 . nil) .
```

Similarly, passing a . 3 .ni l we would expect to fail.

testvar2(a . 3 . nil).

1MS FAIL

We have seen a variety of control constructs available in Prolog. Few of them completely fall in line with the ones used in traditional languages. They all knit together to provide quite a flexible assortment. We hope we have shown that criticisms of Prolog's limited control facilities are not as serious as they first appeared. Changes to Prolog's top down, backward-chaining inference method are described in the next section.

3.2 TECHNIQUES AND EXAMPLES

In this section, we look at some general techniques, and we work some examples. In particular, we look at metalevel programming, graph searching, the alpha-beta pruning method for searching game trees, balanced trees, and something that is in some sense the opposite of finding the most general unifier of two terms, namely, finding their most specific generalization.

3.2.1 Meta-level Programming

There is a rather common feeling about Prolog that is expressed something like this: Since Prolog has a fixed method of making inferences, based on top down, left-to-right, depth first search, there must be many symbolic computing tasks for which it is inherently unsuitable. Such tasks might call for, say, forward chaining reasoning, or approximate reasoning with confidence factors. If we look at most of the programs so far in this book, the feeling would appear to be justified. However, we have not yet explored *metalevel programming*. This is a technique in which we not only write rules, but we also write rules about how to use rules. This turns out to be a very powerful technique indeed. Many metaprograms (programs about how to execute programs) are surprisingly succinct when written in Prolog. Extra computing time is used for what is, essentially, a layer of interpretation above Prolog itself. Fortunately, a metaprogram can often be transformed into an equivalent Prolog program that will run faster if needed. Recent work with partial evaluation and source-to-source transformation could make this technique more common. For more on partial evaluation see Komorowski (1981), Bloch (1984), and Takeuchi and Furukawa (1985). For an automated method of producing programs that make suitable source-to-source transformations, see Neumann (1986). In the next sections, we develop, stepwise, a Prolog interpreter in Prolog. At first sight, this might seem to be a rather abstract exercise, but it has two virtues. First, our final interpreter will serve as a debugging tool for the development of programs.

Second, many interpreters, such as the inference engine for an expert system described in Chapter 4, are easy to specify as modifications of Prolog in Prolog.

A Simple Interpreter

We shall now write down a simplified interpreter, in Prolog, for pure Prolog. We then show some step-by-step modifications that remove the simplifications, and that handle some nonpure parts of Prolog.

We saw in Section 3.1, "How to Structure Prolog Programs" how Prolog programs follow the structure of the data. That is also true when the program is itself an interpreter. The interpreter will follow the structure of the language being interpreted. In this case the language is to be pure Prolog itself. So let us look again at the basic structure and meaning of a Prolog program.

- A rule consists of a head and a body (or goal).
- A goal is either a single goal or a conjunction.
- The single goal "true" always succeeds.
- A conjunction succeeds if both parts of the conjunction succeed.
- A single goal succeeds if there is a rule whose head matches the goal and whose body succeeds.

Here is an outline of a predicate `succeeds(Goal)` that succeeds if `Goal` succeeds. To encourage an English-like reading, "succeeds" is declared to be a suffix operator. Other infix operators are defined as needed. They bind more strongly than &.

A predicate `clause(Head <- Body)` is used to define the program to be interpreted. `Body` is the body of a clause whose head matches `Head`. For simplicity, facts are specified by having a special body consisting of the single goal `true`.

The clauses that say Socrates is human, and all humans are mortal, are rendered as follows.

```
clause(human(socrates) <- true)).
clause(mortal(X) <- human(X)).
```

The metainterpreter for executing such logic programs is simple:

```
op("succeeds", suffix, 45).

"true" succeeds.
(A & B)  succeeds  <- A succeeds & B succeeds.
A succeeds  <-
    clause(A <- Goal) & Goal succeeds.
```

This simplified interpreter for the core of Prolog has only three rules. This is not just a trick program. It actually makes reasoning about programs, and manipulating them, much more straightforward than in other languages. Understanding this interpreter will also help us understand what is essential in

Prolog and what is not. Of course, we must elaborate on the interpreter to account for built-in procedures and other "gadgets" we want to add to the language, but we start with this basic core.

So far, we have kept matters declarative, both at the *metalevel* (consisting of our three rules) and at the *object level*, i.e, the level of the program that will be interpreted by our three rules. Now it is time for procedural considerations at both levels.

Our interpreter does not yet handle special cases, such as built-in routines, predicates such as `cut` and `retry`, or side effects such as `addax` and `delax`. These require an extra rule each. The interpretation of these extra-logical items is best handled with the extra-logical facilities of Prolog itself. Finally, we need to take care of the "only-if" nature of the rule patterns. Note that our definition includes a final catchall clause. To include the `cut()`, `label(P)` and `cut(P)`, we can write:

```
cut(P)     succeeds <- cut(P).
"true"     succeeds <- /.
(A & B)    succeeds <- / & A succeeds & B succeeds.
A succeeds <-
     clause(A<-Goal) & Goal succeeds.
```

The rule for `cut(P)` is easier to implement than `/()` with no argument. `cut(P)` contains an explicit label reference to P. We can assume that a suitable label has been made, and simply call `cut(P)` at the Prolog level. For `/()`, the goal must be searched to see if it contains `/()`. If it does, then alternatives for the clause will be removed at the time the `/()` is executed. To do this a label is established *before* the subgoal that returns clauses. The label used is `slash`. Then at the time `/()` is to be executed for the metaprogram, `cut(slash)` is performed at the metainterpreter level.

We can avoid looking for `/()` within a goal if the ancestor goals are made explicit in the interpreter, as we shall describe in the next section.

```
op("is_in_conjunction", rl, 45).

/()        succeeds <- cut(slash).
label(P)   succeeds <- label(P).
cut(P)     succeeds <- cut(P).
"true"     succeeds <- /.
(A & B)    succeeds <- / & A succeeds & B succeeds.
A succeeds          <-
     label(slash) &
     clause(A<-Goal) &
     test_for_cut(Goal) &
     Goal succeeds.
```

```
test_for_cut(Goal) <-
     (/() is_in_conjunction Goal) &
     cut(slash).
test_for_cut(*).

P is_in_conjunction (Q & *) <- P == Q & /.
P is_in_conjunction (A & B) <-
     P is_in_conjunction B & /.
P is_in_conjunction Q <- P == Q.
```

Note that == does not bind variables, it just tests whether two terms are literally the same. To see that `cut(P)` works, a `label(here)` and a `cut(here)` are added to the following program for `a(X)`.

```
clause(a(X) <- label(here) &
     b(X) & cut(here) & c(X)).
clause(b(1)<-true).
clause(b(2)<-true).
clause(c(2)<-true).
```

Given this program, the call to `a(*)  succeeds` fails. Since the cut is performed after `b(1)` succeeds, but before `c(1)` fails, the alternative solution `b(2)` is not available. Therefore we expect the call to `a(X)  succeeds` to fail. Without the `cut` and `label` it would succeed with X bound to 2.

     a(*) succeeds.

     OMS FAIL

     To round off our simple interpreter, we can extend it to handle built-in predicates by adding this clause:

```
A succeeds <- built_in(A) & / & A.
```

Here we must go to the trouble of identifying every built-in procedure we want to be able to use in our meta Prolog, such as `built_in(read(*))` and `built_in(write(*))`. This feature can also be used to cause "user built-in" procedures to be executed directly in Prolog, not by the metainterpreter.

A More Elaborate Interpreter.

In the `succeeds` metainterpreter, the program being interpreted is represented as a set of clauses. The program is not represented as an argument to the interpreter. The simple interpreters presented in the last section all relied on the predicate `clause`. This predicate is the one that fetches rules and, consequently, determines the unification and rule-selection strategy. (Note that the rule for `A & B  succeeds` defines the Prolog left-to-right goal selection strategy.) So, if we wish to interpret `addax` and `delax`, we could do so simply by:

```
addax(X) succeeds <- clause_form(X,Y) & addax(Y).
delax(X) succeeds <- clause_form(X,Y) & delax(Y).

clause_form(H<-B,clause(H<-B)) <- /.
clause_form(H,clause(H<-true)) <- /.
```

This is simple and straightforward. However, it turns out that we can even interpret `addaxs` and `delaxs` without actually adding or deleting anything, using a technique described by Bowen and Kowalski (1982). Although what we describe will not be efficient for large object programs, it appears to be a very important step toward a declarative form of updates for knowledge bases. The idea is to make the metalevel interpreter carry the object program as an argument. The `succeeds_with` predicate uses two extra arguments: the object program before and after the predicate succeeds.

The predicate `clause` that selects which clause to try next must be passed the current set of rules, from which it is to choose. A good exercise for the reader is to provide one that implements the Prolog selection rule. One must be careful about binding variables when a rule is selected from the `Clauses` structure. We do not want input arguments from the current goal inadvertently bound to the rule in the set of clauses that becomes a part of `NewClauses`.

To encourage an English-like reading, two prefix operators `adding` and `deleting` are defined, as are the infix operators `to`, `from`, and `gives`. `succeeds_with(Goal, Old_rules, New_rules)` succeeds when `Goal` succeeds using the clauses in `Old_rules`, with the new set of clauses being `New_rules`.

```
succeeds_with(A,Clauses,Clauses) <- built_in(A) &/&...
succeeds_with(addax(P), Clauses, NewClauses) <-/&
    adding P to Clauses gives NewClauses.
succeeds_with(delax(P), Clauses, NewClauses) <-/&
    deleting P from Clauses gives NewClauses.
    ...
succeeds_with(A, Clauses, NewClauses) <-
    pure_core_succeeds(A, Clauses, NewClauses).

pure_core_succeeds(true, Clauses, Clauses)<-/.
pure_core_succeeds(A & B, Clauses, NewClauses)<-/&
    succeeds_with(A, Clauses, MoreClauses) &
    succeeds_with(B, MoreClauses, NewClauses).

pure_core_succeeds(A, Clauses, NewClauses)   <-
    clause(A <- Goal, Clauses) &
    succeeds_with(Goal, Clauses, NewClauses).
```

To give an example of how the database update predicates may be defined, we can represent the set of clauses as a simple list. The update predicates may be simply defined:

```
adding P to Clauses gives (P.Clauses).
deleting P from (P.Clauses) gives Clauses.
deleting P from (*.Clauses) gives NewClauses <-
    deleting P from Clauses gives NewClauses.
```

Of course, this simple definition does not consider everything. For example, we may want to copy P before adding it to the list, just to make sure that retrieving and deleting clauses does not bind variables in other clauses inadvertently. We may also want to include a cut in the definition of deleting to avoid recursion when backtracking. For performance, we may want to maintain a tree structure instead of a list, or store the clauses in a database, and so on. There is considerable scope for elaboration of these predicates.

Computation Trees and Proof Trees

A Prolog program and a goal determine an *and/or* tree. This and/or tree represents the search space for the goal, which is its root. Here is a simple program and its diagrammatic representation for the goal a.

```
a <- b & c.
a <- d.
b <- d.
b <- e.
d.
c.
e.
```

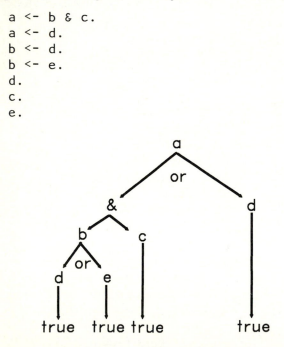

Executing a Prolog program is equivalent to searching for an & subtree, such that

1. Every node inherits the unifiers of its ancestors,

2. Every leaf node is a fact.

The first & subtree found in our example is

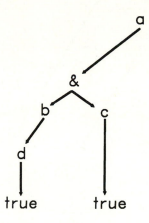

The purpose of a Prolog interpreter is to establish such a tree, which is called a *proof tree*. Thinking of the execution of Prolog programs in this way helps to clear up any confusion about the notion of backtracking.

   During the execution of a Prolog program, there are two pieces of interesting information:

1. What parts of a final proof tree have been constructed, and

2. What or branches of the and/or tree remain to be explored. These are the remaining choice or backtrack points.

The proof tree being constructed has three areas of interest:

1. The entire tree, as accessible from the root,

2. The subtree that is being constructed and will be rooted at the current goal, and

3. The path from the current goal to the root.

We can picture these as

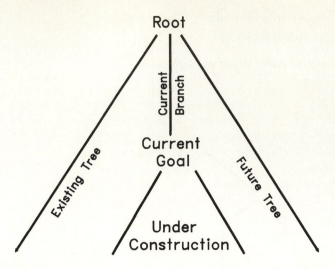

The tree to be constructed by the current goal is a part of the growing proof; the entire proof tree starting at the root can be used to gain access to the results of previous goals; the path to the root can be used to check for cycles and to implement /(). We introduce these three objects one by one into the interpreter. Since this version of succeeds takes two arguments, we do not use the suffix operator form.

1. Under construction from the current goal succeeds(Goal, Proof):

```
succeeds(true, true).
succeeds(A & B, Aproof & Bproof) <-
    succeeds(A, Aproof) &
    succeeds(B, Bproof).
succeeds(A, A<-Proof) <-
    clause(A<-Goal) &
    succeeds(Goal, Proof).
```

2. Adding the entire proof tree

```
    succeeds(Goal, Subproof, Proof_tree):
succeeds(true, true, Proof_tree).
succeeds(A & B, Aproof & Bproof, Proof_tree) <-
    succeeds(A, Aproof, Proof_tree) &
    succeeds(B, Bproof, Proof_tree).
succeeds(A, A<-Proof, Proof_tree) <-
    clause(A<-Goal) &
    succeeds(Goal, Proof, Proof_tree).
```

Look carefully at these rules. Where is the variable Proof_tree bound? Apparently nowhere! But note that the proofs of the current goal (e.g, Aproof) must be parts of the entire proof tree. Note that the proof of the root is the entire proof tree. To construct `Proof_tree`, the initial call to `succeeds` must be

```
succeeds(Goal, Proof, Proof).
```

In a call to a subproof `Goal succeeds`, the argument `Proof` is actually part of the structure pointed to by the argument `Proof_tree`. This is an example of making structures available in a number of places through use of the logical variable. When the original call to `succeeds` terminates, it will return the entire proof. As the Prolog program executes, parts of the data structure representing the proof have been constructed already , parts will be constructed by the current goal, and parts are yet to be defined by siblings to the ancestors of the current goal. This partially defined structure is available as the third argument to `succeeds`. If we were to call a program to look at the unbound leaves of this structure, we would find the second argument appearing there. The second argument is actually a part of the third argument!

3. Adding a list of ancestors:

```
succeeds(Goal, Subproof, Proof_tree, Ancestors)
```

The ancestor list is maintained in reverse order, from the current node to the root.

```
succeeds(true,true,Proof_tree, Ancestors).
succeeds(A & B, Aproof & Bproof,
        Proof_tree, Ancestors) <-
    succeeds(A, Aproof, Proof_tree, Ancestors) &
    succeeds(B, Bproof, Proof_tree, Ancestors).
succeeds(A, A<-Proof, Proof_tree, Ancestors) <-
    clause(A<-Goal) &
    succeeds(Goal, Proof,
            Proof_tree, A.Ancestors).
```

We could now revise the last rule so that it checks the ancestor list to see if the current goal is an ancestor of itself, and fails if it is. This might be useful for controlling some of the looping problems we have discussed. The questions are, does this work and in what cases is it correct?

If the current goal is the same as an ancestor that is ground (i.e, contains no variables) then we know we have an infinite recursion. If the current goal is not more specific than an ancestor, then we have an infinite recursion, since whatever happened for that ancestor can happen for the current goal.

In general, there is no way of curing all such problems, since if such a cure existed it would solve a fundamental problem of computer science called the *halting problem*, that we know to be unsolvable. However, if we think not about all Prolog programs, but just about pure Prolog programs that do not use function symbols to manipulate data structures, then the problem is solvable. We might then begin to look at various methods of cutting off a recursion based on the tree above a current goal. However, Brough and Walker (1984) showed that any such method that relies on the Prolog top down mechanism plus a cutoff using ancestor information has a fundamental flaw: Either the cutoff is too strong and misses some answers, or it is too weak and allows some unbounded recursions. Fortunately, the difficulty lies in using only top down information. As shown in Apt et al. (1986), the addition of a little bottom up information solves the problem, at least in principle. These points are discussed further in Appendix B.

A Debugging Aid

IBM Prolog has built-in facilities for simple tracing of predicates. (These are discussed in Appendix A.) It has a number of features to support building your own debugging tools. Here we present the skeleton of a tracing metainterpreter, which can be elaborated to control program execution in a flexible manner. Here is a simple tracing debugger. It will display the CALL, EXIT, FAIL, and REDO points of execution of a predicate, as described on page 71. These points are developed one at a time.

Call:

```
succeeds(true) <- /.
succeeds(A & B) <- / & succeeds(A) & succeeds(B).
succeeds(A) <- note_call(A) &
    clause(A<-Goal) & succeeds(Goal).

note_call(A) <-write(call(A)).
```

Exit: Replace the last call for succeeds with

```
succeeds(A) <- note_call(A) & clause(A<-Goal) &
    succeeds(Goal) & note_exit(A).
```

And add the following rule

```
note_exit(A)<-write(exit(A)).
```

Fail: Note from the definition that a predicate fails if all rules for it fail. This will cause backtracking into the note_call predicate. So add a second rule that is there to note failure by a write side effect, and then continue the failure:

```
note_call(A) <- write(call(A)).
note_call(A) <- write(fail(A)) & fail.
```

Alternatively, another clause for succeeds can be added to note failure:

```
succeeds(A) <- note_fail(A) & fail.
```

The / in the clause for succeeds(A & B) will keep this last clause from being invoked for A & B when A or B fails. We only want notification of the failure of individual goals, not of conjuncts. Otherwise, if C fails in

```
A & B & C.
```

we would see fail(C), fail(B & C), and fail(A & B & C).

Redo: The rule that returns the goal for a given head can be changed to notice when backtracking is invoked. The predicate clause must be changed to clause1, which now calls clause and makes a note of this.

```
clause1(A<-Goal) <-
    clause(A <- Goal) & note_redo(A).
```

```
   . . .
```

```
succeeds(A) <- note_call(A) & clause1(A<-Goal) &
    succeeds(Goal) & note_exit(A).
```

```
   . . .
```

```
note_redo(A).
note_redo(A) <- write(redo(A)) & fail.
```

Here is a listing of the Prolog metainterpreter that traces execution, which we have been developing in stages.

```
succeeds(true) <- /.
succeeds(A & B) <- / &
    succeeds(A) & succeeds(B).
succeeds(A) <- note_call(A) & clause1(A<-Goal) &
    succeeds(Goal) & note_exit(A).

clause1(A<-Goal) <-
    clause(A <- Goal) & note_redo(A).


note_call(A) <-write(call(A)).
note_call(A) <-write(fail(A)) & fail.
note_exit(A) <-write(exit(A)).
note_redo(A).
note_redo(A) <- write(redo(A)) & fail.
```

Here is an example program:

```
clause(a(X) <- b(X) & c(X)).
clause(a(X) <- d(X)).
clause(b(1) <- true).
clause(b(2) <- true).
clause(c(2) <- true).
```

and here is its execution

succeeds(a(*)).

```
call(a(V1)) .
call(b(V1)) .
exit(b(1)) .
call(c(1)) .
fail(c(1)) .
redo(b(1)) .
exit(b(2)) .
call(c(2)) .
exit(c(2)) .
exit(a(2)) .
3MS SUCCESS
 <- succeeds(a(2)) .
```

This trace is a bit hard to read. Indentation would help distinguish the different subprocedures. Adding the depth as an argument to the procedures allows us to accomplish this. We will use the IBM Prolog built-in predicates tab, which writes a certain number of spaces, and writech which writes a term without an ending period or line feed. We also want to see the clause when it is selected, so we will add a note_clause(A <- Goal) procedure.

```
succeeds(true, D) <-/.
succeeds(A & B, D) <- / &
    succeeds(A, D) & succeeds(B, D).
succeeds(A, D) <- note_call(A, D) &
    clause1(A<-Goal, D) & sum(D,1, D1) &
    succeeds(Goal, D1) & note_exit(A, D).

clause1(A<-Goal, D) <- clause(A <- Goal) &
    note_clause(A<-Goal, D) & note_redo(A, D).
```

```
note_call(A, D) <- tabit(D) & write(call(A)).
note_call(A, D) <-
     tabit(D) & write(fail(A)) & fail.
note_exit(A, D) <- tabit(D) & write(exit(A)).
note_redo(A, D).
note_redo(A, D) <-
     tabit(D) & write(redo(A)) & fail.
note_clause(A <- true, D) <- /.
note_clause(A <- Goal, D) <-
     tabit(D) & write(clause(A<-Goal)).

tabit(D) <- tab(D) & writech(D) & writech(' ').
```

This is starting to give a nicer trace.

```
succeeds(a(*),0).

0 call(a(V1)) .
0 clause(a(V1) <- b(V1) & c(V1)) .
 1 call(b(V1)) .
 1 exit(b(1)) .
 1 call(c(1)) .
 1 fail(c(1)) .
 1 exit(b(2)) .
 1 call(c(2)) .
 1 exit(c(2)) .
0 exit(a(2)) .
3MS SUCCESS
 <- succeeds(a(2),0) .
```

Next we look at some variations on the normal Prolog execution methods, specifically, breadth first evaluation, Query-the-User, and term reduction (i.e, expression evaluation). We use our Prolog interpreter in Prolog techniques as the point of departure.

Breadth-First

The standard Prolog strategy is a depth first search. The body of a rule is stacked in front of any other goals that may be on the goal stack. To get the effect of breadth first search, a goal *queue* can be used instead of a stack. The body of a rule can be placed at the end of the queue. The only problem is how to handle failure. The queue of goals is actually structured; a failure may require some other goals (descendants of siblings) to be taken off of the queue also.

The approach taken will be to explicitly maintain the and/or tree, growing it in a breadth first fashion.

A difference list (see page 136) is kept, which has on it all of the conjunctions to be proven. It starts with the initial goal. A conjunction is selected (there is only one initially), and a single goal is selected from that conjunction. For each unifying clause, a new conjunction is added to the list. Each new conjunction consists of the old conjunction with the selected goal replaced by the body of the corresponding clause.

The basic process is quite simple. The only complication arises in maintaining the bindings of variables. The built-in unification of the base Prolog cannot be used, since many alternatives to a given goal may all need different bindings to the same variable, and we want to expand these alternatives simultaneously. We will discuss that below. Here we describe the basic algorithm for the propositional case (no variables). We use the following object program as an example.

```
a <- b & c.
a <- d.
b <- a.
b.
c <- c1.
c.
b1.
c1.
```

```
Initial goal list: a . *
```

Note the potential infinite recursion with a and b. There are two clauses that unify with a, giving a new list of conjunctions: (b & c). d . *. If the first conjunction (b & c) is selected, and b is selected from that, then again two clauses unify. These are

```
b <- a.
b.
```

Substituting the body of the first clause for b in (b & c) gives the goal (a & c). The second clause has an empty body, so substituting that for b in (b & c) produces the goal c. The new conjunctions are placed at the end of the list to give a round-robin scheduling effect. If it were placed at the beginning of the list, the standard Prolog depth first strategy would be duplicated. This gives the new list of conjunctions

```
d . (a & c) . c . *
```

Continuing in this way, the goal d fails to unify, so it is removed from the list entirely, and the process is repeated. The goal list is now: (a & c) . c . *. With (a & c) selected and with a selected from within that, the two clauses for a generate c. (b & c & c) . (d & c) . *.

The goal c unifies with two clauses, one of which has no body. The one with no body causes the original goal to be completely solved, so we could quit there, with success. However, it is easier programming to put the special token `true` on the goal list, and stop when it comes to the front. So the new goal list is

(b & c & c) . (d & c) . c1 . true. *

The goal b in (b & c & c) is replaced with the bodies of its two clauses,

c1 . true . (a & c & c) . (c & c) . *

The goal c1 gets replaced with its (empty) body, causing the special token "true" to get placed in the list of goals to be tried.

true . (a & c & c) . (c & c) . true . *

However, the next goal in the list is `true`, so we stop, realizing that we have succeeded in finding at least one solution to the original goal a. The potential difficulty with the infinitely recursive b<-a, a<-b has been no problem.

Here is a console listing of the execution:

success(a.X - X).

```
1MS SUCCESS
<- success(a .
(b & c) . d .
(a & c) . c .
(b & c & c) . (d & c) . c1 . true .
(a & c & c) . (c & c) . true . V1 -
(b & c) . d .
(a & c) . c .
(b & c & c) . (d & c) . c1 . true .
(a & c & c) . (c & c) . true . V1) .
```

The binding for X is a list of all the goals that were added to the initial stream (a.X - X) during the course of finding a solution to a. Looking at the first five goals in the list: a is the initial goal. It reduces to (b & c), and (d . (b & c)) reduces to (a & c), and c . d cannot reduce.

Here is the program for a breadth first ground (propositional) theorem prover. Success(Goal_difference_list) succeeds when there is a solution to one of the goals on the goal list, using clause(Goal <- Body) to define the ground Prolog program. Each goal may be a conjunction of subgoals. A solution is indicated by reducing a goal to the single atom `true`:

success(true.* - *).

Otherwise, select some one of the alternatives, select a subgoal from that one, compute the set of bodies of clauses whose heads unify with the subgoal, add to the list all the new alternative goals just generated, and repeat until a success is found.

```
success(Goal.Goals - MoreGoals) <-
   select_a_goal(Goal, Head, Rest) &
   set_of(Body, clause(Head <- Body), Bodies) &
   make_more_goals(Bodies, Rest, MoreGoals - Y) &
   success(Goals - Y).
```

To select a goal, simply select the first goal in the list of alternatives. To select a subgoal from that, select the first conjunct. Use the special marker no_more to signal that a conjunction is exhausted. (This plays the role that nil plays in lists.)

```
select_a_goal(G&B,G,B)<-/.
select_a_goal(B,B,no_more).
```

Each matching clause found by set_of gives rise to another alternative. If N clauses match, then N alternatives are generated by the predicate make_more_goals. It replaces the selected subgoal with the body of each of the N clauses. These N alternatives are added to the end of the list of alternatives. This predicate also turns the regular list produced by the set_of predicate into a difference list. If there are no (more) of these goals to make, then we generate the empty difference list.

```
make_more_goals(nil,*,X - X).
```

If the replaced subgoal was the last in its alternative goal, then we have only to make the regular list into a difference list.

```
make_more_goals(B.Bodies, no_more, B.Bods - X)<-
   make_more_goals(Bodies, no_more, Bods - X).
```

In the general case, we have to add each body onto the front of the conjunction of the remaining subgoals. We do this by recursing down the list of bodies, using conjunct(B,R,G) to add a body B onto the front of the remaining subgoals R to produce the conjunct G.

```
make_more_goals(Body.Bodies,Rest,Goal.Goals - X) <-
   conjunct(Body, Rest, Goal) &
   make_more_goals(Bodies, Rest, Goals - X).
```

conjunct(Conjunct1,Conjunct2,Conjunct3) puts Conjunct1 and Conjunct2 together to make Conjunct3, similarly to append for lists. However, there is no nil end-of-list marker, and the token true needs special handling.

```
conjunct(true, C, C) <- /.
conjunct(A & B, C, A & D) <- / & conjunct(B, C, D).
conjunct(A, C, A & C).
```

Note the / used because of the final catchall clause.

This interpreter continues to reduce goals even after a solution has been found. It stops when the token true comes to the front of the list of alternatives. This token must have been placed there by a previous step. In order to stop immediately upon computing a success, `success(Goals - Y)` can be replaced by

```
(MoreGoals is true.* & / | success(Goals - Y))
```

in the last subgoal in the second clause for `success`. This will cause the predicate to immediately succeed without a final cycle through the list of goals.

What we have not shown is how to keep track of variable bindings. Because each selected goal can give rise to more than one alternative goal, we cannot use only the underlying Prolog unification mechanism. We leave this as an exercise for the reader.

Query-the-User

We described Query-the-User on page 115. The user and the program are both viewed as capable of answering queries about whether a certain goal is true. If the program cannot prove something, it has the option of asking the user if there is a true instance. This is a simple addition to our interpreter.

```
succeeds(true) <-/.
succeeds(A & B) <- / & succeeds(A) & succeeds(B).
succeeds(A) <-
    clause(A<-Goal) &
    succeeds(Goal).
succeeds(A) <- query_the_user(A).
```

In the example on page 115 we wrote several rules to explicitly Query-the-User. These can be eliminated if the interpreter supports this function directly.

Term Reduction and Expression Evaluation

It is often convenient to use expressions that can be evaluated to give a solution. In IBM Prolog, we can write expressions such as `A := B+C`, which succeeds when A can be unified with the sum of B and C. However, we cannot call a goal such as `p(X, B+C)` and have the expression B+C evaluated. We have to use a temporary variable and an extra predicate call such as `A := B+C & p(X,A)`. Except for special built-in procedures such as `:=`, Prolog does not evaluate arguments to procedures.

Such evaluations can be established in a metainterpreter. Let `eval(Expression, Value)` actually perform the evaluation. For example,

```
eval(A+B,C) <-  C := A + B.
eval(A-B,C) <-  C := A - B.
```

(These two clauses can be generalized as `eval(E,V) <- V:=E`. However, we may also want to evaluate expressions containing operators that are not built in.)

If we have an interpreter with this kind of modification, we can write programs to run on this interpreter that include evaluable functions, such as

```
p(X, N) <- p(X, N-1).
```

rather than the standard IBM Prolog

```
p(X, N) <- N1:=N-1 & p(X, N1).
```

The interpreter evaluates every term in a goal before looking for a rule to match. If no evaluations can be performed, then a term evaluates to itself:

```
succeeds(true) <-/.
succeeds(A & B) <- / & succeeds(A) & succeeds(B).
succeeds(A) <-
    evaluate_term(A, ValA)  &
    clause(ValA <- Goal) &
    succeeds(Goal).

evaluate_term(A, ValA) <-
    (A =.. F.Args) &
    evaluate_term_list(Args, Evaluated_args) &
    (Evaluated_A =.. F.Evaluated_args) &
    final_evaluation(Evaluated_A, ValA).

final_evaluation(Evaluated_A, ValA) <-
    eval(Evaluated_A, ValA).
final_evaluation(Evaluated_A, Evaluated_A).
```

We leave it as an exercise to write the predicate `evaluate_term_list`.

"Compiling" Meta-level Functions

Instead of running our programs using a metalevel interpreter, we can often compile them so that they run as they would have, but with the efficiency of direct execution in Prolog. Here we do this for Query-the-User and two other metadeclarations, and for proof-tree extraction.

The compiler translates a predicate P if the source program contains the fact `askable(P)`, which says that predicate P should be asked of the user if it cannot be otherwise proven (see page 115). In addition, the declaration `unique(P)` says that P is to give only one solution. The declaration `assertable(P)` says that P is to be remembered whenever it is successfully proven. `convert(P, Q)` converts all goals G in the body of P to an appropriate goal that takes into consideration the effects of the declarations. Unit clauses are unchanged. If a clause has a body, then we call `convert_body`.

```
convert(P<-Body,P<-QtuBody) <-
    convert_body(Body, QtuBody).
```

If a clause has no body, then it is unchanged. The IBM Prolog built-in predicate A =/ B succeeds when A does not unify with B.

```
convert(P,P)<- (P =/ (*<-*)).
```

We make the simplifying assumption that the body of a clause is either a single goal, or a conjunction. If the body is a conjunction, call convert_goal for the first single goal in the conjunction, and call convert_body recursively for the rest of the conjunction.

```
convert_body(A & B,QA & QB) <-
    convert_body(A,QA) &
    convert_body(B,QB).
convert_body(A,QA) <- (A =/ (* & *)) &
    convert_goal(A,QA).
```

Since there are three declarations, askable, assertable and unique, there are eight possible combinations for each procedure. This table gives the correspondence between each combination and the converted procedure. Assume that the goal to be converted is P.

askable	assertable	unique	converted procedure
no	no	no	P
no	no	yes	unq(P)
no	yes	no	asrt(P)
yes	no	no	qtu(P)
no	yes	yes	unqa(P)
yes	yes	no	qtua(P)
yes	no	yes	qtuu(P)
yes	yes	yes	qtuua(P)

To convert a goal, we consider the eight possible combinations of declarations according to the above table.

```
convert_goal(A,qtuua(A))<-
    askable(A) &  unique(A) & assertable(A).
convert_goal(A,qtua(A)) <-
    askable(A) & ¬unique(A) & assertable(A).
convert_goal(A,unqa(A)) <-
    ¬askable(A) &  unique(A) & assertable(A).
convert_goal(A,asrt(A)) <-
    ¬askable(A) & ¬unique(A) & assertable(A).
```

```
convert_goal(A,qtuu(A)) <-
    askable(A) &  unique(A) & ¬assertable(A).
convert_goal(A,qtu(A))  <-
    askable(A) & ¬unique(A) & ¬assertable(A).
convert_goal(A,unq(A))  <-
    ¬askable(A) &  unique(A) & ¬assertable(A).
convert_goal(A,   A )  <-
    ¬askable(A) & ¬unique(A) & ¬assertable(A).
```

These procedures are defined as follows.

```
unq(P) <- P & /.

asrt(A) <- A & remember_assertable(A).

qtu(P)<-P.
qtu(P)<-query_user(P,*).

qtuu(P)<-qtu(P) & /.

unqa(P) <- unq(P) & remember_assertable(P).

qtua(P)<-qtu(P) & remember_assertable(P).

qtuua(P)<-qtuu(P) & remember_assertable(P).
```

The next interesting development in compiling metalevel functions is the definition of `remember_assertable(P)`. The basic idea is that we will keep the solution of an assertable goal as a unit clause with the *clause name* `proved`. We could alternatively have used `proved` as a predicate name, but in IBM Prolog using a clause name is slightly more efficient, and has other benefits. See Appendix A for more discussion of clause names. As a refinement, we will not record a solution if it is an instance of an already recorded solution.

The goal `instance(P,Q)` succeeds whenever P is an instance of Q. If there is a unit clause with the clause name `proved` that unifies with P, then we do nothing. Otherwise, we add the unit clause P with the clause name `proved`. There is an IBM Prolog built-in predicate `ax(P,Q,N)` that succeeds when Q is a clause whose head unifies with P, with clause name N. The goal `addax(P,N)` adds the clause P to the current rule set with clause name N.

```
remember_assertable(P) <-
    ax(P,Q,proved) &
    instance(P,Q) & /.
remember_assertable(P) <- addax(P,proved).
```

Being an instance of something is more restrictive than unifying with something. Substitutions may go only one way: Only variables in the more general Q may be bound when unifying with P.

We give two definitions, one for `instance`, and one for the related predicate mg, for "more general." Here and in Appendix B we use the IBM Prolog built-in routines `copy` and `=*=` to define the predicate mg(Q,P), which succeeds when Q is more general than P.   P `=*=` Q succeeds when P and Q are the same term except for renaming of variables.

```
mg(Q,P) <- copy(Q,QQ) & copy(P,PP) &
    QQ = PP &
    P =*= PP & ¬(Q =*= QQ).
```

After the terms are copied, the copies are unified. Unifying the copies avoids having to bind variables in the input terms. Q is more general than P if the unification binds only variables in Q. P `=*=` PP says that no variables in P were bound. ¬(Q `=*=` QQ) says that some variable in Q was bound. The goal mg(Q,P) differs from `instance(P,Q)` when Q and P are the same. In that case mg fails but `instance` succeeds.

It is possible to write `instance` without resorting to these special IBM Prolog built-in routines. To underscore the difference in implementation and the slight difference in meaning, we use the name `instance`, rather than mg. We want `instance(P,Q)` to succeed when P is an instance of Q. To accomplish this, we bind all the variables in P to ground terms not appearing in P or Q, then unify with Q. In order not to exit the predicate with terms bound, we enclose the body in the ¬¬ predicate. ¬¬(A) succeeds if A succeeds, but no variables are bound.

```
instance(P,Q) <- ¬¬(make_ground(P) & Q = P ).
```

To make P ground, we get a list of its variables and recurse down the list. We want to bind the variables of P to terms that should never appear in Q.

```
make_ground(P) <-
    listvar(P,L) & bind_var_list(L,1).

bind_var_list(nil,*).
bind_var_list("//##**@@"(N).Xs, N) <-
    N1 := N+1 & bind_var_list(Xs,N1).
```

On page 164 we saw how to write an interpreter that, when it succeeds in proving some predicate P, also provides a proof tree for P. Here we show how to translate a program automatically into a new program that will provide proofs of success when run directly in Prolog.

The idea is to translate each rule into another rule that will return its proof, if it succeeds. An extra argument is used to carry the proof along. The proof of a fact is just the fact itself. The proof of A & B is more interesting; it is ProofA & ProofB, where ProofA is a proof of A, and ProofB is a proof of B.

The predicate convert(Clause,NewClause) succeeds when NewClause is like Clause, but contains an extra argument that collects a proof.

```
convert(Head<-Body, NewHead<-NewBody) <-
    convert_unit(Head, NewHead, BodyProof) &
    convert_body(Body, NewBody, BodyProof).

convert(UnitClause, NewUnitClause) <-
    convert_unit(Head, NewHead, Head).
```

When convert_unit(Head,NewHead,BodyProof) succeeds, NewHead is like Head, with BodyProof as the first argument.

```
convert_unit(Head, NewHead, BodyProof) <-
    (Head =.. P.HeadArgs) &
    (NewHead =.. P.BodyProof.HeadArgs).

convert_body(B1 & B2,
             NewB1 & NewB2,
             ProofB1 & ProofB2)
    <- / &
    convert_unit(B1, NewB1, ProofB1) &
    convert_body(B2, NewB2, ProofB2).
convert_body(B1, NewB1, ProofB1) <-
    convert_unit(B1, NewB1, ProofB1).
```

So far this is fairly straightforward. Conversion of programs containing | is more interesting. The same variable Proof is used in both translated disjuncts, since in the final proof only one of them will be needed.

```
convert_body(B1 | B2,
             (NewB1 & (Proof = Pb1))
              | NewB2 & (Proof = Pb2)),
             Proof) <-
    convert_body(B1, NewB1, Pb1) &
    convert_body(B2, NewB2, Pb2).
```

We leave it as an exercise to see how the programs for proof tree extraction and metadeclaration can be combined.

3.2.2 Graph Searching

Many problems, particularly in symbolic processing, are naturally written down and solved using graphs. Nodes in a graph can represent different situations, as in the water jug problem on page 55. The connections among the nodes can represent allowable actions that take us from one state to another, such as pouring water in the jug problem.

For example, in a chess-playing program, the nodes may represent positions and the connections represent legal moves; in a parsing problem, the nodes may represent different partial parses for a string and the connections represent grammatical extensions of a given parse for a given string; planning the strategy for a legal defense in court can be represented as different possible legal situations (discovery, trial, appeal, etc.) and the conditions that must hold to get from one to another.

In these examples, solving a problem means starting at a given node (the *initial state*) and following the connections (also called *arcs* or *edges*) until a node is found that satisfies a given condition. The sequence of nodes or arcs that are traversed is called, naturally enough, a *path*. Whether we are interested in the nodes or the connections depends on the nature of the problem. Since a given graph is mathematically *dual* with one made by turning nodes into connections and connections into nodes, the distinction between nodes and connections is no real problem.

Much attention has been given to graph-searching algorithms for such problems as: how to find a path to a satisfactory node in the least time; how to find the shortest path to a satisfactory node. There are many refinements to graph searching that can be expressed in terms of knowledge about a particular problem being represented. For example, in the Chess problem, one could look last at any paths that lead to substantial disadvantage in materiel. This strategy would make sacrifice plays the last to be considered. Whether a node is an advantage or not is something that no general graph-searching algorithm can decide; it is *domain-specific knowledge*.

Next we examine just the basics of how to represent and search a graph. Later we look at the *alpha-beta* algorithm for game playing, in Section 3.2.4, "Playing Games and Alpha-beta Pruning."

Representing a Graph

As discussed in 3.1, "How to Structure Prolog Programs," the first decision to be made is whether to represent the graph as facts or as a term. We will first consider a graph represented as facts. If the graph does not change, then that poses no logical problem. If the situation requires frequent changes to the graph, then representing the graph as a term avoids the use of `addax` and `delax`. The detailed structure of a node is not important for the discussion of general graph searching, although it may be important for search strategies requiring knowledge of the problem.

In these examples a node is represented by the fact

```
node(Id, State)
```

and a legal transition by the fact

```
arc(ArcId,Id1,Id2)
```

which names the connection between two nodes. The transitions are directed; there is an arc from Id1 to Id2. A *path* between two nodes is represented by a list of arcs taken to get from one node to the other.

Paths in a Graph

The predicate `path(Start_node,Path,End_node)` expresses the fact that `Path` is a path that originates at `Start_node` and terminates at `End_node`. Consider the following graph

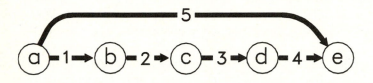

represented as five facts:

```
arc(1,a,b). arc(2,b,c). arc(3,c,d).
arc(4,d,e). arc(5,a,e).
```

In this example,

```
path(a,1.2.3.4.nil,e)
path(a,5.nil,e)
```

are both true, indicating the fact that there are two paths from node a to the node e. The following rules define this relation declaratively.

```
path(Node, nil, Node).
path(Node1, Arc.Arcs, NodeN) <-
    arc(Arc, Node1, Node2) .&
    path(Node2, Arcs, NodeN).
```

Procedurally, this definition will start at Node1, and explore in a depth first fashion nodes reachable from Node1.

Let us say that a satisfactory node is one that satisfies the predicate

```
satisfactory(Node) <- ....
```

To find a path from one node to another node having a desired property;

```
find_goal(Start, Path, Goal) <-
    path(Start, Path, Goal) &
    satisfactory(Goal).
```

Graphs containing cycles need special attention (recall the water jug problem). Although the above rules for path finding are logically correct, they are also satisfied by infinite paths. Prolog may well start exploring an infinite path before it looks at others. Of course, it will never stop exploring the infinite path. To avoid this, we can add the condition that the arc to be explored does not lead to any node that has already been visited.

Thinking about this as a process in time may help. The path returned by the predicate represents the sequence of arcs to take *in the future* to get from this node to some other. We must keep a *history* of the arcs already tried, which are to be avoided. The revised predicate can be read:

```
path(Start, Path, Goal, Seen)
```

succeeds when Path leads from Start to Goal, avoiding all arcs in Seen.

```
path(Node, nil, Node, Seen).
path(Node1, Arc.Arcs, NodeN, Seen) <-
      arc(Arc, Node1, Node2) &
      ¬member(Node2, Seen) &
      path(Node2, Arcs, NodeN, Node1.Seen).
```

Consider the following graph derived from the previous example by adding arc(6, b, a). If this is used before arc(2, b, c), then our first version of path would get stuck in the loop in this graph.

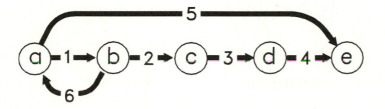

Here are some of the ways the procedure succeeds for the graph given above:

```
path(a, 1 . 2 . 3 . 4 . nil, e, nil) .
path(b, 6 . nil, a, nil) .
path(a, 5 . nil, e, nil) .
```

Representing cyclic graphs as term structures is discussed on page 186.

Breadth-First

The above programs search a graph in a depth first order. The current path is extended until the goal or a dead end is reached. Since Prolog executes in a depth first manner, there is no need to explicitly maintain the list of paths to be extended. That information is implicitly maintained in the interpreter's internal control information.

We shall describe a graph searching program that explicitly maintains a record of paths to be extended. When the record is maintained as a *stack*, then we get depth first search. When it is maintained as a *queue*, we get breadth first search. As the depth first strategy is rather similar to our Prolog interpreters in 3.2.1, "Meta-level Programming," we will describe just the breadth first approach here. Having reached a node N by some path P, N has now become one of our *frontier* nodes. If there are arcs from it to nodes N1, . . . ,Nk, then path P can be extended to paths P1, . . . ,Pk. P1 extends P by adding N1, and so on. N1, . . . Nk become part of the new frontier. Associated with each node in the frontier is the path used to reach it. Since a node is uniquely determined by the path leading to it, our list of frontier nodes is actually a list of paths — each path leading to a frontier node. We can picture this as

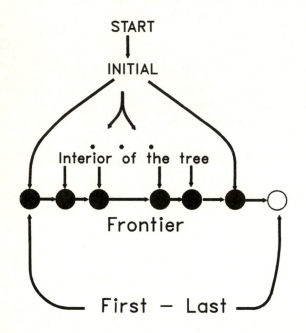

Each path may in general be extended in several ways. Each way of extending the path gives rise to a new path. We will pick the path at the head of the list and extend it to several new paths. Each of these new paths is added to the list, and the path that was just extended is deleted. As mentioned earlier, we wish to add the new paths to the end of the list. This makes a queue the appropriate structure to represent this list.

An efficient way to represent a queue is by using a difference list. The list will contain all the paths corresponding to the current frontier. Although the list conceptually contains entire paths, in structure-shared Prolog implementations only the most recent element in a path is actually generated at each successive step. The previous path is pointed to as part of the newly extended path. Thus a list of the most recent element in each path represents the frontier of the tree being grown through the graph from the initial node. Note the following design decisions, which affect the structure of the Prolog program.

1. The paths that can be extended are kept on a difference list. This allows appending new elements by using unification only (see page 136).

2. Since we do not append individual paths together, each path is represented by an ordinary list, whose elements are *arcs*. A representation of a path as a list of nodes would have been simpler, but contains less information (since we allow more than one arc between two nodes). The initial case must be represented by a dummy arc between a special "start" node and the true initial node with which the search is to begin. This arc by convention is labeled 0.

3. An arc is represented by an identifying number. The result of this decision is that the "from" and "to" nodes are not directly available by unification in a call, but require a goal in the body to return these nodes.

In addition there is one more major decision to be made; whether to generate all extensions to a path at once, or one at a time.

1. Generating all extensions to a given path requires that the `extend` predicate return a difference list. Here we use a predicate called `bag_of`, which is like the `set_of` predicate discussed on page 79, except that it does not eliminate duplicates from the list items of items it produces. The definition of `bag_of` is

   ```
   bag_of(V,G,L) <- compute(list,V,G,nil,L) & /.
   bag_of(V,G,nil).
   ```

   This generates the list in standard form, and we then convert it to a difference list.

2. Generating one extension at a time requires that the search routine keep track of which extensions remain, but does not require use of a `bag_of` predicate. This can conveniently be done by keeping a standard list of what extensions have been made from the current path. If the branching factor is small, searching this list is not expensive. However, some other technique could be used to represent this information.

Shown below is an implementation that generates all extensions at once. Observe the use of difference lists. Note how the description makes dealing with the data structure simpler than in some procedural languages. In effect, we simply have to draw a picture (using terms) of the data structures before and after. The use of difference lists makes the rule very concise, so that the English describing the predicate sounds wordy. In these examples, it is worth studying how an `append` is done by unifying the list extension in the head of the rule.

We define two infix operators:

```
op(";", rl, 50).
op("is_in_path", rl, 50).
```

The "`;`" operator is used to form the difference list of paths to the frontier. Each path in this list is itself a list formed from the conventional "`.`" operator. `search` takes two arguments, a `Frontier` and a `Path` to a satisfactory node. `search(Frontier, Path)` succeeds when `Path` is an extension of one of the `Frontier` nodes. `Frontier`, a difference list of paths from root, has this structure: `((Arc.Path);Otherpaths) - Tail`.

The first clause covers the basis case, where the current path leads to a satisfactory node. This occurs if the current `Arc` goes into a satisfactory node. This clause is the one that actually binds output.

```
search(List , Arc.P) <-
    ¬emptylist(List) &
    List = ((Arc.P);*)-* &
    arc(Arc, From_Node, To_Node) &
    satisfactory(To_Node).
```

The second clause tells us that `Path` leads to a satisfactory node *if* the current path is extended to some new paths *and* the path in the `Frontier` extended with new paths leads to a satisfactory node.

```
search( ((Path;Frontier) - New_paths), Good_path) <-
    extend(Path, New_paths - Future) &
    search(Frontier - Future, Good_path).
```

A path whose most recent addition is `Arc` and whose earlier additions were `Path` can be extended to a set of `New_paths` *if*

- `Paths` is the list of all extensions where

  - `Arc` leads into `Current_node`, and
  - `New_arc` leads from the `Current_node` to `New_node`, and
  - `New_node` is not in the earlier `Path`, and
- `New_paths` is the difference list form of `Paths`.

Expressing this definition in Prolog:

```
extend(List, New_paths) <-
    ¬var(List) &
    List is (Arc.Path) &
    bag_of(New_arc.Arc.Path,
        arc(Arc, From_node, Current_node) &
            arc(New_arc, Current_node, New_node) &
            ¬(New_node is_in_path Path),
        Paths) &
    makedifflist(Paths, New_paths).
```

Here are the subroutines used in the above program.

```
makedifflist(nil, A - A).
makedifflist(A.B, (A;C) - X) <-
    makedifflist(B, C - X).

emptylist(X - X) <- var(X).

(New_node is_in_path Arc.nil)  <-
    arc(Arc, *, New_node).
(New_node is_in_path Arc.Path) <- / &
    arc(Arc, New_node,*).
(New_node is_in_path Arc.Path) <-
    New_node is_in_path Path.
```

Given the following graph and the fact that node f is a satisfactory node, we show how this program executes.

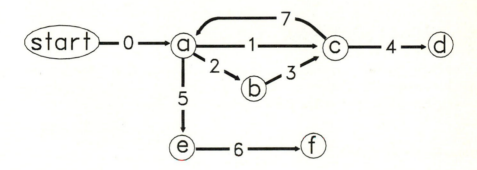

```
satisfactory(f).

arc(0,start,a).
arc(2,a,b). arc(1,a,c). arc(5,a,e). arc(3,b,c).
arc(7,c,a). arc(4,c,d). arc(6,e,f).
```

Arc number 0 from start into a indicates a is the initial frontier:

```
    test(P) <- search(((0 .nil);X) - X, P).
```

Here we find all nonrepeating paths to the satisfactory node f.

```
    test(L) & write(L) & fail.

(6 . 5 . 0 . nil) .
FAIL
```

Solutions involving paths with cycles can be found by removing the check
¬(New_node is_in_path Path) from the extend procedure. In that case
we get the following behavior:

test(L) & write(L) & fail.

```
(6 . 5 . 0 . nil) .
(6 . 5 . 7 . 1 . 0 . nil) .
(6 . 5 . 7 . 3 . 2 . 0 . nil) .
(6 . 5 . 7 . 1 . 7 . 1 . 0 . nil) .
(6 . 5 . 7 . 3 . 2 . 7 . 1 . 0 . nil) .
(6 . 5 . 7 . 1 . 7 . 3 . 2 . 0 . nil) .
(6 . 5 . 7 . 1 . 7 . 1 . 7 . 1 . 0 . nil) .
(6 . 5 . 7 . 3 . 2 . 7 . 3 . 2 . 0 . nil) .
(6 . 5 . 7 . 3 . 2 . 7 . 1 . 7 . 1 . 0 . nil) .
(6 . 5 . 7 . 1 . 7 . 3 . 2 . 7 . 1 . 0 . nil) .
(6 . 5 . 7 . 1 . 7 . 1 . 7 . 3 . 2 . 0 . nil) .
(6 . 5 . 7 . 1 . 7 . 1 . 7 . 1 . 7 . 1 . 0 . nil) .
. . .
```

We have done a breadth first search of the graph, using difference lists to avoid
the expense of appending lists. We have used the bag_of predicate as an easy
and efficient way of generating all extensions to a given path. This is more
complex to express than the previous program which used a depth first strategy,
because that is Prolog's inherent search method.

Graphs as Cyclic Data Structures

The above search routines searched static graphs. Because the graphs did not
change during computation, they were most conveniently represented by
collections of facts. Now we look at representing changing graphs as data
structures. We could use the metainterpreter technique from page 161, which
implemented addax and delax by passing the current set of clauses as an
argument. However, this is a good place to illustrate how to use cyclic data
structures. As we shall see, it can be done, but not quite as naturally as in
languages that can reassign bound variables.

Here are some routines that construct and manipulate a linked list of values.
Each node is represented by a term of the form

node(Location, Left_link, Right_link, Value).

Nodes at the ends of the list have a variable in the appropriate link. In this
example, new nodes can be added only at the ends of the linked list. Trying to
change the linked list by adding a link between a and b, say, causes an error.

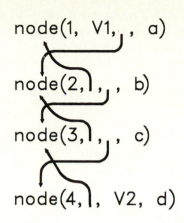

node(1, V1, , , a)

node(2, l, , , b)

node(3, l, , , c)

node(4, l, , V2, d)

The predicate `addi(Location, Value, Linked_list)` holds if a `Linked_list` has a certain `Value` at a specified `Location`. The list is ordered by `Node_id`. First we define some infix operators:

```
op("<",lr,100).
op(">",rl,100).
op("is",rl,50).

(A < B)   <- lt(A,B).
(A > B)   <- lt(B,A).
(A is A).
```

A list L with no nodes is represented simply by an unbound variable. So for the basis case, we make one entry with value V and `node_id` V, with unbound left and right pointers.

```
addi(N,V,L) <- L is node(N,*,*,V) & /.
```

In the recursive case, we test to see if the N to be inserted is less than or greater than the `node_id` K of the node currently pointed to in the list. If N is less than K, then we insert to the left:

```
addi(N,V,L)<-
    L is node(K,Left,Right,*)  &
    N < K &
    addi(N,V,Left) & /.
```

If N is greater than K, then insert to the right.

```
addi(N,V,L)<-
        L is node(K,Left,Right,*)  &
        N > K &
        addi(N,V,Right).
```

Cycles are produced in the structures because the `Left` value is a pointer to a term whose `Right` pointer is the original term. Naturally, `addi` can be used in several ways. We can check that an element is in a particular place, or we can add a new element at an end of the list. Here are some examples of `addi` in execution. IBM Prolog represents cyclic structures by using `n@` to point to the nth enclosing term. In `f(g(1,2@))`, `2@` refers to the term beginning with `f`. It is a finite representation of the term

```
f(g(1, f(g(1, f(g(1, . . .)))))).
```

Here is a clause to test `addi`.

```
additest(L) <-  /* add nodes in this order */
    addi(4,d,L) & addi(3,c,L) & addi(5,e,L) &
    addi(2,b,L) & addi(6,f,L) & addi(1,a,L).
```

Setting the goal `additest(L)` should set up the following structure.

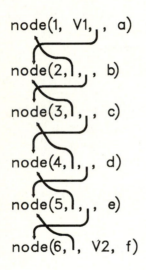

```
node(1, V1, , a)



node(2, l, , b)



node(3, l, , c)



node(4, l, , d)



node(5, l, , e)



node(6, l, V2, f)
```

If we now actually issue the goal at the terminal, we get the following result. (For easier reading, we have indented the output to show the nesting structure.)

```
additest(L).

1MS SUCCESS
 <- additest(
  node(4,
        node(3,
             node(2,
                  node(1,V1,2@,a),
                  2@,
                  b),
             2@,
             c),
        node(5,
```

```
                    2@,
                    node(6,2@,V2,f),
                    e),
           d)) .
```

additest(L) & addi(2,V,L) & write(V) & nl.

```
2MS SUCCESS
 <- additest(
 node(4,
       node(3,
             node(2,
                   node(1,V1,2@,a),
                   2@,
                   b),
             2@,
             c),
     . . .
```

addi(1,a,L) & addi(2,b,L).

```
OMS SUCCESS
 <- addi(1, a,node(1, V1, node(2,2 @ ,V2,b),a)) &
 addi(2,b,node(1, V1, node(2,2 @ ,V2 ,b),a)) .
```

addi(1,a,L) & addi(3,c,L).

```
1MS SUCCESS
 <- addi(1, a,node(1, V1, node(3,2 @ ,V2,c),a)) &
 addi(3,c,node(1, V1, node(3,2 @ ,V2 ,c),a)) .
```

Trying to add node 2 between nodes 1 and 3 causes an error.

addi(1, a,L) & addi(3,c,L) & addi(2,b,L).

```
* local stack overflow *
912MS ERROR
```

One can write a similar de l i predicate, which deletes a node from a linked list. However, de l i will cause all of the list to be copied: In order to delete a link, or to add a node in between two others already established, neighboring nodes must be modified. Since Prolog variables cannot be reassigned, new ones that point to each other must be created. But then *their* neighbors must be modified to point to the new nodes, and so on.

Except for variable assignment, linked structures of this kind cannot be modified without copying. That is usually an expensive operation. The fact that a variable cannot have its value changed once it is bound (except by backtracking), is a cornerstone of Prolog's declarative reading. Here, however, this feature causes considerable inefficiency.

This problem can be partially solved by recognizing that each pointer in a linked list is not just one pointer, but a sequence of pointers. This is in fact the dominant "message-stream" programming methodology used in Concurrent Prolog, as described in Shapiro and Takeuchi (1983). By binding a variable to a pair `Value.Future`, where future is a variable that can be assigned a new value, lists can be dynamically modified. This is only a partial solution, since old values are still reachable, and cannot be garbage collected.

Here are routines that use this "sequence-of-pointers" idea. In the `replace(Old,New)` predicate, `Old` and `New` are two linked lists that are the same, except that the starting node of `Old` has been replaced by `New`. The internal representation of a node is not visible except to the predicates `left_node` and `right_node`. `left_node(Node, Left)` holds when `Left` is the node to the left of `Node` in the linked list; similarly for `right_node(Node,Right)`. We now represent a node as

```
n(Left, Value, Right)
```

where `Left` and `Right` are considered to be *pointers* to the appropriate neighbors in the linked list. For a three-node linked list of a, b, and c, this could be visualized as:

$$n(nil, a, \quad) \qquad n(\quad, b, \quad) \qquad n(\quad, c, nil)$$

We picture a sequence of pointers as a vertical stack, with the most recent assignment next to the bottom. The bottom is an unbound variable that sometime in the future will get assigned to the next pointer and a new "future" variable:

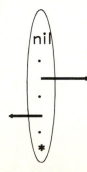

Then the above graph can be represented as

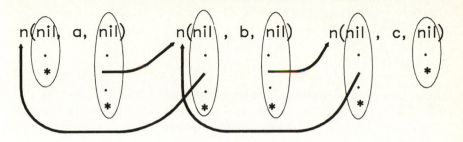

Here, the ending variables are used to "replace" values. "Replacing" b with d would result in

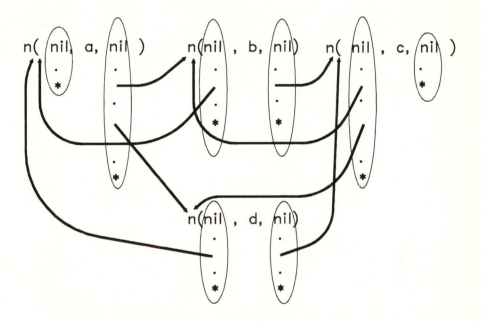

The current structure can be found by taking the most recent nonvariable entry on every pointer sequence. By tagging the pointer with a "context" key, the structure associated with any particular context could be reconstructed. For example, if the linked data structure represented a game board, then the context could represent the move that established a particular value. In this way the state of the board at any given move could be determined.

Here is the program. insert(Old, New) inserts the list New into the list Old just to the left of the node pointed to by Old.

```
insert(Old,New) <-
  find_leftmost_node(New,LM) &
  left_node(Old,Left) &
  link(Left,LM) &
  find_rightmost_node(New,RM) &
  link(RM,Old).
```

As we see, replace(Old,Node) makes Node into a linked list with all the elements of Old, except for the node pointed to by Old. In effect, Node replaces the top node in Old, when viewed by the Node pointer. The Old pointer gives the original value.

```
replace(Old,Node) <-
  left_node(Old,Left) & link(Left,Node) &
  right_node(Old,Right) & link(Node,Right).
```

The following predicates are used with our linked-list data representation. (Recall that a node is of the form n(Left,Value,Right).) Left and Right are sequences of pointers. The most recent pointer is the last nonvariable in the sequence. The sequence ends with a variable that can be bound to future values. Since Prolog variables cannot be overwritten, a sequence of values is used, rather than a single value. To find the leftmost node in a list, move to the left until the next node to the left is empty.

```
find_leftmost_node(Node,Node) <-
    left_node(Node,L) &
    empty_node(L) & /.
find_leftmost_node(List,Node) <-
    left_node(List,Left) &
     find_leftmost_node(Left,Node).
```

We find the rightmost node in a similar way.

We can join together two linked lists Left and Right. The right pointer of Left must be made to point to Right, and the left pointer of Right must be made to point to Left. Note that the operation is symmetric from the point of view of Left and Right. Unlike more "normal" Prolog programs, there is no third argument which is used to represent the result. Either of the pointers Left or Right may now be used to access the joined list.

This program has the interesting property that two lists can be joined before either one is created. We leave it as an exercise for the reader to see what happens when one or the other list is empty, and also what happens when both are empty?

```
link(Left,Right) <-
    left_seq(Right,Left_of_right) &
    extend(Left_of_right,Left) &
    right_seq(Left,Right_of_left) &
    extend(Right_of_left,Right).
```

In addition to `left_node` and `right_node`, the following procedures are needed to implement this particular representation of a node:

```
get_value(n(*,Value,*),Value).

/*   node is linked list of 1 element */
make_node(Value, n(L,Value,R)) <-
    empty_sequence(L) & empty_sequence(R).

/*  Left is to the left of Node  */
left_node(n(LL,*,*), L) <-  find_last(LL,L).

right_node(n(*,*,RR), R) <- find_last(RR,R).

left_seq(n(LL,*,*), L) <-  find_last_seq(LL,L).

right_seq(n(*,*,RR), R) <- find_last_seq(RR,R).
/* Item is the last item in Seq */

find_last(A.B,A) <- var(B).
find_last(*.B,A) <- ¬var(B) & find_last(B,A).

find_last_seq(A.B,A.B) <-var(B).
find_last_seq(*.B,A) <- ¬var(B) &
    find_last_seq(B,A).

empty_node(nil).
empty_sequence(nil.X) <- var(X).

extend(Value.* , Value) <- /.
extend(*.Sequence, Value) <-
    extend(Sequence, Value).
```

We define the following tests:

```
inserttest <-
    make_node(a,A) & make_node(b,B) &
    make_node(c,C) & insert(C,B) &
    insert(B,A) & write(A).

reptest <-
    make_node(a,A) & make_node(b,B) &
    make_node(c,C) & insert(C,B) &
    insert(B,A) & write(B) & nl &
    make_node(d,D) & replace(B,D) &
    write(D).
```

We can use the programs as follows.

```
inserttest.

n(nil . V1, a,nil . n(nil . (6 @) . V2,b,nil .
n(nil . (6 @) . V3,c,nil . V4) . V5) . V6) .
1MS SUCCESS
 <- inserttest() .
```

```
reptest.

n(nil . n(nil . V1, a,nil . (6 @) . V2) . V3,b,nil.
n(nil . (6 @) . V4,c,nil . V5) . V6) .

n(nil . n(nil . V1, a,nil . n(nil . (6 @) . V2,b,
nil . n(nil . (6 @) . (13 @)     . V3,c,
nil . V4) . V5) . (7 @) . V6) . V7,d,
nil . n(nil . n(nil . n(nil . V1, a,
nil . (6 @) . (13 @) . V6) . V2,b,
nil . (6 @) . V5) . (7 @) . V3,c,nil . V4). V8) .
4MS SUCCESS
 <- reptest() .
```

3.2.3 Balanced Trees

The time it takes to search a tree to locate a value can be kept proportional to the smallest integer not less than log N, where N is the number of nodes in the tree and the base of the logarithm is the branching factor of the tree. This is done by *balancing* the tree as it is built. Whenever an item is to be inserted into the tree, it is done in such a way that the difference in depth of all paths from root to leaf is never more than one. If the new item would be inserted in the tree so as to unbalance it, then a new root node is found that makes the tree balanced. The old root is then inserted in the tree.

It takes extra computations to construct balanced trees. But searching for an element in an unbalanced tree has worst case behavior of order N, whereas in a balanced tree it is log N. So it pays to balance large trees. The point at which it becomes economical depends on the cost of balancing the tree, the maximum depth, the branching factor, and so on. For a detailed discussion of maintaining tree structures, see Knuth (1973).

We define the *depth* of a nonempty tree to be 1 plus the maximum of the depths of its subtrees. An empty tree (nil) has depth 0.

A tree is *balanced* if all of its immediate subtrees are balanced, and the depth of any of these subtrees is no more than 1 greater than the depth of any other of these subtrees. The empty tree is balanced.

A tree is *full* if all its subtrees are full and are of exactly the same depth. The empty tree is full. Adding an element to a full tree will increase its depth by

1. So given a choice between two trees of the same depth, we should add an element to the one that is not full (if there is one). We can change the representation of a node to keep the relevant information about depth and number of empty slots. Although the results are similar for general trees, we will discuss the case for binary trees:

node(Left, Value, Right, Depth, Empty_slots)

where Depth is the depth of the tree, and Empty_slots is the number of places that remain to be filled in the leaves of the tree. If Empty_slots=0 then adding an element will increase the depth. Let us assume that we are to fill the left subtree before we fill the right subtree.

Where we can add a node and still keep a tree balanced depends on whether the subtrees are full. Suppose the element to be added should ordinarily go in the left subtree, but it is full. If the right subtree is also full, then we add the element to the left subtree. This will increase the depth of the left subtree, and hence the depth of the current tree. But if the right subtree is *not* full, then we add the root node value to the right subtree, and reorder the left subtree to accommodate the new node, making the maximum value of the left subtree the root of the new tree.

Here is an unbalanced binary tree containing all the digits from 1 to 9, except for 5 and 6. Note that there are unused slots at depths 3, 4, and 5.

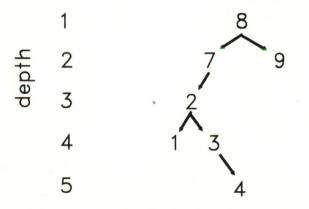

Adding the element 6 to this tree can be done easily by putting it into the empty slot to the right of 4. This does not use one of the unused slots at level 3, 4, or 5, but increases the depth of the tree.

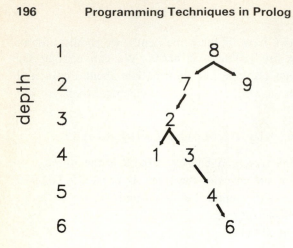

The depth of the tree is an indication of the worst case behavior for tree searches. It is better to have shallower trees. For example, finding whether 5 is in the tree requires looking at six nodes. Adding 5 to the tree would increase its depth again, since it must go to the right of 4 but to the left of 6. We could have added 6 in one of the unused slots, but only if we had some more complicated insert algorithm that would arrange values already in the tree. For example, we could have put 6 where 7 is at level 2, and pushed 7 to the right of 6 into what had been an empty slot.

Here is a completely full balanced binary tree of depth 3 containing the same original elements — all the digits except for 5 and 6:

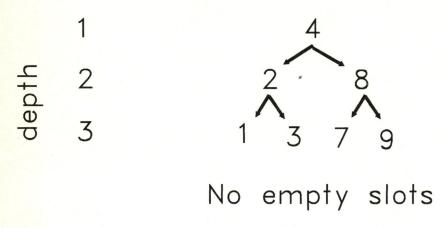

Since it is full, adding 5 to this tree must increase its depth to 4. A binary tree at depth 4 has room for eight nodes on the bottom level of the tree. Since the new tree has only one node filled, its `Empty_slots` = 8 − 1 = 7:

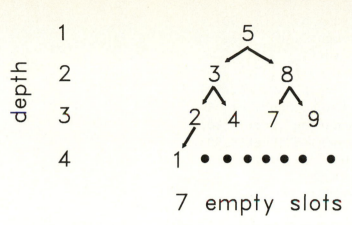

7 empty slots

Notice that 5 is now the root. Let us follow this example through. We start with a tree whose current Value=4. Since the tree is full (Empty_slots=0), any insertions will be into the left subtree. Inserting into a full tree will increase the depth, creating a whole new layer of empty places. Our algorithm always fills these from the left. However, the element to be inserted, 5, is greater than Value, and so should be put in the right subtree, not the left. In this case the right subtree is reordered to include Value and exclude the minimum value in the reordered tree plus Value In our example, the minimum of 5, 7, 8, and 9 is 5, so the reordering does not change anything.

The minimum value, 5, becomes the new root. The displaced old root, which is less than the new root, is then inserted into the left tree. Remember that every element in the right subtree of a balanced tree is greater than the root. That is why the extracted minimum value replaces the root.

This process is repeated on the left subtree. Now the root Value is 2. Again, 4 is to be inserted into the right subtree. The minimum now is 3, which becomes the new root, while the single node 4 makes up the right subtree; 4 has replaced 3, 3 has replaced 2, and 2 is to be inserted in the left subtree.

Inserting 2 into the tree containing the single node 1 is an interesting exercise in base cases. Since 2 is greater than 1, the (empty) right subtree is reordered to include 2 and exclude the minimum element. Since 2 itself is the only element, it constitutes the excluded minimum. So the empty right subtree remains empty, 2 displaces the root 1, and 1 is inserted into the left subtree.

Since the left subtree is empty, inserting 1 into it is trivial. The main thing that happens is that the depth of the trees increases by 1, and the Empty_slots factors are appropriately adjusted. So in the end, 5 has replaced 4, 4 has replaced 3, 3 has replaced 2, 2 has replaced 1, and 1 has moved into an empty slot.

For the program, we use the following operator declarations:

```
op("is_the_same_as", rl, 50).
op("with_element", rl, 50).
op("added", suffix, 51).
op("is_full", suffix, 51).
op("is_same_depth_as", rl, 50).
op("is_shallower_than", rl, 50).
op("max_reordering",prefix,50).
op("min_reordering",prefix,50).
op("to_include",rl,51).
op("gives",rl,52).
op("with",rl,53).
```

Newtree is_the_same_as Oldtree with_element A added
succeeds when Newtree is a balanced tree having the same elements as
Oldtree with the new element A added.

Reordering subtrees to include a new element A and exclude the minimum is
done by min_reordering Oldtree to_include A gives Newtree
with Minimum. A similar rule exists for the maximum.

Here is the program for cases where the new value (A) is less than the value
of the current node (Value). That is, the new value must go into the left
subtree. We have the following cases:

1.   The tree is empty.

2.   A<Value, Left: full, Right: full, Right samedepth Left.

3.   A<Value, Left: full, Right: ¬full.

4.   A<Value Left: ¬full.

5.   A<Value, Left: full, Right: full, Right shallower Left.

These cases give us the following clauses.

The tree is empty

```
        node(nil, A, nil, 1, 0)
        is_the_same_as nil with_element A added.
```

A<Value, Left: full, Right: full, Right samedepth Left
        Put A in the left tree, opening up a new level. The depth will increase by 1.

```
(node(NewLeft, Value, Right, D1, F1)
 is_the_same_as
 node(Left, Value, Right, D, F)
 with_element A added)
     <-
     A < Value &
     Left   is_same_depth_as Right &
     Right is_full   &   /*by assumption so is Left*/
     nth_power_of_2(D, P2) &
     F1 :=(F + P2 - 1) &
     D1 :=(D + 1) &
     NewLeft is_the_same_as Left with_element A added.
```

A<Value, Left: full, Right: ¬full. The depth D does not change.

```
(node(NewLeft, MaxLeft, NewRight, D, F1)
 is_the_same_as
 node(Left, Value, Right, D, F)
 with_element A added)
     <-
     A < Value &
     Left is_full  &
     ¬(Right is_full)
     /*note: Left is full else Right depth less*/
     F1 := F - 1 &
     NewRight is_the_same_as Right
         with_element Value added &
     max_reordering Left to_include A
         gives NewLeft with MaxLeft.
```

A<Value Left : ¬full. Depth D does not change.

```
node(NewLeft, Value, Right, D, F1) is_the_same_as
                    node(Left, Value, Right, D, F)
                    with_element A added
     <-
     A < Value &
     ¬(Left is_full)  &
     F1 := F - 1 &
     NewLeft is_the_same_as Left with_element A added.
```

A<Value, Left: full, Right: full, Right shallower Left. Depth D does not change.

```
(node(NewLeft, MaxLeft, NewRight, D, F1)
   is_the_same_as
   node(Left, Value, Right, D, F)
   with_element A added)
   <-
   A < Value &
   Left   is_full &
   Right  is_full &
   Right is_shallower_than Left &
   F1 := F - 1 &
   NewRight is_the_same_as Right
        with_element Value added &
   max_reordering Left to_include A
        gives NewLeft with MaxLeft.
```

Here are definitions of some of the subroutines.

```
nil is_full.
node(*,*,*,*,0) is_full.

node(*,*,*,Depth, *)
      is_same_depth_as node(*,*,*,Depth, *).
nil    is_same_depth_as nil .

Left is_shallower_than Right <-
    depth(Left, DepthLeft) &
    depth(Right, DepthRight) &
    DepthLeft < DepthRight.

depth(node(*,*,*,Depth,*), Depth).
depth(nil,0).

nth_power_of_2(0,1).
nth_power_of_2(N,1)<-(N<0) & /.
nth_power_of_2(N,P) <-   N1 := N - 1 &
    nth_power_of_2(N1, P1) & P := 2 * P1.
```

We leave it as an exercise for the reader to complete the definition for the case where the value to be inserted is greater than the value in the current node of the tree.

The definition of the reordering predicate is interesting. For empty trees, it in effect puts one node in, then takes out the maximum, leaving an empty tree. The maximum is the node we had previously added.

```
max_reordering nil to_include A gives nil with A.

max_reordering node(Left, Value, Right, D, F)
     to_include A
     gives node(NewL, MaxL, NewR, D, F)
     with MaxR
     <-
     A < Value &
     max_reordering Left to_include A
        gives NewL with MaxL &
     max_reordering Right to_include Value
        gives NewR with MaxR.

max_reordering node(Left, Value, Right, D, F)
     to_include A
     gives node(Left, Value, NewR, D, F1)
     with MaxR
     <-
     A > Value &
     max_reordering Right to_include A
        gives NewR
        with MaxR.
```

We have shown one way to maintain a balanced tree. Such data structures are useful in many applications. Lists are a bit easier to work with, but in general require more time to locate a specific element. This is an example where the specification by cases translates naturally into the corresponding Prolog clauses.

Next we look at a program that inspects game trees. In this case, however, the trees are not represented as terms, but as collections of facts.

3.2.4 Playing Games and Alpha-beta Pruning

The type of game we consider here is played by two persons. What one person wins the other must lose. Each player has the same information about the game as the other — for example, there are no hidden cards. Finally, the outcome is determined solely by decisions of the players — there is no element of chance involved. These games are called *two-person, zero-sum, perfect-information* games. Examples are chess, go, nim, and checkers. A technique for playing these types of games, called *alpha-beta pruning*, has been shown to be optimal in a certain sense, explained below. For a more detailed look at the development of the algorithm, see Nilsson (1980), or Knuth and Moore (1975). A specification of the algorithm in Prolog seems to be much clearer than those written in other languages.

A *game tree* is a directed graph that represents the moves of the game. The nodes are positions, and the arcs are the moves.

Given an initial node, a path leads to a *satisfactory node* if the final position is a win for the side whose turn it is to move at the initial node. It is assumed that there is a *static evaluation function* that can determine the value of final positions for each side. The *true value* (sometimes called "minimax" value) of a node can be defined recursively:

1. If a node is a terminal position (a win, lose, or draw), then its value is the value of the static evaluation function.

2. If a node has successor legal moves, then its value is the maximum taken over the negative values of all successors.

This definition can be turned into a Prolog specification. Its big disadvantage is that it searches all nodes in the graph reachable from the initial node. This is a very large number for any but the most trivial games. Even a game with only two possible moves at each stage would have over a million nodes to search after only 20 moves.

Alternative algorithms have been developed that do not look at every node in a game tree. This is called *pruning* the game tree. Some of these are guaranteed to give the "true value" of a node, and some are not. The "true value" of a node is the value that the minimax algorithm would have given if it could have finished.

One such algorithm is the so-called *alpha-beta* algorithm. It is guaranteed to find the true value of a node, and in many cases it does so by looking at far fewer nodes than does minimax. In fact, there is always an ordering of a tree for which the alpha-beta algorithm visits no more nodes than any algorithm that is also guaranteed to give the true value of a node. In this sense, the alpha-beta algorithm is optimal. The trick, of course, is to find the right ordering of the tree.

Even with the efficiencies available with alpha-beta, games like chess or go have so many nodes that it is impossible to search to the bottom of a full game tree. So further pruning of the tree occurs by introducing an *approximation* or *estimation* function, which will make a guess at the true value of a node. Alpha-beta can be used to some reasonable depth, at which time the value of the node is estimated, and the algorithm continues. Of course, in general these estimation functions are not exact. They are not guaranteed to give the true value of a node. If they were, we could just estimate the value of the top node and be done. So alpha-beta with pruning of this sort is not guaranteed to get the true value of a node. There is a large amount of research on using knowledge of particular games to improve the accuracy of the estimation functions. These issues, interesting as they are, will not be discussed further here.

The essence of the alpha-beta algorithm is simple: Suppose we are looking ahead at a node somewhere down in the tree trying to maximize our score. Let alpha be the best value that our opponent can get to by making some particular choice at a previous node. Let beta be the best value that we can get to by having made a previous choice. It is always the case that alpha is less than or equal to `beta`. Let `t` be the value we have just determined for this node. There are three cases to consider. Either

1. `t < alpha`,
2. `alpha ≤ t < beta`, or
3. `beta ≤ t`.

We must say what to do with the descendants of a particular node in each of these cases.

1. If the value of this node (`t`) is less than what we know we already can achieve elsewhere (`alpha`), then we continue looking at the other siblings of this node to see if we can do better.

2. If the value of this node (`t`) is between these two values, then see what our siblings have to offer, with `t` as our new lower bound (`beta`).

3. If the value of this node (`t`) is better for us than what our opponent can force us to on an alternate path (`beta`), then we forget about any siblings, because our opponent will never give us the opportunity to have that choice. The value of the node is the beta value. This is called *beta cutoff*.

Suppose that `successors` determines the list of legal successors to a position. If there are none, then the list is `nil`. For nodes without successors, let `static` determine the value of the node (e.g, win, lose, or draw).

This formulation tries to maximize the score of the side whose turn it is to move, and minimize the score of the opponent. As in the minimax algorithm, the basic objective is to find the maximum of all successors. But the value for a successor is a minimum value. In order to write just one procedure, a maximizing one, it is noted that the maximum of the minimums of a set is the maximum of the negatives of the maximums of the set of negative values:

$$f(p) = max(min(f(p11),\ldots,f(p1n)), \ldots ,$$
$$min(f(pm1),\ldots,f(pmn)))$$
$$= max(-max(-f(p11),\ldots,-f(p1n)), \ldots)$$

where `f(pnm)` is the true value of the Mth successor of the Nth successor of p. For example

$$max(min(1, 2), min(3, 4)) = 3 =$$
$$max(-max(-1, -2), -max(-3, -4))$$

In this way, there do not have to be two procedures, one that maximizes and one that minimizes.

In the following program some small liberties are taken with the syntax for numeric functions and predicates: `ab(First, -T, ...)` is short-hand for `ab(First, MT, ...) & T := -MT`. Also, A < T < B is short-hand for A < T & T < B.

V is the true value of position P given initial values of A (`alpha`) and B (`beta`) in `ab(P,V,A,B)`.

```
ab(P,V,A,B) <-
    successors(P ,nil) &
    static(P,V).
ab(P,V,A,B) <-
    successors(P ,First.Rest) &
    ablist(First.Rest,V,A,B).

ablist(nil,A,A,B).
ablist(First.Rest,V,A,B) <-
    ab(First,-T,-B,-A) &
    abcases(Rest,T,V,A,B).

abcases(Rest,T,T,A,B) <-
    B ≤ T & /.
abcases(Rest,T,V,A,B) <-
    A < T < B & / &
    ablist(Rest,V,T,B).
abcases(Rest,T,V,A,B) <-
    T ≤ A &
    ablist(Rest,V,A,B).
```

The following example is taken from Knuth and Moore (1975). Suppose there is a nice symmetric game with a uniform branching factor of 3 and a depth of 5 (counting the initial node as 1). Then there are a total of 81 possible final positions in the game, with a total of 121 nodes. Minimax would look at all 121 nodes to determine the value of the initial node. Alpha-beta could look at substantially fewer.

Knuth uses the digits of π to 80 decimal places to assign "random" values to the 81 terminal nodes. If we label each node by the inverse path back to the initial node (let us call that node "1"), then we get the following tree:

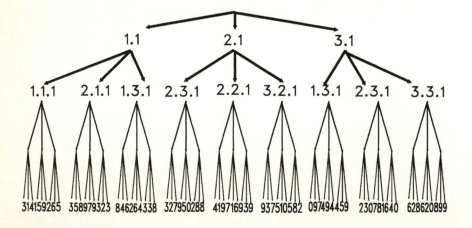

We assign the digits of π (314159...) to the terminal nodes (e.g 1 . 1 . 1 . 1 . 1, 3 . 2 . 2 . 1 . 1, ...). These values are those returned by ab at level 5 in the trace beginning on page 206. They can be found by examining the EXIT trace points. Taking the liberties out of the program notation and defining successors appropriately gives us the following program. V is the true value of position P given initial values of A (alpha) and B (beta).

```
ab(P,V,A,B) <-
    successors(P ,nil) &
    static(P,V) .
ab(P,V,A,B) <-
    successors(P ,First.Rest) &
    ablist(First.Rest,V,A,B) .

ablist(nil,A,A,B) .
ablist(First.Rest,V,A,B) <-
    MB := -B & MA := -A &
    ab(First,MT,MB,MA) &
    T := -MT  &
    abcases(Rest,T,V,A,B).

abcases(Rest,T,T,A,B) <- B ≤ T &/ .
abcases(Rest,T,V,A,B) <-
    A < T & T<B & / &
    ablist(Rest,V,T,B) .
abcases(Rest,T,V,A,B) <-
    T ≤ A &
    ablist(Rest,V,A,B) .

successors(N,(1 .N) . (2 .N) . (3 .N) . nil) <-
    size(N,L) & L<5 .
successors(N,nil) <- size(N,L) & L=5 .
successors(N,nil) <- size(N,L) & L>5 .

size(Node.Nodes, Length) <-
   size(Nodes, Ln) & Length := Ln+1 &/.
size(X,1).
```

Executing ab(1,*,0,10) with tracing on for ab(*,*,*,*) gives an interesting trace. The call points indicate when a node is to be evaluated. By inspecting the trace, we can follow the change in alpha and beta values.

The exit points indicate when the alpha-beta algorithm (the ab procedure) has successfully computed a value for a node. By observing the pattern of call and exit, we can see how the algorithm examines the tree. Level 5 nodes are the leaf nodes, and the static values are assigned to them at that level.

Only 31 of the possible 81 leaf nodes are evaluated, and only 55 of the total of 121 nodes are evaluated.

We begin the trace of alpha-beta at node 1, with initial values of alpha and beta equal to 0 and 10, respectively. Note the values of alpha and beta at alternate levels. At level 2 alpha is -10 and beta is 0.

```
1 : call ==> ab(1, V1, 0,10) .
 2 : call ==> ab(1 . 1, V1, -10,0) .
  3 : call ==> ab(1 . 1 . 1, V1, 0,10) .
   4 : call ==> ab(1 . 1 . 1 . 1, V1, -10,0) .
```

At level 5 we hit our first static value. The value of node 1.1.1.1.1 is 3.

```
5 : call ==> ab(1 . 1 . 1 . 1 . 1, V1,0,10) .
5 : exit ==> ab(1 . 1 . 1 . 1 . 1, 3,0,10) .
```

Back at level 4, the value returned for MT is 3, so the value for T is -3. This is between the level 4 value of alpha (-10) and beta (0), so we proceed with the siblings with a new level 4 alpha value of -3. This produces level 5 values of alpha and beta of 0 and 3, respectively.

```
5 : call ==> ab(2 . 1 . 1 . 1 . 1, V1,0,3) .
5 : exit ==> ab(2 . 1 . 1 . 1 . 1, 1,0,3) .
```

The computation that decides whether or not to invoke another call to ab takes place at the next level up from the level that just exited. At this level the roles of alpha and beta are reversed, and negated. This last node has returned a value for MT of 1, or for T of -1. This is between the new level 4 alpha and beta values of -3 and 0, so -1 becomes the new level 4 alpha value. This shows up at level 5 as the new beta value, as computation continues with the other level 5 siblings.

```
5 : call ==> ab(3 . 1 . 1 . 1 . 1, V1, 0,1) .
5 : exit ==> ab(3 . 1 . 1 . 1 . 1, 4,0,1) .
```

Now the level 4 value of the last sibling is -4. This is less than -1, which is the current level 4 alpha value, so nothing happens. We would continue with other siblings if this were not the last one. Since it is, we return the value of MT = -1 (or T = 1) to level 3 for node 1 . 1 . 1 . 1.

```
4 : exit ==> ab(1 . 1 . 1 . 1, -1, -10,0) .
```

This is between level 3 alpha (0) and beta (10), so we continue with level 4 siblings with a new level 3 value of alpha. This new value is reflected at level 4 as the negated beta value.

```
4 : call ==> ab(2 . 1 . 1 . 1, V1, -10,-1) .
```

Since this node is not a leaf node, we must look at descendants.

```
5 : call ==> ab(1 . 2 . 1 . 1 . 1, V1, 1, 10) .
5 : exit ==> ab(1 . 2 . 1 . 1 . 1, 1, 1, 10) .
```

Now we return a value for T to level 4 that is equal to beta at level 4; namely -1.

```
4 : exit ==> ab(2 . 1 . 1 . 1, -1, -10,-1) .
```

Level 3 takes over now, determines that alpha and T are the same, and continues
with the next level 4 sibling.

```
4 : call ==> ab(3 . 1 . 1 . 1, V1, -10,-1) .
```

When level 4 calls level 5 successors, the first sibling narrows the field
considerably, forcing the local value to lie between 1 and 2, inclusive. Successive
sibling values of 6 and 5 do not change that range.

```
5 : call ==> ab(1 . 3 . 1 . 1 . 1, V1, 1, 10) .
5 : exit ==> ab(1 . 3 . 1 . 1 . 1, 2,1, 10) .
5 : call ==> ab(2 . 3 . 1 . 1 . 1, V1, 1, 2) .
5 : exit ==> ab(2 . 3 . 1 . 1 . 1, 6,1, 2) .
5 : call ==> ab(3 . 3 . 1 . 1 . 1, V1, 1, 2) .
5 : exit ==> ab(3 . 3 . 1 . 1 . 1, 5,1, 2) .
4 : exit ==> ab(3 . 1 . 1 . 1, -2,-10,-1) .
```

So the level 4 value of this node is returned as -2. Since that is the last sibling at
this level, the value (negated) is passed up to level 3 as the current value of node
1 . 1 . 1.

```
3 : exit ==> ab(1 . 1 . 1, 2,0,10) .
```

We can proceed at level 3 with this new beta cut-off value.

```
3 : call ==> ab(2 . 1 . 1, V1, 0,2) .
 4 : call ==> ab(1 . 2 . 1 . 1, V1, -2,0) .
  5 : call ==> ab(1 . 1 . 2 . 1 . 1, V1, 0,2) .
  5 : exit ==> ab(1 . 1 . 2 . 1 . 1, 3,0,2) .
  5 : call ==> ab(2 . 1 . 2 . 1 . 1, V1, 0,2) .
  5 : exit ==> ab(2 . 1 . 2 . 1 . 1, 5,0,2) .
  5 : call ==> ab(3 . 1 . 2 . 1 . 1, V1, 0,2) .
  5 : exit ==> ab(3 . 1 . 2 . 1 . 1, 8,0,2) .
 4 : exit ==> ab(1 . 2 . 1 . 1, -2,-2,0) .
3 : exit ==> ab(2 . 1 . 1, 2,0,2) .
3 : call ==> ab(3 . 1 . 1, V1, 0,2) .
 4 : call ==> ab(1 . 3 . 1 . 1, V1, -2,0) .
  5 : call ==> ab(1 . 1 . 3 . 1 . 1, V1, 0,2) .
  5 : exit ==> ab(1 . 1 . 3 . 1 . 1, 8,0,2) .
  5 : call ==> ab(2 . 1 . 3 . 1 . 1, V1, 0,2) .
  5 : exit ==> ab(2 . 1 . 3 . 1 . 1, 4,0,2) .
  5 : call ==> ab(3 . 1 . 3 . 1 . 1, V1, 0,2) .
  5 : exit ==> ab(3 . 1 . 3 . 1 . 1, 6,0,2) .
 4 : exit ==> ab(1 . 3 . 1 . 1, -2,-2,0) .
3 : exit ==> ab(3 . 1 . 1, 2,0,2) .
```

A better value than 2 has not been established, so this is passed up to level 2
(negated) as -2:

```
2 : exit ==> ab(1 . 1, -2,-10,0) .
2 : call ==> ab(2 . 1, V1, -10,-2) .
 3 : call ==> ab(1 . 2 . 1, V1, 2,10) .
  4 : call ==> ab(1 . 1 . 2 . 1, V1, -10,-2) .
   5 : call ==> ab(1 . 1 . 1 . 2 . 1, V1, 2,10) .
   5 : exit ==> ab(1 . 1 . 1 . 2 . 1, 3,2,10) .
   5 : call ==> ab(2 . 1 . 1 . 2 . 1, V1, 2,3) .
   5 : exit ==> ab(2 . 1 . 1 . 2 . 1, 2,2,3) .
```

Here the value of T at level 4 is -2. This is equal to the beta value, so a beta
cut-off occurs. The next sibling is not explored. Level 4 returns its value of -2.

```
  4 : exit ==> ab(1 . 1 . 2 . 1, -2,-10,-2) .
  4 : call ==> ab(2 . 1 . 2 . 1, V1, -10,-2) .
   5 : call ==> ab(1 . 2 . 1 . 2 . 1, V1, 2,10) .
   5 : exit ==> ab(1 . 2 . 1 . 2 . 1, 9,2,10) .
   5 : call ==> ab(2 . 2 . 1 . 2 . 1, V1, 2,9) .
   5 : exit ==> ab(2 . 2 . 1 . 2 . 1, 5,2,9) .
   5 : call ==> ab(3 . 2 . 1 . 2 . 1, V1, 2,5) .
   5 : exit ==> ab(3 . 2 . 1 . 2 . 1, 0,2,5) .
  4 : exit ==> ab(2 . 1 . 2 . 1, 0,-10,-2) .
  4 : call ==> ab(3 . 1 . 2 . 1, V1, -10,-2) .
   5 : call ==> ab(1 . 3 . 1 . 2 . 1, V1, 2,10) .
   5 : exit ==> ab(1 . 3 . 1 . 2 . 1, 2,2,10) .
```

Here is another good example of a beta cut-off. This time it is immediately after
the first sibling. Level 4 returns a value of -2 without looking at any more level 5
siblings.

```
  4 : exit ==> ab(3 . 1 . 2 . 1, -2,-10,-2) .
 3 : exit ==> ab(1 . 2 . 1, 2,2,10) .
2 : exit ==> ab(2 . 1, -2,-10,-2) .
2 : call ==> ab(3 . 1, V1, -10,-2) .
 3 : call ==> ab(1 . 3 . 1, V1, 2,10) .
  4 : call ==> ab(1 . 1 . 3 . 1, V1, -10,-2) .
   5 : call ==> ab(1 . 1 . 1 . 3 . 1, V1, 2,10) .
   5 : exit ==> ab(1 . 1 . 1 . 3 . 1, 0,2,10) .
  4 : exit ==> ab(1 . 1 . 3 . 1, 0,-10,-2) .

  4 : call ==> ab(2 . 1 . 3 . 1, V1, -10,-2) .
   5 : call ==> ab(1 . 2 . 1 . 3 . 1, V1, 2,10) .
   5 : exit ==> ab(1 . 2 . 1 . 3 . 1, 4,2,10) .
   5 : call ==> ab(2 . 2 . 1 . 3 . 1, V1, 2,4) .
   5 : exit ==> ab(2 . 2 . 1 . 3 . 1, 9,2,4) .
   5 : call ==> ab(3 . 2 . 1 . 3 . 1, V1, 2,4) .
   5 : exit ==> ab(3 . 2 . 1 . 3 . 1, 4,2,4) .
  4 : exit ==> ab(2 . 1 . 3 . 1, -4,-10,-2) .
```

```
4 : call ==> ab(3 . 1 . 3 . 1, V1, -10,-4) .
 5 : call ==> ab(1 . 3 . 1 . 3 . 1, V1, 4,10) .
 5 : exit ==> ab(1 . 3 . 1 . 3 . 1, 4,4,10) .
4 : exit ==> ab(3 . 1 . 3 . 1, -4,-10,-4) .
3 : exit ==> ab(1 . 3 . 1, 4,2,10) .
```

Here we see the alpha value for level 3 successors narrowing, from -10 to -4:

```
3 : call ==> ab(2 . 3 . 1, V1, 2,4) .
 4 : call ==> ab(1 . 2 . 3 . 1, V1, -4,-2) .
  5 : call ==> ab(1 . 1 . 2 . 3 . 1, V1, 2,4) .
  5 : exit ==> ab(1 . 1 . 2 . 3 . 1, 2,2,4) .
```

Because the value at level 5 for this node is 2, the level 4 value is -2. With a level 4 beta value of -2, this causes another beta cut-off.

```
 4 : exit ==> ab(1 . 2 . 3 . 1, -2,-4,-2) .
 4 : call ==> ab(2 . 2 . 3 . 1, V1, -4,-2) .
  5 : call ==> ab(1 . 2 . 2 . 3 . 1, V1, 2,4) .
  5 : exit ==> ab(1 . 2 . 2 . 3 . 1, 7,2,4) .
  5 : call ==> ab(2 . 2 . 2 . 3 . 1, V1, 2,4) .
  5 : exit ==> ab(2 . 2 . 2 . 3 . 1, 8,2,4) .
  5 : call ==> ab(3 . 2 . 2 . 3 . 1, V1, 2,4) .
  5 : exit ==> ab(3 . 2 . 2 . 3 . 1, 1, 2,4) .
 4 : exit ==> ab(2 . 2 . 3 . 1, -1, -4,-2) .

 4 : call ==> ab(3 . 2 . 3 . 1, V1, -4,-2) .
  5 : call ==> ab(1 . 3 . 2 . 3 . 1, V1, 2,4) .
  5 : exit ==> ab(1 . 3 . 2 . 3 . 1, 6,2,4) .
  5 : call ==> ab(2 . 3 . 2 . 3 . 1, V1, 2,4) .
  5 : exit ==> ab(2 . 3 . 2 . 3 . 1, 4,2,4) .
  5 : call ==> ab(3 . 3 . 2 . 3 . 1, V1, 2,4) .
  5 : exit ==> ab(3 . 3 . 2 . 3 . 1, 0,2,4) .
 4 : exit ==> ab(3 . 2 . 3 . 1, 0,-4,-2) .
3 : exit ==> ab(2 . 3 . 1, 2,2,4) .
```

Level 2 applies a beta cutoff here, and does not go on to search 3 . 3 . 1:

```
 2 : exit ==> ab(3 . 1, -2,-10,-2) .
1 : exit ==> ab(1, 2,0,10) .
```

The final value turns out to be 2.

3.2.5 Most-Specific Generalizations

One interesting issue is how to get computers to learn. One way that has been proposed is to get them to generalize from their experience. As we mentioned in Chapter 1, a specific application of this proposal is induction from examples. In

Prolog, that involves generalizing terms as well as finding instances of them. Shapiro (1983) discussed this in terms of error location and correction.

Unifying two terms produces the *most-general instance*, which is an instance of both terms. For some problems, we may be interested in the dual operation, the *most-specific generalization* (MSG) of two terms. Sometimes it is also called the *least-general generalization*. This is the dual operation to unification, if we consider the lattice formed by terms under the *instance* relation. Here are some pairs of terms and their MSGs.

T1	T2	MSG
X	X	X
X	Y	Z
a	a	a
a	b	X
f(X)	g(X)	Y
f(X,1)	f(2,Y)	f(X,Y)

Let two terms T1 and T2 be *type-similar* if neither is a variable, and

- They are the same constant, or
- They are structured terms that have the same arity and same function symbol.

A term T is the MSG of terms T1 and T2 as determined by the following cases.

1. T is T1, if T1 and T2 are the same variable.
2. T is a new variable, if T1 and T2 are both variables.
3. T is T1, if T1 is a variable and T2 is not a variable.
4. T is T2, if T2 is a variable and T1 is not a variable.
5. T is a new variable, if neither T1 nor T2 is a variable, and T1 and T2 are not type-similar.
6. T is T1, if T1 and T2 are the same constant.
7. T is the term constructed from the function symbol of T1 and the list of MSGs of the arguments of T1 and T2, if T1 and T2 are type-similar and are not constants.

A program to compute the MSG of two terms follows. Notice that there are seven clauses, one for each part of the definition. There are also the subprocedures, `type_similar`, `msg_list`, and `constant`.

In addition to identifying the predicates, we must identify the objects and decide on their representation. These are

- Constant, represented as a Prolog integer or atom. We define the procedure `constant` in terms of IBM Prolog's built-in predicates `int` and `atom`.

- Variable, represented as a Prolog variable. We use the built-in predicate `var`.

- Structure, represented as a Prolog term. We use `=..` to gain access to function symbols and sub structures. We use `length` to test the arity of a term. The IBM Prolog built-in `prlen` would work also, except that it fails if the arity is 0. We want to succeed with a value of 0. We define `msglist` to recursively process arguments.

Below is a program that implements the above decisions. When T is the MSG of T1 and T2 `msg(T,T1,T2)` is true. To keep the specification as general as possible, special IBM Prolog equality tests are not used.

1. T is T1, if T1 and T2 are the same variable. If they are both variables, they are the same variable if we cannot bind them to different constants:

   ```
   msg(T1,T1,T2) <-var(T1) & var(T2) &
       ¬((a = T1) & (b = T2)) & /.
   ```

2. T is a new variable, if T1 and T2 are both variables:

   ```
   msg(*,T1,T2) <- var(T1) & var(T2) & /.
   ```

3. T is T1, if T1 is a variable and T2 is not a variable:

   ```
   msg(T1,T1,T2) <- var(T1) & ¬var(T2) & /.
   ```

4. T is T2, if T2 is a variable and T1 is not a variable:

   ```
   msg(T2,T1,T2) <- var(T2) & ¬var(T1) & /.
   ```

5. T is a new variable, if neither T1 nor T2 is a variable, and T1 and T2 are not type-similar:

   ```
   msg(T3,T1,T2) <- ¬var(T2) & ¬var(T1) &
       ¬type_similar(T1,T2) & /.
   ```

6. T is T1, if T1 and T2 are the same constant:

   ```
   msg(T1,T1,T2) <- constant(T1) & constant(T2).
   ```

7. T is the term constructed from the function symbol of T1 and the list of MSGs of the arguments of T1 and T2, if T1 and T2 are type-similar and are not constants:

   ```
   msg(T,T1,T2) <- type_similar(T1,T2) &
       ¬constant(T1) &
       T1 =.. (F.T1args) & T2 =.. (F.T2args) &
       msg_list(Targs, T1args, T2args) &
       T =.. (F.Targs).
   ```

We present without comment some subroutines.

```
msg_list(nil,nil,nil).
msg_list(T.Ts,T1.T1s, T2.T2s) <-
    msg(T,T1,T2) & msg_list(Ts,T1s,T2s).

type_similar(A,A)<-constant(A) & /.
type_similar(T1,T2) <-
    T1 =.. (F.T1s) & T2 =.. (F.T2s) &
    length(T1s,N) & length(T2s,N).

constant(A) <-
    int(A) | atom(A) | string(A) | floatp(A).

msgtest <- write('enter term 1:') & read(Term1) &
    write('enter term 2:') & read(Term2) &/&
    msg(Msg, Term1, Term2) &
    writech('Generalization:') & write(Msg).
```

Here is a sample of how MSG works.

```
enter term 1: f(a).
enter term 2: f(b).
Generalization: f(V1) .

enter term 1:.f(a).
enter term 2: f(a).
Generalization: f(a) .

enter term 1: f(g(1, h(X))).
enter term 2: f(g(*,h(1))).
Generalization: f(g(V1, h(V2))) .

enter term 1: f(g(1, h(1))).
enter term 2: f(g(1, k(1))).
Generalization: f(g(1, V1)) .
```

Unification can bind variables, whereas generalization can create them. The bulk of the code for `msg` involved the use of the `var` built-in routine. If we had chosen to represent variables other than as Prolog variables, then we would have had to provide a similar routine. An interesting exercise for the reader would be to program unification, and to compare its use of `var` with that of `msg`.

3.3 SUMMARY OF PROLOG PROGRAMMING PRINCIPLES

There are many different ways of thinking about the usefulness of a programming language. Prolog seems at present to be used more for symbolic than for numeric computation. One of the most important features is that it has a *declarative* as well as a *procedural* meaning.

A Prolog program can be assigned an English reading that captures its declarative meaning, as long as it avoids the side effects that are common to other languages. These side effects are

1. System predicates — specifically, input and output (`read`, `write`).
2. Workspace modification (`addax` and `delax`).
3. Execution control (`cut`, `retry. . .`).

Few interesting programs can be written that do not require use of some of these features for pragmatic reasons. Some simple conventions and a little care in structuring a Prolog program can maximize the benefits of the declarative style. Primarily, one must separate the *logic* part from the *side effect* part.

Some guidelines are

1. Pass needed data as parameters, not by setting global values.
2. Structure the program into small, readable pieces, using as many predicates as necessary (but no more!).
3. Make the flow of control pass *across* a conjunction, and not down *into* a subgoal (except for recursion).
4. Write out in English what each predicate and each clause means before writing the Prolog code.
5. Define declarative predicates that imbed any necessary side effects (`query_the_user`, `read_object`, global value assignment, etc.).
6. A program's structure follows the structure of the terms with which it deals. Take care to define the data structures first.
7. An informal proof that a program is correct can be relatively easily established; it follows the structure of the program.
8. Unification has subtle features that can make it both a bane and a blessing; look carefully at some of the examples, and make full use of the power of the logical variable. In particular, self-referential structures (like difference lists) can be very useful, demonstrating the power of unification.
9. Cyclic terms can be dealt with in Prolog, but their use requires care. They often require copying large structures.
10. We may write our own forms for different types of control, including "forward-chaining" or "bottom up" inference, as well as traditional forms such as `do-while`.
11. Meta-interpreters are easy to write if we want to extend the power of the Prolog language.

We emphasize that Prolog should be used declaratively as far as possible. We are convinced that following these guidelines will make your Prolog programming tasks easier, especially for large projects. Meta-level programming is important in Prolog, and is not widely available in other languages. Unification allows some very interesting data representations. Direct manipulation of the machine is difficult in Prolog; however, as we shall describe in Appendix A, IBM Prolog has several ways of working with the operating system, and with software written in other languages. We can use the fact that recursive programs follow the structure of recursive data to write elegant and practical programs.

Prolog is in essence a very simple language. It pays always to keep this simplicity in mind. If a program is becoming too complex to handle, one should stop and think if there is a better, a more declarative, way of approaching the problem. The more you work on a Prolog program, the simpler the program should become.

EXERCISES

1. Write a procedure that turns a difference list (see page 136) into a standard list, and vice versa. Watch out for empty lists (page 185).

2. Write the definition of the `adding` and `deleting` predicates on page 162 using the list handling predicates we defined on page 133.

3. Extend the interpreter `succeeds(Goal)` on page 167:

    a. to handle all the extra-logical special predicates of Prolog (`retry`, `ancestor`, etc.).

    b. to handle Prolog built-in routines (`read`, `write`, etc.).

    c. with a recursion depth counter for the `succeeds` predicate.

    d. to use the depth counter to indent the trace messages.

    e. to ask at each step if the user is ready to continue.

    f. to become active only at certain user-supplied breakpoints. (partial solution, page 168.)

4. For the metainterpreter on page 166, revise the procedures `note_exit`, etc., to print out `exit(A <- Goal)`, but not `exit(A & B)`.

5. Extend the breadth first propositional interpreter `success(Goal - List)` on page 171 so that it will interpret an object program containing predicates with arguments. Your interpreter will need to keep track of binding environments. Since variables are not lexically identified, different invocations of a clause can have the same variable names. Variables must therefore be identified, e.g by clause activation. You may find the IBM Prolog built-in predicate `copy(Term,Newterm)` useful.

6. Modify the interpreter on page 173 to ask the user for information only for those goals specified by the author of a program, and to have the author supply the procedures to ask the question and receive the answer.

7. Modify the interpreter to ask *before* attempting a proof, and then to give the author the option of asking the user either before or after attempting a proof.

8. Write a `query_the_user` predicate that will

   a.   Determine whether a goal is ground or not.

   b.   If ground, present the goal to the user and ask "true or false?."

   c.   If not ground, ask for a true instance.

   d.   Allow for backtracking to get other instances.

   e.   Prompt the user when this occurs.

   f.   Allow the user to somehow say "no more solutions."

9. Have the interpreter on page 173 take note of the results of proving certain specified predicates, and use these results if possible before trying for another proof.

10. Write the predicate

    `evaluate_term_list(Args,Evaluated_args)`

    for the interpreter `succeeds(Goal)` on page 174.

11. Write `eval` predicates for the arithmetic primitives plus, minus, times, and integer division. You may use the built-in routine `:=`.

12. Write `eval` predicates for the Lisp primitives `car`, `cdr`, `cons`, `cond`, `eq`, and `atom`.

    Answer:
    ```
    eval(car(A.B), A).
    eval(cdr(A.B), B).
    eval(cons(A, B), A.B))
    eval(cond(List), Val) <- cond_val(List, Val).
    eval(eq(A,B),true) <- eq(A,B).
    eval(eq(A,B),nil) <- ¬eq(A,B).
    eval(atom(A),true) <- ¬var(A) & ¬(A is *.*).
    eval(atom(A),nil)  <- ¬var(A) & (A is *.*).

    cond_val(nil,nil).
    cond_val((Cond.Expr).*), ExprVal) <-
        eval(Cond, true) & eval(Expr, ExprVal).
    cond_val(*.List, ExprVal) <-
        cond_val(List, ExprVal).
    ```

13. Define the `eval` predicates for the Lisp primitives `getprop`, `putprop`, `remprop`, `eval`, and `apply`.

14. On page 178 we ask "How can the programs for proof-tree extraction and metadeclaration be combined?"

15. Extend the conversion routine on page 178 that compiles proof tree extraction to handle built-ins and extra-logical constructs.

16. Adapt the `search` procedure on page 184 to perform breadth first as does `success` on page 171, by defining `satisfactory` and `arc` appropriately.

17. Write routines to maintain and search a grid, not just a list as on page 187. In addition to `Left` and `Right` pointers, it should have `Up` and `Down` pointers.

18. Use the predicates defined in the previous problem to write a mini-text editor. Each character in the text should be represented as an element in a two-dimensional array. The text editor will have the concept of a "current line." Define the following predicates.

   a. `newline(Old_text, New_text)` adds a blank line after the current line.

   b. `list(N,Old_text)` lists N lines of text starting with the current line.

   c. `next(Old_text,New_text)` the current line in `New_text` is the one following the current line in `Old_text`.

   d. `back(Old_text,New_text)` the current line in `New_text` is the one preceding the current line in `Old_text`.

19. What would we change if we had to maintain the concept of a current *column*? Both column and row?

20. Complete the definition of `is_the_same_as` on page 200 for the case where the value to be inserted is greater than the value in the current node of the tree.

21. How does the definition of adding to a balanced tree on page 198 change if duplicate values are included? Answer: Add

```
node(NewLeft, Value, Right)
    is_the_same_as
    node(Left, Value, Right)
    with_element A added     <-
        A = Value &
        NewLeft is_the_same_as Left
        with_element A added.
```

22. If we wanted the sort routine `sorted(List1,List2)` on page 145 to include duplicates, how would the definition of a balanced tree on page 198 be changed?
   Answer: Add

```
node(Left, Value, Right)
    is_the_same_as node(Left, Value, Right)
    with_element A added   <-
        A = Value.
```

23. Write the definition of the `adding` and `deleting` predicates on page 162 using the balanced binary tree programs from page 198. Use the predicate

name, sequence in predicate, and first argument (or principle functor of the first argument if it is a term) as a key.

24. Using the balanced tree programs on page 198, write an indexer for rules in `succeeds(Goal,Clauses,NewClauses)` on page 161 where the key is the value of the first argument.

25. Define `min_reordering` analogous to `max_reordering` on page 200.

26. Draw the game tree on page 204 and label the nodes with exit values. Compare this with Knuth and Moore (1975).

4

Expert Systems in Prolog

Adrian Walker

> "A syllogism is discourse in which, certain things being stated, something other than what is stated follows of necessity from their being so."

Aristotle, *Prior Analytics*.

It is said that during a recent territorial conflict between two countries—let us call them country X and country Y—the armed forces on both sides were using similar computer assisted radar systems for detecting aircraft. During tests before the conflict, the story goes, country X discovered a way of fooling the software in their own system into losing track of four planes at a time. This was done by flying the planes in close formation toward the radar, and, at a critical distance, fanning them out. Initially the radar system regarded them as one object, as they fanned out it focussed on the central point where the object should have been, and finally it lost track of all four.

Country X used the tactic during the conflict. When country Y realized what the tactic was, they set about correcting the gap in the software. Although the real world knowledge needed to do this was present in the disputed area, the necessary programming skills were elsewhere. There was a substantial delay before the program was extended to avoid the trap.

Fortunately, keeping a program in line with real world knowledge is not always such a pressing matter. Yet, if it is easy for a person who is not a programmer to change the knowledge used by a program, that program can be very useful, perhaps in topics that we would not have the time or ability to cover otherwise.

An expert system is a program. It differs from a conventional program in that the knowledge it uses can be changed by a person who is not a programmer. Ideally, it is possible for a nonprogrammer to add knowledge about a completely new topic. As noted in Chapter 1, there are other important differences between expert systems and conventional programs. For example, if an expert system gives advice, then it is important that it be able to explain its reasons for the advice. Few people would be willing to change their investments, or to replace their car rather than repair it, without an explanation of why this is the best course of action.

In writing down knowledge for use in a computer, it would be nice to know how we humans represent the knowledge. Some of the efforts made in artificial intelligence can be viewed as hypotheses about how we think. Other efforts, such as most of the chess-playing programs, try to mimic our performance, but use methods that are clearly different from ours.

There is typically a key difference between a scientific theory and an expert system. In constructing a scientific theory, one may try to build a predictive model of a set of situations (for example accelerating objects in mechanics), and be satisfied if one finds a succinct model (e.g the well-known formula Force = Mass times Acceleration). This approach is enormously powerful in subjects in which such elegant models exist, and in which we know how to find the models. However, suppose that, in some subject (e.g medicine) we must find practical answers to practical questions before a complete theory is developed. (We may even be unsure that a succinct theory exists at all.) Then we can proceed to build a computer model of the reasoning that experts do in the area, and the model may be more useful if it has the characteristics of an expert system (see page 4) than if it lacks them. The power of taking this step is that we are no longer limited to succinct models. Current expert systems typically contain between a few hundred and a few thousand facts and rules. Current databases contain up to about one hundred million facts. It is a goal of the Japanese Fifth Generation project to provide computer hardware to allow the effective use of many more than one hundred million facts and rules.

To make knowledge available to a computer we need a notation, or representation, for writing it down. Section 4.1, "Knowledge Representation and Use" surveys some representations that are used in expert systems. Once we have a notation, we can begin to build systems.

Section 4.2, "Syllog—an Expert and Data System Shell" describes an expert system shell called Syllog. Syllog is designed to deal with both knowledge and data; we give an example of the use of Syllog in manufacturing. Section 4.3, "Plantdoc" describes an expert system shell called Plantdoc. When provided with rules annotated with confidence weights, Plantdoc asks questions, and then makes a judgmental diagnosis. We give a simple example of the use of Plantdoc to diagnose a house heating system that is not working properly. In Section 4.4, "Generating Useful Explanations" we look at techniques for generating useful explanations; it turns out that some of these techniques can be quite general—they work for a range of tasks. Then in Section 4.5, "Checking Incoming Knowledge" we describe some knowledge acquisition techniques—techniques that help an expert system shell to accumulate and check knowledge.

4.1 KNOWLEDGE REPRESENTATION AND USE

As we mentioned in Chapter 1, there are many schools of thought about how to represent knowledge usefully. Evidence about how people actually represent knowledge is interesting, but at present suggests techniques, rather than spelling them out in detail. (For some interesting work in this direction, see de Callatay 1985.) Artificial intelligence researchers have suggested that knowledge can be represented in *frames*, in *scripts*, in *semantic nets*, in *causal graphs*, as *actor-like objects*, in *rules*, and in *logic*, to mention but a few notations. One of the problems with this proliferation of notations is that there has been little work so far on comparing and contrasting their virtues and shortcomings on standardized tasks. As long as each system of notation resides in its own large, complicated, experimental system, with no general concepts shared with other notations, this situation is likely to continue. Happily, logic programming and Prolog seem to offer both a conceptual common ground (logic theory), and a practical technology to allow us to compare and contrast the different knowledge representations. Furthermore, we seem to be able to do this in Prolog without excessive amounts of experimental programming effort. Each of the well known artificial intelligence notations fits rather smoothly into Prolog (we shall see some examples in this chapter.) To the extent that Prolog is a declarative, rather than a procedural language, some of the algorithms for using artificial intelligence notations (e.g to get advice from an expert system) are just special cases of Prolog's built-in logical inference and pattern matching. When this is not the case, there is a conceptually powerful technique, called metainterpretation, that captures algorithms (such as an EMycin-style inference engine) in just a few Prolog rules. We introduced metainterpretation in Chapter 3, and we shall have more to say about it this chapter and in Appendix B.

4.1.1 Rules

Knowledge is represented as *rules* in systems such as Syllog (see Section 4.2) and EMycin (see Section 4.3). For example, a Syllog rule reads

```
site eg_number has eg_type rock in suitable form
eg_group fossils have been found at site eg_number
eg_group fossils are characteristic of the eg_p period
there are known reserves in eg_type rock from the eg_p period
------------------------------------------------------------
some evidence for oil at site eg_number
```

Here, the conclusion below the line is established if all of the premises above the line are true. The `eg_` items are variables that make the rule general. Judgmental reasoning is carried explicitly and symbolically in phrases such as "suitable" and "some evidence." An EMycin-style rule reads

```
if "plant is wilting" and
    not "leaves have yellow spots"
              then "there is not enough water" : 60.
```

The number **60** indicates that we have 60% confidence in the rule and is used in a numerical form of judgmental reasoning.

Like all viable knowledge representations, rules tend to suggest ways in which they can be used. The two main ways of using rules are called *forward chaining* and *back chaining*.

- To forward chain, a system makes sure it has established all of the premises of a rule, and then notes that the conclusion therefore holds. During this step, particular values (such as `site 3` for the Syllog rule above) may be passed through from the premises to the conclusion.

- To backchain, a system treats the conclusion of a rule as a goal to be established, and sets itself the subgoal of establishing each of the premises of the rule. These subgoals may in turn give rise to subsubgoals, but in a successful back chain deduction, some goals will eventually match with known facts. Then, values may be passed from the facts through several layers of rules and into the original goal. These values *instantiate* variables in the original goal (such as `site eg_number` in the Syllog rule above) to particular values (such as `site 3`).

The EMycin system, and many expert system shells use back chaining as their main mode of deduction. Indeed, Prolog itself works in this way. However, forward chaining is the basis for the OPS family of shells (Brownston et al. 1985) so clearly both directions have their uses.

A simple forward chaining interpreter can be written in Prolog like this:

```
forward(K1,K3) <- step(K1,K2) & forward(K2,K3).
forward(K1,K1).

step(K,B.K) <- rule(if A then B) &  (A true_in K)  &
    ¬(B true_in K).

(A & B true_in K) <- (A true_in K) & (B true_in K).
A true_in (A.Anything).
A true_in (Anything.K) <- (A true_in K).
```

The first rule says that we can start with a list of facts **K1**, and forward chain to get a larger list of facts **K3**, if we can **step** forward to get one new fact in K2 then forward chain again from K2 to get K3. The next line says that, if step yields nothing new, then we are done.

The rule for step says that we can establish a new fact B if there is a rule

```
if A then B
```

A is true in K, and B is not already true in K.

For example, suppose we have the rules

```
rule(if b & c then a).

rule(if d & e then b).
```

and we start with the facts d, e and c. This we do by asking

```
forward(d.e.c.nil,K)
```

In the first step, b is established, in the next step, a is established, then nothing new can be established, so forward stops with the answer

```
K = a.b.d.e.c.nil
```

It is intriguing to notice that although this is a forward chaining interpreter, the underlying mechanism is back chaining in Prolog. Note also that the forward chaining interpreter will establish everything that it can before stopping. In this respect, forward chaining mechanisms are sometimes called *trigger happy* because even though we may only be interested in, say, a above, if there are extra rules the interpreter will insist on proving all of the possible consequences.

As mentioned in Chapter 3 (page 158) a simple back chaining interpreter can be written in Prolog along the following lines:

```
"true" succeeds.

(A & B)  succeeds  <- A succeeds & B succeeds.

A succeeds  <-
     clause(A<-Premise) & Premise succeeds.
```

The key rule here is the last one. It replaces the goal of showing that A can succeed by the Premise of a rule that could be used to establish A; then it tries to establish the Premise. Actually, these rules are *metarules*—rules about how to use rules— but they run in Prolog just the same way as ordinary rules.

4.1.2 Frames

Among the virtues that we seek in a knowledge notation is that it should allow us to write down knowledge succinctly, and to change the knowledge easily. In our everyday lives, we find taxonomies and classifications a help. We name groups of things, such as cars, and classes of methods for changing the state of things, such as driving. This seems to help us to reason about our surroundings and our activities. For example, once we know that a car, in general, has four wheels, we know that it is a good working assumption that any particular car has four wheels, unless we are told the contrary. In artificial intelligence terminology, a particular car *inherits* a property (having four wheels) from the general class of cars. Similarly, if we say that Fred drove from New York to Toronto, we assume that he drove on the right, since this is an instance of a general method of driving in North America. We can think of a *frame* as a way of writing down some general properties of a situation. To see how frames work as a succinct way of representing things and their properties, here is an example (continued from Chapter 1) that looks like a simplified fragment of a real-estate listing. Suppose that, in general, a house in the listing is on Main Street, has two bathrooms, a basement, white walls, and wood floors. We can write this in Prolog as

```
house has
    (street_name : main &
    number_of_bathrooms : 2 &
    basement : yes &
    wall_color : white &
    floor_surface : wood).
```

(Here has is declared as an operator.) This is a frame. Of course, some groups of houses may have additional features, or may differ from the norm. Type A houses could have 8 bedrooms. Type B houses could be on Delaware rather than on Main Street, and could have 4 bedrooms.

```
type_A_house has
    number_of_bedrooms : 8.

type_B_house has
    (street_name : delaware &
    number_of_bedrooms : 4).
```

Then, individual houses may have their own peculiarities.

```
house1 has
    (street_name : delaware &
    basement : no &
    wall_color : green).

house2 has
    floor_surface : tile.
```

To link all this together, we say that house1 is a type A house, and type A houses are of course houses; similarly for house2 and type B.

```
type_A_house is_a house.

type_B_house is_a house.

house1 is_a type_A_house.

house2 is_a type_B_house.
```

(Here is_a is an operator.)

So far, we have written down facts about houses, using operators such as has and is_a that show roughly how we intend to use the facts. However, we have not yet spelled out this use. That is done in the rules:

```
Attr of Object is Value <-
    description_says Attr of Object is Value.

Attr of Object is Value <-
    Object is_a Object1 &
    Attr of Object1 is Value &
    ¬description_says Attr of Object is SomeValue.
```

An example of the first rule is that the wall color of house1 is green, because the description of house1 says so directly. Here, wall color is an *attribute* of the *object* house1, and it has the *value* green.

The second rule is more subtle, and it captures our notion of an object inheriting properties of its class unless otherwise stated. For example, we can use the two rules to reason that house1 has 2 bathrooms, because it is type A, which is a house, which has 2 bathrooms. The reasoning goes through because neither house1 nor type A houses have a number of bathrooms listed, so the number is inherited from the prototypical house. Notice that the second rule is used twice here.

The rest of the program looks like this. We define some operators so that we can write items like `Attr of Object is Value` directly in Prolog.

```
op("has",rl,35).          op("of",rl,100).
op("is",rl,100).          op("is_a",rl,100).
op("is_in",rl,35).        op(":",rl,95).
op("description_says",prefix,50).
```

Finally we need a rule to say what it means for the description to say that an atrribute of an object has a value.

```
description_says Attr of Object is Value <-
    Object has Description &
    Attr : Value is_in Description.
```

When we run the program, it will confirm statements such as

```
number_of_bathrooms of house1 is 2.
street_name of house is main.
number_of_bedrooms of type_A_house is 8.
street_name of type_B_house is delaware.
street_name of house1 is delaware.
```

Even in this fairly simple example, it may not be obvious why the program has concluded say, that `house1` has 2 bathrooms. So, instead of running the program with the ordinary Prolog interpreter, we can run it with a metainterpreter written in Prolog that produces explanations of its answers. An *explanation* of a "yes" answer can consist of a successful line of reasoning that leads to the answer. An explanation of a "no" answer can consist of a line of reasoning containing some assumptions that, if true, would be enough to yield a "yes" answer. We shall look at just how these explanations can be found in Section 4.4, "Generating Useful Explanations." In the meantime, here are some questions, with explanations of the answers, for our simple knowledge of frames about houses.

```
Question: number_of_bathrooms of house1 is *.

Answer: Yes

Explanation:

number_of_bathrooms of house1 is 2
  house1 is_a type_A_house
  number_of_bathrooms of type_A_house is 2
    type_A_house is_a house
    number_of_bathrooms of house is 2
      description_says number_of_bathrooms of house is 2
```

Here the main answer `number of bathrooms of house1 is 2` is explained to be true because `house1 is a type A house` and `number of` bathrooms of type A house is 2. The first of these is given as a fact, while the second gets further explanation, and so on.

If we ask whether the number of bathrooms of house1 is 3, the answer will be "no." Nevertheless, it may be interesting to see what kind of assumptions might otherwise lead to a "yes" answer.

```
Question: number_of_bathrooms of house1 is 3.
```

```
Answer: No
```

```
Explanation:
```

```
number_of_bathrooms of house1 is 3
 house1 is_a type_A_house
 number_of_bathrooms of type_A_house is 3
  type_A_house is_a house
  number_of_bathrooms of house is 3
   description_says number_of_bathrooms of house is 3?
```

The question mark in the last line indicates our assumption. It says that, if the description of a house were to say that there were three bathrooms, then the rest of the reasoning would go through to give a "yes" answer.

In our section on representing knowledge as rules, we used metainterpreters to describe the use of rules by back chaining and forward chaining. In this section, we have used a metainterpreter to describe the way in which items in frames inherit properties from parent frames. There are just three rules that describe this metainterpreter:

```
Attr of Object is Value <-
    description_says Attr of Object is Value.
```

```
Attr of Object is Value <-
    Object is_a Object1 &  Attr of Object1 is Value &
    ¬description_says Attr of Object is SomeValue.
```

```
description_says Attr of Object is Value <-
    Object has Description  &
    Attr : Value is_in Description.
```

So, although the underlying inference mechanism is that of Prolog, and the underlying knowledge representation is just rules and facts, we can quite easily represent inheritance and frames. Similar experience with other knowledge representations leads us to think that *logic*, using a metalevel where necessary, may be the *missing link* between a number of apparently diverse methods of building expert systems. Moreover, as we shall see next, there is a very simple problem for which *only* logic seems useful.

4.1.3 Logic

There is a further reason for supposing that logic programming and Prolog provide a sensible approach to the proliferation of knowledge representation methods. Although each method has been shown experimentally to work well on the kinds of tasks for which it was designed, there is a simple problem (Moore 1975) in common sense reasoning for which *none* of the known methods other than logic seems appropriate. We shall simplify it further here.

Let us suppose that we are redecorating a house, and that one of our tasks is to lay a line of blue and green tiles. We start the line from its two ends, and (as so often seems to happen) end up one tile short. The tiles either side of the gap are A, which is green, and C which is blue. Our design calls for us to buy another tile B to put in between A and C, so that in the sequence ABC there is a green tile next to a tile that is not green. What color should we choose for B?

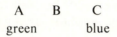

Some thought tells us that the color of B does not matter. For (i) if B is green, then it is a green tile next to C, and (ii) if B is not green, then A is green and next to B.

The surprising thing about this example is that, while it is very simple, logic seems to be the only suitable artificial intelligence notation in which to pose and answer it on a machine. One way of writing the example is shown in the following Prolog program. In the program we ask the question "is there a green tile next to a tile that is not green?" without specifying the color of B. We say that the answer to the question is "yes" if there is no counter example. There *is* a counter example if, for some color of B, we cannot prove that there is a green tile next to a tile that is not green. We can prove that there is a green tile next to a tile that is not green (for some given color of B) by showing that there are neighboring tiles X and Y such that X is green and Y is not green. The two negations (no counter example, no proof) effectively cause the program to check the possible colors of B, making sure that for each color the answer to the question is "yes."

```
question <- ¬counter_example.

counter_example <-  has(ColorB) &
    ¬prove( green_next_non_green, given(ColorB) ).

green_next_non_green <-
    ( next_to(X,Y) | next_to(Y,X) ) &
    color(X,green) &  not_color(Y,green).


next_to(a,b).     next_to(b,c).

color(a,green).

fact( color(b,green) | color(b,blue) ).

color(c,blue).

not_color(X,C) <- color(X,CC) & C=/CC.

has(S) <- fact(F) & member_or(S,F).
```

The first rule says that the answer to our question is "yes" if there is not a counter example. The second rule says that there is a counter example if, for some color of B, we cannot prove that something green is next to something nongreen. The third rule says that there is something green next to something nongreen if X is next to Y, or Y is next to X, and further, X is green and Y is not green. Finally, there is some knowledge about the problem statement. If we run the program, with suitable definitions of member_or(X, Y) and prove(U, given(V)) we get the following.

```
prove(green_next_non_green),given(color(b,green)).

prove(green_next_non_green),
    given(not_color(b,green)).
```

Although the statement of the problem in English is simple, the statement in Prolog is somewhat more complicated than it would be in logic. The example serves to remind us that Prolog is a specialized form of logic. This specialization accounts for the efficiency of Prolog, but it also makes the expression of some problems less direct. In logic, our tiling problem can be written like this:

```
next_to(a,b).          color(a,green).
next_to(b,c).          color(c,blue).
color(b,green) | color(b,blue).
~color(b,green) | ~color(b,blue).
```

Here we are using ~ to stand for *not*, since the way that negation is established in logic differs from Prolog's normal method of arriving at a ¬. (We shall return to this point in the next section and in Appendix B.) The first two lines are just as in Prolog. Although the third line can be regarded as a Prolog term, Prolog's built-in inference method will not reason with it directly. It says that b is green *or* b is blue, which we may think of as an indefinite statement. Prolog statements are more definite; something is so (a fact or an unconditional rule) or something is so if something else is so (a conditional rule). To turn the third line into a Prolog statement we wrote it as

```
fact( color(b,green) | color(b,blue) ).
```

and we provided an extra rule

```
has(S) <- fact(F) & member_or(S,F).
```

about how to use it. Although we have written down our tiling problem in logic, we have yet to ask our question. We want to know whether there are tiles X and Y such that X is green, Y is blue, and X is next to Y. (This is a slight simplification of Moore's problem, but it serves to illustrate our logical approach.) So we can write

```
∃(X,Y) :
    next_to(X,Y) & color(X,green) & color(Y,blue).
```

One way to show that this is so is to assume the opposite, namely

```
~∃(X,Y) :
    next_to(X,Y) & color(X,green) & color(Y,blue).
```

and then to show that the assumption leads to a contradiction. We will then be able to conclude that the answer to our original question must be yes.

The nonexistence of X and Y with some property is the same as saying that for all pairs X and Y the property does not hold. So we can write our assumption as

```
∀(X,Y) : ~ (next_to(X,Y) &
    color(X,green) & color(Y,blue)).
```

and then, noting that ~ (a & b & c) is the same as (~a | ~b | ~c), our assumption becomes

```
∀(X,Y) : (~next_to(X,Y) |
    ~color(X,green) | ~color(Y,blue)).
```

Finally, taking the ∀(X,Y) as understood, we can write

```
~next_to(X,Y) | ~color(X,green) | ~color(Y,blue).
```

So now we are ready to reason from

```
next_to(a,b).            color(a,green).
next_to(b,c).            color(c,blue).
color(b,green) | color(b,blue).
~color(b,green) | ~color(b,blue).
~next_to(X,Y) | ~color(X,green) | ~color(Y,blue).
```

to find a contradiction. If we can find one, we shall have answered "yes" to the original question.

Our method of reasoning is called *resolution*. It is due to Robinson (1965) and it can be summarized by a general scheme

```
A1 | ... | Am | ~B
B | C1 | ... | Cn
------------------------------
A1 | ... | Am | C1 | ... | Cn
```

This means that if we are given (A1 | ... | Am | ~B) and (B | C1 | ... | Cn), we can conclude (A1 | ... | Am | C1 | ... | Cn). This is really shorthand, since B and ~B may contain variables that are bound when the two items are matched, and these bindings may affect the A's and C's also.

In the scheme, if m=0 and n=0 then from B and ~B we get *nothing* which is understood as a *contradiction*—just what we shall be looking for. Although the resolution step may not appear obvious, it is actually like a more general form of the Prolog inference step. For example, from the rule e <- f and the fact f we are happy to conclude e. If we think of e <- f as (e | ~f), then resolution says the same thing—from (e | ~f) and f we can conclude e.

We can now use resolution to solve the tiling problem. We do this by listing some resolution steps that lead us to a contradiction (remember, we assumed the opposite of our question).

```
next_to(b,c)
~next_to(X,Y) | ~color(X,green) | ~color(Y,blue)
-----------------------------------------------------
~color(b,green) | ~color(c,blue)

next_to(a,b)
~next_to(X,Y) | ~color(X,green) | ~color(Y,blue)
-----------------------------------------------------
~color(a,green) | ~color(b,blue)
```

```
~color(b,green) | ~color(c,blue)
color(c,blue)
-----------------------------------
~color(b,green)

~color(a,green) | ~color(b,blue)
color(a,green)
-----------------------------------
~color(b,blue)

color(b,green) | color(b,blue)
~color(b,blue)
-----------------------------------
color(b,green)

~color(b,green)
color(b,green)
---------------
contradiction
```

We have looked at the simple tiling problem, and we have shown how to solve it somewhat indirectly in Prolog, and directly in logic. The problem is interesting in that, though it is simple to state, it has no straightforward solution in the main knowledge representations used for expert systems, other than logic. This, together with the fact that the known representations fit rather well in logic, give us some evidence that logic is a good way of representing knowledge.

4.1.4 Summary

On the one hand, many useful artificial intelligence methods for representing knowledge fit neatly into logic, and executably into Prolog. On the other hand, there is a simple problem for which logic seems to be the only useful notation.

4.2 SYLLOG—AN EXPERT AND DATA SYSTEM SHELL

We have mentioned that many expert systems can be usefully written in terms of rules— even some that do not appear at first to represent knowledge in rules (see 4.1.2, "Frames"). Prolog programs also contain rules. So what then is the difference between rule-based expert systems and Prolog programs? The distinction is that Prolog, while a very advanced language, is for use by programmers. It should be possible for a person who is not a trained programmer to change the knowledge in an expert system. Ideally, an expert system shell can also be adapted to entirely new tasks without reprogramming.

As we mentioned in Chapter 1, *learning by being told* is a relatively simple technique that can be surprisingly useful. For most learning by being told tasks, the notation used must at least resemble a natural language, such as English, rather than a programming language. We can pick different shades along the spectrum from English, at one extreme, to logic or Prolog at the other. This section looks at a system called Syllog. Syllog's language is English-like, and it allows the system to learn by being told.

4.2.1 Introduction to Syllog

It would be good to be able build one's own knowledge system without doing any programming. Once the knowledge system is written, we need a way of finding out what it is about, if people other than the writer are to use it. (Even the writer may forget some details.) Of course it should also be possible to change the facts, and the knowledge about how to use the facts, without doing any programming. If we are using a knowledge system, say, to order materials for building a house, then it is important that the system should explain the reasons for the advice that it gives; few people would be happy about ordering a ton of concrete without an explanation of why it is needed.

To do this without programming, we settle for a language that we can use in an English-like way, rather than full English. This turns out to have both disadvantages and advantages. A disadvantage is that we have to remember some conventions about how the language stops short of English, and we may sometimes have to think for a while to cast our thoughts, written in English, into a restricted form of the language. An advantage is that the underlying technology is simplified so much that it actually does not matter whether we put in knowledge in English-like language, in a jargon, or in a French-like language, and so on. As long as we use words and phrases consistently, it does not matter what words and phrases we use!

Most of us are familiar with syllogisms, which are logical implications written in English. For example

> All rooms have doors.
> This is a room.
> Therefore it has doors.

It turns out that such syllogisms can be read in two different ways. In mathematical logic, the normal reading is this. If the first two sentences are true, then so is the third; if one of the first two sentences is false, then the third one could be true or false. Often, in ordinary English use, the reading is different; the third sentence is true if the first two are, but otherwise the third sentence is false.

For example, suppose we know that bedroom and study are rooms, and we also know the syllogism above, but that is all that we know. Under the first reading, an object that we do not know about, such as a car, might or might not have doors. Under the second reading, a car is assumed not to have doors, because we cannot reason from what we know to show that it has.

The second reading looks slightly strange with this example, because the two facts and the syllogism are very much less than we humans know. If we think of a bigger example, with all of the relevant knowledge about things with doors, then we may be confident in using the second reading to conclude, say, that beds do not have doors. The second reading saves us from having to include, in a knowledge system, explicit notes about the very large number of things that do not have doors.

The first reading is conveniently called the *open world assumption*, the second the *closed world assumption*. (We use different symbols for *not* to signal which assumption is being made. Say ~ when using the open world and ¬ when using the closed world assumption.)

Here is how our simple example would be written in Syllog.

The syllogism is written

```
eg_place is a room
-------------------------------
eg_place has one or more doors
```

and the fact that `bedroom` and `study` are rooms is written

```
eg_place is a room
==================
bedroom
study
```

In the syllogism, the dotted line divides an IF part from a THEN part. The phrase `eg_place` is a way of indicating that we are talking about any place, that is the `eg_` stands for a variable. In the facts about bedroom and study, the double dotted line separates a heading sentence from the actual facts. We can think of this as a table with one column. From the user's point of view, Syllog reasons directly with syllogisms and facts in these forms.

If we actually type the syllogism and facts on the screen, then Syllog can reason with them right away. To remind us about the knowledge in the system, Syllog prompts with the sentences it has seen.

```
eg_place has one or more doors
eg_place is a room
```

If we choose the second sentence, and press the appropriate key, then Syllog understands this as asking for the table of facts. The screen changes to

```
eg_place is a room
==================
bedroom
study
```

If we choose the first sentence and press the appropriate key, then we are asking for the places, known to the system, that have one or more doors. The answer is

```
eg_place has one or more doors
===============================
bedroom
study
```

If we would like to see why the system has reasoned that a bedroom has one or more doors, we can leave this

```
bedroom has one or more doors
```

on the screen. The system answers like this

```
bedroom has one or more doors
-----------------------------

    Yes, that's true.

    Because....

bedroom is a room
-----------------------------
bedroom has one or more doors
```

The system shows the relevant instance of the syllogism by way of explanation.

On the other hand, if we ask the system whether, according to its knowledge, a car has doors

```
    car has one or more doors
```

the answer is

```
    car has one or more doors
    -------------------------

    Sorry, no.

    Because....

    car is a room?
    -------------------------
    car has one or more doors
```

In the explanation, the system is indicating that, if a car were a room, then the system could reason that it has doors. The system is using the closed world assumption (by saying "no," rather than "don't know"), but it is also explaining what it is doing. Of course the answer is wrong, because the knowledge is incomplete. In this kind of situation, an explanation is often a help in finding a place where some knowledge should be added.

Although Syllog works with English-like sentences, there is no need to build a dictionary, or a grammar, when new parts of English (e.g for law or manufacturing) are needed. One simply types in sentences, and the system is immediately ready to use them. In fact, the language used can equally well be French, German, most other natural languages, or even an artificial language. Syllog makes logically correct inferences based on what it is told. However, it *knows* little of the language concerned, when compared with natural language understanding programs, such as those described in Chapter 5. This lack of knowledge has both advantages and disadvantages. The advantages are that one can easily add knowledge to the system in the language of one's choice, and that one need not instruct the system about the details of the language one is using. The disadvantages are that one is limited to simple declarative sentences, and these use the special *example* words starting with eg_. Also, one must either consistently use the same sentence to mean the same thing, or provide syllogisms to say that different sentences have the same meaning. Syllog supports this approach by prompting with a menu of the sentences that are in the knowledge base. In the menu, the sentences are grouped and ordered in a helpful way.

One can type almost any sentence into Syllog, and have the system reason with it. A sentence may contain one or more words starting with eg_, and it must have at least one word that does not start with eg_. Beyond this, there are a few reserved phrases, such as not followed by a colon, which must be used at the start of a sentence.

In our manufacturing example in the next section, we talk about the number of items per day that can be handled on a test machine of a certain type, when some percentage of the items spend a longer "burnin" time than others on the tester. We say this in Syllog as

```
can handle eg_c of eg_item pd,
    with eg_p % burnin, on eg_testm machine.
```

Inside Syllog, the sentence is represented simply in the form

```
p3(V1,V2,V3,V4)
```

in which p3 is an arbitrarily chosen predicate name and V1 to V4 are variables corresponding to eg_c to eg_testm. Of course the English-like form that we see on the screen must also be kept along with the p3 form, so that the system can understand questions and show explanations. This is a simple and robust device, that gives us a lot of language flexibility as users of Syllog. Nevertheless, the internal programming of the translation between the two forms takes some thought. For example, a knowledge base with the above English-like sentence may also contain the sentences

```
can handle 99 of eg_item pd, with eg_p % burnin, on eg_testm machine.
```

```
can handle eg_c of eg_item pd, with eg_p % burnin, on a50 machine.
```

When we load the knowledge base, all three sentences must be translated to the predicate p3. If only the last two sentences are in the knowledge base, then the loading process must construct the first sentence..

Some simple sets of syllogisms can be thought of as English-like forms of expressions in relational algebra—a database retrieval language (Codd 1971, Date 1977) with some arithmetic processing allowed. However, syllogisms can be recursive, (that is, they may be defined ultimately in terms of themselves) and they sometimes need to be. In our manufacturing knowledge base in the next section, we define a parts explosion hierarchy, and the definition is recursive. Recursion allows us to express concepts that cannot be written down in the nonrecursive relational algebra (Aho and Ullman 1979). Although recursive syllogisms are quite readable, and have a simple common sense meaning (corresponding to their models in mathematical logic), it is not entirely straightforward to interpret them both declaratively (order does not matter), and efficiently. For example, it is not enough to compile recursive syllogisms into Prolog and then execute them using Prolog's built-in inference engine, for reasons set out in Section 4.2.3, "Inside the Syllog Shell."

Instead, the Syllog system, which is written in Prolog, contains its own inference engine. This engine computes correctly with many sets of recursive syllogisms that are outside the scope of Prolog itself. Some related ways of computing with recursive logic statements are discussed in Appendix B and are given a formal treatment in Brough and Walker (1984).

We have introduced the idea of representing knowledge as English-like syllogisms, by means of a simple example about rooms and doors. To see that this approach works more generally, we can try a more interesting example.

4.2.2　A Manufacturing Knowledge Base in Syllog

Our example is a knowledge base about manufacturing. This section describes a prototype knowledge base for manufacturing planning, which we have built using Syllog. We describe a Tester Capacity Planning and Yield Analysis task, knowledge needed for a part of the task, and the use of the knowledge in the Syllog system. Our manufacturing task concerns the testing of electronic items in a production line before they are plugged into larger assemblies. We wish to plan the numbers of various types of testing machines that are needed to meet a production target. Accurate estimates of the numbers of machines are important, since too little capacity can cause production delays, while too much is wasteful. The numbers of machines needed, the times when they should be available, and their locations, depend in a complex way on the bill of materials for the items to be manufactured, on previous experience of the yields of good items from testing, on previous experience of the rates at which items can be tested, on the space available, and on several other considerations.

The information needed for planning consists of facts and of equations and rules for using the facts. The facts are held in some form of database, and increasingly are collected automatically by manufacturing instrumentation. An equation or rule typically reads as a piece of common sense knowledge about the planning task. However, the ways in which the facts and rules combine to give answers are complicated, and our knowledge base allows us to keep a clear view of the process.

One might consider writing conventional database application programs for our task. However, as rules change, or as new rules are added, such application programs tend to get out of step with reality and to become hard to maintain. In our tester capacity planning task, timely expert advice is needed. Since the users are not programmers, the expertise is best captured and maintained without programming. In addition, while the facts and rules may be correct, the answers that they produce may sometimes not be obvious. So for the planning team, it is useful to have explanations of the answers provided by a planning tool. If an answer provided by such a planning tool is positive, then an explanation provides a means of checking that the rules that caused the answer are correct. If an answer provided by a planning tool is negative, then an explanation can help in determining what additional facts or rules are needed.

Next we describe our manufacturing planning task. Then we show the process of building a part of a knowledge base for the task, in Syllog. We also describe how the knowledge can be used for manufacturing planning by asking questions, by trying *what-if* questions, and by getting explanations.

The Tester Capacity Planning Task

This section describes a simplified version of a planning task that is of importance to manufacturing test engineers. Although the facts that we use in this section are just samples, the knowledge is about a real manufacturing planning task (Fellenstein et al. 1985).

A major step in electronics manufacturing is the testing of individual cards before they are plugged into a larger assembly, (e.g a controller), generally called a product, or box. Typically, a flow of cards must be checked on a battery of specialized test machines. Another important step is to test the components, such as resistors and chips, that will be placed on a card. For this step, test machines are also needed. In each step, some of the items (cards or components) that are tested will fail.

So, if there is a production goal to manufacture, say, 1000 boxes during the third quarter of the year, we must plan to allocate enough test machines of the right kinds. This is the tester capacity planning problem. To solve the problem, we need three kinds of knowledge.

First, we need a bill of materials for a box, showing the number of each type of card needed, and the number of each type of component needed for each card. Second, we need an estimate of the percentage of each batch of items that will pass testing. Third, we need to know the capacity of each kind of tester on each kind of item, that is, the rates at which items can be tested.

The bill of materials for a box can be supplied as a table showing, for each item, how many subitems of a given type there are. From this, we need to find

how many components of each kind are in a box, using the information about
how many components are on a card, and how many cards of each kind are in a
box. This is the well-known *parts explosion* hierarchy. In addition, we need to
estimate the larger numbers of each component and card that are actually
needed for a batch of boxes, based on expected yields of good items (cards and
components) during the two levels of testing.

Next, we need to know the expected yield of each of the items, based on
previous testing. This information is extracted from detailed reports of test
batches in earlier production runs.

Finally, in order to estimate the number of test machines needed to meet a
production goal, we need to know the rate at which each tester can test each type
of item. We usually have an estimate of the capacity of a tester from earlier
experience, and this estimate improves with time. However, the capacity is not
fixed for a given item, but depends on how we choose to test. For example, we
may choose to test some percentage of items with a *burnin* period, which takes
longer, but gives better results. We get this knowledge by summarizing previous
test records for the same items, where available.

What we have described so far is a simplified form of the actual task. This
form is convenient for illustrating the kinds of knowledge and reasoning that are
needed. We shall describe this simplified task knowledge as a set of syllogisms
and tables. Syllog will then be used to answer the question *how many test
machines of each type will be needed to support the manufacture of a certain
number of boxes over a given time period?* We shall how *what-if* questions
about tester capacity can be posed and answered in Syllog, and how the
knowledge and estimates can be checked using Syllog's built-in explanation
mechanisms. We note that Syllog is task independent; that is, different tasks
within a certain range can be performed just by loading different sets of facts
and syllogisms. So we do not need to change the Syllog system itself in order to
work with facts and knowledge about tester capacities.

We mentioned that, for our simplified tester capacity and yield analysis task,
we need knowledge of three kinds. We need to know about the parts hierarchy
(bill of materials) for the box to be manufactured, about the expected yield of
each item from testing, and about test machines and their individual capacities.

The Parts Hierarchy

First, we shall write the facts and syllogisms for the parts hierarchy, using the
Syllog language of facts and rules.

A group of related facts is written for Syllog in the form of a table. The
table is like a table in a relational database, except that it is headed by a sentence
in English (or French, German etc), containing one or more *example elements*.
Thus, we can enter (or load) the table

```
eg_item has eg_number of the immediate part eg_subitem
=========================================================
box1          2                             card1
box1          3                             card2
card1         5                             resistor1
card1         7                             chip2
card1         6                             capacitor1
card2         8                             chip1
card2         5                             resistor7
card2         6                             capacitor2
```

The English sentence has an example element eg_item, which we can think of as *an item* or *some item*; likewise for eg_number and eg_subitem. So the whole sentence above the double line can be read as *an item has a number of the immediate part subitem.* The line separates the sentence, which serves as a heading, from the body of the table. The first row of the table can be read as the fact that *box1 has 2 of the immediate part card1*, and similarly for the other rows. So, a row in a Syllog table corresponds to a fact in the ordinary sense.

We write down knowledge for Syllog in the form of syllogisms. A syllogism consists of one or more sentences, a line, then a single sentence, as in

```
eg_item has eg_4 of the part eg_subitem
eg_subitem has eg_6 of the part eg_subsubitem
eg_4 * eg_6 = eg_24
-----------------------------------------------
eg_item has eg_24 of the part eg_subsubitem
```

As for a classical syllogism, the meaning is: *IF each of the sentences above the line is true, THEN the sentence below the line is true.* In each sentence the example elements serve as place holders. Here eg_4 stands for some number, and it stands for the same number in two places in the syllogism. (We could equally well have written eg_x for eg_4, eg_y for eg_6, and eg_z for eg_24; the choice is a matter of style.) We refer to a syllogism as a rule, for short. We can read the above rule as *if an item has x of some subitem, each such subitem has y of some subsubitem, and x times y is z, then the item has z of the subsubitems.* (We are assuming for simplicity that each kind of item appears in just one place in the parts hierarchy.)

We need another similar rule. If an item has a number n of the immediate subitems of some kind, then it has n subitems of that kind. In Syllog, we write this as the rule

```
eg_item has eg_5 of the immediate part eg_subitem
-------------------------------------------------
eg_item has eg_5 of the part eg_subitem
```

Once we have typed the table of facts, and the two rules, into Syllog, the system responds with a prompt

```
eg_item has eg_4 of the part eg_subitem
```

```
eg_item has eg_5 of the immediate part eg_subitem
```

consisting of the sentences it has seen so far. (There are just two sentences in the prompt, since the other important sentences in the knowledge can be obtained from these by renaming the eg_ example elements.) If we want to see how many of each card and component are in box1, we select the first sentence

```
eg_item has eg_4 of the part eg_subitem
```

of the prompt, and change eg_item to box1, thus

```
box1 has eg_4 of the part eg_subitem
```

If we press the appropriate key, the screen changes to

```
box1 has eg_4 of the part eg_subitem
=====================================
         2                  card1
         3                  card2
         10                 resistor1
         14                 chip2
         12                 capacitor1
         24                 chip1
         15                 resistor7
         18                 capacitor2
```

Thus, our question to Syllog is the sentence that we chose from a menu of sentences and specialized by typing box1. (If we do not know in advance a particular value that we want to ask about, such as box1, we can open a window of possible values on the screen and select a value from it.) When we press the appropriate key, Syllog fills in the table.

The system has used the table of immediate parts and the two rules to reason that, among other things, box1 contains 10 of resistor1. To get an explanation of the reasoning for this we can move the cursor to the third row of the answer table, then press an "explanation" key. The screen then changes to

```
box1 has 10 of the part resistor1
----------------------------------

    Yes, that's true

    Because...

box1 has 2 of the part card1
card1 has 5 of the part resistor1
2 * 5 = 10
----------------------------------
box1 has 10 of the part resistor1
```

```
box1 has 2 of the immediate part card1
---------------------------------------
box1 has 2 of the part card1


card1 has 5 of the immediate part resistor1
-------------------------------------------
card1 has 5 of the part resistor1
```

The explanation, below **Because...**, consists of the instances of the rules that have been used to establish the answer. The first rule instance gives the main conclusion, while the last two rule instances show why the premises of the first rule instance hold. In general, Syllog explanations may be longer than one screen, so it is useful to see the main reasoning first, and then to scroll to subsidiary justifications as needed.

Now that the system can reason about the numbers of cards and components in a box, we need to add knowledge about the numbers actually needed, given that not all items will pass their tests. This will depend on the number of boxes we plan to ship, the length of time we are given to manufacture the boxes, and the expected yield of each item at each test. We can write the knowledge in Syllog as

```
we plan to ship eg_100 of eg_product in quarter eg_q
eg_product has eg_2 of the immediate part eg_card
the expected yield of eg_card is eg_75 %, based on past experience
eg_100 * eg_2 = eg_200
eg_200 divided by eg_75 (normalized and rounded up) is eg_267
------------------------------------------------------------
we shall set up testers for eg_267 of eg_card in quarter eg_q


we shall set up testers for eg_10 of eg_card in quarter eg_q
eg_card has eg_2 of the immediate part eg_comp
eg_10 * eg_2 = eg_20
the expected yield of eg_comp is eg_50 %, based on past experience
eg_20 divided by eg_50 (normalized and rounded up) is eg_40
----------------------------------------------------
we shall set up testers for eg_40 of eg_comp in quarter eg_q


eg_y - 1 = eg_y1
eg_x * 100 = eg_x100
eg_x100 + eg_y1 = eg_x100_plus_y1
eg_x100_plus_y1 / eg_y = eg_z
---------------------------------------------------------
eg_x divided by eg_y (normalized and rounded up) is eg_z
```

The first rule tells us how many cards to plan tester capacity for, given how many boxes we want to ship, and the expected yield of good cards from testing. The second rule does the same for each component, making use of the conclusion of the first rule. The third rule just does normalized, rounded up division. In order to use the first two rules, we need know the expected yield of each item during testing, based on past experience. For the moment, we shall assume that this is given as

```
the expected yield of eg_item is eg_y %, based on past experience
=================================================================
                       card1        88
                       card2        95
                       resistor1    90
                       chip2        85
                       capacitor1   90
                       chip1        93
                       resistor7    94
                       capacitor2   95
```

Later, we shall show how the yield information is extracted from more detailed shop floor reports.

If we now select the conclusion of our first rule, and ask for a table, we get

```
we shall set up testers for eg_267 of eg_card in quarter eg_q
=============================================================
               2273        card1         3
               3158        card2         3
               12628       resistor1     3
               18719       chip2         3
               15154       capacitor1    3
               27166       chip1         3
               16798       resistor7     3
               19946       capacitor2    3
```

If we wish, Syllog will give us an explanation of any row of the table. If we pick the fourth row, we get:

```
we shall set up testers for 18719 of chip2 in quarter 3
-----------------------------------------------------------

    Yes, that's true

    Because...

we shall set up testers for 2273 of card1 in quarter 3
card1 has 7 of the immediate part chip2
2273 * 7 = 15911
the expected yield of chip2 is 85 %, based on past experience
15911 divided by 85 (normalized and rounded up) is 18719
-----------------------------------------------------------
we shall set up testers for 18719 of chip2 in quarter 3

we plan to ship 1000 of box1 in quarter 3
box1 has 2 of the immediate part card1
the expected yield of card1 is 88 %, based on past experience
1000 * 2 = 2000
2000 divided by 88 (normalized and rounded up) is 2273
-----------------------------------------------------------
we shall set up testers for 2273 of card1 in quarter 3
```

The bottom of the explanation also contains the reasons for the rounded division result; we omit such details from explanations from now on. They are always available in Syllog by scrolling down through the screens of the full explanation.

At this point, we can predict the numbers of items that we shall need to test, based on some assumed yield figures. Next, we show how the yield figures are found. Then, we shall add knowledge about testers, so that we can find out how many testers of each type are needed.

Yield Analysis

In the last section we used the table of assumed yield figures on page 243. These figures are actually found from shop floor reports of earlier test runs. The kinds of facts that are available are about test jobs. A job has some number of items (cards or components). Some of these items fail test, and the number of failures is noted. Also, the day on which each job is started, and the day on which it is finished, is tabulated. So, the kinds of facts that are available are:

```
job eg_j has eg_number of eg_item
==========================================
```

eg_j	eg_number	eg_item
1	100	card1
2	200	card2
3	500	resistor1
4	700	chip2
5	600	capacitor1
6	800	chip1
7	500	resistor7
8	600	capacitor2

```
in job eg_j the fallout was eg_f items
========================================
```

eg_j	eg_f
1	12
2	10
3	50
4	100
5	55
6	50
7	28
8	30

```
job eg_j was completed during the days eg_d1 through eg_d2
============================================================
```

eg_j	eg_d1	eg_d2
1	1	31
2	1	3
3	3	20
4	1	1
5	3	12
6	51	70
7	1	365
8	1	365

These facts are summarized using the two rules

```
in days eg_d1 thru eg_d2 yield of eg_item was eg_y % in job eg_j
---------------------------------------------------------------
the expected yield of eg_item is eg_y %, based on past experience

job eg_j was completed during the days eg_d1 through eg_d2
job eg_j has eg_number of eg_item
in job eg_j the fallout was eg_f items
eg_number - eg_f = eg_net
eg_net is eg_y as a percent of eg_number
---------------------------------------------------------------
in days eg_d1 thru eg_d2 yield of eg_item was eg_y % in job eg_j
```

Once we have entered these three tables and two rules into the system, we can ask for an explanation of how the first row of the expected yield table on page 243 was found:

```
the expected yield of card1 is 88 %, based on past experience
----------------------------------------------------------------


    Yes, that's true

    Because...

in days 1 thru 31 yield of card1 was 88 % in job 1
------------------------------------------------------------
the expected yield of card1 is 88 %, based on past experience


job 1 was completed during the days 1 through 31
job 1 has 100 of card1
in job 1 the fallout was 12 items
100 - 12 = 88
88 is 88 as a percent of 100
--------------------------------------------------------
in days 1 thru 31 yield of card1 was 88 % in job 1
```

So far, we have knowledge about the parts hierarchy, about the number of items we shall need to test, about the number of components needed, and about the expected yield of each item that we shall test. It remains to plan the number of test machines.

Planning the Number of Test Machines

We can now predict the number of items that we shall need to test in quarter 3, based on shop floor reports of yields in earlier production runs. We still need to add knowledge about the test machines themselves, and facts about how many items will be burnt in during testing, so that we can plan the actual number of each kind of test machine.

We start with the facts. We shall plan to burn in items at the rates

```
eg_p % of eg_item are burnt in
===============================
50          card1
60          card2
50          resistor1
70          chip2
60          capacitor1
40          chip1
50          resistor7
60          capacitor2
```

and, later, we shall try some *what if* questions about the effects of these rates on the testers needed. Testing an item on a machine takes different times, depending on whether or not we burn in the item:

```
test of eg_item on eg_m machine takes times eg_t1 (nb) and eg_t2 (b)
====================================================================
          card1       a50                   20              40
          card2       t20                   36              62
          resistor1   cr10                  2               10
          chip2       nb40                  3               20
          capacitor1  cc20                  2               15
          chip1       nb50                  5               50
          resistor7   cr20                  2               9
          capacitor2  cc30                  3               20
```

Here, eg_t1 (nb) and eg_t2 (b) are the times for testing without and with burnin, respectively. The table consists of estimates, that we normally obtain by using rules to summarize more detailed reports. For example, with a little more detail on the time taken to complete each job, the times given in the above table could be found from shop floor reports about individual jobs.

We shall use the facts with three rules that tell us how many test machines we shall need:

```
we shall set up testers for eg_num of eg_item in quarter eg_q
eg_num divided by 60 (and rounded up) is eg_rate
-------------------------------------------------------------------
the daily going rate for eg_item for quarter eg_q is eg_rate
```

Here, we are assuming that there are 60 working days per quarter.

```
test of eg_item on eg_m machine takes times eg_t1 (nb) and eg_t2 (b)
eg_p % of eg_item are burnt in
the rounded eg_p % weighting of eg_t1 and eg_t2 is eg_t
480 divided by eg_t (and rounded up) is eg_c
-------------------------------------------------------------------
can handle eg_c of eg_item pd, with eg_p % burnin, on eg_m machine
```

The 480 in this rule is the number of minutes in a working day.

```
the daily going rate for eg_item for quarter eg_q is eg_rate
can handle eg_c of eg_item pd, with eg_p % burnin, on eg_testm machine
eg_rate divided by eg_c (and rounded up) is eg_number
-------------------------------------------------------------------
we need eg_number of the eg_testm test machine in quarter eg_q
```

In the first of the above three rules, the sentence

```
we shall set up testers for eg_num of eg_item in quarter eg_q
```

refers to the rules on page 242 for the volume of items for which test machines are needed. In the second rule, the first and second sentences refer to tables in this section. The last rule makes use of the first two to tell us how many test machines of each type we need.

If we now select the conclusion of the last rule, Syllog fills in a table

```
we need eg_number of the eg_testm test machine in quarter eg_q
===============================================================
```

3	a50	3
6	t20	3
3	cr10	3
10	nb40	3
6	cc20	3
22	nb50	3
4	cr20	3
9	cc30	3

showing the numbers of each test machine needed. To see how the knowledge in the system has contributed to the table, we can ask for an explanation of the sixth row:

```
we need 22 of the nb50 test machine in quarter 3
-------------------------------------------------


    Yes, that's true

    Because...


the daily going rate for chip1 for quarter 3 is 453
can handle 21 of chip1 pd, with 40 % burnin, on nb50 machine
453 divided by 21 (and rounded up) is 22
-------------------------------------------------------------
we need 22 of the nb50 test machine in quarter 3

we shall set up testers for 27166 of chip1 in quarter 3
27166 divided by 60 (and rounded up) is 453
-------------------------------------------------------------
the daily going rate for chip1 for quarter 3 is 453
```

```
test of chip1 on nb50 machine takes times 5 (nb) and 50 (b)
40 % of chip1 are burnt in
the rounded 40 % weighting of 5 and 50 is 23
480 divided by 23 (and rounded up) is 21
-------------------------------------------------------------
can handle 21 of chip1 pd, with 40 % burnin, on nb50 machine

we shall set up testers for 3158 of card2 in quarter 3
card2 has 8 of the immediate part chip1
3158 * 8 = 25264
the expected yield of chip1 is 93 %, based on past experience
25264 divided by 93 (normalized and rounded up) is 27166
-------------------------------------------------------------
we shall set up testers for 27166 of chip1 in quarter 3

we plan to ship 1000 of box1 in quarter 3
box1 has 3 of the immediate part card2
the expected yield of card2 is 95 %, based on past experience
1000 * 3 = 3000
3000 divided by 95 (normalized and rounded up) is 3158
-------------------------------------------------------------
we shall set up testers for 3158 of card2 in quarter 3
```

(The explanation continues with more detail, but we have stopped it here.) Once we have checked the knowledge in the rules by looking at several such explanations, we can start to ask *what-if* questions. Recall that the present answers are based on the burnin percentages

```
eg_p % of eg_item are burnt in
==============================
50        card1
60        card2
50        resistor1
70        chip2
60        capacitor1
40        chip1
50        resistor7
60        capacitor2
```

If we have this table on the screen, we can increase the burnin percentages for the cards to

```
eg_p % of eg_item are burnt in
==============================
70          card1
80          card2
70          resistor1
90          chip2
80          capacitor1
60          chip1
70          resistor7
80          capacitor2
```

and ask again how many test machines are needed. For the new burnin percentages:

```
we need eg_number of the eg_testm test machine in quarter eg_q
==============================================================
          3                a50                          3
          6                t20                          3
          4                cr10                         3
          12               nb40                         3
          7                cc20                         3
          31               nb50                         3
          5                cr20                         3
          12               cc30                         3
```

Once again, we can ask for an explanation, if we so wish.

So, we have written down some knowledge in Syllog. We have written a bill of materials and parts hierarchy, an estimate of the yield of items from each phase of testing, and an estimate of the rate at which each item can be tested on a given test machine. The Syllog system has applied the knowledge to plan the number of test machines of each type needed, and also to plan an inventory requirements list of components to be purchased to meet the production goal.

4.2.3 Inside the Syllog Shell

So far we have spoken about Syllog as something of a "black box"; we put in knowledge, and the system reasons with it and provides explanations of the reasoning. In fact Syllog is designed to be used in that way— it should normally not be necessary to look inside to see how it works. However, for those of us who wish to *write* shells like Syllog it is interesting to look inside, and that is what we shall do in this section.

The idea of a shell as a black box is closely tied to the notion of declarative knowledge. If we can provide knowledge declaratively, without much concern about how it is to be executed, then (as users of the shell) we need not look into the internal reasoning procedures. However, we do need some confidence that these procedures, whatever they are, yield results that correspond to the declarative meaning of the knowledge that we provide. The declarative meaning of a few rules and facts can often be seen just by common sense. Yet common sense by itself is not really a satisfactory way of judging an inference engine— we need a precise standard so that we can say exactly whether or not our inference engine lives up to it. Moreover, our precise standard should probably not be a procedure, since different people may think of different procedures, and we cannot be sure that they will always produce the same results.

The most useful declarative standard appears to be one based on *model theory* in logic. For our purposes, a *model* of a knowledge base is a set of variable-free facts with two particular properties:

- Each fact in the knowledge base is in the model,
- If the premises of a rule in the knowledge base can be instantiated with facts in the model, then the corresponding instance of the conclusion of the rule is also in the model.

In Appendix B, Logical Basis for Prolog, we look at the notion of a model in detail, and we show how it can be used to assign a declarative meaning to Syllog knowledge bases and to Prolog programs, particularly to knowledge bases and programs containing negation. Ideally, we would like to be able to *prove* that a procedural inference engine computes as required by the declarative model of a knowledge base. This is in fact possible when the engine is simple, as shown in (Apt et al. 1986). However, the more efficient engines tend also to be more complicated, and we usually verify them by extensive testing on carefully chosen examples.

Although this section is about an inference engine, we note that the Syllog shell consists of a number of components:

- A screen-manager, for menu selection etc,
- A language file, for tailoring the system messages into English, French, and so on,
- A loader, to prepare and check a knowledge base,
- An update component, for changes to the knowledge,
- An inference engine,
- An interface to a database management system, and
- An explanation generator.

Here we shall concentrate on the inference engine. Prolog by itself is efficient, but it does not always assign the declarative meaning that we want. For example, Prolog will loop if it attempts to use the rule

```
a(X, Z) <- a(X, Y) & b(Y, Z).
```

In fact we show on page 442 that no strictly top down left to right method of interpretation of knowledge (such as Prolog) is satisfactory for our purpose, even when supplemented by loop trapping. Thus, our options are to write a metainterpreter in Prolog, or to find a way of compiling the knowledge provided by a user so that it will run directly in Prolog. The interpreted and compiled approaches are really just extreme points on a spectrum, and they can be mixed. Here we shall talk about an interpreted approach.

Since a pure top down interpreter will not produce the required declarative meaning, our interpreter will have both a top down (back chaining) and a bottom up (forward chaining, iterative) component. The method described here is a simplified version of the *backchain iteration* method first implemented for Syllog (Walker 1981). As often seems to be the case, our simplified backchain iteration interpreter is slower than the more complicated versions. However, we shall indicate some ways to increase its speed. It should be mentioned that the idea of giving improved declarativeness for Prolog-like programs, while retaining as much of the speed of Prolog as possible, has received much attention recently. Many other inference methods (most of which, like backchain iteration, are actually *classes* of methods) have been proposed. For example, Bancilhon and Ramakrishnan (1986) list 10 classes of methods. In Appendix B (page 446) we describe an interesting method called *Earley Deduction*.

We should mention that it is quite hard to compare the practical efficiency of different methods, unless the efficiencies differ by at least an order of magnitude. One method may be better for a class A of knowledge bases, another for a class B. Small programming decisions about each method may reverse the situation. If we measure the successful rule firings per second, we also need to measure how many of these contribute to an answer, and how many represent unnecessary search.

Section 3.2.1, "Meta-level Programming" described several metainterpreters written in Prolog. We now use the same general approach to describe a simplified backchain iteration interpreter. It will be convenient to follow the working of our interpreter on a simple Prolog-like example, namely:

```
a(X, Y) <- b(X, Y).
a(X, Z) <- a(X, Y) & b(Y, Z).
b(1, 2).  b(2, 3).   b(3, 4).   b(4, 5).
```

We say that this example is Prolog-like, since the left recursion in the second rule would cause Prolog to loop.

We describe our interpreter top down, starting with our main predicate:

```
demo(Question, Answer) <-
    backchain(Question, Rules) &
    iterate(Question.Rules, nil, Lemmas) &
    set_of(Question,
            member(Question, Lemmas), Answer).
```

The demo predicate takes as input a Question, such as a(1,Z) and produces an Answer list, such as

```
a(1,2).a(1,3).a(1,4).a(1,5).nil.
```

The method here is to first backchain through the rules from the Question to find a list Rules of relevant instances of rules. The next step is to use the list of rules to iterate forward to find all of the consequences

(Lemmas) relevant to the Question. Finally, the Lemmas that actually match the Question are chosen as the Answer.

Let's now follow what happens with the example program when the Question is a(1,Z). The first step of demo,

```
backchain(a(1,Z), Rules)
```

works backward from a(1,Z) to find a list of rule instances that are needed to answer the question. In this example Rules consists of the list

```
(a(1,V1) <- b(1,V1)) .
    (a(1,V2) <- a(1,V3) & b(V3,V2)) . nil
```

The next step of demo is

```
iterate(Question.Rules, nil, Lemmas)
```

The original Question has been added to the list of Rules in case it matches a fact directly. Now, starting with an empty list nil of lemmas, iterate finds all the lemmas that it can by forward chaining using the Rules. In this case Lemmas is

```
a(1,2) . a(1,3) . a(1,4) . a(1,5) . nil
```

Finally, the relevant answers are extracted from Lemmas— in this case all of them.

Both backchain and iterate operate by repeatedly trying for more items (rule instances and lemmas, respectively) until no more are found. Since there is only a finite number of items in each case, the process is bound to terminate, at what is called a *fixed point*. It turns out that fixed points also provide a way of talking about the meaning of a knowledge base, see Apt et al. (1986).

The backchain predicate is defined as

```
backchain(Question,Rules) <-
    backchain1(Question.nil,nil,Rules).

backchain1(Questions,Rules,NewRules) <-
    set_of(A<-Bs,
            member(A,Questions) &
            rule(A<-Bs) & ¬in_gen(A<-Bs,Rules),
            Rs) &
    Rs=/nil & append(Rs,Rules,IntRules) &
    frontier(Rs,Qs) &
    backchain1(Qs,IntRules,NewRules).
backchain1(Questions,Rules,NewRules) <-
    most_gen(Rules,NewRules).
```

Here backchain1 takes a list of Questions and a list Rules of rule instances found so far (initially, just nil), and finds a list Rs of new rule instances that match a question in Questions. (The predicate rule finds a rule in the program being interpreted. The predicate in_gen treats a rule instance as new if it is not already in Rules, or if there is not already a more general item in Rules.) If there is at least one new rule (Rs=/nil), then the Rs are appended to Rules to form an intermediate list IntRules. Also, frontier collects all of the positive literals on the right of rules in Rs into a new list of questions Qs. Then backchain1 starts again with Qs and IntRules. Eventually, Rs will be nil, and the second rule for backchain1 then saves the most general rule instances from Rules in NewRules, and this is what the main backchain predicate returns.

The call backchain(Question,Rules) is followed by

```
iterate(Question.Rules,nil,Lemmas)
```

which forward chains on the Rules to find the Lemmas. The iterate predicate is defined as

```
iterate(Rules,Lemmas1,Lemmas3) <-
    execute(Rules,Lemmas1,Lemmas2) &
    Lemmas1=/Lemmas2 &
    iterate(Rules,Lemmas2,Lemmas3).
iterate(Rules,Lemmas,Lemmas).
```

Note that the rules for iterate have a similar structure to those for backchain1—in each case the first rule recurses as long as new items are being discovered, and then control goes to the second rule. The first rule of iterate uses execute to augment the list Lemmas1 to form a new list Lemmas2. So long as Lemmas2 contains at least one new lemma, proved by executing the rules and using Lemmas1, iterate calls itself again. Eventually there will be no new lemmas, so everything found so far is returned as the answer.

The iterate predicate uses execute to find lemmas. Here are the rules for execute:

```
execute(Rule.Rules,Lemmas1,Lemmas3) <-
    execute1(Rule,Lemmas1,Lemmas2) &
    execute(Rules,Lemmas2,Lemmas3).
execute(nil,Lemmas,Lemmas).

execute1(A<-Bs,Lemmas1,Lemmas3) <- / &
    set_of(A,
            execute2(Bs,Lemmas1) | fact(A),
            Lemmas2) &
    union(Lemmas1,Lemmas2,Lemmas3).
execute1(A,Lemmas1,Lemmas3) <- / &
    set_of(A,fact(A),Lemmas2) &
    union(Lemmas1,Lemmas2,Lemmas3).
```

```
execute2(B&Bs,Lemmas) <- / &
    execute2(B,Lemmas) & execute2(Bs,Lemmas).
execute2(¬B,*) <- builtin(B) & / & ¬B.
execute2(¬B,*) <-
    demo(B,Answer) & / & ¬member(B,Answer).
execute2(B,*) <- builtin(B) & / & B.
execute2(B,*) <- fact(B).
execute2(B,Lemmas) <- member(B,Lemmas).
```

The first two rules just say that to `execute` a list of rules, we `execute1` each
rule in turn. Actually, the list of rules also contains the original `Question`, so
`execute1` has two cases, the first when we are dealing with a rule of the form
`A<-Bs`, the second when we are dealing with a simple goal A. In `execute1`, the
predicate `fact` finds a fact in the program being interpreted. To `execute1` a
rule of the form `A<-Bs`, we `execute2` the body `Bs`, using previously established
lemmas in the list `Lemmas1` as needed. We also look to see if there are any facts
matched by A. This gives us a set of lemmas (proven instances of A) called
`Lemmas2`, and we take the `union` of the lists `Lemmas1` and `Lemmas2` to get
`Lemmas3`.

To `execute2` a rule body of the form `B&Bs`, we first `execute2` the goal B,
then the rest of the goals `Bs`. In `execute2`, the evaluation of built-in predicates
(such as `sum`, `diff` and so on) is simply handed to Prolog. We can also prove a
goal B by finding a fact for it, or by matching it with a previously proved lemma
in `Lemmas`.

Perhaps the most interesting part of `execute2` is the third rule, which deals
with the goal ¬B when B is not a built-in predicate:

```
execute2(¬B,*) <-
    demo(B,Answer) & / & ¬member(B,Answer).
```

The first thing to note is that we do not use any prior lemmas. The call to `demo`
always succeeds (possibly with an `Answer` that is `nil`), so the effect of the cut
(`/`) is to commit the execution to ¬`member(B,Answer)`. Thus to evaluate ¬B,
we *call the whole interpreter recursively* using `demo`, and we say that ¬B is
established if B does not match anything in the `Answer`. This way of treating
Prolog negation is designed for use with programs that are *stratified*, in the sense
that one cannot chain through the program being interpreted from some
predicate p, through a negation, and back to p again. The notion of a stratified
program is discussed in more detail on page 279 and in Appendix B. Programs
that are not stratified are rare, and their meaning can be somewhat problematic.

Apart from some utility predicates, such as `in_gen` and `frontier`, this
completes the description of how our simplified backchain iteration interpreter
works. The whole program, with details about how to run it, is in Section
A.2, "Detailed Programming of a Metainterpeter." The interpreter can be made
more efficient in several ways. The main considerations are to make as much use
as possible of constants in the question (since these tend to reduce the search
space), and to avoid re-proving lemmas.

Recall that when we asked the question a(1,Z), backchain produced the relevant rule instances

```
(a(1,V1) <- b(1,V1)) .
    (a(1,V2) <- a(1,V3) & b(V3,V2)) . nil
```

These are fine for this question. However, if we ask the more specific question a(1,5), backchain produces the same rule instances; the information that 5 appears in the question is lost, and this results in general in extra and unnecessary computation. So backchain can be improved to avoid this loss of information.

If we look again at execute1:

```
execute1(A<-Bs,Lemmas1,Lemmas3) <- / &
    set_of(A,
                execute2(Bs,Lemmas1) | fact(A),
            Lemmas2) &
    write(lemmas2=Lemmas2) &
    union(Lemmas1,Lemmas2,Lemmas3).
execute1(A,Lemmas1,Lemmas3) <- / &
    set_of(A,fact(A),Lemmas2) &
    union(Lemmas1,Lemmas2,Lemmas3).
```

and we insert the write statement as shown in the first rule, we can see that the same lemma is typically proved several times while answering a question. One way of cutting down on this duplication is to maintain three sets of lemmas, which we can call Old, Last and New. Then we insist that the proof of any New lemma must use at least one lemma from Last, as well as any number of lemmas from Old. At the end of an iterate cycle, Old is augmented with Last, and Last is set to the New just found, while New starts empty for the next cycle. This is a useful device to reduce the number of re-proofs of lemmas.

This section has described a simplified backchain iteration interpreter, and has sketched how to make it more efficient. We have noted that there are now many classes of methods, besides backchain iteration, whose aim is to interpret declarative knowledge correctly and efficiently. Some of these methods contain significant amounts of compilation. We have also noted that it is difficult to make close comparisons of the efficiency of different interpretation and compilation methods, since their speed depends on detailed decisions made in programming them, and on the knowledge bases used to test them.

It is worth remembering that when we write a system such as Syllog, we make a number of decisions that are essentially engineering trade-offs. Our choice of inference engine may be influenced by the fact that we not only need to make deductions from knowledge, but we also need to produce explanations of the deductions that we make. We may drop a fast engine for totally pure programs in favor of a slower one that deals satisfactorily with an open-ended library of built-in predicates. We may choose one inference method over another because it is easier to link it efficiently to a relational database of facts, perhaps by using the sql predicate in IBM Prolog. So while the inference engine is the heart of the system, there are many criteria for deciding which inference method to choose.

4.2.4 Summary of Syllog

Without knowledge, a shell system such as Syllog is just that—a shell. So, the development of such a system raises two related questions. The first question is "how easy is it to acquire knowledge for the shell?" The second is "what are the mathematical and engineering characteristics of the internals of the shell?" Clearly, the second question can be answered more precisely than the first. As we mentioned in Chapter 1, *knowledge acquisition* is a large topic in its own right. The main concerns are how to inform a system of the concepts it needs, and then how to instruct it in the use of the concepts. Knowledge acquisition can proceed by being told, by induction from examples, and by observation and discovery. Indeed, these methods can be combined.

For the present Syllog system, the approach is acquisition by being told, with three techniques for assisting the person who is providing the knowledge. A measure of the success of the first technique is that the person should not notice it! Syllog supports the acquisition of *declarative* knowledge. This means that the person putting in knowledge is largely freed from considerations about how the knowledge will be used in a computation. By contrast, programming in a conventional language is a *procedural* activity, in which we tell the computer a sequence of steps it is to take.

The second technique is the automatic provision of explanations. Since knowledge may be supplied in any order, perhaps by different people, the answers produced from the knowledge can be unexpected. So explanations are useful both for checking the answers and for checking the knowledge on which the answers are based. The third technique is the checking of the incoming syllogisms and facts to make sure that they are in a correct form, and also, to some extent to check their meaning. Some of these checking techniques are described in Section 4.5, "Checking Incoming Knowledge."

We have noticed that the combination of declarative English-like language with explanations tends to encourage direct interactive experimentation with sample knowledge bases, in Syllog, relatively early in the process of knowledge acquisition. For our prototype manufacturing knowledge base, knowledge acquisition was straightforward.

As we mentioned on page 251 the internals of the Syllog shell consist of seven main components, including an inference engine, an interface to a database management system, and an explanation generator. We described a simplified inference engine in the form of a backchain iteration interpreter. We mentioned that the requirements of Syllog essentially set us the goals of (a) getting deduction according to a declarative model of knowledge and (b) doing this efficiently using relational database technology as a component. A number of major research groups in several countries are now actively working on this goal.

We shall look further at explanation generation in Section 4.4, "Generating Useful Explanations."

Even for the simple manufacturing knowledge base in the section starting on page 237 it is clear that the facts and knowledge are complicated enough to make Syllog an attractive planning method, compared with treatment by pencil plus spreadsheet program, or with standard application programming over a database. In Syllog, the knowledge is modular and self documenting. Hence it is relatively easy to change the knowledge for what-if studies, and to extend the knowledge.

We mentioned on page 238 that the manufacturing task we have described is part of a larger task. For example, we would also like to know

- How many testers will be required for the new and concurrent production of other products?

- When will these quantities of testers be required?

- How many more testers will be required, and when, just for the new product?

- When are the new testers to be acquired, considering the time required to install and program them?

These questions can be answered by straightforward extensions of the simplified knowledge base. Some further questions are:

- How much floor space and rearrangement will be required for the new testers?

- Is there sufficient floor space and sufficient time to acquire the new testers to meet the production schedules?

- Should the new testers be placed at a vendor shop, or should some of the test workload be placed at a vendor who already has testers?

These further questions are partly about constraint satisfaction (a kind of knowledge that works well in a logic based system such as Syllog), and partly about the kind of knowledge we have dealt with in the simplified knowledge base.

4.3 PLANTDOC

This section describes an expert system shell that is in some ways similar to Syllog. The system, called Plantdoc, was first written to work with rules for diagnosing some common ailments of garden plants. It is modeled on the by now classical EMycin system developed at Stanford university (Buchanan and Shortliffe 1984).

Like Syllog, Plantdoc reasons using rules. However, the facts that are needed are gathered from the user, rather than gleaned from a database. Also, a Plantdoc rule does not contain the Syllog `eg_` elements (i.e, it has no variables), and the rules cannot be recursive.

4.3.1 Using Plantdoc

As in Syllog, the rules containing the knowledge for Plantdoc are English-like, and are separate from the system shell. So we can use Plantdoc for diagnosing things other than plants, by writing new sets of rules. In this section, we show a simple example of how to diagnose a faulty heating system for a house.

Each rule for Plantdoc has a number attached to it, that indicates how confident we are that the rule is indeed valid. Here is an example rule:

```
if "have been using the heating a lot recently" and
    not "furnace lights when thermostat is turned up high" and
    not "heating oil tank filled in last 3 months" then
  "heating oil tank is empty" : 70.
```

The 70 means that we are 70% confident that this is a valid rule.

Plantdoc uses rules of this form to ask questions, such as,

```
have been using the heating a lot recently?
```

on which to base a diagnosis. During a session with the system, these questions can be answered with "yes," "no," "unknown," or a percentage confidence between -100 (synonymous with "no") and +100 (which means "yes"). The confidences in the answers are then combined with the rule confidences to produce a final weighting for the diagnosis reached by the system. The way in which confidences are combined allows conflicting evidence about a possible diagnosis to be balanced. The method for this comes from the EMycin system, and we discuss it later in this section.

First, let's look at our simple example rules for diagnosing a house furnace.

```
if  "house is too cold" and
    "thermostat is at 65 or above" and
    "heating oil tank filled in last 3 months" and
    not "installed new furnace filters in last 12 months" then
  "weak hot air flow" : 90.

if "have been using the heating a lot recently" and
    not "furnace lights when thermostat is turned up high" and
    not "heating oil tank filled in last 3 months" then
  "heating oil tank is empty" : 70.

if "weak hot air flow" then "replace furnace filters" : 100.

if "heating oil tank is empty" then
    "reorder heating oil" : 100.
```

The rules contain advice for correcting, as well as diagnosing, a fault. If we run the Plantdoc system with these rules, we get a dialogue in which the system asks questions until it can reach a diagnosis:

```
house is too cold? yes
thermostat is at 65 or above? yes
heating oil tank filled in last 3 months? 90
installed new furnace filters in last 12 months? -70

My diagnosis is:

   weak hot air flow
   It is probable (63%) that it is suitable to
   replace furnace filters
```

In this session, we have given definite answers to the first two questions. The third answer, 90, means we are pretty sure the correct answer is yes. The fourth answer, -70, means that we suppose that the answer is no. As in Syllog, we can get explanations of answers. In this case, the explanations contain confidence weights. For the session above, the explanation is

```
It is probable (63%) that replace furnace filters
because weak hot air flow

 It is probable (63%) that weak hot air flow
 because house is too cold
 and thermostat is at 65 or above
 and heating oil tank filled in last 3 months
 and it is not the case that
   installed new furnace filters in last 12 months

   It is definite (100%) that house is too cold
   because you said so.

   It is definite (100%) that thermostat is at 65 or above
   because you said so.

   It is definite ·(90%) that heating oil tank filled in last 3 months
   because you said so.

   It is probably not the case (70%) that
   installed new furnace filters in last 12 months
   because you said so.
```

This is often called a *how* explanation, since it shows how the system reached a conclusion. Apart from the confidence factors, it is close in spirit to a mathematical proof. When the system asks us a question, we can answer with *why*, meaning "why did you ask me that question." What appears next on the screen is called, of course, a *why* explanation. We shall see one below.

First, though, there is something to note about the session. The system could have asked questions to find out whether the oil tank was empty. It did not, because it had reasoned ahead and discovered that these questions are irrelevant,

once we are confident that the oil tank has been filled recently. We call this
mechanism the useless question filter of Plantdoc. If we run the system with the
same rules, but with the filter disabled, we get

```
house is too cold? yes
thermostat is at 65 or above? yes
heating oil tank filled in last 3 months? 90
installed new furnace filters in last 12 months? -70
have been using the heating a lot recently? why

(i.e why is it important whether:
 have been using the heating a lot recently?)

 because..

  if     have been using the heating a lot recently
  and    it is not the case that:
         furnace lights when thermostat is turned up high
  and    it is not the case that:
             heating oil tank filled in last 3 months

  then   it is probable that: heating oil tank is empty

continue (con) or more explanation (why)? why

(i.e why is it important whether: heating oil tank is empty?)

 because..
  if     heating oil tank is empty
  then   it is definite that: reorder heating oil

have been using the heating a lot recently? yes
furnace lights when thermostat is turned up high? no

My diagnosis is:

 weak hot air flow
 It is probable (63%) that it is suitable to replace furnace filters
```

The conclusion is the same, but the system has asked two extra questions. Along
the way, we asked the system why it was asking a question, and then asked it
why concerning its first explanation. As no further "whys" are possible for these
rules, the system then asked us the question again.

We note that the example is simplified from real life, since there are several
reasons, apart from an empty tank, why a burner may not light. However, we

now have an idea of what the Plantdoc system does. The next step is to look at some of the techniques used inside the system.

4.3.2 The Plantdoc Inference Engine

Firstly, Plantdoc rules are actually in Prolog—we have simply declared `and`, `if`, `then`, and so on to be Prolog operators. The core of the Plantdoc inference engine can be thought of as an extension of a Prolog interpreter in Prolog to handle such matters as confidence factors and the filtering of questions. The system decides to ask a question about an item if it has

- no rule for the item,
- no prior answer for the item, and
- it calculates that an answer could change a diagnosis.

The top level of the Plantdoc inference engine looks for a list of triples of the form

    Goal.Confidence.Explanation

in which `Goal` is one of the diagnoses the system can make, `Confidence` is the confidence with which it can make it, and `Explanation` is an explanation. Here is the first rule.

```
set_of((G.C.E),
       top(G) & plausible(G,20) &
       demonstrate(G,20,C,E) & ge(C,20),
                                    GCEs) &
qsort(GCEs,SGCEs) & say(SGCEs).
```

For simplicity, a potential suggestion is just a *top goal*, in the sense that it does not act as a premise for any rule in the knowledge base. The predicate `top(G)` finds such a goal `G`.

Next, the predicate `plausible` is used to check that it is possible in principle to establish `G` with a confidence of `20` or more. This is our "useless question filter"; we only go ahead and ask the user questions about `G` if it could potentially be a suggestion, in the light of any questions already answered. If it could, we go ahead with

    demonstrate(G,20,C,E) & ge(C,20)

to see if `G` can in fact be suggested, with some confidence `C` greater than `20` and an explanation `E`. The predicate `demonstrate` normally causes some questions to be asked. It is defined by the rule

```
demonstrate(G,T,C,E) <-
    set_of(pair(CF,EF),
              demo(G,T,CF,EF,nil,*) & in_range(CF,T),
              Pairs) &
    split(Pairs,Cs,Es) &
    pick(Cs,Es,E) & result(Cs,C).
```

The action here is to collect a set of pairs each of the form

```
pair(Confidence_factor, Explanation)
```

for the various significant ways of showing that G holds. A confidence factor is in_range if it lies between -100 and -20, or between +20 and +100.

Once we have the list of pairs, we split it into two lists Cs and Es of confidence factors and explanations. The confidence factors Cs are combined into a single result confidence C, while the explanations are kept so that we are able to answer a *how* question.

The main "workhorse" predicate is demo, which has arguments as in demo(G,T,C,E,Rs,CR). The first argument G is the goal we are currently working on. T is the threshold for significant deductions, usually set at 20. C is a confidence that demo assigns to G, and E is an explanation. The Rs are a stack of rules used in getting from a potential suggestion to the current goal A—they are used to show *why* the inference engine is asking a question. Finally, CR can carry the confidence of a rule currently being worked on. It is there for a scheme to cut off unfruitful deductions. Here are the rules for demo, plus a rule for a predicate called ok.

```
demo(A and B,T,C,EA & EB,Rs,CR) <-
    ok(A,T,CA,EA,Rs,CR) &
    demo(B,T,CB,EB,Rs,CR) & min(CA,CB,C).

demo(A and B,T,0,A,Rs,CR) <- / &
    ¬ok(A,T,CA,EA,Rs,CR).

demo(not A,T,C,¬E,Rs,CR) <- / &
    demo(A,T,CN,E,Rs,CR) &
    diff(0,CN,C) & in_range(C,T).

demo(A,T,C,A,Rs,CR) <- given(A,C).

demo(A,T,C,A<-EB,Rs,*) <- (if B then A : CR) &
    demo(B,T,CB,EB,(if B then A : CR).Rs,CR) &
    times(CB,CR,C) & in_range(C,T).

demo(A,T,C,A,Rs,CR) <-
    ask_user(A,C,Rs) & in_range(C,T).

ok(A,T,CA,EA,Rs,CR) <-
    demo(A,T,CA,EA,Rs,CR) & times(CA,CR,CACR) &
    in_range(CACR,T).
```

The first two rules deal with processing a conjunct. The idea here is that the confidence in a conjunct is the minimum of the confidences in its components. The first rule says that, if A is ok, in the sense that its confidence times the CR of the rule we are about to use is in_range, then we can proceed with the rest of the conjunct. Otherwise, second rule, the confidence in A is 0.

The third rule allows us to demo not A by establishing A and reversing the sign of the confidence factor we get. The fourth rule says that we can demo A by looking up a prior answer to a question about A.

In the fifth rule, we demo A by finding a rule

```
if B then A : CR
```

in the knowledge base, demoing B with confidence CB, and multiplying CB by the confidence CR in the rule to get the resulting confidence C in A.

Finally, sixth rule, we can ask the user about A, although only if there is no rule that concludes with A and we have not already asked.

We mentioned that useless questions are avoided. This is done by using a slight variation on the demo predicate, which we call demo1. Before a possible suggestion or diagnosis is allowed to trigger any questions, a trial run is made with demo1 to see if the goal could in principle be established with a confidence above the threshold of 20. In place of ask_user (see above), demo1 assumes temporarily that the answer for a positive rule premise is "yes," and for a negated premise is "no." In our furnace example, once we have said that the heating oil tank has been filled in the last 3 months, the potential questions

```
have been using the heating a lot recently?
```

```
furnace lights when thermostat is turned up high?
```

remain unasked, because the diagnosis that they support (heating oil tank is empty) is blocked.

When a suggestion can be established with more than one confidence, the confidences are combined into a single result. We look at this next.

4.3.3 Weighing the Evidence

In our simple example, there was just one rule that concluded about each item. In general, though, there may be many, and each rule may confirm or deny a conclusion with a certain confidence factor. These confidence factors can be combined to get a single resulting confidence. One way of combining two confidences C1 and C2 to get a resulting confidence C is given in Buchanan and Duda (1982). They suggest that

```
C = C1 + C2 - (C1*C2)/100    if C1, C2 > 0

C = C1 + C2 + (C1*C2)/100    if C1, C2 <= 0

C = (C1 + C2) * 100  /  (100 - min( |C1|, |C2| ))
otherwise
```

If there are several confidences, then they are successively combined pairwise. The section of the Plantdoc inference engine that does this is

```
result(C.Cs,R) <- result1(C,Cs,R).

result1(C,nil,C).
result1(C1,C2.Cs,R) <-
    update(C1,C2,C) & result1(C,Cs,R).

update(C1,C2,C) <- ge(C1,0) & ge(C2,0) & / &
    sum(C1,C2,S) & norm_prod(C1,C2,P) & diff(S,P,C).
update(C1,C2,C) <- lt(C1,0) & lt(C2,0) & / &
    sum(C1,C2,S) & norm_prod(C1,C2,P) & sum(S,P,C).
update(C1,C2,C) <-  / &
    sum(C1,C2,S) & abs(C1,A1) & abs(C2,A2) &
    min(A1,A2,A) & diff(100,A,D) &
    prod(S,100,S100) & quot1(S100,D,C).

norm_prod(X,Y,Z) <- prod(X,Y,XY) & quot(XY,100,Z).
```

Although this approach using a fixed way of combining confidence factors sometimes works well in practice, it is difficult to provide any further justification for it. In fact, task experts are often reluctant to assign numbers to rules, perhaps because the way in which the numbers will be used is not clearly the same as their own implicit methods of weighing evidence. Actually, there is no need to assume that there is always just one way of combining confidences, and that it must be calculated by a formula built in to the inference engine. We can also combine confidences symbolically or numerically in each rule, and then see in an explanation an explicit record of the approximate reasoning that has been used to reach a conclusion. When we use an expert system in this way, it need not have a built-in method of combining confidences.

4.3.4 Summary of Plantdoc

Plantdoc is a shell modeled on the well-known EMycin system. Plantdoc was originally written for diagnosing certain common ailments of plants. However, as in Syllog, we can write down knowledge about various subjects in the form of English-like rules. In the case of Plantdoc, we write a number next to each rule to indicate the confidence we have in it. Plantdoc normally asks us questions while it is deciding what its advice should be. We can answer "yes," "no," or type in a number for something in between, such as "most likely so." The numbers in the rules and in our answers are combined into a single number that signals the confidence rating that Plantdoc attaches to its advice.

Before asking a question, Plantdoc reasons ahead. It only asks the question if the reasoning ahead tells it that the answer could affect the advice that it gives. This is time consuming for the computer, but saves time for the person answering the questions. Like EMycin, Plantdoc can produce an explanation of *why* it is asking a question, and of *how* it reached a conclusion.

When we write a syllogism for the Syllog shell, we can use example elements that stand for variables. We can also write syllogisms that are recursive, for example to specify a parts hierarchy in manufacturing. Plantdoc has neither variables nor recursion, yet it is useful for diagnostic and decision-making kinds of tasks. Some tasks can make good use of Plantdoc's approximate reasoning using confidence factors, and of the way in which rules cause Plantdoc to ask questions. Our answers to those questions are the basis for the advice that Plantdoc gives.

4.4 GENERATING USEFUL EXPLANATIONS

In this chapter, we have talked about two expert system shells; Syllog and Plantdoc. Each system can explain its advice when asked to do so, and indeed this is a very important feature for a shell.

The explanation component of each shell does not depend on the particular subject for which the shell is being used. This an advantage, in that we can use a shell for many different tasks without having to tailor the explanation component. It can be a disadvantage too; sometimes explanations that come from such a fixed component look odd in the context of a specific subject, and may not be as helpful as possible. Nevertheless, it is interesting to see how far we can go in providing explanations in a subject-independent way; this allows us to study the nature of useful explanations in general, and to write what we find out as a component of a shell. Once we have some general techniques, we can specialize them as necessary, for example by adding information that only certain parts of explanations are interesting—perhaps just those that have not recently been mentioned.

So, what *is* an explanation? In ordinary life it can be a sequence of reasoning steps used to convince a person that something is so. In systems such as Syllog and Plantdoc, the situation is similar; an explanation produced by the shell can help to convince us that what the system is suggesting follows from what we have told it. So, is an explanation simply a list of all the steps a system has taken in reaching a conclusion—an execution trace? Not in general, since the system may have followed many blind alleys before finding a path to the conclusion, and it is at most this path that we are interested in. In logic, this path amounts to a proof.

So we begin to form the idea that a *trace* is more detailed than a *proof*, which in turn may be more detailed than an *explanation*. This is a useful point of view, at least for the case when a system reaches a positive conclusion. Indeed, for systems such as Plantdoc, this even works for a negative conclusion, which could be treated simply as a positive conclusion that something can be shown to have a confidence factor of -100. However, for systems such as Syllog, which use the *closed world assumption*, (see page 234) it is not quite so straightforward to generate an explanation of a negative conclusion. What we can do is to find an explanation of *what would be needed* to change the negative conclusion to a positive one.

In this section, we use metainterpreters to extract explanations from Prolog-like deductions. We start with a simple metainterpreter that produces explanations of "yes" answers. These explanations stop short at a negated item. We then extend the metainterpreter to explain "no" answers. Finally, we extend it so that it will pursue explanations that pass through a negated item and continue further.

4.4.1 Explaining Yes Answers, Stopping at a Negation

Our point of departure is a metainterpreter that is very like the Prolog interpreter itself. Recall that we can write a simplified Prolog interpreter in Prolog like this:

```
demo(A & As) <- / & demo(A) & demo(As).
demo(¬A) <- / & ¬demo(A).
demo(A) <- builtin(A) & / & A.
demo(A) <- fact(A).
demo(A) <- rule(A<-B) & demo(B) .
```

This interpreter actually differs from Prolog in that it will always look for a fact for a goal A before trying a rule, and in that it does not handle cuts in the program being interpreted. However, it serves nicely as a basis for extracting explanations. We can modify it so that it keeps an explanation tree if the interpretation of a goal succeeds. The resulting interpreter will be quite similar to the one on page 164, but we shall need an argument to hold a *yes* or a *no*. In this section we use the argument with a *yes* only.

```
demo_expl(A & B,EA & EB,yes) <- / &
    demo_expl(A,EA,yes) & demo_expl(B,EB,yes) .
demo_expl(¬A,¬A,yes) <-
    builtin(A) & / & ¬guarded_call(A).
demo_expl(¬A,¬A,yes) <- ¬demo(A) & /.
demo_expl(A,A,yes) <- pos(A) & fact(A).
demo_expl(A,A,yes) <-
    pos(A) & builtin(A) & / & guarded_call(A).
demo_expl(A,A <- EB,yes) <-
    pos(A) & rule(A<-B) & demo_expl(B,EB,yes).
```

The first rule says that an explanation of a conjunct A & B consists of an explanation of A and an explanation of B. Note that this rule can deal with conjuncts of more than two items by calling itself recursively. For example demo(b & c & d, EA & EB) starts with b bound to A and (c & d) bound to B, then a second call of the same rule deals with the remaining conjunct (c & d). The second and third rules say that an explanation of ¬A can be just ¬A itself, and that this is the case if the goal A fails either as a built-in predicate, or in the call demo(A). This is in the spirit of negation as failure, but as we shall see, we can do better. We shall be able to supply information about why an attempt to demo A fails. In the case of a built-in predicate such as sum, we use guarded_call to fail, rather than giving an error, if the arguments are not instantiated enough, e.g in sum(X,Y,10).

The fourth and fifth rules say that an explanation of A is just A itself, if A is a fact in the program being interpreted, or if A is a built-in predicate for which a guarded call succeeds. The predicate pos(A) checks that A is positive, i. e. that it does not have a negation sign in front of it.

The last rule says that an explanation of A consists of A<-EB if there is a rule A<-B in the program being interpreted, and EB is an explanation of B. Here we can think of the arrow as saying that A holds *because* of the explanation EB of B.

Suppose we try the interpreter on this simple example.

```
q <- b & c.
b <- d & e.
c <- f & ¬g.
g <- h.
d. e. f.
```

In the example, the first rule leads to an explanation of q via b & c. Further, b is proved because d and e are facts, while c is proved because f is a fact and g *cannot* be proved. If we load the program into IBM Prolog in such a way that the interpreter can get at it via the fact and rule predicates (see pages 415 and 417) then we ask the question demo_expl(q(),E,yes), we get the explanation

```
q <- (b <- d & e) & (c <- f & ¬g)
```

(Actually, IBM Prolog will print q as q() and so on, but we can suppress the parentheses for readability.) The explanation can be read: q because b and c; b because d and e; and c because f and ¬g. The explanation corresponds to a tree of the form

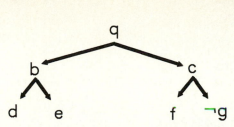

If we do not choose to show an explanation as a tree, it is often best to show it in a breadth first form, so that one can see the main reasons (b & c) for the conclusion (q) first, then look at the reasons for b and for c, and so on. One way of showing our tree breadth first is this:

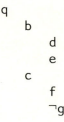

A similar idea is used in showing Syllog explanations, although in that case the method is to line up the reasons down the screen in a form corresponding to

```
b & c => q
d & e => b
f & ¬g => c
```

where => stands for implication.

4.4.2 Explaining Yes and No Answers, Stopping at a Negation

So far, we have shown how to get an explanation of a "yes" answer, although the explanation is partial in that it does not continue through a negation. Continuing with the same interpreter and example program, if we ask the question

```
demo(g(),E,yes)
```

then we simply get a failure, and no value is supplied for the explanation E. Yet there is a rule g <- h in the program, and it would be informative to know that g cannot be proven because there is no rule or fact for h. In a Syllog explanation, we would indicate on the screen that g is *not proven* because h is *missing*. Internally in Prolog we can represent this situation by an annotation of g <- h. Here we choose to write

```
? g <- ?? h
```

One question mark means *not proven*, two question marks together mean that the item is *missing*. We use the operator definitions

```
op("?",prefix,50).
op("??",prefix,50).
```

to make ? g <- ?? h a valid Prolog term.

Now we are in a position to explain a "no" answer. The most important metarules for this are the following:

```
demo_expl(A,? A<-EB,no) <- pos(A) &
    rule(A<-B) &  demo_expl(B,EB,no).
demo_expl(A,?? A,no) <- pos(A) &
    ¬rule(A<-*) &  ¬fact(A).
```

These two metarules will in fact produce the Prolog term ? g <- ?? h, which contains the information necessary to drive a screen display that will show the explanation.

There are some more details needed to handle negation and built-in predicates, so altogether we can explain "no" answers (stopping short at a negation) using the rules

```
demo_expl(¬A,? ¬A <- A,no) <-
    builtin(A) & / & guarded_call(A).
demo_expl(A & B,EA & EB,no) <- / &
    decide(YN1,YN2,no) &
    demo_expl(A,EA,YN1) & demo_expl(B,EB,YN2).
demo_expl(A, ? A<-EB ,no) <- pos(A) &
    rule(A<-B) &  demo_expl(B,EB,no).
demo_expl(A,?? A,no) <-
    builtin(A) & / & ¬guarded_call(A).
demo_expl(A, ?? A,no) <- pos(A) &
    ¬rule(A<-*) &  ¬fact(A).
demo_expl(¬A, ? ¬A,no) <- demo(A).

decide(yes,no,no).
decide(no,yes,no).
decide(no,no,no).
```

The first rule explains a "no" answer to ¬A by saying that ¬A is not proven because A, a built-in predicate, is proven.

The second rule explains a "no" answer to A & B. When we call demo_expl, we like to do so with the last argument bound to either yes or no. This helps, for example, in the case where we are looking for multiple "yes" explanations by making the interpreter backtrack. When we reach the last "yes" explanation, we do not want the next backtrack to produce a "no" explanation! So in the second rule above, decide is used to assign definite values to YN1 and YN2. These values may later be undone by backtracking, but they will be bound before each call of demo_expl in the body of the second rule.

Rule three allows us to explain that A is not proven when there is a rule A<-B and EB is an explanation of why B is not proven, or is missing. The fourth and fifth rules explain that A is missing if it is a failing call of a built-in predicate, or otherwise if there is no fact or rule for A.

Finally, since we are not yet continuing explanations through negations, the sixth rule explains that ¬A is not proven if we can demo A.

So far, we have defined demo_expl for the two cases when the last argument is yes or no, and we have mentioned that we like the last argument to be bound to one of these values before demo_expl is called. This can be ensured as by using demo to decide whether to call demo_expl with a "yes" or a "no":

```
explain(A) <- demo(A) & / & explain1(A,yes).
explain(A) <- explain1(A,no).
explain1(A,YN) <-
     demo_expl(A,E,YN) & write(E) & again.
explain1(A,YN).

again <- readch(A) & A=";" & / & fail.
again.
```

In the first rule, if demo(A) succeeds then there must be at least one "yes" explanation, so we commit to finding "yes" explanations. If demo(A) fails, we find "no" explanations. The explanations are actually found via explain1. When demo_expl produces an explanation E, it is printed, and then we can ask for another explanation by typing in a semicolon. If we type anything else, or if we type a semicolon and there are no more explanations, then again, explain1 and explain all succeed.

To see how this works, we can look at some more examples:

```
a1<-b1 & c1.
b1.

a2<-b2 & ¬c2.
b2.

a3<-b3 & c3.
a3<-d3 & e3.
b3.
e3.

a4 <- ¬b4.
b4 <- ¬c4.
c4.
```

It is easy to see that a1 fails, a2 succeeds, and that a3 fails and has two "no" explanations. The goal a4 in fact succeeds, but we may need an explanation to convince us!

If we run these examples, we get just one explanation for a1, namely

```
? a1 <- b1 & ?? c1
```

that is, a1 is not proven because, although b1 is a fact, c1 is missing, i.e there is no rule or fact for c1.

We also get just one explanation for a2:

```
a2 <- b2 &  ¬c2
```

that is a2 is proven because there is a fact for b2 but nothing for c2.

For a3, there are two "no" explanations:

```
? a3 <- b3 & ?? c3
? a3 <-  ?? d3 & e3
```

The first says that a3 is not proven because, although b3 is a fact, c3 is missing; the second that d3 is missing, and e3 is a fact.

For a4 there is a "yes" explanation:

```
a4 <-  ¬b4.
```

However, since we have not provided a way for the explanations to continue through a negation, this explanation has stopped short.

4.4.3 Full Explanations of Both Yes and No Answers

In Section 4.4.1, "Explaining Yes Answers, Stopping at a Negation" we saw that our interpreter can explain why q follows from the rules

```
q <- b & c.
b <- d & e.
c <- f & ¬g.
g <- h.
d. e.  f.
```

The explanation is

```
q <- (b <- d & e) & (c <- f &  ¬g)
```

and it stops short at ¬g.

We saw above that the interpreter will explain why a4 follows from

```
a4 <- ¬b4.
b4 <- ¬c4.
c4.
```

The explanation is

```
a4 <-  ¬b4
```

and it stops short at ¬b4. If we now give the goal b4 we can get an explanation of why it fails:

```
? b4 <-   ? ( ¬c4)
```

This can be read as: b4 is not proven because ¬c4 is not proven. However, it should not be necessary to ask for the explanation in of a4 in two stages. It would be better to have the interpreter give us

```
a4 <-   ¬b4 <-   ? b4 <-   ? ( ¬c4) <- c4
```

This can be read as "a4 because ¬b4, because b4 is not proven, because ¬c4 is not proven, because c4 is given as a fact." Clearly, this notation gets harder to read as the explanations get longer, but the thing to remember is that the notation contains all of the information needed to make a more friendly display.

Now let's see how we can adapt the interpreter to follow both "yes" and "no" explanations through a negation. Our program is based on a method developed at IBM by Oded Shmueli. For the "yes" part, we replace the rule

```
demo_expl(¬A,¬A,yes) <- demo(¬A) & /.
```

with the rule

```
demo_expl(¬A,¬A<-E,yes) <- demo_expl(A,E,no) .
```

For the "no" part, we replace the rule

```
demo_expl(¬A,? ¬A,no) <- demo(A).
```

with the rule

```
demo_expl(¬A,? ¬A<-E,no) <- demo_expl(A,E,yes).
```

There is a nice symmetry about the two new rules, in that the "yes" rule calls demo_expl with the last argument no, while the "no" rule calls demo_expl with the last argument yes.

Now we are ready to put all of the pieces of our explanation program together. Recall that the main pieces are the predicates explain, demo, and demo_expl. The last of these really works as two predicates, since it is always called with its last argument bound to a yes or to a no. Here is the whole program so far:

```
explain(A) <- demo(A) & / & explain1(A,yes).
explain(A) <- explain1(A,no).

explain1(A,YN) <- demo_expl(A,E,YN) & write(E) &
      pretty_print(E) & again.
explain1(A,YN).

demo(A & As) <- / & demo(A) & demo(As).
demo(¬A) <- / & ¬demo(A).
demo(A) <- builtin(A) & / & A.
demo(A) <- fact(A).
demo(A) <- rule(A<-B) & demo(B) .
```

```
demo_expl(A & B,EA & EB,yes) <- / &
    demo_expl(A,EA,yes) & demo_expl(B,EB,yes) .
demo_expl(¬A,¬A,yes) <-
    builtin(A) & / & ¬guarded_call(A).
demo_expl(¬A,¬A <- E,yes) <- demo_expl(A,E,no) .
demo_expl(A,A,yes) <- pos(A) & fact(A).
demo_expl(A,A,yes) <-
    pos(A) & builtin(A) & / & guarded_call(A).
demo_expl(A,A<-EB,yes) <- pos(A) &
    rule(A<-B) & demo_expl(B,EB,yes).

demo_expl(¬A,? ¬A <- A,no) <-
    builtin(A) & / & guarded_call(A).
demo_expl(A & B,EA & EB,no) <- / &
    decide(YN1,YN2,no) &
    demo_expl(A,EA,YN1) & demo_expl(B,EB,YN2).
demo_expl(A ,? A <- EB,no) <- pos(A) &
    rule(A<-B) &  demo_expl(B,EB,no).
demo_expl(A,?? A,no) <-
    builtin(A) & / & ¬guarded_call(A).
demo_expl(A,?? A,no) <- pos(A) &
    ¬rule(A<-*) &  ¬fact(A).
demo_expl(¬A,? ¬A <- E,no) <- demo_expl(A,E,yes).

decide(yes,no,no).
decide(no,yes,no).
decide(no,no,no).
```

We leave it as an exercise for the reader to write the predicate guarded_call, which fails rather than giving an error if a built-in predicate is called with too few arguments instantiated.

So far we have found explanations only from programs that do not contain recursion, so now we can try the interpreter on a simple recursive program:

```
a(X,Y) <- b(X,Y).
a(X,Z) <- b(X,Y) & a(Y,Z).
b(1,2).    b(2,3).    b(3,4).
```

If we ask for an explanation of why a(1,4) follows from the program, we get

```
a(1,4) <-
    b(1,2) & (a(2,4) <- b(2,3) & (a(3,4) <- b(3,4)))
```

and if we ask for another explanation, the interpreter indicates that there are no more. On the other hand, if we ask about a(1,5), we can get several explanations of why it cannot be concluded:

```
? a(1,5) <-  ?? b(1,5)

? a(1,5) <- b(1,2) & ( ? a(2,5) <-  ?? b(2,5))

? a(1,5) <- b(1,2) &
   ( ? a(2,5) <- b(2,3) & ( ? a(3,5) <-  ?? b(3,5)))
```

The first explanation says that a(1,5) could be concluded if b(1,5) were a fact, the second shows that b(1,2) is a fact, and that therefore a(1,5) would follow if b(2,5) were a fact, and so on.

In general, it's clear that there may be a number of explanations of why a conclusion follows from a program, and that there may be a very large number of explanations of why a desired conclusion does not follow. One way of managing this situation is to present a single explanation, and to provide a way of asking for the next explanation if it is needed. However, it's interesting to see if there are general rules about the order in which the explanations are best presented. The following ideas are often appropriate:

■ If the answer to a question is "yes," show the shortest explanation first.

■ If the answer to a question is "no," first show the longest explanation in which nothing is repeated.

The justification for a short explanation of a "yes" answer is that, for instance, if the question matches a fact in the program, then it's interesting to know this right away, even if the answer can also be deduced using the rules. The justification for a long explanation of a "no" answer is that the program may be able to make considerable progress toward a "yes," and it is often useful to see this.

Of course, these ideas about the order in which explanations may be presented do not take particular subject matter into account—they may work better in, say, a manufacturing knowledge base than in one about oil exploration. It is interesting to try out these ideas in practice, on real knowledge bases.

4.5 CHECKING INCOMING KNOWLEDGE

So far in this chapter we have looked at knowledge representation, at the Syllog system, at the Plantdoc system, and at techniques for generating useful explanations. In all of this discussion, we have mentioned knowledge that is written down as rules and facts. If these rules and facts are part of a Prolog program, then they may have been written by a programmer (or perhaps by a program written by a programmer). If the rules and facts are in the Syllog form, then we hope that they can be written by people who are not programmers.

As we mentioned in Section 1.6, "Some Trends in Knowledge Acquisition," we can group methods by which a machine can acquire knowledge under three headings:

■ Learning by being told,

- Learning by induction from examples, and
- Learning by observation and discovery.

This section looks at some ways of using general and specific knowledge to support learning by being told.

One of our aims in building an expert system shell is to make it easy to change the subject-specific knowledge that the shell uses. If we are really successful in this, and it is indeed easy to change the knowledge, then we have the prospect that users of the system (who need not be programmers) can keep the knowledge base up to date. It is particularly helpful if a user can add or change a small item of knowledge, such as a rule or fact, without having to read through the whole knowledge base. However, there is a danger here. In making changes, it is easy to make mistakes. To some extent it is practical to have the *system* check that the incoming knowledge is valid, and of course the system can scan as much of the knowledge base as is needed to do this.

For learning by being told, we can group the kinds of checking of incoming knowledge like this:

- Subject-independent checking of individual rules
- Subject-independent checking of the knowledge base
- Subject-dependent checking of the knowledge base

The first two kinds of checking can be built into a shell, in such a way that the user can call them up when needed. The last kind of checking depends on *constraints* supplied by experts in the subject concerned. For example, we may wish to exclude from a knowledge base the possibility that a person has two different salaries from the same company in the same year. These constraints can usually be written as rules, just like the rest of the knowledge, but it may be a good idea to ensure that only a privileged group of users can change the constraints. We look at the three kinds of checking next.

4.5.1 Subject-Independent Checking of Individual Rules

We often want to restrict the form that a rule can take. For instance, in a Syllog knowledge base, it is usually best if each `eg_` element in a conclusion of a syllogism appears in a sentence in the premise—preferably a sentence without a "not" at the beginning. So for example we would usually want to warn the user if he or she types in either of the following syllogisms:

```
eg_person2 is married to eg_person3
-----------------------------------
eg_person1 is married to eg_person2

not: the manager of eg_person1 is eg_person2
--------------------------------------------------------
eg_person1 is the chief executive officer of the company
```

In the first syllogism, `eg_person3` should be `eg_person1`. Although we cannot make this kind of correction automatically while staying independent of the subject matter, we can warn the user that there is probably something wrong. The second syllogism can lead to a problem because of the way in which simple negation as failure works in practice. In Prolog notation, the syllogism becomes

```
ceo(X) <- ¬manager(X,Y).
```

Suppose we also add the facts

```
manager(fred,jane).
employee(fred).
employee(jane).
```

Then in Prolog, the answer to the question `ceo(U)` is `fail` (i.e "no") while the answer to the question `ceo(jane)` is "yes." The first answer should have been "yes, `U=jane`." We can avoid this problem by changing the rule to

```
ceo(X) <- employee(X) & ¬manager(X,Y).
```

So in general, it is good if the system can issue a warning if a premise of a rule contains a negated literal, none of whose variables have been mentioned earlier in a positive literal. In fact, the safest situation is the one in which all of the variables in a negated literal have been mentioned earlier in a positive literal.

So we would like to have a way of checking a Prolog rule to make sure that

- each variable in the head appears in an earlier positive literal in the body, and
- each variable in a negative literal in the body has appeared in a positive literal to the left.

Here is the main part of a simple Prolog program to do this.

```
checks <-
    set_of(R:Error,
            rule(R) & check(R, Error), REs) &
            show(REs).
check(A<-Bs,h) <-
    and_list(Bs,LBs) &
    vars(A,Xs) & member(X,Xs) &
    ¬positive_occurs(X,LBs).
check(A<-Bs,b) <-
    split(Bs,Left,¬PXs,Right) &
    vars(PXs,Xs) &
    ¬(member(X,Xs) & positive_occurs(X,Left)).

error(h,"each variable
    in the head should occur positively in the body").
error(b,"some variable
    in each neg lit should occur first in a pos lit").
```

```
split(Bs,Left,¬PXs,Right) <-
    and_list(Bs,LBs) & append(Left,(¬PXs).Right,LBs).

positive_occurs(X,L) <- member(PYs,L) & pos(PYs) &
    vars(PYs,Ys) & member(Y,Ys) & X==Y.

pos(¬P) <- / & fail.
pos(*).

vars(PXs,Xs) <- (PXs =.. P.Xs).

and_list(B & Bs,B.L) <- / & and_list(Bs,L).
and_list(B,B.nil) <- B =/ (* & *).
```

The program looks up in the predicate `rule` a rule to be checked, and tries the two `checks` indicated by `h` and `b`. The h check looks for a variable X that appears in the head A of a rule but not in a positive literal of the body Bs of the rule. The b check nondeterministically `splits` the body Bs of a rule into a `Left` part, a negated literal `¬PXs` and a `Right` part, then tries to find a variable X in PXs that has not appeared in a positive literal in the `Left` part. The result is a list of pairs of the form `R:Error`, where R is a rule and `Error` is an h or b error. Of course a single rule may contain both kinds of error.

To find the variables in a literal, the predicate `vars` uses the IBM Prolog built-in `=..` which flattens a simple predicate into a list, for example

```
p(X,Y) =.. p.X.Y.nil
```

It is convenient to convert the body of a rule to a list form, using `and_list` before splitting it up. The predicate `positive_occurs` uses the IBM Prolog built-in `==`, which checks whether two variables are literally the same, or are cross bound to one another.

If we run the program on the two rules

```
married(X,Y) <- married(Y,Z).
ceo(X) <- ¬manager(X,Y).
```

we get the results

```
married(V1,V2) <- married(V2,V3)
each variable in the head
   should occur positively in the body

ceo(V1) <-  ¬manager(V1,V2)
each variable in the head
   should occur positively in the body

ceo(V1) <-  ¬manager(V1,V2)
some variable in each neg lit
   should occur first in a pos lit
```

In the Syllog system, one has the option of loading a knowledge base with this kind of checking.

So far, we have looked at two kinds of checking that can be done on individual rules, independently of the subject matter. This kind of simple checking is often very helpful.

4.5.2 Subject-Independent Checking of the Knowledge Base

In principle, individual rules can be checked by inspection, but it is nice to have a program that will do the checking. Sometimes we want to check to see if there is a particular pattern of rules. This is can be much harder to do by hand, and so a checking program can be almost essential. In Syllog, we usually want to avoid knowledge bases in which we can form a path from a sentence to itself via a negation, by chaining through the syllogisms. For example, it's not clear what the following syllogism should mean:

```
eg_person is an employee
not: eg_person has a window office
---------------------------------
eg_person has a window office
```

The syllogism seems to try to conclude that someone has a window office if she does not have one! In general, a path that goes from a sentence to itself via a negation might use several rules, perhaps scattered through a knowledge base, so it is good to be able to check for this automatically, rather than by hand. In Appendix B we outline a general theory for the meaning of a knowledge base that does not contain this kind of path, so the checking puts us on safe ground.

Let's change to Prolog notation, and look at an example in which a path through a negation uses two rules:

```
good_tempered  <- window
window <- employee & ¬manager
manager <- window
good_tempered <- interruptible
interruptible <- good_tempered
```

The problem path here is from `window` via `¬manager` and back to `window`, using the second and third rules. We can check for such paths by actually chaining through the rules. In fact, a simple checker is rather like a metainterpreter (such as the one on page 267), in which we look for a repeated goal that gives us the completion of a path. We must also look for a negation along the path. Here is a program that does this:

```
loop_check <-
    set_of(Path,
            rule(A<-*) & find(A,Path) & Path=A.*,
            Paths) &
    write(paths:Paths).
```

```
find(A,Path) <-
    reachable(A,nil,Path,Sign) & Sign==neg.

reachable(A&As,Gs,P,Sign) <- / &
    (reachable(A,Gs,P,Sign) |
     reachable(As,Gs,P,Sign)).
reachable(¬A,Gs,A.Gs,neg) <- member(A,Gs) & /.
reachable(A,Gs,A.Gs,Sign) <- member(A,Gs) & /.
reachable(¬A,Gs,P,neg) <- / &
    rule(A<-B) & reachable(B,A.Gs,P,neg).
reachable(A,Gs,P,Sign) <-
    rule(A<-B) & reachable(B,A.Gs,P,Sign).
```

The first rule finds all of the paths that

- start with the head A of a rule in the program being checked,
- are `reachable` from A,
- contain at least one negation, and
- end with A.

The rules for `reachable` follow the outline for a Prolog metainterpreter in Prolog (see demo on page 267). In the body of the first rule a disjunction (|) replaces a conjunction (&), since we want to follow paths through the rules rather than execute them. The predicate `find` calls `reachable` with a free variable `Sign` in the last argument. If `reachable` passes through a negation, `Sign` is set to `neg`, and `find` tests for this to see if the `Path` contains a negation.

If we run the program to check the five rules about `good_tempered`, `window`, `employee`, `manager`, and `interuptible`, we get the paths

```
manager . window . manager . nil
window . manager . window . nil
```

The loop between `good_tempered` and `interruptible` is not flagged as a problem, since there is no negation in it, but the loop between `manager` and `window` is a problem, and this is indicated.

The program checks a knowledge base to see that it does not contain a recursion through a negation. To do this, we must look at all of the rules in the knowledge base. We have run the program on a simple example without variables. It is an interesting exercise to see if the program needs to be changed to deal with knowledge bases that do contain variables.

Although this kind of checking is global, it is still independent of the subject matter of the knowledge base. That is, the same checking program can be used for a knowledge base about managers and windows, for a knowledge base about manufacturing planning, and so on. This means that the checking can be built into a shell (such as Syllog) and used when appropriate.

In addition, we often need checking that is linked to particular subjects, and we look at this next.

4.5.3 Subject-Dependent Checking of the Knowledge Base

So far we have looked at subject-independent checking of individual rules and of a whole knowledge base. Our next step is to look at checking that depends on the particular subject. For this, we need rules that can work as *constraints* on the allowable situations in a knowledge base—for example a physical object cannot be in two places at once. It is interesting that in Prolog and in Syllog we cannot derive a contradiction directly from a program or from a knowledge base, because all of the conclusions that we can draw are positive. Thus there is no possibility (as long as we stick to programs with firm semantics) of concluding some item P and also ¬P. However, we can still use Prolog and Syllog to write down constraints and to reason with them. In Prolog we could write

```
impossible <- at(Object,Posn1) &
     at(Object,Posn2) & Posn1=/Posn2.
```

to say that it is impossible for an `Object` to be at two different positions called `Posn1` and `Posn2`. Then if we ask the question `impossible` and get the answer "yes," we know that there is a problem. We can even arrange matters so that the question `impossible` is asked whenever the knowledge changes. In fact, as we mentioned on page 18 we can be quite systematic about this kind of checking, at least for small knowledge bases. We can examine an incoming item to see if it is deducible from or inconsistent with the current knowledge. If neither of these is the case, then the item can be assimilated. If the item is a general rule, it may cause some redundancy, and it may be a good idea to trim the knowledge base.

We can write this down in Prolog.

```
op("plus",r1,10).
op("minus",r1,10).

assim(KB,Input,KB) <- demo(KB,Input) & known_input.
assim(KB,Input,KB) <-
     member(impossible(Situation),KB) &
     demo(KB plus Input,Situation) &
     rejected_input(Situation).
assim(KB,Input,NewKB) <-
     trim(KB plus Input,NewKB) & accepted_input.
```

The first rule says that assimilation of an `Item` into a knowledge base `KB` leaves `KB` unchanged if we can show, using a `demo` predicate, that the `Item` is deducible from `KB`. The second rule says the `KB` is also unchanged if an impossible situation would be deducible from the `KB` plus the incoming `Item`. The third rule accepts the input, doing some trimming if needed, and changes `KB` to `NewKB`.

The demo predicate is similar to others that we have looked at, except that it carries the `KB` from which it makes deductions in its first argument.

```
demo(KB plus I,J) <- / & demo(I.KB,J).
demo(KB minus I,J) <-
     pick(I,KB,Rest) & / & demo(Rest,J).
demo(KB minus I,J) <-  / & demo(KB,J).
demo(KB,X & Y) <- / & demo(KB,X) & demo(KB,Y).
demo(KB,¬X) <- demo(KB,X) & / & fail.
demo(KB,¬X).
demo(KB,X) <- built_in(X) & X.
demo(KB,X) <- lookup(KB,X).
demo(KB,X) <- lookup(KB,X<-Y) & demo(KB,Y).
```

This demo also allows us to talk about KB plus I and KB minus I, which is useful for keeping track of the way assim works. The predicate pick picks an item from the KB, and yields the rest of the KB as Rest. The predicate lookup finds a fact or a rule in the KB, but it is careful not to change the KB.

Next, we need to be able to sort through a knowledge base and trim off the items that are deducible from general rules.

```
trim(KB plus Input,NewKB) <- / &
     trim(Input.KB,NewKB).
trim(KB,NewKB) <-
     pick(I,KB,RestOfKB) & I=/impossible(*) &
     demo(KB minus I,I) & trim_drops(I) &
     trim(RestOfKB,NewKB).
trim(KB,KB).
```

In doing this, we give the constraints special status—we assume that we shall not want to trim them. If we do decide to drop an item, then we use trim_drops(I) to make a note of this for a user to read.

Suppose we have a simple knowledge base about blocks that can be stacked on top of one another. To keep things simple, we can talk about just a horizontal and vertical coordinate for the position of each block. For example here

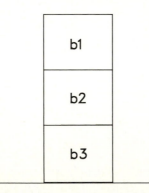

the block b1 is on top of b2, which is on top of b3. We can say that the positions of b1, b2, and b3 are 1:3, 1:2, and 1:1, respectively, and that this is an initial situation:

```
initial(at(b1,1:3)).
initial(at(b2,1:2)).
initial(at(b3,1:1)).
```

We can also write down some subject-specific constraints about what cannot happen in the world of stackable blocks.

```
initial(impossible(at(P1,XY) & at(P2,XY) & P1=/P2)).
initial(impossible(at(P,XY1) &
        at(P,XY2) & XY1=/XY2)).
initial(impossible(above(X,Y) & above(Y,X))).
initial(
   impossible(at(P,X:Y) & gt(Y,1) &
      diff(Y,1,Y1) & ¬at(P1,X:Y1))).
```

These constraints say that we cannot have two blocks in the same place at once, that no block can be in two different places at once, that we cannot have both X above Y and Y above X, and that a block that is not on the floor must be supported by another block.

We can also have some initial knowledge about being "above" and being "on" something:

```
initial(on(B1,B2) <-
     at(B1,X:Y1) & at(B2,X:Y2) & diff(Y1,Y2,1)).
initial(above(B1,B2) <- on(B1,B2)).
```

So now we have the essential core of a general assimilation program, augmented with specific knowledge about blocks. We can set up the program so that we can hold a conversation like this. The program prompts with ">>," we type in an item, and the program then says what its reaction is.

```
>> on(b1,b2).
I already knew that

>> above(b1,b2).
I already knew that

>> above(b1,b3).
OK, input accepted

>> above(X,Z) <- on(X,Y) & above(Y,Z).
item above(b1,b3)is redundant, so it is dropped
OK, input accepted

>> above(b1,b3).
I already knew that
```

```
>> above(b3,b1).
Rejected, because it yields the impossible situation:
above(b3,b1) & above(b1,b3) .

>> at(b4,1:2).
Rejected, because it yields the impossible situation:
at(b4,1 : 2) & at(b2,1 : 2) & b4 =/ b2 .

>> at(b1,2:1).
Rejected, because it yields the impossible situation:
at(b1,2 : 1) & at(b1,1 : 3) & 2 : 1 =/ 1 : 3 .

>> at(b4,2:2).
Rejected, because it yields the impossible situation:
at(b4,2 : 2) & gt(2,1) &
      diff(2,1,1) &  ¬at(V1,2 : 1).
```

The first item we typed in, on(b1,b2), is deducible from the initial situation, so the assimilation program says "I already knew that"; similarly for the second item, above(b1,b2). The third item, above(b1,b3), is not deducible, so the program accepts it as a new fact and the KB is changed.

The fourth item is the rule

```
above(X,Z) <- on(X,Y) & above(Y,Z).
```

Our simple assim predicate is mainly useful for filtering incoming facts. Detecting redundancy in incoming rules needs a much fuller treatment. For now, we treat an incoming rule as redundant if we can match it directly to a rule in the knowledge base. (Strictly we should be checking the relative generality of the incoming rule and a rule that it matches.) So the above rule is accepted. However, it allows us to deduce above(b1,b3), so we drop this as an explicit fact in the KB. The next item just checks that we can indeed deduce above(b1,b3) from the revised KB. The last four items show that the various constraints we have put in the initial knowledge are indeed active—blocks cannot be simultaneously above and below one another, two blocks cannot be in the same place at the same time, a block cannot be in two places at once, and a block has to be supported by something.

This simple kind of subject-dependent checking can be very useful, particularly the constraints that warn us if we try to put in facts that describe something that cannot happen. However, if we consider checking incoming rules, then it is not always clear exactly what checking we should be doing. Also, in a real knowledge base, one must usually strike a balance between the checking that can easily be specified and the checking that can be done efficiently.

4.6 SUMMARY

We can distinguish between conventional programming, and the construction of knowledge systems. Conventionally, we write a fixed program containing knowledge about how to process certain kinds of facts—for example a program to invert matrices of numbers. It may be possible to adjust the knowledge in the program slightly, perhaps by setting some parameters, but it will usually be hard to make a radical change without rewriting the program. Also, unless we know the algorithm (perhaps it is spelled out in comments) it may be a matter of some effort to read the program and to find out how it works. In fact, quite a few people are reluctant to read other people's programs.

In an expert system shell, it is not only the facts that act as input parameters to the program, but also the knowledge about how to use the facts—hence the name "shell." We think of a shell as initially empty, waiting to be primed with knowledge about a particular subject. For an expert system, we write down rules and facts about a subject. For a natural language understanding program, we write down dictionaries of facts, and rules about syntax and semantics of the language. Moreover we often want to add new facts or rules without doing any programming.

This means that we have to shift our knowledge representation. Conventionally, knowledge is either a fact (cell x of the memory contains the value 33), or an instruction about how to change the memory (x:=22), perhaps conditionally (if y>5 then x:=22). In most knowledge systems, we move our representation away from snapshots of the state of the computer hardware toward notations that are closer to natural language. Prolog is a step in this direction, a Frame system written in Prolog is a further step, as are Plantdoc and Syllog, and the ultimate is of course English itself.

There is quite a choice of representations, and it turns out that the choice is very important. A good choice is one that keeps the task description conceptually simple (so that we don't get lost in the details when reading it) yet is efficient when used to answer questions. Since efficiency and conceptual simplicity sometimes steer us in opposite directions, there is much interest in techniques that shift the knowledge representation tacitly and automatically, while allowing us to view the system as though it works directly with knowledge in the form that we write it down.

Our logical approach turns out to be very useful for writing expert systems. It gives us exact reasoning methods that we can compare with declarative standards of correctness. Even though logic is exact, there are several ways to use it as a firm basis for judgmental reasoning. There are some quite general techniques for explaining why an answer to a question follows from whatever knowledge is in the system, and indeed for finding out what would have to be changed to get a desired answer that is not forthcoming. We can also check incoming knowledge, both in ways that are built into a knowledge system shell and do not depend on the current subject we are reasoning about, and also to make sure that we do not step outside subject-dependent knowledge about what is possible in the real world.

As we mentioned, there is a nice progression from representing knowledge in a conventional program, to Prolog, to shells that reason logically and declaratively with more or less English-like forms of knowledge, to English itself. In this chapter we have looked at two shells, at how to use them, and at some of the techniques used to write them. In Chapter 5 we turn to natural language processing, specifically getting a computer to understand English.

EXERCISES

1. In 4.1, "Knowledge Representation and Use" we described some ways of representing knowledge. Exactly how we represent knowledge about a problem can be very important in solving it. The following example, due to John McCarthy, shows this. Suppose we have a chess board, and we cut out a square at one corner, and another square at the opposite corner. We are next given a box of dominoes. Each domino can exactly cover two squares of the board. Is it possible (assuming we have enough dominoes), to cover the altered chess board with dominoes, leaving no square uncovered, without a domino half on the board?

    The first part of the exercise is to write a Prolog program to try various ways of covering the board. However, the program is likely to be slow, and it may not be worth trying to make it faster.

    The second part of the exercise is to note that any domino placed on the board must cover one red and one black square. Since the mutilated board does not have the same number of red and black squares, the answer to the question is "no." Write an efficient program which, for any chess board with some squares removed, finds out whether it can be tiled with dominoes.

2. In 4.1.3, "Logic" we used a predicate `prove(X,given(Y))`. One way to write this predicate is to temporarily add Y to the Prolog workspace, then delete it when we are done. However, this is not good Prolog practice.

    The normal Prolog `addax` changes the program that is currently executing, i.e, whatever is `addax`ed is not removed if the program later backtracks.

    Implement a predicate called `assume`, which adds its argument only temporarily, and undoes the add upon backtracking. See D. S. Warren (1984) for the formal semantics of such a predicate. See also McCord's report (1982b).

    Use your `assume` predicate in a rule

    ```
    prove(X,given(Y)) <- assume(Y) & X.
    ```

    and test this rule with the tiling problem on page 228.

3. Write a Prolog metainterpreter to do simple resolution theorem proving, as described on page 231. Use your theorem prover to find the chain of reasoning on page 231 for the tiling problem in logical notation. Then use the IBM Prolog `time` predicate to compare the speed of execution of your metainterpreter with that of the Prolog program on page 228.

4. On page 236 we mentioned the part of Syllog that transforms sentences in a Syllog knowledge base into a Prolog-like form.

(i) Write a program that reads a sentence such as

```
can handle eg_c of eg_item pd,
    with eg_p % burnin, on eg_testm machine
```

into a form such as

```
p3(V1,V2,V3,V4).
```

To do this, you will need to be able to generate distinct names p1, p2, p3, and so on for predicates.

(ii) Next, modify your program from part (i) so that if it reads in these two sentences,

```
can handle 99 of eg_item pd,
    with eg_p % burnin, on eg_testm machine.
```

```
can handle eg_c of eg_item pd,
    with eg_p % burnin, on a50 machine.
```

it produces the sentence

```
can handle eg_c of eg_item pd,
    with eg_p % burnin, on eg_testm machine.
```

Make your program general enough so that it will read all three sentences in any order and still produce just the last sentence mentioned above.

5. Section 4.4.3, "Full Explanations of Both Yes and No Answers" described a way of getting comprehensive explanations from programs containing negations. Complete the program on page 273 and test it with the examples given. The program is a metainterpreter, and it may be useful to refer to Appendix A for details of how to set up and run such a program in VM/Prolog.

6. On page 266 we talked about the idea that an explanation may consist of just the interesting parts of a proof. Write a sample knowledge base on a topic of interest to you, and run it using the full explanation interpreter in the last exercise. Note places where the explanations seem to contain more information than is really needed.

7. Write a predicate interesting(E1,E2) that edits an explanation E1 produced in the previous exercise, to leave only the interesting parts in E2. Then, use your interesting predicate to prune an explanation step by step as is it produced by your interpreter.

8. What aspects of the interesting predicate in the previous exercise are subject-specific? Isolate the subject-independent parts, where possible, and test these on further sample knowledge bases.

9. On page 275 we mentioned that it is often a help if the system chooses the order in which explanations are shown. Specifically

    ■ If the answer to a question is "yes," show the shortest explanation first.

    ■ If the answer to a question is "no," first show the longest explanation in which nothing is repeated.

    Adapt the program on page 273 to do this, in such a way that one can ask for different explanations, if needed, by causing a Prolog backtrack. Test your program on the example in Section 4.1.2, "Frames."

10. Even with the ordering suggested in the previous exercise, one may have to look at several explanations of why something is not so before finding an informative one. If the answer to a question is "no," it can sometimes be a help to show first a negative explanation that differs as little as possible from a positive explanation of a similar question for which the answer is "yes."

    Design working definitions of the words "differ" and "similar" in the last sentence. Then starting from the program on page 273, program an explanation generator based on these definitions.

11. On page 277 we looked at a problem with rules of the form

    ```
    ceo(X) <- ¬manager(X,Y).
    ```

    and we suggested instead

    ```
    ceo(X) <- employee(X) & ¬manager(X,Y).
    ```

    The rule

    ```
    ceo(X) <- ¬manager(X,Y) & employee(X).
    ```

    has the same declarative meaning, although procedurally Prolog treats it differently.
        Starting with the simple metainterpreter on page 267, write an interpreter that delays a negated goal in the body of a rule until as many of its arguments as possible have been evaluated in a positive goal. Test your interpreter to make sure that it gives the same answers for the questions ceo(X) and ceo(jane) when either of the last two rules are used with the facts

    ```
    manager(fred,jane).
    employee(fred).
    employee(jane).
    ```

12. On page 279 we described a program that checks a knowledge base to see whether it is possible to follow the rules from a goal, through a negated literal, and back to the same goal again.
        We showed that the program works for a knowledge base that is *propositional*, in the sense that it contains no variables.

Write a sample knowledge base containing rules with variables, including a recursive loop through a negation, and see whether the same program works correctly and identifies the loop.

Will the program work correctly in general for knowledge bases with variables?

13. In Syllog, one can ask a question and get an answer as a table, or one can ask for the syllogisms that conclude about a sentence. If we have a table of facts on the screen, or if we have some syllogisms on the screen, we are free to change them.

However, if we have on the screen a table of answers that have been deduced using rules, it is not always clear what is meant by a change made to the screen. For example, deleting something deducible might mean "restrict the rules so that they don't deduce this," or it might mean "remove some (minimal) number of underlying facts so that the deleted line is no longer deducible."

In relational database theory this is called the *view update problem*, and it is widely studied, see for example Fagin et al (1986), though usually without treating recursion in the rules.

Write a program, based on a Prolog metainterpreter, that interviews a person who suggests such a deletion to find out what the intention is. To what extent can the program be made independent of the subject matter of the knowledge base it is used with?

14. As we mentioned on page 18, one may set up a knowledge system so that each item in it has an associated start time. Then, instead of deleting an item, we note the time at which it ends. Adapt the `assim` predicate on page 281 so that it assimilates information in this way. Design the adaptation so that we can ask whether some item is currently true, and also whether it was true at some specified time in the past.

15. In Section 4.1.2, "Frames," we looked at the idea that descriptions of houses could be grouped using a frame structure, so that a particular house is the same as a prototypical house, with some noted exceptions. In *object oriented programming*, a similar notion allows us to apply a prototypical rule for reasoning about an object, unless an exception rule is provided.

Choose a subject, (such as combinatorial logic circuits), in which there are many copies of the same computation to be done, and write a metainterpreter that causes an object (e.g a logic gate) to inherit its computation method from a more general object.

5

Natural Language Processing in Prolog

Michael McCord

"The structure of every sentence is a lesson in logic."

John Stuart Mill *Inaugural Address at St. Andrews.*

Prolog has special applicability to natural language processing in three ways. First, natural language grammars can be written almost directly as Prolog programs, so that analysis and synthesis of natural language can be performed efficiently by direct Prolog execution. Second, semantic representations of natural language text in logic are natural to produce with Prolog because of Prolog's close connection to logic. Finally, inference with these logical representations (say, for question answering) can often be done by Prolog inference, or by inference procedures built on top of Prolog. In the initial development of Prolog in Marseille in the early 1970s, these possibilities were seen by Alain Colmerauer, with some input from Robert Kowalski, and were in fact a major motivation for Colmerauer in his work on Prolog. An early Prolog-based natural language system was described in Colmerauer et al.(1972). The papers by Colmerauer (1975, 1978) describe his Metamorphosis Grammars, which can be translated directly into Prolog; and a version of logical semantic representation is given in Colmerauer (1979, 1982).

This chapter presents a systematic approach to the application of Prolog to natural language processing, based on a type of grammar called Modular Logic Grammar (MLG) designed for a modular treatment of syntax and semantics (McCord 1985a).

In general, the purpose of a natural language grammar is to associate *analysis structures* with sentences. Analysis structures might be *semantic representations*, which give the meanings of sentences and are used in inference (say, for an expert system or a database query system). Analysis structures might also be *syntactic structures* (or *syntactic analyses*), which represent the division of a sentence into phrases, subphrases, subsubphrases, etc. Some grammars associate both types of analysis structures with sentences, and the grammar may be divided into a *syntactic component*, which produces syntactic analyses, and a *semantic interpretation component*, which takes syntactic analyses and produces semantic representations. Other types of grammars may not produce syntactic analyses, but just produce semantic representations directly. Modular Logic Grammars are capable of being used in either way. They have a clear separation into a syntactic component and a semantic interpretation component, but these two components can be used either in a serial or an interleaved way.

The formalism used for semantic representation in this chapter is a version of predicate logic called LFL (Logical Form Language). The aim of LFL is a good, general representation of the meanings of natural language sentences, including an adequate treatment of quantification and related constructions involving scoping. Since the semantic representation language is the "target" language of a grammatical system, it has a great influence on what specific grammars look like. We therefore take a rather goal-directed approach to exposition in this chapter, devoting the first section to a discussion of LFL. This section is mainly descriptive and involves very little implementation.

The next four sections are the methodological core of the chapter. The first of these, 5.2, "Logic Grammars," begins with a discussion of Definite Clause Grammars (DCGs), which are a special case of Colmerauer's Metamorphosis Grammars, mentioned above. Then our main grammatical formalism, Modular Logic Grammars (MLGs) (more precisely, the *syntactic* portion of MLGs) is introduced as an augmentation of the DCG formalism. We show how to implement rule compilers for both DCGs and MLGs.

The next Section, 5.3, "Words," describes a collection of techniques for the treatment of words in a large grammar. The form of the lexicon, with special emphasis on slot frames, and a scheme for representing semantic types, are discussed.

Section 5.4, "Syntactic Constructions" deals with interesting syntactic phenomena in English grammar and with methods for covering them with a Modular Logic Grammar.

The final methodological Section, 5.5, "Semantic Interpretation," describes techniques for getting LFL analyses of sentences, assuming that syntactic analyses have already been obtained (by the methods of the preceding sections). Issues of scoping for quantifiers and other modifiers are dealt with.

The last section of the chapter, 5.6, "Application to Question Answering," takes a specific database (dealing with university records) represented in Prolog, and applies the techniques of the preceding sections for answering natural language questions about the database. Sentences such as

> Which graduate students majoring in mathematics has Anderson had in an undergraduate computer science course?

are translated by a Modular Logic Grammar into LFL forms representing their meanings, then into Prolog goals that are executed to obtain answers.

Although not dealt with in this chapter, another application of some of the methods is an experimental English-German machine translation system, LMT (Logic-based Machine Translation), currently under development (McCord 1985c, 1986).

5.1 THE LOGICAL FORM LANGUAGE

In this section we discuss a logical language LFL (Logical Form Language), which we will use as a meaning representation language for natural language. Meanings of sentences are *logical forms* and these are expressions in LFL. LFL expressions are represented as Prolog terms and can be produced by Prolog programs that we will describe in this chapter. For some natural language applications (including many database query applications), LFL expressions can be treated as Prolog goals and executed directly by Prolog to answer queries. However, in general, LFL is a more powerful logical language than Prolog, and one must write a separate inference procedure for LFL.

5.1.1 The Formation Rules for LFL

There is actually a version of LFL for each natural language, because the main predicates in LFL are *word senses* in the given natural language. Word senses correspond roughly to the distinct senses of words listed in a standard dictionary, although standard dictionaries generally do not make enough distinctions. We will elaborate on this notion in succeeding subsections. We deal only with English, but the basic ideas appear to apply to all natural languages.

As an example, the logical form for

```
John believes that each man knows Bill.
```

might be written as

```
believe1(john,each(man1(X),know2(X,bill))).
```

Here `believe1` is one of the senses of the verb "believe", `man1` is one of the senses of the noun "man", and so forth. Even the quantifier `each` is considered a predicate of LFL, being a sense of the determiner "each".

In addition to word senses, there are a small number of *nonlexical* predicates in LFL. These are predicates that do not correspond directly to words. Sometimes their presence is signaled by inflections of words, as in the case of `past`:

```
John saw Bill.
past(see(john,bill)).
```

Other nonlexical predicates are signaled by syntactic constructions, as in the case of yesno:

```
Does John see Bill?
yesno(true,see(john,bill)).
```

(The significance of the first argument of yesno will be explained later.) Still other nonlexical predicates are more "abstract" and have to do with emphasis and discourse function, although their presence is often signaled by syntax and by stress patterns in spoken language.

Each predicate of LFL takes a fixed number of arguments. Note (in the above examples) that arguments might be variables, constants, or other logical forms. With this said, we can give the formation rules for logical forms (expressions of LFL) as follows:

- If p is a predicate of LFL (either a word sense or a nonlexical predicate) taking n arguments, and each of x1, .., xn is either a constant or a logical form (as required by p for that argument) or is a variable, then p(x1, .., xn) is a logical form.

- If P and Q are logical forms, then P & Q is a logical form.

- If P is a logical form and E is a variable, then P:E (read "P indexed by E") is a logical form.

In the last rule, ":" is called the *indexing operator*. When an indexed logical form P:E appears as part of a larger logical form Q, and the index variable E is used elsewhere in Q, E can be thought of roughly as standing for P together with its "context." Contexts include references to time and place that are normally left implicit in natural language. When P specifies an event, as in see(john,mary), writing P:E and subsequently using E will guarantee that E refers to the *same* event. Indexing will be discussed in more detail in Section 5.1.11, "The Indexing Operator."

For some applications, it is sufficient to ignore contexts, and in such cases we just think of P:E as verifying P and binding E to an instantiation of P. In fact, for Prolog execution of logical forms without contexts, ":" can be defined by the single clause

```
P:P <- P.
```

In the next few sections, we will get a more detailed picture of LFL by looking at different parts of speech and how their senses are represented. While looking at the different word classes, we will say something about English syntax, because (not surprisingly) the syntax has a close (but not always so simple) connection to logical form.

5.1.2 Verbs

The verb is the heart of the sentence; or perhaps we should say "the head," because we follow the notion that every noncompound sentence or phrase has a well-defined *head word*. The head of the sentence "John knows the old man" is the verb "knows", and the head of the noun phrase "the old man" is the noun "man".

Clustered around the head verb of a sentence are its *modifiers*. For the sentence

John probably knows the old man.

the modifiers of "knows" are the subject noun phrase "John", the adverbial "probably", and the object noun phrase "the old man". Modifiers are of two types: *complements* and *adjuncts*. Subjects and objects (both direct and indirect) are examples of complements, and adverbials are examples of adjuncts. In the logical form of the sentence, a word sense predicate for the head verb will appear, with one argument for each complement of the verb. Thus the syntactic notion of *complement* is closely tied to the semantic notion of *argument* in word sense predications.

Let us look at some examples.

John laughs.
laugh1(john).

John sees Mary.
see1(john,mary).

John gives Fido to Mary.
give1(john,fido,mary).

John gives Mary Fido.
give1(john,fido,mary).

John believes in Mary.
believe_in(john,mary).

John trusts Mary.
trust1(john,mary).

(*Note:* The names we choose for word sense predicates are arbitrary; what really counts is having a different name for each word sense and, of course, having suitable axioms that involve these predicates. But for readability it is useful to choose minor variations of the citation form of the word. In subsequent examples, we will often just use the citation form, using variations only when we want to distinguish senses.)

The most important thing to note in these examples is that some complements are introduced by prepositions like "to" and "in". The phrase "to

Mary" in the third example plays the same role semantically as the indirect object "Mary" does in the fourth. Note that "believe in" is close in meaning to "trust". In this usage, "in" has the function of introducing a complement (logically, an argument) similar to a direct object.

Of course prepositions can introduce adjunct modifiers as well. This happens in the sentence "John walks in the park". The main clue for this is that "in" has its own independent meaning (containment) in this sentence.

A word sense is called *intensional* if at least one of its arguments is a logical form. Many verbs have intensional senses.

```
John believes that Mary knows Bill.
believe(john,know(mary,bill)).

John wants to see Mary.
want(john,see(john,mary)).

John asks Bill to find Mary.
ask(john,bill,find(bill,mary))
```

Such words are called *intensional* because they can "look at" whole logical forms and do things with their senses (intensions).

For a passive sentence such as

```
John is seen by Mary.
```

we use the analysis

```
be_passive(john,see(mary,john)).
```

Here be_passsive(X,P) means roughly that P describes what happens to X. Note that P itself in this example captures the meaning of the corresponding active sentence "Mary sees John". But the active sentence does not mean exactly the same thing as the passive sentence, so the logical form should capture the difference. In some applications, though, it would be satisfactory to ignore the difference and define

```
be_passive(X,P) <- P.
```

or even to replace be_passive(X,P) by P while transforming the logical form to a more efficient executable form.

A small number of verbs have senses that are predicates with 0 arguments. For example, the sentence "It snows" could have the simple logical form snow. Here "It" is a sort of dummy subject for the verb "snows". We have given examples of verb senses with 0, 1, 2, and 3 arguments. It appears that verb senses never have more than 3 arguments.

5.1.3 Nouns

Most typically, a noun sense is a 1-place predicate, like man, which classifies entities. But some nouns are relational, as in

```
brother(X,Y)
"X is a brother of Y"
```

Many nouns are derived from verbs, and such nouns normally have a complement structure similar to that of the verb.

```
John believes that Mary knows Bill.
believe(john,know(mary,bill)).

John's belief that Mary knows Bill.
belief(john,know(mary,bill)).
```

Proper nouns correspond to constants in LFL. In most cases we represent these as atoms or numbers in Prolog, but it is also useful sometimes to use (variable-free) compound terms when proper nouns have structure.

A noun phrase does not have an isolated meaning (a closed logical form) of its own, but only contributes to the meaning of the sentence in which it appears. Proper noun phrases contribute by binding a variable to the associated constant. All other noun phrases have an associated quantifier, and this has an argument that comes from (part of) the remainder of the sentence. In the above example with "belief", the contribution of the noun phrase actually looks like

```
the(belief(john,know(mary,bill)):E, P)
```

where P is what is to be said about the belief.

The quantifiers associated with noun phrases come mainly from determiners, and we look at these next.

5.1.4 Determiners

The main types of premodifiers of nouns are determiners, adjectives, and other nouns. Determiners form a *closed class* of words — a small class that rarely accepts new members in the growth of the language. (Verbs and nouns form *open classes*.) Examples of determiners are

```
a, an, the,
each, all, some, no, few, many, ...
his, her, its, ...
this, that, these, those,
which, what, whose, ...
```

Syntactically, a characteristic of determiners is that they normally come first in the noun phrase; they cannot be preceded by adjective and noun premodifiers. (There are certain *predeterminers*, like "all" in "all the men", but these also function semantically as determiners.)

Semantically, determiners are basically quantifiers. Their senses, as predicates in LFL, have in most cases two arguments, which are filled by logical forms. The first argument is called the *base* of the determiner, and the second is called the *focus*.

```
determiner(Base,Focus)
```

The pair (Base,Focus) is called the *scope* of the determiner(-sense). Examples:

```
Each man knows Bill.
each(man(X), know(X,bill)).

Each boy eats several apples.
each(boy(X), several(apple(Y), eat(X,Y))).

Each man that knows Mary knows Bill.
each(man(X)&know(X,mary), know(X,bill)).

Each man that owns a car washes it.
each(man(X)&car(Y)&own(X,Y), wash(X,Y)).
```

We can define each(P,Q) for execution of queries in Prolog by the clause

```
each(P,Q) <- ¬(P & ¬Q).
```

Because of the implementation of ¬ as failure to prove, this works out to mean procedurally: "For each way of proving P (with resulting instantiation of variables in P), Q can be proved." The reader should verify that this works.

The standard universal quantifier in first-order predicate logic has two operands: all(X,P) means "for all X, P holds." With this standard quantifier, we would use the analysis

```
Each man knows Bill.
all(X, man(X)->know(X,bill)).
```

So the standard universal quantifier all(X,P) specifies a single variable (X) to quantify over, and the proposition P is supposed to hold for every value of X. The single form P is the scope of the quantifier. The quantifiers in LFL are different in two ways. (1) The scope of the quantifier is split into two parts, the base and the focus, so that we write all(P,Q) (or each(P,Q)) instead of all(X,P->Q). (2) Quantification can be over several variables simultaneously, as in the example analysis above for "Each man that owns a car washes it". The quantification is over all free variables appearing in the base of the quantifier.

If we were dealing only with universal and existential quantification, it would be sufficient to use the standard quantifiers; but to handle natural language quantifiers like few and most, it seems necessary to use something like LFL quantifiers. First, it is necessary to split the scope into two parts, because `few(P,Q)` basically says that the number of ways P & Q holds is small relative to the number of ways P holds. Consider the example:

```
Few tigers are tame.
```

If we followed the pattern of the standard universal quantifier and wrote

```
few(X,tiger(X)->tame(X)).
```

with the usual meaning for `->`, we would be in trouble, because the proposition in the second argument would hold vacuously for *most* things in the universe since most things are not tigers.

On the other hand, using the analysis

```
few(tiger(X),tame(X)).
```

we can give a reasonably good definition of this base/focus version of `few` by

```
few(Base,Focus) <-
    card(Base, B) &
    card(Base&Focus, BF) &
    small(BF,B).
```

Here, we could define `card(P,N)` ("the *cardinal number* of P is N") by the rule

```
card(P,N) <- set_of(P,P,S) & length(S,N).
```

The predication `set_of(X,P,S)` means that the set of all X such that P holds is S. And `small(M,N)` might be defined by requiring that the quotient M/N be less than a certain fraction.

It seems necessary to use the LFL method of simultaneous quantification over several variables, because of examples like the following.

```
Most people writing a letter mail it.
most(person(X)&letter(Y)&write(X,Y), mail(X,Y)).
```

Here the quantification is over cases of persons writing letters, not just persons or letters separately. David Lewis (1975) has made a similar point for adverbs of quantification (like "always" and "often"). We deal with these in the next section. A simple definition of `most(Base,Focus)` would be similar to that of `few(Base,Focus)`, but would require that the number of ways Base&Focus holds is some very large fraction of the number of ways Base holds.

The definitions just indicated for quantifiers like `few`, `most`, and `many`, are not actually adequate for all uses of these quantifiers. Consider the sentence

```
John knows many people.
```

What should the logical form be, and how should the use of `many` in it be defined? The most obvious logical form might be

```
many(person(X),know(john,X)).
```

A definition of this along the lines indicated above would require the conditions

```
card(person(X),B) & card(person(X)&know(john,X),BF)
  & large(BF,B).
```

In other words, the number of people John knows is a large fraction (say, over half) of the total number of people. This is actually a possible sense of "many" in the sentence, (especially if we understand some limited world); let us call it the *absolute* sense. But there is another sense that is probably more common, the *relative sense*, namely, that the number of people John knows is large in comparison with the numbers of people known by other people. To be more precise, let `friends(X)` be the set of people known by X. What we need to do then is to compute

- the cardinality J of `friends(john)`, and
- the list C of cardinalities of the sets `friends(X)` for all possible X,

and we want to require that J be large with respect to C; say, J is over twice the average of C.

To express this in IBM Prolog, we can use very conveniently the built-in procedure

```
compute(Type,X,P,Y,L).
```

Basically, this procedure computes L as the *list* or the *set* (depending on whether Type equals `list` or `set`) of all X such that P holds. If there is no X such that P holds, then `compute` fails. In particular, we can define `set_of(X,P,S)` ("the set of X such that P holds is S") by

```
set_of(X,P,S) <- compute(set,X,P,nil,S).
set_of(X,P,nil).
```

(As we mentioned on page 79, this is a simple definition, and it should not be used in a program that will backtrack into it. If such a use is needed, then we can add a cut at the end of the first rule for `set_of`.)

The fourth argument Y of `compute` is in general a list of variables, called *cross-sectional* variables, that are held fixed in the computation of the aggregate. If we make the computation

```
compute(set,X,know(Y,X),Y.nil,S),
```

then the cross-sectional variable Y will be instantiated to some particular person, and S will be the set of all persons X that Y knows; in other words, S is the set `friends(Y)`. If we backtrack into the call to `compute`, then the cross-sectional variable Y will be instantiated to other persons. We can get the set T of all sets `friends(Y)` by the computation

```
compute(set,S,compute(set,X,know(Y,X),Y.nil,S),nil,T).
```

To give a general definition of `many` and other such quantifiers, we need an auxiliary predicate:

```
cardlist(X,P,Y,L) <-
   compute(list,N,
                compute(set,X,P,Y,S) & length(S,N),
           nil,L).
```

Thus L will be the list of cardinalities for all sets S, where S is the set of all X such that P holds and Y is a list of cross-sectional variables. For example, if we ask for

```
cardlist(X,know(Y,X),Y.nil,L),
```

then L will be the list C described above consisting of all cardinalities of sets `friends(Y)`.

With this, we can define a general sense of many by

```
many(X,Base,Focus,Y) <-
   cardlist(X,Base,Y,B) &
   cardlist(X,Base&Focus,Y,BF) &
   large(BF,B,Y).
```

Here we are being explicit in the predication `many(X,Base,Focus,Y)` in naming the *counting variables* X and the *cross-sectional variables* Y. Note that B and BF are now *lists* of numbers. We could take the condition `large(BF,B,Y)` to mean that the average of the numbers in the list BF is larger than K times the average of the numbers in the list B, where K = 2 if Y is nonnull (the relative case), and K = 1/2 if Y is null (the absolute case).

Now we can return to the sentence

```
John knows many people.
```

in the second (more common) sense indicated above, and give it the logical form

```
many(X.nil, person(X)&know(Y,X), Y=john, Y.nil).
```

From the definition of many just given, this will be equivalent to

```
cardlist(X.nil, person(X)&know(Y,X), Y.nil, B) &
cardlist(X.nil, person(X)&know(Y,X)&Y=john,
         Y.nil, BF) &
large(BF,B,Y).
```

Note that BF will turn out to be a list with one member, the number of people John knows. And we are saying that this number is large compared to the numbers of people that other people know.

Note: Two representations for "many" were given independently by Saint-Dizier (1986). These correspond to the absolute reading, as in "Many tigers are wild", and the relative reading, as in "John knows many people", just described. Saint-Dizier's formulas for these two different types of readings were rather different from each other. The general formula for many given above includes them both as special cases; the dichotomy between the absolute and relative cases is expressed in the definition of `large`.

There are cases where BF, in the formula for many, has more than one member, as for the sentence

```
Politicians know many people.
```

with logical form

```
many(X.nil, person(X)&know(Y,X),
     politician(Y), Y.nil),
```

which would mean that the numbers of people known by politicians are large compared to the numbers of people known by people in general.

The original, simple, sense of many, as in

```
Many people own a car.
```

has no cross-sectional variables:

```
many(X.nil, person(X), car(Y)&own(X,Y), nil).
```

We have defined a general sense of many that has four arguments. Two of the arguments are the base and the focus, and the other two represent explicitly the counting variables and the cross-sectional variables. It is actually not necessary to specify these extra variable-list arguments in logical form, because they can in fact be determined from the complete logical form of the sentence. We will not give complete details, but the rough idea is as follows. We want to specify the cross-sectional variables and counting variables for a quantifier form P=quant(Base,Focus), which may be part of a larger logical form. First we make a recursive definition: A variable X is *bound* by P provided that (1) X is not bound by any quantifier form containing P and (2) X has an occurrence in P that is outside any quantifier form within P. Now, a variable X will be *cross-sectional* for P (if this is relevant for the given quantifier) provided that X is bound by P and X is related by an equality or by the indexing operator to a variable that is bound by a quantifier form containing P. A variable X will be a *counting variable* for P provided that X is bound by P, X is not cross-sectional, and X occurs in the base of P.

As an example, consider the sentence

```
Everybody that knows many people knows Bill.
```

We can give the following analysis with two-place quantifiers:

```
every(person(X) & many(person(Y)&know(X0,Y), X0=X),
      know(X,bill)).
```

Clearly, the every form has X as its single counting variable. The many form has X0 as a cross-sectional variable since it is related by an equality to a higher bound variable (X). And finally, Y is a counting variable for the many form.

For the sentence

```
John knows many people.
```

with the cross-sectional reading, the actual logical form shows "John" as the *topic* of the sentence (in the sense of the Section below, 5.1.10, "Nonlexical Predicates in LFL"), and this accounts for the cross-sectional character of the variable associated with "John".

The *articles* "a" (with variant "an") and "the" are tricky determiners. It is interesting that some languages (e.g, Chinese, Japanese, and Russian) get by without articles. The indefinite article "a" is sometimes used existentially:

```
Mary owns a cat.
ex(cat(X),own(mary,X)).
```

For Prolog queries we can just define ex by

```
ex(P,Q) <- P & Q.
```

In other cases, the best view of the indefinite article is that it has a null contribution to logical form, and the real quantification over its head noun is determined elsewhere. In examples like

```
A cat always likes Mary.
always(cat(X),like(X,mary)).
```

which means essentially the same as "All cats like Mary", the real quantification comes from "always", and "a" has a null contribution. Note that we get essentially the same meaning with the plural form

```
Cats always like Mary.
```

which has no determiner. Similarly, in the example given above

```
Each man that owns a car washes it.
each(man(X)&car(Y)&own(X,Y), wash(X,Y)).
```

the "a" has a null contribution, and the control lies with "each".

The definite article "the" is the most common word in the English language. The basic meaning of the(P,Q) is that P holds uniquely and Q holds. An example analysis is

```
John likes the cat that Bill owns.
the(cat(X)&own(bill,X), like(john,X)).
```

For some applications, it would be correct to define the by

```
the(P,Q) <- card(P,1) & P & Q.
```

But there are complications. One is that in many uses of "the", the literal base given for "the" does not actually hold uniquely. Example:

```
A cat came to our house last night.
The cat was starving.
```

To get an accurate logical form in such cases, we can arrange for one of the following three things: (1) The contribution of the definite noun phrase can simply be a variable that is quantified elsewhere, as in

```
John owns a cat.
John likes the cat.
ex(cat(X), own(john,X) & like(john,X)).
```

(2) The contribution can be a constant that represents the desired referent of the definite noun phrase. (3) We could simply fill out the information that will make the base of the hold uniquely. The problem of incomplete specification of noun phrases exists also for determiners other than "the". For these, method (3) must be used.

Another complication for "the" is that many uses of it *presuppose* existence and uniqueness for the base instead of asserting it. For example, if someone asks:

```
Is the cat Bill owns Siamese?
```

and Bill owns no cats or owns more than one cat, it is misleading to answer "No." We will have more to say about presuppositions in Section 5.1.10, "Nonlexical Predicates in LFL." For some applications, however, it is satisfactory to ignore the uniqueness condition for "the", and just define

```
the(P,Q) <- P & Q.
```

With careful use of English, the scoping of quantifiers reflects syntactic structure in a simple way; in particular, if two noun phrases NP1 and NP2 modify the same verb and NP1 precedes NP2, then the determiner of NP1 will have wider scope than that of NP2. But there are cases where this direct relation between syntax and semantics is violated. The sentence

```
Some woman loves every man.
```

has two possible readings:

```
ex(woman(X), all(man(Y), love(X,Y))).
all(man(Y), ex(woman(X), love(X,Y))).
```

There is a similar problem of interaction of quantifiers with other modifiers:

```
Everybody isn't here yet.
not(yet(all(person(X),here(X)))).
```

5.1.5 Pronouns

Pronouns form a closed class that has features in common with both nouns and determiners. Many pronouns are homographs of determiners (have the same spelling). Pronouns include

```
he, she, it, ...,
himself, herself, itself, ...,
this, that, these, those,
each, all, some, no, few, many, ...,
everybody, somebody, nobody, ...,
which, what, who, ... .
```

The *definite pronouns* (indicated in the first three lines) have something in common with the definite article ("the"); e.g, "he" is similar in meaning to "the male person". As with noun phrases introduced by "the", definite pronouns show up in logical form as (1) variables, (2) constants, or (3) completely specified the forms. Examples:

```
Every man likes himself.
every(man(X), like(X,X)).

Bill owns a cat.  He likes it.
ex(cat(X), own(bill,X) & like(bill,X)).

That belongs to Bill.
the(object(X)&point_to(speaker,X), belong_to(X,bill)).
```

The problems of determining pronoun reference are difficult, and have been the subject of much investigation in linguistics and natural language processing (see, *e.g*, Hobbs 1978, Reinhart 1985).

Indefinite pronouns essentially consist of a determiner with an understood base. For example, "everybody" appears in logical form as `every(person(X),_)`, although the base may need further qualification from the context.

5.1.6 Adverbs and the Notion of Focalizer

Adverbs form an open class of words that can modify verbs, adjectives, and other adverbs. They are all intensional (take logical forms as arguments). Some take a single argument and say something about the time of validity of the logical form in the argument.

```
Yesterday John bought a cat.
yesterday(ex(cat(X),buy(john,X))).
```

We will concentrate here on adverbs that are examples of *focalizers*. Our first examples of focalizers were the determiners. Recall that determiners have two logical form arguments called the *base* and the *focus*. The reason for the name *base* is probably clear; it specifies the base or range of items quantified over. The reason for the name *focus* will now be explained. There are quantificational adverbs that are analogous to most of the quantificational determiners (they are close in meaning), namely, "always", "often", "usually", "sometimes", "seldom", and "never". The word sense predications for these adverbs take the form

```
adverb(Base,Focus).
```

In spoken language, the part of the sentence that produces the Focus is often stressed (emphasized); it receives phonological focus. In each of the following groups of examples, the first sentence has a focalizer adverb and its logical form follows it; the second sentence is a paraphrase with the related determiner and its logical form follows it. Note that the two logical forms in the group are essentially the same.

```
John always buys books at Smith's.
   always((book(X)&buy(john,X)):E, at(smith,E)).
All John's book purchases are at Smith's.
   all((book(X)&purchase(john,X)):E, at(smith,E)).

John always buys books at Smith's.
   always(at(smith,buy(john,X)), book(X)).
All John's purchases at Smith's are books.
       (He could buy books elsewhere too.)
   all(at(smith,purchase(john,X)), book(X)).

John often buys books at Smith's.
  often((book(X)&buy(john,X)):E, at(smith,E)).
Many of John's book purchases are at Smith's.
  many((book(X)&purchase(john,X)):E, at(smith,E)).

John often buys books at Smith's.
  often(at(smith,buy(john,X)), book(X)).
Many of John's purchases at Smith's are books.
  many(at(smith,purchase(john,X)), book(X)).
```

These examples illustrate that two sentences consisting of the same sequence of words, but differing in focus, can have quite different meanings. It is important to capture these differences in logical form.

Closely related focalizer adverbs are "only", "even", "just", "too", and "also". Phonological focus is particularly noticeable with "only" and "even". Note, in the following examples, the similarity between "only" and "always".

```
John only buys books at Smith's.
  only((book(X)&buy(john,X)):E, at(smith,E)).

John only buys books at Smith's.
  only(at(smith,buy(john,X)), book(X)).
```

In fact, only(P,Q) means essentially the same as always(P,Q) (and all(P,Q)). The difference is in presupposition. The predication `always(P,Q)` normally presupposes that there is a case where P holds, whereas `only(P,Q)` normally has the stronger presupposition that there is a case where P & Q holds.

Many adverbs and adjectives concern comparison or degree along some scale of evaluation. These degree adverbs and adjectives are also focalizers. The base specifies the base of comparison, and the focus singles out what is being compared to the base. This shows up most clearly in the *superlative* forms of the words (with "-est" or "most"). Consider the adverb "fastest" in the sentence

> `John ran fastest yesterday.`

If the focus is on "yesterday", then the meaning is that, among all the events of John's running (this is the base), John's running yesterday was fastest. For this reading, the logical form would be

> `fastest(run(john):E, yesterday(E)).`

If on the other hand the focus is on "John", then the meaning is that among all the events of running yesterday (there is an implicit location for these events), John's running was fastest. For this, the logical form would be

> `fastest(yesterday(run(X)), X=john).`

For a definition of `fastest(Base,Focus)`, we might take something like the following:

```
fastest(Base,Focus) <-
  superlative(Speed,Base&speed(Base,Speed),Focus).

superlative(X,Base,Focus) <-
  set_of(X,Base,B) &
  set_of(X,Base&Focus,BF) &
  maximum(B,BF).

maximum(Set,Max) <-
  "Max has a single member which is >=
     every number in Set".
```

Thus

> `fastest(yesterday(run(X)), X=john).`

would reduce to

```
set_of(S, yesterday(run(X))&
        speed(yesterday(run(X)),S), B) &
set_of(S, yesterday(run(john))&
        speed(yesterday(run(john)),S), BF) &
maximum(B, BF).
```

Here `speed(E,S)` needs to be able to look at a logical form E representing an event of motion and say what its speed S is.

As another example, consider "best" (the superlative of the adverb "well").

```
John sang best yesterday.
best(sing(john):E, yesterday(E)).
```

```
John sang best yesterday.
best(yesterday(sing(X)), X=john).
```

We might define best by

```
best(Base,Focus) <-
    superlative(Value,Base&quality(Base,Value),Focus).
```

Here quality(Act,Value) would have definitional clauses tied to different types of acts. (Evaluating *singing* is different from evaluating *wrestling*, etc.)

The regular forms (like "fast") of degree adverbs are also focalizers, although the associated phonological focus is not as noticeable. For the sentence

```
John ran fast yesterday.
```

we could get analyses

```
fast(run(john):E, yesterday(E)).
fast(yesterday(run(X)), X=john).
fast(run(X):E, yesterday(E)&X=john).
```

Here the idea of fast(Base,Focus) is that, compared to the speeds of events Base, the speed(s) of event(s) Focus is (are) relatively high.

```
fast(Base,Focus) <-
    high(Speed, Base&speed(Base,Speed), Focus).

high(X,Base,Focus) <-
    set_of(X,Base,B) &
    set_of(X,Base&Focus,BF) &
    large(BF,B).
```

For large(BF,B) we might require that the average of the set BF be greater than a certain constant times the average of the set B.

5.1.7 Adjectives

Adjectives are open-class words that can modify nouns and can be complements of certain verbs like "be" and "seem". The majority of adjectives have corresponding adverbs, formed with an "-ly" ending.

The semantically simplest adjectives are extensional (nonintensional), and are similar to the majority of nouns in having a single argument representing an entity. Examples are "red", "solar", and "symphonic".

```
John sees a red house.
ex(house(X)&red(X), see(john,X)).
```

The simplest intensional adjectives take a single argument coming from the head noun and possibly other modifiers. These include "former", "future", "fake", "non", "true", "real", ...

```
John meets his former teacher.
ex(former(teacher(X,john)), meet(john,X)).
```

```
John owns a fake diamond.
ex(fake(diamond(X)), own(john,X)).
```

Another class of intensional adjectives are focalizers that are closely related to adverbial focalizers like "only". These include "only" (as an adjective), "main", "chief", and "particular". The following is an example with "only". Paraphrases with the adverb form are given.

```
John is the only child of Bill.
only(child(X,bill), X=john).
```

```
Only John is a child of Bill.
```

```
John only is a child of Bill.
```

The majority of adjectives are degree words and are focalizers that are similar to the degree adverbs discussed in the preceding section. Examples are "fast" (as an adjective), "good", and "tall".

```
John is a good singer.
good(singer(X), X=john).
```

```
John hears a good singer.
ex(good(singer(X),X=X1), hear(john,X1)).
```

```
John is good as a singer,
  but bad as a pianist.
but(good(singer(X), X=john),
    bad(pianist(X), X=john)).
```

We can define good(Base,Focus) using the same auxiliary predicates high and quality that we used above in defining the adverb senses fast and best.

```
good(Base, Focus) <-
    high(Value, Base&quality(Base,Value), Focus).
```

5.1.8 Prepositions

Prepositions are closed-class words introducing *prepositional phrases*, that consist of a preposition (pre-position!) followed by a noun phrase. Examples of prepositions are "of", "in", "out", "on", "off", "to", "from", "with", "without", ... Prepositional phrases can modify open-class words — verbs, nouns, adverbs, and adjectives.

A preposition sense is a 2-place predicate. The first argument corresponds to the noun phrase associated with the preposition, and the second corresponds to the phrase modified by the prepositional phrase. Example:

```
John sees the man with Mary.
the(man(X)&with_loc(mary,X),see(john,X)).
```

When a prepositional phrase modifies a verb, the second argument of the preposition sense will be a logical form.

```
John sees the star with a telescope.
the(star(X),ex(telescope(Y),with_use(Y,see(john,X)))).
```

Having a logical-form argument gives the preposition a chance to scope higher than other predicates, as in

```
In the book John wrote, everybody knows everybody.
the(book(X)&write(john,X), in_context(X,
    all(person(Y),all(person(Z),know(Y,Z))) )).
```

```
In 1975, John knew all Mary's friends.
in_time(1975, all(friend(X,mary),know(john,X))).
```

When a prepositional phrase modifies a verb, it may be a complement or an adjunct modifier.

```
John decided on a car.   (Complement)
past(decide_on(john,car(X))).
```

```
John decided on the train.  (Adjunct)
past(the(train(X),on_loc(X,decide(john,*)))).
```

As indicated above in the subsection on verbs, the main criterion for whether a preposition introduces an adjunct is whether it has its own independent meaning. In "decide on the train", there is a clear meaning that the location of the decision is *on* the train, whereas in "decide on a car", "on" has no independent meaning. In fact, "decide on" here is closely related to "select", which clearly is followed by a complement (direct object). There are cases that are not so clear, because it is not clear how general (or diverse) the meanings of prepositions should be made. An example is "agree with", although it appears that "with" introduces a complement here.

In the case of motion verbs, "to" and "from" introduce destination and origin, and these are general notions for motion events (as are other notions like path and speed), so we view these prepositions as introducing adjunct modifiers.

```
John went to Chicago.
past(to(chicago,go(john))).
```

```
Flight 205 goes from L. A. to New York.
from(l.a,to(new.york,go(flight.205))).
```

The predication `from(X,P)` says that X is the origin of an event of motion described by the logical form P. The form P may itself have further qualification by modifiers (like `to`), but the rules for `from` can be written to find the underlying event. In some cases, the underlying event might not be described by a single verb predication, as in

```
John walked and rode a bicycle
     from New York to Poughkeepsie.
```

Thus it is reasonable to view `to` and `from` as predicates in their own right, and not as introducing complements to verbs.

5.1.9 Conjunctions

Conjunctions are closed-class words of two types, *coordinating conjunctions* and *subordinating conjunctions*.   Their senses all take two logical forms as arguments.

The coordinating conjunctions are "and", "or", "nor", and "but". One of the first things to note is that the natural language "and" does not always translate into the logical & (which is an operator of LFL). In the example

```
John opened the door and entered the room.
past(and(the(door(X),open(john,X)),
         the(room(Y),enter(john,Y)) ))
```

the "and" is used in the sense of "and then" (with an implication of time sequence). It is not equivalent to say

```
John entered the room and opened the door.
```

So, there is a predication `and(P,Q)` that is not the same as P & Q. However, in some cases it would be correct to translate "and" into &.

```
John likes Mary and loves Sue.
like(john,mary) & love(john,sue).
```

As is well known, "or" can be used in natural language as the *inclusive or* or the *exclusive or*, so there are predicates `or` and `exor`. The conjunction "nor" is used with "neither", and the combination translates into a form `not(or(P,Q))`. The meaning of `but(P,Q)` is similar to `and(P,Q)`, but (!) signals that there is a contrast between P and Q.

One complexity in dealing with coordinating conjunctions is that there can be *ellipsis* (omission of material) in the two phrases being conjoined. This happens in the preceding example, where the subject "John" is omitted in the second conjunct. In the logical form, john must be repeated. But if the omitted material has a quantifier, we do not repeat the quantifier in the logical form. The sentence

```
Somebody likes Mary and loves Sue.
some(person(X), like(X,mary)&love(X,sue)).
```

is not equivalent to

```
Somebody likes Mary and somebody loves Sue.
some(person(X), like(X,mary)) &
    some(person(Y), love(Y,sue)).
```

The subordinating conjunctions include "if", "when", "before", "after", "as", "although", ... These are all 2-place predicates taking logical forms as arguments. The first argument corresponds to a *subordinate clause* in a larger clause and the second argument corresponds to (part of) the remainder of the larger clause.

```
When John arrived, he was tired.
past(when(arrive(john), tired(john))).
```

The form when(P,Q) is closely related to always(P,Q) (or all(P,Q)). Note the approximate paraphrase:

```
When a cat is hungry, it purrs.
when(cat(X)&hungry(X), purr(X)).

A hungry cat always purrs.
always(cat(X)&hungry(X), purr(X)).
```

In the "when" sentence, it is in fact better to think of the "cat" noun phrase as universally quantified, so that the pronoun "it" naturally has "cat" as a coreferent.

The form if(P,Q) is also similar to always(P,Q), but differs in that the latter presupposes that there is a case where P holds (this is also true for when(P,Q)).

The predicates after and before are similar to when, but require inequalities on the times of the situations represented by their arguments.

```
After a cat eats, it sleeps.
after(cat(X)&eat(X), sleep(X)).
```

5.1.10 Nonlexical Predicates in LFL

Some nonlexical predicates are associated with inflections of words. One example, which we have already shown, is past. The form past(P) says that P held in the past (before now). We will have more to say about time in the next section. Note that past can scope over other predicates, as in

```
John knew all Mary's friends.
past(all(friend(X,mary),know(john,X))).
```

Another important nonlexical predicate associated with inflections is `plural`. This is a quantifier that is similar in meaning to `several`.

```
John met people.
past(plural(person(X),meet(john,X))).
```

The plural inflection has a "weakness" similar to that of the indefinite article "a"; it does not always carry its own quantification (`plural`) in logical form, but may defer to other quantifiers, as in

```
All cats have tails.
all(cat(X),ex(tail(Y),have_part(X,Y))).
```

```
Cats always have tails.
always(cat(X),ex(tail(Y),have_part(X,Y))).
```

```
A cat always has a tail.
always(cat(X),ex(tail(Y),have_part(X,Y))).
```

There is another nonlexical predicate, `generic`, which is often associated with plurals and indefinites. The form `generic(P,Q)` means essentially the same as `typically(P,Q)`; i.e, for any typical case of P, Q holds.

```
Cats have tails.
generic(cat(X),ex(tail(Y),have_part(X,Y))).
```

```
A cat has a tail.
generic(cat(X),ex(tail(Y),have_part(X,Y))).
```

Some nonlexical predicates are associated with syntactic constructions and/or phonological focus and are examples of focalizers. One is `yesno`, which is associated with yes/no questions. When a question `yesno(P,Q)` is asked, it is presupposed that a case of P holds, and it is asked whether P & Q holds. Suppose that a speaker is assuming for some reason that John saw several people yesterday. Then the speaker might ask the question:

```
Did John see Mary yesterday?
yesno(yesterday(see(john,X)), X=mary).
```

It is important to separate the two components (base and focus) of `yesno`. If it happened to be true that John saw no one yesterday, it would be misleading to answer "no" to the above question.

For declarative sentences, there is a nonlexical focalizer `dcl(P,Q)` which is analogous to `yesno(P,Q)`. The base P is presupposed and P & Q is asserted. The base of `dcl` is often called the *topic* or the *given* information, and the focus is often called the *comment* or the *new* information. As an example, if again the speaker is presupposing that John saw several people yesterday, he might make the statement

```
John saw Mary yesterday.
dcl(yesterday(see(john,X)), X=mary).
```

(*Note*: Unfortunately, the terminology in the literature concerning *topic* and *comment* is inconsistent. Sometimes our *topic* is called the *focus*. We reserve the term *focus* for the second argument of focalizers. It is often associated with phonological focus (stress), as in the above dcl example.)

The nonlexical focalizers yesno and dcl are *discourse-functional*, in that they concern the way sentences in a discourse are connected. There are others, dealing for example with contrast, which will not be discussed here. The view in LFL is that these nonlexical predicates are involved in logical forms, and do not belong to some separate "pragmatic" domain.

Although the predicates discussed in this section are nonlexical in English, they can be lexical in other languages. For instance, Japanese and Chinese have words (particles) that correspond to yesno.

5.1.11 The Indexing Operator

Natural language sentences describe situations that have an associated time and place of validity, or, let us say, an associated region of space-time, as in Situation Semantics (Barwise and Perry 1983). If we say

```
John saw Mary.
past(see(john,mary)).
```

we are really saying that there exists a space-time location prior to now in which the relation see(john,mary) holds. If we say

```
John toured Greece.

This took 3 weeks.
```

what does "this" refer to? Obviously, we want it to refer to the same particular event (situation) that is referred to in the first sentence, not just a general relation of John touring Greece. In some versions of logical form (see *e.g* McCord 1981), "event variables" are used as extra arguments for predicates, like tour, that describe events (or states). Thus tour(E,X,Y) means that E is an event of touring by X of Y. Values of E could be thought of as unique names that identify events. With this notation, our two sentences could be written as

```
exist(E, tour(E,john,greece) & past(E) &
        duration(E,3.week)).
```

But suppose now we say

```
Dr. Smith saw each of his patients.
This took 6 hours.
```

It is natural to say that the "seeing" relation here (let us call it see_consult) holds only between the doctor and one patient at a time. So there is not a single event of consultation that "this" can refer to. Rather, it is the whole sequence of consultations, specified by the quantified logical form. In LFL we can use the indexing operator on the whole form and write

```
past(each(patient(X,dr.smith),
          see_consult(dr.smith,X))):E &
    duration(E,6.hour).
```

We have seen other examples of the use of indexing in preceding sections, particularly in writing logical forms involving focalizers:

```
John always buys books at Smith's.
always((book(X)&buy(john,X)):E, at(smith,E)).

John ran fastest yesterday.
fastest(run(john):E, yesterday(E)).
```

With this indexing we can be sure that we are referring to the same situation.

In some natural language applications (in particular, some database applications), we have a "timeless" world in which contexts play no part. In such domains, we can view $P : E$ as simply saying that P holds in a particular instantiation and E is bound to the instantiation. Thus we could define ":" in Prolog for such applications simply by

```
P : P <- P.
```

To give an idea of what can be done when space-time contexts are important, suppose that the only contexts we need to worry about are instants in time, and all events are instant events. Then when we say "John sees Mary" (or "John saw Mary"), we really mean that see(john,mary) holds at a certain time, and we can even have a Prolog database with entries of the form hold(P,T), meaning that P holds at time T.

```
hold(see(john,mary), 10:00).
hold(see(bill,joe),  11:00).  ...
```

Suppose then we have sentences

```
John saw Mary.
This was before 11:00.
```

Then (neglecting tense, for convenience) the logical form could be

```
see(john,mary):E & before(11:00,E).
```

To do inference with this directly in Prolog, we could further translate it into

```
hold(see(john,mary),T) & T<11:00.
```

We could write a translator tran(LogicalForm,PrologForm) with rules such as the following:

```
tran(P:(P@T), hold(P,T)).
tran(before(T0,P@T), T<T0).
tran(P&Q, P1&Q1) <- tran(P,P1) & tran(Q,Q1).
```

Here, logical forms with contexts are represented in the form P@T. Thus ":" is a means of linking logical forms so that they have the same context and are treated as different references to the same event.

5.2 LOGIC GRAMMARS

A beautiful characteristic of logic programming is that grammars for natural (and artificial) languages can be expressed easily as logic programs that can be executed to analyze and synthesize the defined languages. Thus analysis and synthesis are forms of inference, and grammars, being simply axiom systems, are declarative in nature, and hence are easier to understand and create. Furthermore, analysis and synthesis can be quite efficient when the logic programming language is Prolog and the grammar is expressed directly as a Prolog program.

Although grammars can be written directly as logic programs, there are some repetitive ingredients in these programs that call for shorthand notation ("syntactic sugar"). It is convenient to define *logic grammar* formalisms, embodying such shorthand, along with means for translating (compiling) logic grammars into logic programs. In this section, two types of logic grammar formalism will be discussed, *Definite Clause Grammars* (DCGs) and *Modular Logic Grammars* (MLGs). DCGs are the earlier and more basic formalism (due to Alain Colmerauer).   MLGs are intended to allow even more compact grammars and to allow greater modularity between syntax and semantics. (*Note:* Colmerauer's logic grammars (Colmerauer 1978) are actually called "Metamorphosis Grammars," and they include DCGs as a special case. DCGs are to Metamorphosis Grammars as context-free phrase structure grammars are to general, type-0 phrase structure grammars.   The name "Definite Clause Grammar" was used by Pereira and Warren (1980), and refers to the fact that these grammars translate into Prolog definite clauses (conditional clauses or unit clauses, as opposed to goal clauses).)

5.2.1 Definite Clause Grammars

Suppose we want to express in logic the statement that a sentence consists of a noun phrase followed by a verb phrase. The most obvious approach is to view grammatical categories like *sentence* as 1-place predicates applied to lists of words. If we agree that

```
s(X)  means that X (a list of words) is a sentence,
np(X) means that X is a noun phrase, and
vp(X) means that X is a verb phrase,
```

then we can express our grammar rule as the Horn clause

```
s(X) <- append(X1,X2,X) & np(X1) & vp(X2).
```

(A Horn clause, named after the logician Alfred Horn, corresponds syntactically to a simple Prolog rule or goal without negation or disjunction.) The call to append expresses the condition that phrase X is the juxtaposition of phrases X1 and X2. After writing similar rules for np and vp, etc., we would then ask Prolog to verify that "Each man loves a woman" is a sentence by giving it the goal

```
<- s(each.man.loves.a.woman.nil).
```

There is an inefficiency in this approach, however, because append will select a candidate noun phrase X1 to be tested by np, which may fail simply because the wrong end point for X1 has been chosen. Needless backtracking results. Greater efficiency is obtained by using difference lists (see page 136) in the representation of word strings. If difference lists are viewed as terms X-Y (where X is a list and Y is a tail end of it), then our grammar rule can be written as the Horn clause

```
s(X-Z) <- np(X-Y) & vp(Y-Z).
```

Now the juxtaposition of the noun phrase X-Y and the verb phrase Y-Z is captured by the condition that the tail end Y of X-Y is the beginning of Y-Z, together with the use of the concatenated list X-Z as the argument of s. It is slightly more efficient still to represent difference lists as pairs of arguments (X,Y) instead of terms X-Y. This is the method we will actually use; our grammar rule finally becomes

```
s(X,Z) <- np(X,Y) & vp(Y,Z).
```

Then to prove that "Each man loves a woman" is a sentence, we would give Prolog the goal

```
<- s(each.man.loves.a.woman.nil, nil).
```

A convenient "syntactically sugared" notation for our grammar rule is simply as follows

```
s --> np: vp.
```

Here the arrow operator is used to separate a *rule head* from a *rule body*. It can be read "consists of." The colon operator is used in rule bodies to represent left-to-right sequencing, and it can be read "followed by." Let these operators be declared as follows.

```
op("-->",rl,15).
op(":",rl,100).
```

Following the terminology for phrase structure grammars, we call symbols like s and np *nonterminals*. Nonterminals define classes of lists of words. We need a notation for *terminal* symbols in a grammar; *i.e.*, symbols that correspond to single words in the word string. Terminals will be indicated in the form +T, where T is the actual terminal symbol. Here   +   is declared as a prefix operator:

```
op("+",prefix,120).
```

With these conventions, we can write a complete (but small) grammar that recognizes sentences such as "Each man loves a woman".

```
s --> np: vp.
np --> det: noun.
vp --> verb: np.
det --> +each.
det --> +a.
noun --> +man.
noun --> +woman.
verb --> +loves.
```

In translating this grammar to a Horn clause program, we replace every nonterminal nt by a 2-place predicate nt(X,Y) meaning that the difference list (X,Y) is a phrase of type nt. Sequencing in a rule body (indicated by the colon operator) is replaced by the use of conjunctions, with difference lists linked appropriately to follow left-to-right order.

How do we translate terminals? One method is just to replace a terminal   + T by the condition X=T.Y on the difference list (X,Y) associated with its position in the rule body. (This would indeed be the condition that (X,Y) consist of the single element T.) With this method, the Horn clause translation of the grammar rule

```
np --> det: noun: +that: vp.
```

would be

```
np(X,V) <-
    det(X,Y) & noun(Y,Z) & (Z=that.U) & vp(U,V).
```

However, it is possible here to execute the condition Z=that.U at compile time instead of waiting till run time; *i.e.*, we just replace Z by that.U in the rule translation, and we get

```
np(X,V) <- det(X,Y) & noun(Y,that.U) & vp(U,V).
```

Thus, the rule

```
noun --> +man.
```

can be given either of the translations

```
noun(X,Y) <- (X=man.Y).
noun(man.Y,Y).
```

and we use the latter, more efficient, one. However, there are cases of rule translation, as we will see below, where it is necessary to keep the equation in the translation.

Now we can give a complete Horn clause translation of the small grammar above, as follows

```
s(X,Z) <- np(X,Y) & vp(Y,Z).
np(X,Z) <- det(X,Y) & noun(Y,Z).
vp(X,Z) <- verb(X,Y) & np(Y,Z).
det(each.X,X).
det(a.X,X).
noun(man.X,X).
noun(woman.X,X).
verb(loves.X,X).
```

This grammar can be used with Prolog both to *recognize* the sentences it defines, and to *generate* all its sentences. The goal

```
<- s(S,nil) & write(S) & fail.
```

will write all the sentences defined by the grammar.

With the methods indicated so far, any context-free phrase structure grammar (CFG) can be translated into a logic program. In a CFG, rules are of the form A `-->` B, where A is a nonterminal and B is a list (using juxtaposition ":") of terminals and nonterminals. (If B is `nil`, then the rule is translated into the unit clause A(X,X)). Terminals and nonterminals are restricted to be atoms in a CFG.

The notion of a *Definite Clause Grammar* (DCG) is basically a simple generalization of that of CFG. The grammar symbols are no longer restricted to be atomic symbols, but can be arbitrary logic terms; *i.e.*, nonterminals (and terminals) can be augmented by arguments. Arguments for nonterminals can be extremely useful; they can hold analysis structures for the phrases defined by the grammar, and they can also express context-sensitive constraints in the grammar. Thus a nonterminal np(N,P) might define a noun phrase with number N (singular or plural) and analysis structure P (say, a logical form).

The extension of the method indicated above for translation to Horn clauses is likewise very simple. Just as atomic nonterminals are given two arguments representing a difference list, so compound nonterminals are given two extra arguments (added at the end) representing a difference list. Thus np(N,P,X,Y) means that the difference list (X,Y) is a noun phrase with number N and analysis structure P. The treatment of terminals is just the same as for CFG's.

There are a few more ingredients in DCGs than we have indicated so far, but before describing them all, we will look at an example and its Horn clause translation.

Let us augment the nonterminals in the sample CFG above, so that the grammar defines analysis structures for its sentences. We could build logical forms or syntactic analysis trees; let us look first at the construction of logical forms (in LFL).

```
s(S) --> np(X,VP,S): vp(X,VP).
np(X,Focus,NP) --> det(Base,Focus,NP): noun(X,Base).
vp(X,VP) --> verb(X,Y,VF): np(Y,VF,VP).
det(B,F,all(B,F)) --> +each.
det(B,F,ex(B,F)) --> +a.
noun(X,man(X)) --> +man.
noun(X,woman(X)) --> +woman.
verb(X,Y,love(X,Y)) --> +loves.
```

According to the method outlined above for translating to Horn clauses, this grammar translates to the logic program

```
s(S, U,W) <-
    np(X,VP,S, U,V) & vp(X,VP, V,W).
np(X,Focus,NP, U,W) <-
    det(Base,Focus,NP, U,V) & noun(X,Base, V,W).
vp(X,VP, U,W) <-
    verb(X,Y,VF, U,V) & np(Y,VF,VP, V,W).
det(B,F,all(B,F), each.U,U).
det(B,F,ex(B,F), a.U,U).
noun(X,man(X), man.U,U).
noun(X,woman(X), woman.U,U).
verb(X,Y,love(X,Y), loves.U,U).
```

If we give Prolog this grammar and ask for a solution of the goal

```
<- s(S, each.man.loves.a.woman.nil, nil).
```

then we get the logical form

```
S = all(man(X),ex(woman(Y),love(X,Y))).
```

To understand how this grammar works, let us look at the original DCG form of it above (not the compiled form). It is interesting that the heart of the construction of logical forms lies with the determiner `det`, even though `det` is called at the deepest level. A call to `det` builds a focalizer expression like

```
all(Base,Focus)
```

in its last argument. The `Base` will be the logical form of the head noun of the noun phrase (like `man(X)`), so that the `np` rule produces a form like

```
all(man(X),Focus)
```

in its last argument. This is the case for the call to `np` in the `s` rule for the sentence "Each man loves a woman". The `Focus` will be the logical form determined by the `vp` "loves a woman". When `np` is called by `vp`, its focus is the material from the verb, `love(X,Y)`, so that the logical form built by `vp` is

```
ex(woman(Y),love(X,Y)).
```

This is filled in as the FOCUS of the subject np, so that the logical form of the whole sentence is

```
all(man(X),ex(woman(Y),love(X,Y))).
```

The reader should try out this grammar in Prolog and do some tracing to gain more familiarity with its workings. Below, we will look at more modular ways of producing logical forms.

The nonterminal arguments in a DCG can be used for building syntactic structures instead of logical forms. For our sample grammar, let us do this in a very systematic way:

```
s(s(NP,VP)) --> np(NP): vp(VP).
np(np(Det,Noun)) --> det(Det): noun(Noun).
vp(vp(Verb,NP)) --> verb(Verb): np(NP).
det(det(each)) --> +each.
det(det(a)) --> +a.
noun(noun(man)) --> +man.
noun(noun(woman)) --> +woman.
verb(verb(loves)) --> +loves.
```

The arguments specifying analysis structures here are completely determinable from the context-free skeleton of the grammar (the CFG obtained by stripping away the arguments). The analysis argument in a rule head is a term whose principal functor is just that of the rule head itself, and whose arguments are the analysis structures of the nonterminals appearing in the rule body. The analysis of the sentence "Each man loves a woman" is now the term

```
s(
  np(
     det(each),
     noun(man) ),
  vp(
     verb(loves),
     np(
        det(a),
        noun(woman) ))).
```

This term, viewed as a tree, is in fact a *derivation tree* for the parse of the sentence; its structure exactly mirrors the way the rules are applied.

The complete regularity of this method of producing analyses invites automation. One could write a Prolog program, for instance, that takes a CFG (or a DCG not producing analysis structures) and adds arguments that build such derivation trees. This sort of automation of analysis-building is one of the ideas behind Modular Logic Grammars, to be discussed below.

Natural language grammars could be written using only the ingredients of DCGs described so far, but the remaining ingredients (there are three of them) are useful in making grammars more compact.

Rule bodies can contain *goals*, which are direct calls to the logic programming interpreter. A goal is indicated in the form $A, where A is a term representing a procedure call. The translation of $A is just A. No extra arguments are added, as in the case of nonterminals. We can declare $ as

```
op("$",prefix,120).
```

The goal facility can be used in our sample grammar to handle lexical entries in a more compact way.

```
s(s(NP,VP)) --> np(NP): vp(VP).
np(np(Det,Noun)) --> det(Det): noun(Noun).
vp(vp(Verb,NP)) --> verb(Verb): np(NP).
det(det(D)) --> +D: $dt(D).
noun(noun(N)) --> +N: $n(N).
verb(verb(V)) --> +V: $v(V).

dt(a).  dt(each).  dt(the). ...
n(man).  n(woman).  n(child). ...
v(loves).  v(sees).  v(knows). ...
```

Here, the translation of a rule like

```
noun(noun(N)) --> +N: $n(N).
```

is

```
noun(noun(N), N.U,U) <- n(N).
```

The value of this for a large number of lexical entries is clear.

Another device allowed in DCG rules is the use of disjunctions, as in

```
postmod --> +that: vp  |  pp.
```

A disjunction in a rule body is translated into the disjunction of the translations of its parts. However, when a terminal symbol is embedded in a disjunction as the leading element of a disjunct (as in the preceding example), the longer form of translation of the terminal mentioned above (involving an explicit equality) must be used:

```
postmod(U,W) <- (U=that.V) & vp(V,W)  |  pp(U,W).
```

Likewise, an occurrence of a goal or of nil as a disjunct, as in

```
postmod(X) --> $test(X) | pp(X).
postmod(X) --> nil | pp(X).
```

requires an explicit equality (U=V) in the translation. Actually, disjunctions are not of particularly great value in writing grammar rules, and in fact style is sometimes improved by avoiding them.

The final ingredient available in DCG rules is the cut symbol (/), that just translates as itself. As with Prolog programming in general, it is good practice to avoid use of the cut in DCGs when it is reasonable to do so.

So far in this subsection, DCGs have been defined and illustrated, and a rough description of their translation to clausal form has been given. Let us now look at a way to do this translation with a Prolog program.

In a Prolog programming environment in which grammars are often used, it is best to make grammar translation as automatic and inconspicuous as possible. In Prolog programs existing in files to be consulted, it is convenient to be able to intermix grammar rules and ordinary clauses. Therefore the procedure that consults files should be modified so that whenever it sees a grammar rule, it immediately translates the rule to clausal form and then adds the clausal form to the workspace. To accomplish this, the consulting procedure can make a call `gtrans(Rule,Clause)` such that when `Rule` is a DCG rule, `Clause` is the translated clause, and otherwise `Clause=Rule`.

For `gtrans` we can write

```
gtrans(A-->B,Clause) <- /&
   dcgtrans(A,Head,X,Y) &
   dcgtrans(B,Body,X,Y) &
   simplify(Head<-Body,Clause).
gtrans(Clause,Clause).
```

Here `dcgtrans(B,C,X,Y)` takes any expression `B` that can be a rule body (including a single nonterminal, which can appear in a rule head), and translates `B` into the proper Prolog goal `C`. The pair `(X,Y)` represents a difference list spanning the portion of the word string covered by `B`. The definition of `dcgtrans` is recursive, and the components of the difference list are manipulated so as to reflect left-to-right sequencing. The procedure `simplify` cleans up superfluous occurrences of `true` produced by `dcgtrans`. For instance, the clause `A<-true` should be simplified to the unit clause `A`.

The following definition of `dcgtrans` is suitable for rules not containing disjunctions:

```
dcgtrans(B1:B2,C1&C2,X,Z) <- /&
   dcgtrans(B1,C1,X,Y) & dcgtrans(B2,C2,Y,Z).
dcgtrans(+T,true,T.X,X) <- /.
dcgtrans(nil,true,X,X) <- /.
dcgtrans($P,P,X,X) <- /.
dcgtrans(/,/,X,X) <- /.
dcgtrans(NT,NT1,X,Y) <-
   cons(Pred.Args,NT) &
   append(Args,X.Y.nil,Args1) &
   cons(Pred.Args1,NT1).
```

Here we can define `cons` as follows.

```
cons(Term.nil,Term) <- atomic(Term) & /.
cons(List,Term) <- Term=..List.
```

We leave it as exercises for the reader to write simplify and to modify dcgtrans so as to handle disjunctions. As indicated above, a terminal +T must sometimes be translated into the condition (X=T.Y), where (X,Y) is the associated difference list, and care must also be taken with goals and nil.

Note: When a DCG is translated into a collection of clauses, these clauses can be executed directly by Prolog's top down inference procedure, so that parsing of sentences is top down parsing. If the collection contains only pure Horn clauses then it also has a declarative meaning that is independent of Prolog. In particular, alternative inference procedures, such as bottom up inference (Kowalski 1979), might be used. Such inference procedures might be implemented in Prolog itself, or one might write more special-purpose parsers in Prolog. An example of this sort appears in Matsumoto, Tanaka and Kiyono (1986).

5.2.2 Modular Logic Grammars

It is probably the case in most natural language applications that the ultimate analyses desired for natural language sentences are semantic analyses (say, logical forms). In writing logic grammars for natural language analysis, then, it would seem reasonable to be as direct as possible and to follow the example of the DCG in the preceding subsection that produces logical forms by manipulating them directly in nonterminal arguments. However, there are some drawbacks to this approach.

One problem is that the connection between logical structure and grammar rule structure can be rather remote and complicated. In Section 5.1.6, "Adverbs and the Notion of Focalizer," the following examples were given:

```
John only buys books at Smith's.
  only((book(X)&buy(john,X)):E, at(smith,E)).
```

```
John only buys books at Smith's.
  only(at(smith,buy(john,X)), book(X)).
```

In both cases, the logical structure differs radically from the syntactic structure that would be associated with any reasonable DCG. Furthermore, the two sentences consist of the same sequence of words, differing only in focus, yet they have quite different logical structures. The two sentences share many of the same syntactic relations (like subject and object), and it would seem reasonable to say that they have nearly the same syntactic structure (the same syntax rules apply in deriving them).

Another example illustrating the remoteness of logical form from syntactic structure is the following.

```
John knows the father of each boy.
each(boy(Y),the(father(X,Y),know(john,X))).
```

Here the "each" form scopes higher than the "the" form, in spite of the fact that the prepositional phrase "of each boy" is a modifier in the noun phrase "the father ..." and lies to the right of "the". On the other hand, the following sentence has a similar syntactic structure, but the quantifier of the whole noun phrase dominates that of the modifying prepositional phrase.

```
Smith handles every request for a car.
every(request(X,Y,car(Y)):E, handle(smith,E)).
```

What seems to be called for is a separate component of the grammar (separate from the syntax rules), a *semantic interpretation component*, which deals with the construction of logical forms and handles problems of scoping such as those just illustrated. Focalizers seem to have a bit of life of their own, showing some independence of syntax.

Having a separate semantic interpretation component means having greater modularity in the grammar, and this can be an advantage for large systems. In a large project, where a grammar with very wide coverage is to be built, it is convenient if syntax rules can be written rather independently of semantic interpretation — at least independently of the problems of scoping.

Another consideration is that it is desirable to be able to build syntactic analysis structures as well as logical forms. Some natural language applications require syntactic analyses (although they may also require semantic information). This is the case for text-critiquing systems — knowledge-based systems that criticize grammar, spelling, and style in documents. It also appears reasonable to use syntactic analyses (embodying some semantic choices, such as word sense disambiguation) in machine translation systems.

Another advantage of producing syntactic structures is that they are useful in debugging large grammars, especially in a modular system (with a separate semantic interpretation component) where the writer of syntax rules is not particularly concerned with the construction of logical forms. By definition, syntactic analysis structures are closely connected with the way grammar rules are applied (if not derivation trees, they are at least close to them). Therefore syntactic analyses are important for monitoring the operation of a grammar.

All of these considerations point to the desirability of a modular grammar system having a syntactic component that can build syntactic analyses and a semantic interpretation component that can build logical forms. A logic grammar formalism — *Modular Logic Grammars* — that has these properties will now be described. In MLGs the building of analysis structures is implicit in the formalism; the grammar rule compiler takes care of adding extra arguments that build up analyses.

The easiest and most uniform way to build syntactic structures automatically would be to build derivation trees. (In the preceding subsection an example of a DCG that builds derivation trees was given, and the format of the analysis arguments there could be automated.) However, there are two problems with using pure and simple derivation trees.

One problem is that in a large grammar there will be many syntax rules that are auxiliary in nature, for example, recursive rules that find the postmodifiers of a verb. It would be undesirable for the application of every such rule to contribute a node to the analysis tree, because (1) the tree would be much larger than is linguistically reasonable (it would be a cluttered thing to look at), and (2) these additional nodes in the tree would complicate the work of the semantic interpretation rules.

To solve this problem, in MLGs there is a distinction between *strong* nonterminals and *weak* nonterminals, where only the strong nonterminals contribute nodes to analysis trees. Formally, the syntax rules are preceded by a clause of the form

```
strongnonterminals(NT1.NT2. ... .NTn.nil).
```

listing the (principal functors of the) strong nonterminals. Every nonterminal not declared to be *strong* is called *weak*. A syntax rule whose left-hand side is a strong (weak) nonterminal is called a *strong* (*weak*) rule. The rule compiler sees to it that whenever a strong rule is applied in analyzing a sentence, a tree node is constructed in the analysis tree, but not when a weak rule is applied. Linguistically, strong nonterminals correspond to major categories like *sentence*, *noun phrase*, *prepositional phrase*, *relative clause*, etc. They introduce major levels of grammatical structure.

A second problem with using pure derivation trees is connected with the existence of left-recursive linguistic constructions, as in

```
John saw the car.
John saw the man's car.
John saw the woman's uncle's car.
John saw the man's wife's uncle's car.
    ...
```

The possessive noun phrases that can introduce a larger noun phrase can be embedded indefinitely in a left-branching manner. The most natural way of covering this construction is with left-recursive grammar rules. However, we are compiling our grammars into Prolog, and the left recursion is of the sort that would result in an infinite loop. Fortunately, these constructions can be covered with right-recursive grammar rules, with only a bit of extra work; but (unfortunately) then a derivation tree gives the wrong linguistic structure. (It should be left-branching; this is necessary, for example, to get the correct logical form in a reasonable way.) In order to let the rule compiler see to the correct construction of these left-branching trees, the MLG formalism contains a device called the *shift operator*. In this section, we specify the formal use of the shift operator in MLG syntax rules, but we delay a real treatment of it to the Section below, 5.4.4, "Left-Recursive Constructions." In fact, for the sake of simplicity, we will describe here a version of the rule compiler that ignores the shift, and postpone till a later section the modification of the compiler that deals with it.

The MLG syntactic formalism can be considered an extension of the DCG formalism. All of the ingredients available for DCG rules are available for MLG rules (terminals, nonterminals, nil, goals, the cut, the sequencing operator : and the *or* operator |). As with DCG rules, an MLG rule consists of a rule head, that is a nonterminal, connected by an arrow to a rule body. For MLG rules, we use a different arrow, `==>`, so that the rule compiler will know that it is looking at an MLG rule. This is declared in the same way as the DCG arrow `-->`.

For MLGs there are three ingredients that are not present in DCGs: (1) the declaration of *strong nonterminals*, (2) the *shift operator*, and (3) *logical terminals*. We have already specified the format of the declaration of strong nonterminals, which precedes all the syntax rules. The other two ingredients can appear in rule bodies.

The shift operator is a binary infix operator declared as follows

```
op("%",rl,120).
```

A rule body can contain a *shifted nonterminal*, which is of the form `Label%NT`, where `NT` is a weak nonterminal and `Label` is any Prolog term. Using the shift operator has no effect on the success or failure of the analysis of a sentence, but it does have an effect on the syntactic structure tree that is built automatically in analysis. As we will see below in Section 5.4.4, "Left-Recursive Constructions," a shift `Label%NT` causes the construction of a left-embedded tree node, and `Label` is the label on this node.

The body of an MLG rule can contain *logical terminals*. Formally, these are terms of the form

```
Op-LF.
```

The term `LF` should be a logical form, typically a predication (like `see1(X,Y)`) associated with a sense of a word ("see"). The term `Op` is called an *operator*, and it is used by the semantic interpretation component in combining `LF` with other logical forms in building up the complete semantic interpretation of a sentence. The semantic interpretation component works more generally with *semantic items*, which are of the same form as logical terminals, except that the logical form component can be a complex form (resulting from the combination of several semantic items). Examples of logical terminals are

```
1-man(X).
Q/P-each(P,Q).
```

Here the operator 1 ("left-conjoin") causes its associated logical form to be left-conjoined (during semantic interpretation) to the logical form of the semantic item it is modifying. The operator `Q/P` causes `P` to be unified with the logical form of the semantic item it is modifying. If the "each" item modifies the "man" item (as it would for the noun phrase "each man"), the result is the item `@P-each(man(X),P)`. Here `@P` is a new operator that causes `P` to be unified with the logical form of the item being modified. When `@P-each(man(X),P)` modifies `1-live(X)`, the result is the semantic item `1-each(man(X),live(X))`. All this would happen in the semantic interpretation of the sentence "Each man lives". We would finally discard the operator of the top level semantic item, getting the logical form `each(man(X),live(X))`.

In the syntactic analysis trees that are built automatically for MLGs, the terminal (leaf) nodes will be logical terminals. The semantic interpretation component takes these trees and builds up a logical form analyzing the whole sentence. The logical terminals lying at the terminal nodes are the basic building blocks in this construction.

When contrasting logical terminals (of the form `Op-LF`) with ordinary terminals (of the form `+T`), we may call the ordinary terminals *surface terminals*. The idea is that surface terminals are building blocks for the word stream and these go over into logical terminals, which are building blocks for logical form.

Now let us look at the syntactic component of a sample MLG. Its coverage extends that of the sample DCGs in the preceding section. Nouns can be postmodified by a relative clause of the form "that"+vp, as in "each man that loves a woman", and a noun phrase can consist of a proper noun. The grammar now defines an infinite number of sentences.

```
strongnonterminals(s.np.det.relclause.nil).

s ==> np(X): vp(X).
np(X) ==> det: noun(X): relclause(X).
np(X) ==> name(X).
vp(X) ==> verb(X,Y): np(Y).
relclause(X) ==> +that: vp(X).
relclause(*) ==> nil.
det ==> +D: $dt(D,B,F,P): F/B-P.
noun(X) ==> +N: $n(N,X,P): 1-P.
name(X) ==> +X: $nm(X).
verb(X,Y) ==> +V: $v(V,X,Y,P): 1-P.

dt(each,B,F,each(B,F)).
dt(a,B,F,ex(B,F)).
n(man,X,man(X)).   n(woman,X,woman(X)).
nm(john).   nm(mary).
v(loves,X,Y,love(X,Y)).
```

Together with its semantic interpretation component, which will be given in the Section below (5.5, "Semantic Interpretation") this grammar associates logical forms with the sentences in its coverage, the following being examples:

```
John loves Mary.
love(john,mary).

Each man loves Mary.
each(man(X),love(X,mary)).

Each woman that loves John loves a man.
each(woman(X)&love(X,john), ex(man(Y),love(X,Y))).
```

Note that the nonterminals in this grammar contain no arguments that represent and manipulate logical forms, although the arguments X — as in np(X) — do play a role in logical forms. Only the *building blocks* for logical forms are specified in the rules, through the occurrence of logical terminals in the rules for det, noun, and verb.

For comparison, we give a DCG having the same coverage as this MLG and extending the DCG of the preceding section which manipulates logical forms directly in nonterminal arguments.

```
s(S) --> np(X,VP,S): vp(X,VP).
np(X,F,NP) --> det(B,F,NP): noun(X,B0):
                    relclause(X,B0,B).
np(X,NP,NP) --> name(X).
vp(X,VP) --> verb(X,Y,VF): np(Y,VF,VP).
relclause(X,B,B&VP) --> +that: vp(X,VP).
relclause(*,B,B) --> nil.
det(B,F,P) --> +D: $dt(D,B,F,P).
noun(X,P) --> +N: $n(N,X,P).
name(X) --> +X: $nm(X).
verb(X,Y,P) --> +V: $v(V,X,Y,P).
```

```
/* Lexical clauses same as in MLG */
```

The purpose of the remainder of the current section is to describe the rule compiler for MLGs, which translates MLGs to Prolog programs that associate syntactic structures with sentences.

What about the format of the syntactic structure trees? In the previous section, we showed a DCG that produces syntactic structures of such a uniform format that the production of these could easily be automated. The tree node produced by the application of a rule of the form

```
nt(...) --> B1: B2: ...
```

is a term of the form nt(X1,X2,...), where Xi is the structure associated with Bi. Thus the node label of a tree is just the principal functor of the Prolog term representing the tree, and the daughters of the node are the arguments of the term.

For MLGs, the tree node associated with a rule of the above form, where nt is a *strong* nonterminal, will be a term of the form

```
syn(nt:Arg, Daughters)
```

where `Arg` is the first argument of the term `nt(...)` (if `nt` has no argument, `Arg` will be `nil`), and where `Daughters` is the list of nodes produced by the body of the rule. Each strong nonterminal in the rule body contributes a single `syn` element to the daughter list, whereas a weak nonterminal in the rule body contributes a sublist to the daughter list (that could be empty). Each logical terminal in the rule body contributes a single element, namely itself. Goals, surface terminals, and the cut contribute nothing.

With the `syn` representation of syntax tree nodes, nodes can be examined more easily (without using `cons`). More importantly, the node label is allowed to be a compound term — `nt:Arg`. The point of including the contents (`Arg`) of an argument of `nt` is that `Arg` can contain additional syntactic information obtained in the course of the analysis. This is important, for instance, for semantic interpretation in large grammars, and it is important for applications that are keyed to the syntactic analysis tree itself. In larger grammars, it is convenient to make this first argument, `Arg`, of strong nonterminals a structure exhibiting "features" of the node.

When the sample MLG above is compiled by the rule compiler described below in this section, the `syn` structure produced for the sentence "Each man loves a woman" is as follows. (We display it in a way that exhibits the tree structure.)

```
syn(s:nil,
    syn(np:X,
        syn(det:nil,
            F1/B1-each(B1,F1).
            nil).
        1-man(X).
        syn(relclause:X,
            nil).
        nil).
    1-love(X,Y).
    syn(np:Y,
        syn(det:nil,
            F2/B2-ex(B2,F2).
            nil).
        1-woman(Y).
        syn(relclause:Y,
            nil).
        nil).
    nil) .
```

We leave it as an exercise to write a Prolog procedure that prints out `syn` trees in a nice indented format. It is convenient not to show so much information as above. To print (starting in a certain column) a `syn` term whose node label is `nt:Arg`, print `nt` in the given column, then print all the daughters on successive lines, but indented over three more columns. To print a logical terminal `Op-LF`, just print `LF`. It is convenient also to ignore `syn` terms whose daughter list is `nil`. When this is done for the preceding example `syn`, the result should be the following.

```
s
    np
        det
            each(B1,F1)
        man(X)
    love(X,Y)
    np
        det
            ex(B2,F2)
        woman(Y)
```

In compiling DCGs to Horn clauses, each nonterminal gets two extra arguments holding the difference list that represents the word string analyzed by the nonterminal. For MLGs, every nonterminal will also get these two arguments (added at the end). In addition, we need to add arguments representing analysis structures. If the nonterminal is *strong*, it will get *one* analysis structure argument representing the `syn` associated with expansion of that nonterminal. If the nonterminal is *weak*, it will get *two* analysis arguments representing the difference list of nodes produced by expansion of the nonterminal. As examples, we have the following translations of a strong rule and a weak rule from the above MLG.

```
s ==> np(X): vp(X).
s(syn(s:nil,Syn.Mods), U,W) <-
    np(X, Syn, U,V) &
    vp(X, Mods,nil, V,W).

vp(X) ==> verb(X,Y): np(Y).
vp(X, Mods1,Mods2, U,W) <-
    verb(X,Y, Mods1,Syn.Mods2, U,V) &
    np(Y, Syn, V,W).
```

Logical terminals are added into the analysis lists in the same way that surface terminals are added into the word lists. We get the following translation

```
det ==> +D: $dt(D,B,F,P): F/B-P.
det(syn(det:nil, F/B-P.nil), D.U,U) <- dt(D,B,F,P).
```

In order to make translation of MLG rules an automatic part of consulting files, we augment the procedure `gtrans`, defined in the preceding section, as follows. (The first clause recognizes DCG rules and the second recognizes MLG rules.)

```
gtrans(A-->B,Clause) <- /&
   dcgtrans(A,Head,X,Y) &
   dcgtrans(B,Body,X,Y) &
   simplify(Head<-Body,Clause).
gtrans(A==>B,Clause) <- /&
   mlgtransh(A,Head,Mods1,Mods2,X,Y) &
   mlgtransb(B,Body,Mods1,Mods2,X,Y) &
   simplify(Head<-Body,Clause).
gtrans(Clause,Clause).
```

Here, `mlgtransh` translates the head A of the MLG rule and `mlgtransb`
translates the body B. The pair of arguments (`Mods1`,`Mods2`) represents the
difference list of syntactic structures associated with the *body* of the rule. For
defining `mlgtransh`, we need to make a distinction between strong and weak
nonterminals, as indicated above. The procedure `strongnt(NT)` holds if `NT` is
a member of the list given in the declaration of strong nonterminals. We can
define `mlgtransh` as follows

```
mlgtransh(A,Head,Mods,nil,X,Y) <-
   cons(Pred.Args,A) &
   strongnt(Pred) &/&
   (Args=Arg1.* &/ | Arg1=nil) &
   append(Args,syn(Pred:Arg1,Mods).X.Y.nil,Args1) &
   cons(Pred.Args1,Head).
mlgtransh(A,Head,Mods1,Mods2,X,Y) <-
   cons(Pred.Args,A) &
   append(Args,Mods1.Mods2.X.Y.nil,Args1) &
   cons(Pred.Args1,Head).
```

The definition of `mlgtransb` is as follows.

```
mlgtransb(B1:B2,C1&C2,M,N,X,Y) <- / &
   mlgtransb(B1,C1,M,P,X,Z) &
   mlgtransb(B2,C2,P,N,Z,Y).
mlgtransb(+T,true,M,M,T.X,X) <- /.
mlgtransb(Op-LF,true,(Op-LF).M,M,X,X) <- /.
mlgtransb(nil,true,M,M,X,X) <- /.
mlgtransb($P,P,M,M,X,X) <- /.
mlgtransb(/,/,M,M,X,X) <- /.
mlgtransb(NT,NT1,Syn.M,M,X,Y) <-
   cons(Pred.Args,NT) &
   strongnt(Pred) &/&
   append(Args,Syn.X.Y.nil,Args1) &
   cons(Pred.Args1,NT1).
mlgtransb(NT,NT1,M,N,X,Y) <-
   cons(Pred.Args,NT) &
   append(Args,M.N.X.Y.nil,Args1) &
   cons(Pred.Args1,NT1).
```

In these definitions, we have made two simplifying assumptions: that neither disjunctions nor shift operators are present in the rules. We leave it as an exercise to modify `mlgtransb` so as to handle disjunctions. (The extension is similar to that for `dcgtrans` above.) The extensions necessary for handling the shift will be discussed in Section 5.4.4, "Left-Recursive Constructions."

Note: More details on the MLG syntactic formalism and the rule compiler can be found in (McCord 1985a, 1986). A related syntactic formalism with automatic structure-building, but with a rule interpreter and other differences, was described in Dahl and McCord (1983).

5.3 WORDS

In this section, we discuss several topics involving the treatment of words in a large grammar, with special emphasis on the shape of the lexicon. These topics are largely preparatory for the succeeding section on techniques for writing the syntactic component of an MLG.

5.3.1 Tokenizing

For the sake of efficiency, it is best for logic grammars to analyze lists of words, but it would certainly be inconvenient to have to input sentences in the form `each.man.loves.mary.nil`. The user should be allowed to input sentences in a normal way. So what we need is a *tokenizer*, which converts natural input, in character string form, into a list of words (tokens) for the grammar to analyze.

There is the initial question of getting a complete input sentence into a character string. (What Prolog reading mechanism should be used?) The sentence may be long and may extend over several lines. If the sentence were required to be surrounded by quotes and followed by a period, then we could just use `read`. But it is better not to require the quotes. A good method is to use `readli` to read in the lines, concatenating them into one long string, and stopping when the last nonblank character on the line is a sentence terminator (say ".", "?", or "!"). We leave it as an exercise to write a procedure to do this.

It is convenient to write the main part of the tokenizer as a DCG, whose "input word list" is the list of *characters* in the input sentence, and whose analysis structure is the desired list of words or tokens. So if the input procedure of the previous paragraph produces a data structure of type `string`, it should be converted to a list of characters to be given to the tokenizer DCG.

Most tokens will be words in the normal sense, and will be represented as Prolog atoms (with lower case spelling). But some tokens are not normal words, and deserve special marking — for the convenience of the syntactic component. A capitalized word (except at the beginning of the sentence) can be represented as a term `cap(W)`, where `W` is the corresponding atom in lower case form. Thus the input word "John" will produce `cap(john)`. A number `N` can be represented as the token `num(N)`. And a punctuation character `C` can be represented as `punc(C)`.

With these conventions, we can write the top level of a tokenizer DCG as

```
words(Word.Words) --> word(Word): /: words(Words).
words(Words) --> +C: words(Words).
words(nil) --> nil.

word(W) --> lowercaseword(W1): $li_to_at(W1,W).
word(cap(W)) --> capitalized(W1): $li_to_at(W1,W).
word(num(N)) --> digits(N1): $li_to_at(N1,N).
word(punc(C)) --> +C: $punc(C).
```

The predicate `li_to_at(L,A)` is defined, in terms of other IBM Prolog built-in predicates, to convert a list L of characters to an atom A (or a number, if appropriate). The completion of the definition of the tokenizer is left as an exercise for the reader.

5.3.2 Inflections

Many words have variant forms, or *inflections*, such as the past tense of a verb or the plural of a noun. In this section, we set up terminology for inflections and discuss their treatment in the lexicon. The various inflectional forms of a word share lexical information, so we want to factor this out and avoid duplication in a large system. One of the forms is chosen as the *citation form* (for example, the infinitive form of a verb), and this is used as the indexing form in the lexicon.

It is convenient in a grammar to associate *features* (represented as Prolog terms) with the inflectional forms of a word and to manipulate these features in arguments of nonterminals in order to exercise constraints in the grammar. For example, the verb "be" in the passive sense requires that its complement verb be a past participle (as in "be taken"). A suitable use of the feature `en` (indicating a past participle) can exercise this constraint. This will be illustrated below in Section 5.4, "Syntactic Constructions."

English verb forms can be classified as either *finite* or *nonfinite*. The nonfinite inflectional features and their full names are as follows (we also give a sample verb form for the verb "take").

```
inf - infinitive - take,
ing - present participle - taking,
en - past participle - taken,
```

The finite verb forms are the forms having a tense (present or past); they also (can) show variation for person and number. (We ignore in this discussion the question of subjunctive mood as in "John requests that you *be* there".) For finite forms, we use a feature that is a compound term

```
fin(Pers,Num,Tense)
```

where `Pers` is `pers1` (first person) or `pers3` (third person), `Num` is `sg` (singular) or `pl` (plural), and `Tense` is `past` or `pres`. (We can do without

"second person", since "you" behaves grammatically like "third person plural".)
Finite verbs are required to agree with their subjects in person and number. This
requirement is enforced conveniently in a logic grammar simply by unification of
variables like Pers and Num.

For most English verbs, there are only three distinct finite forms: (1) The
fin(pers3,sg,pres) form has an "-s" or "-es" ending ("breaks", "fixes").
(2) All other fin(*,*,pres) forms are the same as the infinitive form
("break", "fix"). (3) There is a single fin(*,*,past) form ("broke",
"fixed"). The verb "be" has three forms ("am", "is", "are") in the present and
two ("was", "were") in the past. The modal verbs ("can", "may", ...) exist only
in finite forms and have only one present form and one past form.

The infinitive form of a verb is used as the citation form, so we need a
predicate

verbf(V,Vinf,Infl)

which relates a verb form V with inflectional feature Infl to its infinitive form
Vinf. For example, the following relationships should hold:

verbf(sees,see,fin(pers3,sg,pres)).
verbf(saw,see,fin(*,*,past)).

How should the rules for verbf be specified? In a very small system, one
could simply write down unit clauses, but this would be tedious for a system of
any size and would take up too much space. In a system of intermediate size, a
method that works well is to compute verbf from more compact unit clause
specifications of the inflectional forms. For all English verbs except "be" and the
modal verbs, there are at most five distinct inflectional forms:

V	inf
Vs	fin(pers3,sg,pres)
Ved	past
Ven	en
Ving	ing

and we can just specify these in a unit clause

v(V,Vs,Ved,Ven,Ving).

for example

v(take,takes,took,taken,taking).

In fact, for most verbs, the en form is the same as the past form, and we can
just write the unit clause

v(V,Vs,Ved,Ving).

for example

v(make,makes,made,making).

and use the rule

```
v(V,Vs,Ved,Ved,Ving) <- v(V,Vs,Ved,Ving).
```

to get the en form for such verbs. If the lexicon contains v clauses for verbs, then we can preprocess it, adding axioms for verbf. A call to the following procedure, verbinflections, will accomplish this

```
verbinflections <-
  v(V,Vs,Ved,Ven,Ving) &
  addax(verbf(V,V,inf)) &
  addax(verbf(V,V,fin(*,pl,pres))) &
  addax(verbf(V,V,fin(pers1,sg,pres))) &
  addax(verbf(Vs,V,fin(pers3,sg,pres))) &
  addax(verbf(Ved,V,fin(*,*,past))) &
  addax(verbf(Ven,V,en)) &
  addax(verbf(Ving,V,ing)) &
  fail.
verbinflections.
```

If the size of the lexicon would mean that the addition of all these verbf clauses would present a space problem for Prolog, then an alternative would be to create them only for the words that are actually encountered in parsing, or to write conditional clauses for verbf in terms of v.

For an extremely large lexicon, if storage (and creation) of the v clauses presents a problem, then a further alternative would be to take advantage of the regularities that do exist in English for the creation of inflectional forms. One can write rules (morphological rules) that look at the verbs to be analyzed as strings, stripping off affixes like "s" (or "es") in "breaks" (or "fixes"), to recognize the fin(pers3,sg,pres) form of "break" (or "fix"). We refer the reader to Winograd (1972) for an algorithm of this nature. It is an interesting exercise to implement this in Prolog.

For nouns, it is convenient for the grammar to use a predicate

```
nounf(N,Nsg,Num)
```

for example

```
nounf(men,man,pl)
nounf(man,man,sg)
```

relating a noun N to its singular form Nsg (used as citation form) and showing its number Num. In the actual specification of the lexicon, we could give unit clauses

```
n(Nsg,Npl).
```

and add nounf rules by preprocessing, or use conditional rules

```
nounf(Nsg,Nsg,sg) <- n(Nsg,*).
nounf(Npl,Nsg,pl) <- n(Nsg,Npl).
```

Or for a very large lexicon, one could use morphological rules, as indicated above.

5.3.3 Slot Frames

In Section 5.1.2, "Verbs," we discussed the form of the word sense predications for verbs. For instance, a sense of "give" might be a predication `give1(X,Y,Z)`—"X gives Y to Z". The arguments of such a verb sense correspond grammatically to *complements* of the verb in a sentence. Complements include the subject, object, indirect object, prepositional complements (as in "depend on"), and various kinds of clausal complements.

A very direct and useful way of handling verb complements in a grammar is to work with *slots* and *slot frames*. Roughly, slots are names for complement types, together with associated variables that appear in the verb sense predication. An approximation to a slot frame for `give1(X,Y,Z)` is the list

```
(subj:X).(obj:Y).(iobj:Z).nil
```

Here the slots are named `subj` (subject), `obj` (object), and `iobj` (indirect object), and are illustrated in

```
John gives Mary the book.
subj        iobj   obj

John gives the book to Mary.
subj        obj      iobj
```

It is not really standard to call "to Mary" the indirect object in the last sentence, but for the method to be described below for handling complements in the grammar, we do want to use the *same* slot (`iobj`). In both versions of the "give" sentence, the filler of this slot corresponds in logical form to the same (third) argument of the word sense `give1`.

In a natural language grammar of any size, one runs into the problem of ambiguity. Words have multiple senses, and phrases can act as modifiers in multiple ways as in "They saw the man in the park with the telescope". (There is even the ridiculous sense of "saw" that is the present tense of "to saw".)

Resolving ambiguities in general takes nothing less than full-fledged inference with world knowledge. However, a technique that works well in limited domains is to do *type matching*. In the slot frame for a verb sense, the slots can have associated *semantic types*. For example, the subject slot for the verb "see" might have the type `animal`. An actual noun phrase that is a candidate subject for "see" will have its own semantic type, and this must match the type `animal`. A filler for a slot must have a type that matches the required type of the slot. In general, semantic types will not be simply atomic terms like `animal`, but will be compound terms that allow one to deal with hierarchies of types and cross-classification. The *matching* of types will simply be Prolog unification. This will be described in the next section. In the present section we will pretend that types are atoms.

So our slots will actually be *typed*, and will be terms of the form

```
Slotname:X:Type
```

where X is the variable appearing in the verb sense predication corresponding to the slot, and Type is the semantic type for the entity referred to by X. The term X:Type is thought of as a *typed variable*, and is called the *marker* of the slot. Thus the slot frame for give1(X,Y,Z) might be

```
(subj:X:human).(obj:Y:physobj).(iobj:Z:human).nil
```

In slot filling, the marker of a slot is unified with a typed variable associated with the filler (say, a noun phrase), called also the *marker* of the filler.

In a lexical entry for a verb, we want to show a verb sense predication and a corresponding slot frame. Since every verb has a subject (in a finite clause), we will not actually list the subject slot by name, but will just put the subject marker in a separate argument of the lexical entry. An entry will look like this

```
verb(V,Pred,E,X,Slots).
```

```
V     - citation form,
Pred  - verb sense predication,
E     - semantic type of the verb itself,
X     - subject marker,
Slots - slot frame without subject.
```

Example:

```
verb(give, give1(X,Y,Z), action, X:human,
    (obj:Y:physobj).(iobj:Z:human).nil ).
```

The predicate verb is in a form that is convenient to use in a grammar (with the methods described below). However, there is a bit of redundancy in the use of variables, which it would be nice to avoid in the listing of a large lexicon. To avoid this, the raw lexical entries could look like

```
vb(give, give1, action, human,
    (obj:physobj).(iobj:human).nil ).
```

and we could produce the fuller form (for verb) by preprocessing. If some verbs have only one sense and it is satisfactory to use the citation form itself for the verb sense predicate name, then we could give such entries in the form

```
vb(give,action,human,
    (obj:physobj).(iobj:human).nil).
```

Nouns can have complements just as verbs can. Some nouns (like "dependency") are derived from verbs and have corresponding slots. Other nouns (like "brother") are inherently relational. The predicate noun is similar to verb:

```
noun(N,Pred,X,Slots).
```

```
N      - citation form,
Pred   - noun sense predication,
X      - "subject" marker (for main entity
             referred to by the noun),
Slots - slot frame without "subject".
```

Examples:

```
noun(man,man(X),X:human,nil).
noun(father,father(X,Y),X:human,
    (pobj(of):Y:human).nil).
noun(dependence,dependence1(X,Y):E,E:state,
    (pobj(of):X:human).(pobj(on):Y:*).nil).
```

Here the slot `nobj` is a very common noun complement slot that can be filled by an "of"-prepositional phrase in postmodifying position ("the father of John"), or by a possessive in premodifying position ("John's father"). The slot `pobj(Prep)` is filled by a prepositional phrase with head `Prep`. It is used also for verbs (like "depend").

5.3.4 Semantic Types

As indicated in the previous subsection, semantic constraints can be exercised by type matching: The type required by a slot must be matched against the type of a proposed filler. It is convenient to use unification for this type matching. If we do this, then it is not satisfactory to use atoms for types, because then unification will require equality, and the type of a slot may be more or less specific than the actual type of a filler. For example, the verb "see" may require an `animal` subject, and the actual subject may have a more specific type, say, `human`. Or the actual subject may have a less specific marking, as the subject "it" would.

Types exist in a hierarchy of specificity. If they are viewed as 1-place predicates, then the statement that type `t1` is more specific than type `t2` is just equivalent to the Horn clause `t2(X)<-t1(X)`. However, we will use a separate formalism for types, because there are conditions on them that do not fit into Horn clause logic.

In specifying a type hierarchy, we will use two sorts of formulas. The formula

```
t   <=>  t1 | t2 | ... | tn.
```

is read "type t splits into types `t1`, ..., `tn`." If the types were viewed as 1-place predicates, this would be equivalent to the statement:

```
For all X, t(X) iff t1(X) or ... or tn(X).
```

where "or" is the exclusive "or". Examples are

```
animal  <=>  human | nonhuman.
animal  <=>  male | female.
```

Here, nonhuman means "nonhuman animal". Note that with these two splitting statements, the same type can be split in more than one way. This is called *cross-classification*.

The second kind of statement allowed in the specification of a type hierarchy is a simple implication

```
t1  =>  t2.  e.g:
human  =>  intelligent.
```

As indicated above, this is equivalent to a Horn clause when types are viewed as 1-place predicates.

An example of a small hierarchy is the following:

```
entity  <=>  abstract | concrete.
entity  <=>  individual | collective.
abstract  <=>  state | action.
concrete  <=>  living | nonliving.
concrete  <=>  solid | liquid | gas.
living  <=>  animal | plant.
animal  <=>  human | nonhuman.
animal  <=>  male | female.
human  =>  solid.
```

For unification type matching, we will use *type-trees*, which are Prolog compound terms made up out of the atomic types appearing in a type hierarchy such as the one just given. (*Note:* Type-lists (of descending types) were used by Dahl (1977). The purpose of the generalization to trees is to allow cross-classification. Methods similar to ours are used by Bundy, Byrd, and Mellish (1982).) To build a type-tree, one constructs a compound term whose principal functor is the top-level atomic type, entity, and which has as many arguments as there are splitting statements for entity (two arguments, for the above hierarchy). An argument can be either a variable (representing an unspecified subtype), or a *subtype-tree*, selected as follows. For the *i*th argument, the principal functor of the subtree is one of the atomic subtypes appearing on the right-hand side of the *i*th splitting statement for entity. The arguments of the subtree are chosen in a similar way (by looking at further splitting statements), and so on down, until one comes to atomic types that have no splitting statements. We assume that there is no circularity in the subtyping implicit in splitting statements. An implicational statement t1=>t2 imposes a constraint in the choices just described: If t1 is present in the type-tree, then t2 must be also.

Examples of type-trees are as follows

```
entity(*,*).
entity(abstract(state),individual).
entity(concrete(nonliving,solid),*).
entity(concrete(living(animal(human,*)),solid),*).
```

Note that the leaf nodes of a type-tree completely determine the tree. For example, the four preceding type-trees are determined, respectively, by the lists of atomic types:

```
nil
state.individual.nil
nonliving.solid.nil
human.nil
```

(In the last case, we do not even have to specify `solid` because of the implication `human=>solid`.) Because of this redundancy, the specification of types in the lexicon can be compact. We need only specify lists of types at the lowest level of the hierarchy. (A list, like `human.male.nil`, represents a *conjunction* of conditions.) Then before parsing, such type lists can be converted into the type-trees that they determine.

It is left as an exercise to the reader to write a Prolog procedure

```
typetree(List,TypeTree)
```

which converts a `List` of atomic types, assumed to be consistent with respect to the type hierarchy, into the most general `TypeTree` containing the members of that `List` as nodes. Some hints are as follows.

(1) From the split statements (specified as axioms for the `<=>` operator), produce (automatically) axioms for `splits` that would look like the following for the above sample hierarchy:

```
splits(entity,(abstract.concrete.nil).
       (individual.collective.nil).nil).
splits(abstract,(state.action.nil).nil).
splits(concrete,(living.nonliving.nil).
       (solid.liquid.gas.nil).nil).
splits(living,(animal.plant.nil).nil).
splits(animal,(human.nonhuman.nil).
       (male.female.nil).nil).
```

(2) Augment the relation `=>` by adding an axiom `t1=>t2` whenever `splits(t2,L)` holds with `t1` a member of a member of `L`.

(3) Write a procedure `closure(L1,L2)` that takes a list `L1` of atomic types and finds the list `L2` of all atomic types `t2` such that `t1 R t2` for some `t1` in `L1`, where R is the transitive closure of the relation `=>`.

(4) Write `typetree` as

```
typetree(L,Tree) <-
   closure(L,L1) &
   tptree(L1,entity,Tree).
```

where `tptree(L,Node,Tree)` makes use of `splits(Node,*)` to go through the recursive process of type-tree construction.

5.3.5 Lexical Look-up

The lexicon for a Modular Logic Grammar is basically a a list of unit clauses (for predicates like `verb` and `noun`), but it may be too large to be stored entirely in main memory. We discuss here a way to use Prolog to look up lexical entries efficiently in disk files.

Assume that the lexicon is stored in 26 disk files, LEXA, LEXB, ..., LEXZ. Assume that each record of LEXi is a Prolog term of the form

    Word:Clauses.

where `Word` has initial letter `i`, and `Clauses` is the list of all lexical clauses pertinent to `Word`. (A given word may be both a noun and a verb, may have several senses, etc.) These indexing words are in alphabetical order and are not repeated. At lexical look-up time for a given `Word`, we are going to search for the record beginning with `Word` (if it exists) and then assert the corresponding `Clauses` into the Prolog database.

Look-up of a `Word` proceeds in three stages:

1. Determine the appropriate LEXi file by looking at the first letter `i` of `Word`.

2. Search a binary index tree BTREEi associated with LEXi, stored internally in Prolog. This narrows the range of search for LEXi.

3. In the narrowed range, do binary search (with disk reads) in LEXi.

The binary trees BTREEi are defined as follows. The *index tree of depth* N *and range* (L,U) (for LEXi), where N, L, and U are nonnegative integers, is a variable if N=0 or L>U; otherwise it is a term

    btree(Word,LSon,RSon)

where `Word` is the word of LEXi indexing record number M $=$ (L+U)/2 (integer arithmetic), and where `LSon`·is the index tree of depth N−1 and range (L,M−1) and RSon is the index tree of depth N−1 and range (M+1,U). The tree BTREEi is the index tree of a chosen depth (say, N=6) and range (1,U), where U is the number of records in LEXi. We leave it as an exercise to write a Prolog procedure to construct the trees BTREEi for any desired depth. Let us assume that the results are stored as unit clauses:

    index(i,Num,BTREEi).

where `Num` is the number of records in LEXi.

Now, the look-up procedure can be written as follows

```
lookup(Word,Clauses) <-
  firstletter(Word,I) &
  stconc('LEX',I,LEXi) &
  index(I,N,Tree) &
  looktree(Word,1,N,L,U,Tree) &
  dcio(in,input,file,LEXi) &
  lookfile(Word,L,U,Clauses) &
  dcio(in,close).
```

Here the purpose of `looktree` is to compute the range (L,U) of search for the disk file LEXi. It can be defined as follows

```
looktree(Word,L,U,L,U,btree(Word,*,*)) <- /.
looktree(Word,L0,U0,L,U,btree(Word1,Lson,*)) <-
  lt(Word,Word1) &/&
  U1:=(L0+U0)/2-1 &
  looktree(Word,L0,U1,L,U,Lson).
looktree(Word,L0,U0,L,U,btree(*,*,Rson)) <-
  L1:=(L0+U0)/2+1 &
  looktree(Word,L1,U0,L,U,Rson).
```

Finally, the procedure for binary search in LEXi in the narrowed range (L,U) is as follows

```
lookfile(Word,L,U,Clauses) <-
  le(L,U) & Mid:=(L+U)/2 &
  dcio(in,next,Mid) & read(Entry,in) &
  lookfile1(Word,Entry,L,U,Mid,Clauses).

lookfile1(Word,Word:Clauses,*,*,*,Clauses) <- /.
lookfile1(Word,Word1:*,L,*,Mid,Clauses) <-
  lt(Word,Word1) &/& U:=Mid-1 &
  lookfile(Word,L,U,Clauses).
lookfile1(Word,*,*,U,Mid,Clauses) <-
  L:=Mid+1 &
  lookfile(Word,L,U,Clauses).
```

5.4 SYNTACTIC CONSTRUCTIONS

In the preceding two Sections (5.2, "Logic Grammars," and 5.3, "Words") we have laid groundwork for writing the syntactic component of a Modular Logic Grammar. In this section, we will look at some of the specific constructions in English syntax and discuss techniques for handling them. These techniques are relevant to other languages as well.

5.4.1 Verb Phrases, Complements, and Adjuncts

Let us take the small Modular Logic Grammar on page 328 as a starting point and expand it so as to get a reasonable treatment of verb complements. (The reader should review this grammar before proceeding.) The vp and verb rules given there work only for transitive verbs (verbs taking a subject and a direct object). Let us improve vp by using slot frames and slot filling techniques. We will assume now that the lexical information for verbs is given as in Sections 5.3.2, "Inflections" and 5.3.3, "Slot Frames," in entries for verbf and verb. As a first step, let us write the vp rule as follows.

```
vp(Infl,E,X) ==>
  vhead(Infl,E,X,Slots):
  postmods(Slots).

vhead(Infl,E,X,Slots) ==>
  +V: $verbf(V,Vinf,Infl):
  $verb(Vinf,Pred,E,X,Slots):
  l-Pred.
```

The job of vhead is to find a verb with an inflection Infl, subject marker X, verb type E, and list Slots of postverbal slots. To do this, vhead finds a verb V with an inflection Infl and infinitive form Vinf. Then verb is called to get a word sense predication associated with the citation form Vinf. Since the variable X in this call to verb is the marker for the subject of the verb phrase (passed in to vp), this unification takes care of binding the subject argument in Pred.

It is the job of postmods to take the list Slots of postverbal slots and find the corresponding complements of the verb. The slots in the list Slots are of course given in a fixed order. For example, for a verb like "give", the direct object slot obj might be listed before the indirect object slot iobj, whereas the corresponding complements might come in either order. For the moment, though, let us take the easiest route and just write postmods so that it fills the slots in the order they appear in the list Slots.

```
postmods((Slot:X).Slots) ==>
  fill(Slot,X):
  postmods(Slots).
postmods(nil) ==> nil.
```

For filling the obj and iobj slots, we can use the rules

```
fill(obj,X) ==> np(X).
fill(iobj,X) ==> +to: np(X).
```

As indicated in Section 5.1.2, "Verbs," some verb complements are introduced by specific prepositions, as in "John depends *on Mary*" and "John believes *in Mary*". For these complements we can use a slot pobj(Prep), which requires the specific preposition Prep. Its filler rule can be

```
fill(pobj(Prep),X) ==> +Prep: np(X).
```

Some verb complements themselves involve verb phrases. For instance, verbs like "think" and "know" take finite clause complements, as in

```
John thinks that Mary saw Bill.
```

We can give "think" the slot `fincomp` and write the slot-filler rule

```
fill(fincomp,X) ==> compclause(X).
```

```
compclause(X:*) ==> subst(X)-t: +that: s.
```

Here, `compclause` (for "complement clause") should be declared a strong nonterminal.   The operator `subst(X)` means "substitute for X." (The associated logical form `t` is a trivial "true".)   It will cause the logical form produced for the complement sentence `s` to be unified with the variable X, which of course is an argument of the verb whose slot is being filled. We will make `subst(X)` precise below in Section 5.5.2, "Modification." Note that the argument of `compclause` is given in the form `X:*`. This is due to the fact that the markers associated with slots are actually typed variables `X:Type`. The operator `subst(X)` requires X to be the actual argument variable for the verb. (At this point, we neglect using the `Type` itself.)

Some verb complements are nonfinite verb phrases, as in

```
John wants to see Mary.
John wants Bill to see Mary
John likes seeing Mary.
John helped Bill see Mary.
John will see Mary.
John has seen Mary.
John is seeing Mary.
John is seen by Mary.
```

In the last four of these examples, the first verbs ("will", "has", "is") are often called "auxiliary verbs" and are treated as modifiers of the following verbs, which are considered "main verbs." However, with slot-filling techniques, it seems very convenient and natural to view these first verbs as head verbs of their clauses, with the following verb phrases as complements.

A verb phrase (analyzed by the nonterminal `vp`) does not itself include a subject. However, the marker X for the subject of the head of the verb phrase is passed as an argument in `vp(Infl,E,X)`, and this marker is often clearly unifiable with the marker of a noun phrase in the sentence. For instance, in "John wants Bill to see Mary", the logical subject of "see" is "Bill", and in "John wants to see Mary", the logical subject of "see" is "John". In the `vp` rule, we should determine the subject marker of the complement verb phrase and pass it into `postmods`, so that the `fill` rules can call the complement `vp` with the correct subject marker. Let us modify the `vp` rule as follows

```
vp(Infl,E,X) ==>
   vhead(Infl,E,X,Slots):
   $theme(X,Slots,Y):
   postmods(Slots,Y).
```

Here `theme(X,Slots,Y)` takes the subject marker X for the current verb phrase and determines the subject marker Y for possible complement verb phrases by looking at the list `Slots`. (We call Y the *theme* for the postmodifiers.) A definition that works well for `theme` is the following.

```
theme(X,Slots,Y) <- member(obj:Y,Slots) &/.
theme(X,Slots,Y) <- member(pobj(*):Y,Slots) &/.
theme(X,Slots,X).
```

Thus the idea is that the theme Y will be the marker of an `obj` slot or `pobj(*)` slot if either of these slots is present; otherwise the theme is the subject of the head verb. The first cases would occur with "John wants Bill to see Mary" and "John depended on Bill to find Mary". The last case occurs with "John wants to see Mary" and "John promised Bill to see Mary". (The slot frame for "promise" should have an `iobj` slot, not an `obj` slot.)

After making this change to the `vp` rule, we modify `postmods` as follows

```
postmods((Slot:X).Slots,Y) ==>
   fill(Slot,X,Y):
   postmods(Slots,Y).
postmods(nil,*) ==> nil.
```

so that now `fill` has access to the theme. A verb like "try" can be given a `verb` entry like the following:

```
verb(try,try1(X,P),*,X:*,(infcomp:P:*).nil).
```

(We do not specify semantic types in this example.) The slot `infcomp` is filled by infinitival verb phrases (as in "John tried *to see Mary*"), and we can write its filler rule now as

```
fill(infcomp,X,Y) ==> +to: verbph(inf,X,Y).

verbph(Infl,X:E,Y) ==> subst(X)-t: vp(Infl,E,Y).
```

Here `verbph` should be declared as a strong nonterminal. Note that here we do pass into `vp` the type requirement E on the verb of the filler verb phrase.

A sentence like

```
John is seen by Mary.
```

involves the *passive* construction. As indicated above in Section 5.1.2, "Verbs," we want to get a logical form like

```
be_passive(john,see(mary,john)).
```

Here be_passive(X,P) is the passive sense of "be", and its second argument
is filled by the logical form of the passive verb phrase "seen by Mary". Passive
verb phrases can appear without a "be" verb, as in the noun phrase "anyone *seen*
by Mary". In a passive verb phrase, the subject marker X passed into the vp (we
call X the *grammatical subject*) is no longer associated with the first (logical
subject) argument of the head verb of the vp. Rather, one of the postverbal slots
(usually obj) is associated with X, and the logical subject is associated with a
new slot (let us call it actor), that is filled by a "by"-phrase. Thus, in "given
to Mary by the man", the logical subject of "give" is "the man", and the
grammatical subject is the logical object.

We can handle all this in the vp rule by operations on slot lists.

```
vp(Infl,Voice,E,X) ==>
  vhead(Infl,E,Y,Slots):
  $voice(Voice,Infl,X,Y,Slots,Slots1):
  $theme(X,Slots,Z):
  postmods(Slots1,Z).

voice(active,*,X,X,Slots,Slots) <- /.
voice(passive,en,X,Y,Slots,Slots2) <-
  choose(Slot:X,Slots,Slots1) &
  pslot(Slot) &
  append(Slots1,(actor:Y).nil,Slots2).
```

Here the procedure choose(X,L,M) chooses an element X from a list L,
with M as the remainder of L after X is removed. (Writing choose is left as an
exercise.) With unit clauses like

```
pslot(obj).
pslot(iobj).
```

we can declare which slots can be associated with the grammatical subject.

To handle sentences like

```
John is seen by Mary.
```

the passive sense of "be" is selected, and the verb entry for this sense can show
a passive verb phrase complement slot, say pass, with filler rule

```
fill(pass,X,Y) ==> verbph(en,passive,X,Y).
```

(We also modify verbph to have a voice argument.)

So far, we have written postmods so that it fills the slots in the verb's slot
list in exactly the order specified in the list. But they can be filled in different
orders, as in

```
John gave the book to Mary.
            obj        iobj
```

```
John gave Mary the book.
            iobj    obj
```

```
The book was given by John to Mary.
                      actor     iobj
```

```
The book was given to Mary by John.
                      iobj      actor
```

On the other hand, the order is not completely free, and the way of filling a slot can depend on position. We cannot get

```
John gave a book Mary.
            obj     iobj
```

A way of handling this is to use a notion of *states* — as in transition networks. The idea is that as postmods gets the postmodifiers of the verb, it goes through certain states, that are linearly ordered. In filling a slot, one advances (or stays stationary) in the sequence of states, but one never goes backward. States could be represented in the nonnegative integers in standard form 0, 1, 2,..., but it is much more convenient to represent them purely as logic terms, say, 0, +0, ++0,.... We modify the rules for fill so that they name the state *advanced to* by filling a given slot, and we correspondingly give postmods a state argument representing the state advanced to by the next slot filling. In the initial call to postmods from vp, this state argument is just an unbound variable, since the first filling could advance to any state. We modify postmods as follows.

```
postmods(Slots,State,Y) ==>
   $choose(Slot:X,Slots,Slots1):
   fill(Slot,State,X,Y):
   $precede(State,State1):
   postmods(Slots1,State1,Y).
postmods(nil,*,*) ==> nil.

precede(0,*) <- /.
precede(+X,+Y) <- precede(X,Y).
```

Here choose is the same procedure used above in handling the passive construction. We choose a slot, then fill it, advancing to State, then require (through precede) that State precede (not come before) State1, then call postmods recursively with State1 and the reduced slot list.

Sample fill rules are as follows

```
fill(iobj,+0,X,*) ==> np(X).
fill(iobj,++0,X,*) ==> +to: np(X).
fill(obj,++0,X,*) ==> np(X).
fill(actor,++0,X,*) ==> +by: np(X).
fill(infcomp,++0,X,Y) ==> +to: verbph(inf,X,Y).
```

In the next section we will see examples involving states 0 and +++0.

The rule we have given for termination of postmods is

```
postmods(nil,*,*) ==> nil.
```

We use no notion of "final state"; the second argument is just a variable, that could match any state. The first argument is nil, and this requires that all of the slots in the slot list be filled before termination. It is useful to have the notion of *optional slots*. We can declare them with unit clauses:

```
opt(Slot).
```

For example, actor should be declared optional, since we can have both

```
John was seen by Mary.
John was seen.
```

With this notion, we can modify the postmods termination rule by requiring that the slot list be *satisfied*:

```
postmods(Slots,*,*) ==> $satisfied(Slots).
```

Here satisfied(Slots) means that all the members of the list Slots (which could be empty) are optional. It is left as an exercise to write this procedure.

Modifiers that are not complements are adjuncts. For verbs, these include adverbs, prepositional phrases, and subordinate (finite) clauses, as in

```
John ate when he arrived.
```

and various nonfinite verb phrases, as in

```
Having arrived, John started the meeting.
Press this button to start the motor.
```

In general, adjunct modifiers of verbs are called *adverbials*.

Adverbial postmodifiers should be handled by our nonterminal postmods, since they can intermix with complement postmodifiers. We augment postmods as follows

```
postmods(Cat,Slots,State,E,Y) ==>
   $choose(Slot:X,Slots,Slots1):
   fill(Slot,State,X,Y):
   $precede(State,State1):
   postmods(Cat,Slots1,State1,E,Y).
postmods(Cat,Slots,State,E,Y) ==>
   adjunct(Cat,State,E,Y):
   $precede(State,State1):
   postmods(Cat,Slots,State1,E,Y).
postmods(*,Slots,*,*,*) ==> $satisfied(Slots).
```

We have given `postmods` two additional arguments. The first argument `Cat` (standing for "category") will be `vp` if we are working with verb postmodifiers (as we have so far in this section) and will be `np` if we are working with noun postmodifiers. (Nouns can have complements, too, and fortunately we can use the same mechanism, `postmods`, for handling them.)

The fourth argument `E` of `postmods` is the semantic type of the verb that is picked up by `vhead`. The `vp` rule should be modified so as to pass this from `vhead` to `postmods`. This argument is passed to `adjunct` in the second `postmods` rule. It is useful for adverbials to be able to "look at" the verb's type, since they are modifying the verb. Complements do not need to do this (`fill` does not use `E`), because complement slots for a given verb are stored directly in the lexicon with the verb.

Prepositional phrases are very common adjunct modifiers of verbs. As indicated in above in Section 5.1.8, "Prepositions," we want logical form analyses like the following.

```
John waited for 3 hours.
past(for_time(3.hour,wait(john))).
```

The sense `for_time(T,P)` of "for" takes a logical form `P` in its second argument. The semantic interpretation rules will use a semantic item:

```
@P - for_time(X,P)
```

where `@P` unifies `P` with the logical form of the modified item (`wait(john)` in the above example).

We can write an adjunct rule for prepositional phrase modifiers as follows

```
adjunct(vp,++0,E,*) ==> pp(P:E,@P).
```

```
pp(X,Op) ==>
   +Prep: $prep(Prep,Pred,Y,X):
   Op-Pred:
   np(Y).
```

Note that we pass into `pp` the operator `Op` for the logical terminal associated with the preposition. A reason for this is that prepositional phrases that modify nouns can behave differently and require a different operator, as will be shown in the next section. The lexical predicate `prep` can have entries like the following:

```
prep(for,for_time(T,P),T:time,P:event).
```

Here we neglect the fact that the semantic types indicated are part of a larger type-tree. These semantic types for the `for_time` sense of "for" can help disambiguate the two sentences:

```
John waited for 3 hours.
John waited for Bill.
```

Adverbs modify verbs, but adverbs can themselves have modifiers, as in

```
John waited very patiently.
```

So we need to deal with *adverbial phrases*, and we need a nonterminal `avp` for these (which should be a strong nonterminal).

```
adjunct(vp,++0,E,*) ==> avp(E).
```

```
avp(E) ==>
   qualifiers(E):
   +Adv: $adv(Adv,Pred,Op,E):
   Op-Pred.
```

Here `qualifiers` gets words like "very", "quite", and "rather". It is left as an exercise to write the rules for `qualifiers`. The rules should be recursive, since there can be in principle any number of qualifiers. If one wants to do without qualifiers and leave only the "hook," then the following rule suffices:

```
qualifiers(*) ==> nil.
```

Different adverbs can have different operators `Op` associated with them, so we let `adv` return the sort of operator that is appropriate for the given adverb. We could have `adv` entries like the following:

```
adv(yesterday,yesterday(P),@P,abstract).
adv(only,only(B,F),B<F,*).
```

Here the operator B<F is used for adverbial focalizers, and its role in producing logical forms will be discussed below in Section 5.5.2, "Modification."

5.4.2 Left Extraposition

In most cases, the complements of a verb have normal positions as subject or as determined by `postmods` above. But when a complement introduces a *wh-question*, as in

```
Who did John see?
Who did Bill say that John saw?
Who did Mary think Bill said John saw?
```

the complement ("who" in these examples) can be *extraposed* out of its normal place (as the object of "saw") to the left — normally to the front of the sentence. A similar situation exists for the relative pronoun in a relative clause

```
This is the man who John saw.
This is the man who Bill said John saw.
This is the man who Mary thought Bill said John saw.
```

In both wh-questions and relative clauses, the left-extraposed item can (in principle) be arbitrarily far from the its normal "home" as complement of a verb.

How do we handle this? Fortunately, the nonterminals in our grammar can have arguments that can be used to pass information along. When we parse the initial left-extraposed item, we will save relevant information about it in a nonterminal argument, and pass it down until we come to its "home". We will look first at the case of wh-questions, and, in the process, improve the sentence rule so as to handle yes-no questions and subject-verb agreement as well.

To do this, we want the np rule to produce more information. Let us assume that a call to np is of the form

```
np(X:Num:DType)
```

where X is the marker variable (with semantic type) as before, Num is the number of the noun phrase (sg or pl), and DType is the *determiner type*. Of importance to us now is a determiner type wh, which signals a wh-noun phrase, as in "which man" and "who". (In the latter case, there is no overt determiner, but "who" is logically like "which person".) Let us assume that np produces this information now; we will update the np rules below.

We rewrite the s rule as follows

```
s ==>
    topic(Topsubj,Qaux,Topic):
    clause(Topsubj,Qaux,Topic).
```

Here, topic gets the underlined phrases in the following sentences:

```
John saw Mary.
Who saw Mary?
Did John see Mary?
Who did John see?
John I don't like.
```

and clause gets the remainders. The variable Topsubj is either t or f according as the topic contains the subject of the sentence. Thus Topsubj is t in the first three sentences and f in the last two. The variable Qaux will be pre(V) if there is a preposed auxiliary verb V and will be nil otherwise. Thus Qaux is pre(did) in the third and fourth sentences. The variable Topic will be a term hold(X) for the noun phrase np(X) included in the topic.

With these conventions, we can write the rules for topic as follows

```
topic(Topsubj,Qaux,hold(X)) ==>
  np(X):
  mood(X,Mood):
  qaux(Mood,Topsubj,Qaux).
topic(t,pre(V),hold(X)) ==>
  +V: $finiteaux(V):
  np(X):
  (B<<F)-yesno(B,F).

mood(*:*:wh,wh) ==> /.
mood(*,dcl) ==> (B<<F)-dcl(B,F).

qaux(dcl,*,nil) ==> nil.
qaux(wh,t,nil) ==> nil.
qaux(wh,f,pre(V)) ==> +V: $finiteaux(V).
```

Here `finiteaux(V)` means that `V` is a finite auxiliary verb (a finite form of "be", "have", "do", or a modal). The logical terminal involving `yesno(P,Q)` is produced in the case of a yes-no question, and will appear as the outermost predication in the logical form for such a sentence. (See Section 5.1.10, "Nonlexical Predicates in LFL" for a discussion of `yesno`.) For declarative sentences, the form `dcl(P,Q)` is produced by `mood`. (See also the same section for `dcl`.) In many of our sample analyses, we will not show the `dcl` form. To do without it, one should replace the second `mood` rule with

```
mood(*,dcl) ==> nil.
```

The reader should trace through the workings of `topic` for the five sample sentences above.

Now let us look at `clause`. This nonterminal is of use, not only for whole sentences `s`, but also for relative clauses and for clausal verb complements (filling the slot `fincomp`). Clauses always have an overt subject (if `Topsubj` = `f`) or a left-extraposed subject (if `Topsubj` = `t`). The verb of a clause is finite, and must agree in number and person with the subject.

We can write the `clause` rule as follows

```
clause(Topsubj,Qaux,T) ==>
  subject(X:Num:*,Topsubj,T,T1):
  vp(fin(*,Num,*),active,*,X,Qaux,T1).

subject(X,t,hold(X),nil) ==> nil.
subject(X,f,T,T) ==> np(X).
```

The arguments `T` and `T1` are *topic* arguments, and they will often come in pairs behaving somewhat like a difference list. Such a pair `(T,T1)` will always be of one of the forms

```
(hold(X), hold(X))
(hold(X), nil)
(nil, nil)
```

The idea is that when the first topic argument is of the form hold(X), then the item X has been left-extraposed (made a topic) and is "on hold." It can either be left on hold (the first case), or taken off hold (the second case) and replaced by nil (nothing on hold).

Thus in the clause rule, the subject nonterminal will get a subject from hold if Topsubj = t and will get an actual subject with np(X) if Topsubj = f.

Note the way agreement in number between subject and verb is enforced in the clause rule. The number Num of the subject is picked out by the call to subject, and the term fin(*,Num,*) is passed into vp as the inflection of the verb. Thus the verb is required to be a finite verb with the same number Num as the subject. One should also control agreement in person. This is left as an exercise for the reader. (It would be suitable to determine the person of a noun phrase from the determiner type (DType) portion of the np argument X:Num:DType.)

We have given vp two extra arguments for the topic, and an argument Qaux for preposed auxiliary verbs, so we need to update the vp rule

```
vp(Infl,Voice,E,X,Qaux,T) ==>
  vhead(Qaux,Infl,E,Y,Slots):
  $voice(Voice,Infl,X,Y,Slots,Slots1):
  $theme(X,Slots,Z):
  postmods(vp,Slots1,State,E,Z,T,nil).

vhead(Qaux,Infl,E,X,Slots) ==>
  getverb(Qaux,V):
  $verbf(V,Vinf,Infl):
  $verb(Vinf,Pred,E,X,Slots):
  1-Pred.

getverb(nil,V) ==> +V.
getverb(pre(V),V) ==> nil.
```

The changes involve passing the topic argument T into postmods and changing vhead so that it can get a real verb V or one that has been saved as pre(V) because V was preposed in a question sentence.

Now let us modify postmods to take care of the topic arguments. We will just look at the postmods rule that calls fill. (The case of adjuncts is left to the reader.)

```
postmods(Cat,Slots,State,E,Y,T,T2) ==>
  $choose(Slot:X,Slots,Slots1):
  fill(Slot,State,X,Y,T,T1):
  $precede(State,State1):
  postmods(Cat,Slots1,State1,E,Y,T1,T2).
```

Thus `fill` can now have access to topic information. We can have *virtual* filling of slots, where the slot is filled by removing the filler from hold, or *actual* filling, where `fill` actually uses up more of the word string.

An example of a virtual filling rule for the `obj` slot is the following:

```
fill(obj,0,X,*,hold(X:*),nil) ==> nil.
```

This would handle a case like

```
Who did John see?
```

or even

```
Who did John say that Mary saw?
```

(We describe below the passing of topics into complement clauses.)

Our previous actual filler rule for `obj` should be modified as follows (because of the new arguments for `fill`).

```
fill(obj,++0,X,*,T,T) ==> np(X:*).
```

(Note that we also need to break out the marker component `X` in the call to `np` because of the new assumption that the argument of `np` is of the form `X:Num:DType`.)

To handle clause complements with topics passed into them, we modify the filler rule for `fincomp` as follows.

```
fill(fincomp,++0,X,*,T,nil) ==>
  compclause(X,T).

compclause(X:*,T) ==>
  subst(X)-t:
  binder(Topsubj):
  clause(Topsubj,nil,T).

binder(f) ==> +that.
binder(f) ==> +whether.
binder(*) ==> nil.
```

Note that the `binder` partially determines whether the left-extraposed item (the topic) can be the subject of the embedded clause. If the binder is not null (if it is "that" or "whether"), the topic cannot be the subject of the clause. We can say

```
Who did John say that Mary saw?
```

but not

Who did John say <u>that saw Mary</u>?

However, we can say

Who did John say <u>saw Mary</u>?

(with null binder).

What about topics in nonfinite verb phrase complements? We can, for example, modify the filler rule for `infcomp` as follows.

```
fill(infcomp,++0,X,Y,T,nil) ==>
  +to: verbph(inf,active,X,Y,T).

verbph(Infl,Voice,X:E,Y,T) ==>
  subst(X)-t: vp(Infl,Voice,E,Y,nil,T).
```

This slot would get the underlined phrases in the following examples.

John wants <u>to see Mary</u>.
Who does John want <u>to see</u>?
Who does John want <u>to ask Bill to see</u>?

In the last two sentences, the object of "see" will be filled by the virtual `fill` rule for `obj` given above.

[Note: An interesting augmentation of the DCG formalism called *Extraposition Grammars (XGs)*, which is designed to handle left-extraposition more systematically, is described in Pereira (1981, 1983). This formalism obviates the explicit use of topic-pair arguments of the sort used in this subsection (they are added automatically by the rule compiler). However, because they are added indiscriminately to all nonterminals, one must take care to write constraints into the grammar to prevent extraposition from too many places.]

5.4.3 Noun Phrases

Noun phrase syntax involves the constructions discussed in the last two sections. Nouns can have complements, just as verbs can; and noun adjuncts include relative clauses, which involve left-extraposition. We can improve the rules for `np` as follows

```
np(X:Num:def) ==>
  propernoun(X,Num).
np(X:Num:DType) ==>
  pronoun(X,Num,DType).
np(X:Num:DType) ==>
  det(X:Num:DType):
  nhead(Num,X,Slots):
  postmods(np,Slots,State,Num,X,nil,nil).
```

The simplest approach to proper nouns is to assume that they are capitalized in the input string and get converted to terms like `cap(john)` by the tokenizing routines described in Section 5.3.1, "Tokenizing." If we do this, we could write the `propernoun` rule in a simple way as follows

```
propernoun(X:Type,sg) ==> +cap(X).
```

However, this neglects specifying the semantic type and it assumes that the proper noun is singular. It is also not satisfactory always to bind the variable X to the proper noun, because when focalizers are involved, we sometimes need the predicational form X=Noun in logical form, as in

```
Only Mary likes John.
only(like(X,john),X=mary).
```

A more adequate rule for `propernoun` is

```
propernoun(X:Type,Num) ==>
  +Noun: $propern(Noun,Noun0,Num,Type):
  1-(X=Noun0).
```

One can then have a dictionary of proper nouns under `propern`. (This predicate should relate `cap(Noun0)` to `Noun0` in its first two arguments.)

For pronouns, we can use two rules. For definite pronouns (see Section 5.1.5, "Pronouns.") we can use the rule

```
pronoun(X,Num,DType) ==>
  +PNoun: $defpron(PNoun,Pred,X,Num,DType):
  1-Pred.
```

with entries for `defpron` like

```
defpron(he,he(X),X:male,sg,def).
defpron(cap(i),i(X),X:human,sg,pers1).
```

For indefinite pronouns, we use the rule

```
pronoun(X,Num,DType) ==>
  +PNoun: $indefpron(PNoun,Op-LF,Pred,X,Num,DType):
  Op-LF: 1-Pred.
```

Entries for `indefpron` will look like

```
indefpron(everybody,
          P/Q-every(Q,P),person(X),X:human,sg,all).
indefpron(who,P/Q-wh(X,Q&P),person(X),X:human,Num,wh).
```

Note that the lexical predicate `indefpron` includes *two* predications for logical form. This is appropriate because the pronoun is semantically like a determiner plus a noun ("everybody" is like "every person" and "who" is like "which person"). Because of the two semantic items produced by `pronoun`, the sentence

```
Who sees Mary?
```

will get the logical form

```
wh(X,person(X)&see(X,mary)).
```

Now let us turn to the last np rule above, which gets common noun phrases:

```
np(X:Num:DType) ==>
   det(X:Num:DType):
   nhead(Num,X,Slots):
   postmods(np,Slots,State,Num,X,nil,nil).
```

For det, which gets determiners, we can write essentially the same rule as for the smaller grammar on page 328, but we need to show number and determiner type as well, and in some cases, the marker variable.

```
det(X:Num:DType) ==>
   +D: $dt(D,B,F,P,X,Num,DType):
   F/B-P.
```

```
dt(each,B,F,each(B,F),*,sg,all1).
dt(which,B,F,wh(X,B&F),X:*,*,wh).
```

For writing nhead (which gets the head of the noun phrase), we assume the lexical predicates nounf and noun described in Sections 5.3.2, "Inflections" and 5.3.3, "Slot Frames."

```
nhead(Num,X,Slots) ==>
   +Noun: $nounf(Noun,Nsg,Num):
   $noun(Nsg,Pred,X,Slots):
   1-Pred.
```

Now let us look at the noun postmodifiers, as gotten by postmods(np,...), and let us deal first with complements. Fortunately, all the machinery has already been set up with the postmods rule that calls fill. When a noun is derived from a verb (as in "destroy" / "destruction"), the verb's slot frame usually goes over to a slot frame for the noun in a one-to-one fashion, but the noun's slots can have different types of fillers. Verb slots that are filled by noun phrases go over to the pobj(Prep) slot:

The soldiers destroyed the city.
I saw the destruction of the city by the soldiers.
I saw the destruction by the soldiers of the city.

John gave $50 to the fund.
We noted the gift from John of $50 to the fund.

We can write the rules for adjunct(np,...) as follows.

```
adjunct(np,*,*,X) ==> pp(X,r).
adjunct(np,*,*,X) ==> partvp(X).
adjunct(np,*,Num,X) ==> relclause(X,Num).
```

The first of these rules gets prepositional phrases, as in

```
John sees the man with Bill.
the(man(X)&with(bill,X), see(john,X)).
```

Recall (page 350) that a call to pp is of the form pp(X,Op) where we pass in the operator Op that determines the way the prepositional phrase modifies. In the noun adjunct case, the operator is r, for "right-conjoin," which causes the logical form of the prepositional phrase to be right-conjoined to the modificand, as in the preceding example.

The second adjunct rule gets *participial verb phrases* (partvp should be declared a strong nonterminal).

```
partvp(X) ==> vp(ing,active,*,X,nil,nil).
partvp(X) ==> vp(en,passive,*,X,nil,nil).
```

Examples are

```
John noticed the man riding a bicycle.
John saw the bicycle ridden by the man.
```

Finally, we define relative clauses by the rules

```
relclause(X,Num) ==>
  relpron(Topsubj):
  clause(Topsubj,nil,hold(X:Num:wh)).
```

```
relpron(*) ==> +who.
relpron(*) ==> +that.
relpron(*) ==> +which.
relpron(f) ==> +whom.
relpron(f) ==> +nil.
```

Note the analogy between the relclause rule and the s rule, where relpron corresponds to topic. The relpron rules manipulate the Topsubj flag so as to allow the relative pronoun to be the subject (or not) if it is "who", "that", or "which", but to prevent it from being the subject if it is "whom" or is null. We can say

```
This is the man Mary saw.
```

but not

```
This is the man saw Mary.
```

Both relative clauses and participial verb phrases will turn out to be *right*-conjoined in logical form, because of reordering rules that we will discuss below in Section 5.5.3, "Reshaping." Thus we will get logical forms like

```
John likes the woman that Mary knows.
the(woman(X)&know(mary,X), like(john,X))).
```

We have so far neglected *premodifiers* of nouns, other than determiners. Adjectives are of course common premodifiers, and we leave it as an exercise to write rules for handling adjectives. Noun complements can premodify as well as postmodify, as in

I witnessed the soldiers' destruction of the city.

When they premodify, they can appear in possessive form, as in the preceding example, or as simple nouns:

John is a school teacher.

We will discuss the possessive forms in the next section, and will also indicate a method for treating the other forms.

Topics (left-extraposed items) can originate in noun phrases through relative clauses, but they can also be passed into noun phrases, as in

Who did John take a picture of?
Who did John have a suspicion that he'd seen?

This construction is fairly rare. To treat it, the np nonterminal should have topic arguments that can be passed into its call to postmods. (Note that the call to postmods in the above np rule has null topic arguments.) This is left as an exercise for the reader.

5.4.4 Left-Recursive Constructions

In Section 5.2.2, "Modular Logic Grammars" we pointed out the problem with left-recursive constructions such as in the possessive noun phrases:

John saw each boy's teacher.
John saw each boy's brother's teacher.

We indicated that the MLG formalism can handle these constructions with *right*-recursive grammar rules (that are appropriate for direct compilation into Prolog) by use of the *shift* operator %. The reader should review that discussion, on page 326. In this section, we will modify our noun phrase rules in order to handle the above constructions, and we will indicate how to modify the MLG rule compiler so as to treat the shift operator.

Let us modify the np rules given on page 356 as follows

```
np(Feas) =>
  propernoun(X0,Num):
  np2(X0,Num,def,nil,Feas).
np(Feas) ==>
  pronoun(X0,Num,DType):
  np2(X0,Num,DType,nil,Feas).
np(Feas) ==>
  det(DFeas):
  np1(nil,DFeas,Feas).
```

Here the purpose of the (weak) nonterminal np2 is to handle the part of the noun phrase after the head noun, and the purpose of np1 is to handle the part of a common noun phrase after the determiner or after a possessive (that behaves like a determiner). We can write np1 and np2 as follows

```
np1(X0,X1:Num:DType,Feas) ==>
  nhead(Num,X1,Slots):
  $prefill(Slots,X0,Slots1):
  np2(X1,Num,DType,Slots1,Feas).

np2(X0,Num,DType,*,Feas) ==>
  poss:
  (np:X0:Num:DType)%np1(X0,*:*:DType,Feas).
np2(X,Num,DType,Slots,X:Num:DType) ==>
  postmods(np,Slots,State,Num,X,nil,nil).
```

The purpose of prefill (called by np1) is to fill a complement slot of the head noun with an initial possessive noun phrase (if there is one) having marker X0. The nonterminal poss gets a possessive symbol (apostrophe-s or s-apostrophe). We will define prefill and poss below.

Let us look at the workings of this recursive rule system in a rather procedural way. After the head noun has been read (either by one of the first two np rules or by np1), np2 is called. At this time, we can either read a possessive symbol (with poss) and then *shift* back to np1, or we can finish the noun phrase with postmods. Thus, for a series of possessives, the recursion is

```
np -> np1 -> np2 -> np1 -> np2 -> np1 -> ...
```

and the shift operator is used each time np2 calls np1. In more detail, for the noun phrase

```
each boy's brother's teacher
```

the sequence of nonterminals encountered will be

```
      each
np    det


      boy                's
np1   nhead       np2   poss


      brother            's
np1   nhead       np2   poss


  ⌐   teacher
np1   nhead       np2   postmods
```

The rules are thus right-recursive, but the natural syntactic structures for such noun phrases are left-branching. For the sample noun phrase just given, we want a syntactic structure like

```
np
    np
        np
            det
                each(P,Q)
            boy(X)
            poss
        brother(Y,X)
        poss
    teacher(Z,Y)
```

The logical form should be

```
each(boy(X),the(brother(Y,X),the(teacher(Z,Y), Q))).
```

How can we build such syntactic structures while using the right-recursive rules? The idea is to start a *conjecture* of what the final structure of the whole noun phrase will be as soon as we begin np, without *committing* to this conjecture until we actually finish off the noun phrase (in the second np2 rule). But if we choose the first np2 rule, successfully reading a possessive symbol and following the shifted call to np1, then the current conjecture for the structure of the noun phrase becomes a single, initial modifier in the new conjecture. Thus, in the above example, the initial conjecture

```
np
    det
        each(P,Q)
    boy(X)
    poss
    ...
```

becomes the first modifier in the new conjecture:

```
np
   np
      det
         each(P,Q)
      boy(X)
      poss
   ...
```

To handle all this in the compilation of MLG rules to Horn clauses, we can give weak nonterminals still another pair of arguments representing the changing view of the *conjecture* for the syntactic structure of the current (strong) phrase being built. Thus, if a weak nonterminal is of the form

```
nt(X1,...,Xn)
```

then in compiled form we will have a predication

```
nt(X1,...,Xn, Syn0,Syn, Mods1,Mods2, U,V)
```

where (U,V) is the difference list for the word-string, (Mods1,Mods2) is the difference list for the sequence of structures analyzed by nt (as described before in Section 5.2.2, "Modular Logic Grammars"), and (Syn0,Syn) is the new argument pair. The argument Syn0 represents the conjecture for the current tree node as it is *before* encountering nt, and Syn represents the conjecture as it is *after* encountering nt.

Strong nonterminals will get just the same argument configuration as before: one syn structure argument and two string arguments.

In compiling a rule with several nonterminals in its body, the conjecture arguments will be linked across weak nonterminals just as the modifier-list and word-list arguments are — as long as no shifts are involved. To illustrate what happens for a shift, suppose we have a rule

```
a ==> b: c: d: lab%e.
```

where a is the only strong nonterminal. Then the compilation to a Horn clause should give

```
a(Syn, U,Y) <-
   b(syn(a:nil,Mods1),Syn1, Mods1,Mods2, U,V) &
   c(Syn1,Syn2, Mods2,Mods3, V,W) &
   d(Syn2,syn(Lab0,Mods4), Mods3,nil, W,X) &
   e(syn(Lab0,syn(lab,Mods4).Mods5),Syn,
                              Mods5,nil, X,Y).
```

For the nonterminals b, c, d, e, the modifier arguments (third and fourth arguments) and the string arguments (fifth and sixth) are linked a straightforward way, just as before. Note the situation for the structure conjecture arguments. The final structure, Syn, for a appears as the final conjecture argument for e. What happens in between? The initial conjecture syn(a:nil,Mods1) appears as the first argument of b. The conjecture arguments are linked in b, c, and d to a structure `syn(Lab0,Mods4)`, that will just be `syn(a:nil,Mods1)` if no shifts are encountered while processing b, c, and d. The main point to notice is that the new conjecture with which the shifted nonterminal `lab%e` starts out is

```
syn(Lab0,syn(lab,Mods4).Mods5)
```

and here the initial modifier is like the previous conjecture `syn(Lab0,Mods4)`, but with the new node label `lab` indicated in the shift.

To modify the MLG rule compiler so as to handle shifts, let us begin with the `gtrans` rule given on page 332 that handles MLG rules. We can modify it as follows

```
gtrans(A==>B,Clause) <- /&
  mlgtransh(A,Head, Syn0,Syn, Mods1,Mods2, X,Y) &
  mlgtransb(B,Body, Syn0,Syn, Mods1,Mods2, X,Y) &
  simplify(Head<-Body,Clause).
```

We give each of `mlgtransh` and `mlgtransb` an extra argument pair (`Syn0,Syn`) for the structure conjecture. In the definitions of `mlgtransh` and `mlgtransb`, the old arguments are manipulated just as before. One needs just to treat the conjecture arguments (which of course can refer to the other arguments).

We modify the `mlgtransh` rules (page 332) as follows

```
mlgtransh(A,Head, syn(Pred:Arg1,Mods),Syn,
          Mods,nil, X,Y) <-
  cons(Pred.Args,A) &
  strongnt(Pred) &/&
  (Args=Arg1.* &/ | Arg1=nil) &
  append(Args,Syn.X.Y.nil,Args1) &
  cons(Pred.Args1,Head).
mlgtransh(A,Head, Syn0,Syn, Mods1,Mods2, X,Y) <-
  cons(Pred.Args,A) &
  append(Args,Syn0.Syn.Mods1.Mods2.X.Y.nil,Args1) &
  cons(Pred.Args1,Head).
```

The clause for `mlgtransb` that handles a shifted nonterminal of the form `Lab%NT` can be given as follows

```
mlgtransb(Lab%NT,NT1, Syn0,Syn, M,M, X,Y) <- /&
  cons(Pred.Args,NT) &
  Syn0=syn(Lab0,Mods0) &
  ShiftSyn=syn(Lab0,syn(Lab,Mods0).Mods) &
  append(Args,ShiftSyn.Syn.Mods.nil.X.Y.nil,Args1) &
  cons(Pred.Args1,NT1).
```

The modifications for the remainder of the `mlgtransb` rules are straightforward and are left as an exercise.

Let us return to our np rules (above, page 361). We promised a description of poss and prefill.

Let us assume that the tokenizer separates words like boy's into two tokens (atoms), boy and apost_s, and separates boys' into boy and s_apost. Then we can just write poss as

```
poss ==> +apost_s: 1-poss.
poss ==> +s_apost: 1-poss.
```

Now let us consider prefill(Slots,X0,Slots1), which takes the slot list, Slots, of the head noun and tries to fill the initial slot of Slots with X0, with Slots1 as the list of remaining slots. The argument X0 will be nil if the premodifier of the head noun is a simple determiner (obtained by det), but X0 will be the marker of the possessive modifier (which could be complex) if there is one. Thus we can write prefill as follows

```
prefill((Slot:X).Slots,X,Slots).
prefill(Slots,nil,Slots).
```

Consider the result of such filling for a noun phrase like

```
each boy's brother
```

when we have already parsed "each boy's" getting a possessive modifier of the form

```
np
    det
        each(P,Q)
    boy(X)
    poss
    ...
```

so that the marker X0 for this modifier is of the form X:Type. The logical form for "brother" will be of the form brother(Y,Z) and its slot list will be of the form

```
(pobj(of):Z:Type1).nil.
```

Thus the effect of prefill is to unify X with Z (we are talking about brothers of the boys). This then produces the desired pattern of variables in the structure of "each boy's brother":

```
np
    np
        det
            each(P,Q)
        boy(X)
        poss
    brother(Y,X)
```

This is by no means the whole story for noun premodification. Instead of signaling complements, possessives may of course indicate some sense of possession, as in "the boy's cat" or "the boy's plate".

There can be several simple nouns preceding the head noun, which can be bracketed arbitrarily in their modification of each other and of the head noun, forming a *noun compound*, as in "air conditioner department employee". The bracketing tends to be left-embedded, as in

```
(((air conditioner) department) employee),
```

but need not be, as in

```
(((state university) (computer center)) employee).
```

It is left as an exercise to write a small grammar using the shift operator that will build all possible bracketings of a sequence of nouns (without getting into the question of how such modifications will produce logical forms). When one noun compound modifies another, the relationship may just be a slot-filling relationship, as it is with all the modifications in "air conditioner department employee". But the relationship may be a more external relationship — one that is "creative," in the sense of introducing additional predicates in logical form, as in "gold ring", where the "made of" relationship between "ring" and "gold" would not be a complement relationship. A good treatment of noun compounds is not easy; world knowledge is clearly needed. However, in limited domains, one can get by with special lexical entries.

[Note: For further discussion of the syntactic methods described in this section, see (McCord 1982b, 1985a). Additional methods, e.g for handling conjunctions by metarules, are given in McCord (1986).]

5.5 SEMANTIC INTERPRETATION

This chapter on natural language processing began with a section on the nature of the logical form language, LFL. The succeeding sections on *Logic Grammars*, *Words*, and *Syntactic constructions* were basically centered around syntactic analysis. The purpose of the present section is to complete the cycle by defining procedures which produce logical form analyses in LFL, given syntactic analyses.

5.5.1 The Top Level

There are three main data structures dealt with by the semantic interpretation procedures, the first two of which have already been introduced in Section 5.2.2, "Modular Logic Grammars."

- *Syntactic items* are terms of the form syn(Label,Daughters). Here Label is a *node label*, which is of the form Pred:F, where Pred is the principal functor of a strong nonterminal NT and F is either the first argument of NT or nil if NT has no arguments — or Label could be introduced directly by a shift of the form Label%NT1. Daughters is a list consisting of syntactic items and logical terminals.

■ *Semantic items* are terms of the form Op-LF, where Op is a *modification operator* and LF is a logical form. The effect of modification operators in modification of semantic items by other semantic items is determined by the procedure mod described in the next subsection. Logical terminals are special cases of semantic items.

■ *Augmented semantic items* are terms of the form

    sem(Label,Op,LF)

where Label is a node label and Op-LF is a semantic item. In the process of *reshaping* described below, the additional, syntactic information contained in node labels is useful.

The overall idea of semantic interpretation is to take a syntactic item, representing an analysis tree for a sentence, and to produce a logical form representing the meaning of the sentence. In doing this, we manipulate augmented semantic items representing interpretations of subtrees, in the end obtaining a single augmented semantic item for the whole tree. Its logical form component will be the logical form for the sentence (except for some simplification, to be described).

The top-level procedure

    analyze(Sentence,LogicalForm)

can be written as follows

```
analyze(Sent,LF) <-
   s(Syn,Sent,nil) &
   synsem(syn(top:nil,Syn.nil),sem(*,*,LF0).nil,nil) &
   lfsimplify(LF0,LF).
```

Thus, by the call to s, the sentence nonterminal, we get a syntactic analysis tree Syn for the sentence Sent.

A call

    synsem(Syn, Sems1,Sems2)

takes a syntactic item Syn and produces a difference list (Sems1, Sems2) of augmented semantic items representing the semantic structure of Syn. Typically, this list will just have one element, but, as we will see below, daughters of a node can get promoted by the operation of raising to become sisters of the node, and all these sisters will be gathered into the difference list returned by synsem.

In the call to synsem made by analyze, the syntactic item given to synsem is syn(top:nil,Syn.nil), which is just the parse tree Syn with an extra node on top. Thus there is an extra round of interpretation at the top. This is a technical necessity for some of the cases involving focalizers. However, in normal cases, it is not necessary, and we could just have `Syn` in the first argument of the call to `synsem`.

The output of the call to `synsem` is a difference list with a single augmented semantic item `sem(*,*,LF0)` in it. The logical form `LF0` is essentially the desired logical form for the sentence, but it can need a bit of cleaning up, and this is done by `lfsimplify`, which will be described at the end of this subsection.

The definition of `synsem` is as follows.

```
synsem(syn(Label,Mods), Sems2,Sems3) <-
   synsemlist(Mods,Sems) &
   reorder(Sems,Sems1) &
   modlist(Sems1,sem(Label,id,t),
              Sem,Sems2,Sem.Sems3).
```

To interpret a tree node `syn(Label,Mods)`, the first task is to recursively interpret the daughter list `Mods`, and this is done by `synsemlist`.

```
synsemlist(syn(Label,Mods0).Mods,Sems1) <-
   synsem(syn(Label,Mods0),Sems1,Sems2) &
   synsemlist(Mods,Sems2).
synsemlist((Op-LF).Mods,
        sem(terminal:nil,Op,LF).Sems) <-
   synsemlist(Mods,Sems).
synsemlist(nil,nil).
```

The first rule deals with the case of a daughter that is another `syn` structure by calling `synsem` recursively on this daughter. The second rule deals with a daughter that is a logical terminal `Op-LF`, and simply replaces this by the corresponding augmented semantic item with the special label `terminal:nil`.

Let us return to the definition of `synsem`. After getting the list `Sems` of interpretations of the daughters of the syntax tree node, `synsem` calls `reorder` to get a list `Sems1` that is a permutation of `Sems`. This is a *reshaping* operation, that will be dealt with below in Section 5.5.3, "Reshaping." Modifiers need to be reordered when the surface order does not correspond to intended logical order (scoping).

The last step in `synsem` is to call the procedure `modlist`, whose purpose is to combine the elements of the list `Sems1` with one another, through the processes of *modification* and *raising*. A call

```
modlist(Sems,Sem0,Sem,Sems1,Sems2)
```

takes a list `Sems` of (augmented) semantic items and combines them with (lets them modify) the item `Sem0`, producing an item `Sem` (as the combination), along with a difference list `(Sems1,Sems2)` of items that are promoted to be sisters of `Sem`. The leftmost member of `Sems` acts as the outermost modifier. Thus, in the definition of `synsem`, the result list `Sems1` of reordering acts on the trivial item `sem(Label,id,t)` to form a difference list

```
(Sems2,Sem.Sems3)
```

where the result Sem is right-appended to its sisters. The procedure modlist is defined recursively in a straightforward way:

```
modlist(Sem.Sems, Sem0, Sem2, Sems1,Sems3) <-
    modlist(Sems, Sem0, Sem1, Sems2,Sems3) &
    modify(Sem, Sem1, Sem2, Sems1,Sems2).
modlist(nil, Sem, Sem, Sems,Sems).
```

Here modify takes a single item Sem and lets it operate on Sem1, giving Sem2 and a difference list (Sems1, Sems2) of sister items.

The definition of modify is

```
modify(Sem, Sem1, Sem1, Sem2.Sems,Sems) <-
    raise(Sem,Sem1,Sem2) &/.
modify(sem(*,Op,LF),
        sem(Label,Op1,LF1),
        sem(Label,Op2,LF2), Sems,Sems) <-
    mod(Op-LF, Op1-LF1, Op2-LF2).
```

The call

```
raise(Sem,Sem1,Sem2)
```

raises the item Sem so that it becomes a sister of the item Sem1, and Sem2 is a new version of Sem after the raising, although in most cases, Sem2 equals Sem. Raising occurs for a noun phrase like "a chicken in every pot", where the quantifier "every" has higher scope than the quantifier "a". The semantic item for "every pot" gets promoted by raise to be a left sister of that for "a chicken".

The procedure raise is a reshaping operation, and will be discussed below in Section 5.5.3, "Reshaping."

The second clause for modify calls mod, the basic procedure for modification. A call

```
mod(Sem,Sem1,Sem2)
```

lets a (nonaugmented) semantic item Sem modify an item Sem1 to produce a resulting item Sem2. This procedure is the topic of the next subsection.

Note that the reshaping procedures, reorder and raise, work with augmented semantic items, whereas mod works with ordinary semantic items (not using any syntactic information).

The job of lfsimplify(LF0,LF), which is the last call of analyze above, is to get a simplification LF of the logical form LF0. The need for this arises from the fact that the logical form associated with a proper noun N is of the form X=N. Without simplification, we get the analysis

```
X=john & Y=mary & see(X,Y)
```

for "John sees Mary", whereas the form

```
see(john,mary)
```

in which the equalities have been "executed," is preferable. The problem is to do this selectively, because for the sentence "John sees only Mary", we want the analysis

```
only(see(john,Y), Y=mary).
```

The writing of `lfsimplify` is left as an exercise.

5.5.2 Modification

Modification, as expressed in the procedure mod, is the heart of semantic interpretation. The reshaping procedures (`reorder` and `raise`) get semantic items into position to be combined, but the actual combination is done by mod. Let us begin with a small set of clauses for mod that can handle some nontrivial sentences. We will number them for reference below.

```
mod(Sem,id-P,Sem) <- /.              (1)
mod(id-P,Sem,Sem).                    (2)
mod(l-P,Op-Q,Op-R) <- and(P,Q,R).    (3)
mod(r-P,Op-Q,Op-R) <- and(Q,P,R).    (4)
mod(P/Q-R,Op-Q,@P-R).                 (5)
mod(@P-Q,Op-P,Op-Q).                  (6)
mod(subst(P)-t,Op-P,l-t).             (7)
```

The first two rules say that a semantic item of the form `id-P` acts like an identity element for the operation of modification. Note that `synsem` (in the preceding subsection) requires all the daughters of a node (after being interpreted and reordered) to modify a trivial item `sem(label,id,t)`. In doing this, the first call to mod made by `modlist` will use rule (1) for mod.

Rules (3) and (4) deal with the operations *left-conjoin* (1) and *right-conjoin* (r). The left-conjoin operator is very common and has appeared several times in the grammar built up in the preceding section. To make t ("true") act like an identity for conjunction, we let mod call and, defined by

```
and(t,P,P) <- /.
and(P,t,P) <- /.
and(P,Q,P&Q).
```

Rules (5) and (6) are relevant for determiners, since most determiners have the operator P/Q in their logical terminals. Note that the use of P/Q *creates* the operator @P in the result of the modification. The operator @P appears "on its own" in adverbial prepositional phrases.

The operator `subst(P)` ("substitute for P") appeared above in verb phrase complements.

Let us take the simple sentence

```
Each man sees Mary.
```

and trace the process of modification for it. We will actually show augmented semantic items, displaying `sem(Pred:*,Op,LF)` in the form

```
Pred Op LF
```

and we will indicate which `mod` rules are used in combining them. Note that `mod` is called through `modify`, which works with augmented semantic items and can call `raise`. However, `raise` does not apply in the current example.

The syntactic analysis tree produced for the sentence is

```
s
    np
        det
            P/Q-each(Q,P)
        1-man(X)
    1-see(X,Y)
    np
        1-(Y=mary)
```

In doing the noun phrase "each man", `synsem` calls `synsemlist` and gets the following list of augmented semantic items as interpretations of the two daughters of the node

```
det P/Q each(Q,P)
terminal 1 man(X)
```

Reordering has no effect on this list. Then `modlist` is called, to let these two items modify the item

```
np id t.
```

The "man" item modifies this by rule (1) for `mod`, giving

```
np 1 man(X).
```

Then the "each" item modifies this by rule (5), giving

```
np @P each(man(X),P).
```

For the noun phrase "Mary", rule (1) is again used, and the result is

```
np 1 Y=mary.
```

For the s node, `synsem` thus gets the list of interpretations:

```
np @P each(man(X),P)
terminal 1 see(X,Y)
np 1 Y=mary
```

In this case, reordering does have an effect, moving the terminal node to the end:

```
np @P each(man(X),P)
np 1 Y=mary
terminal 1 see(X,Y)
```

Then modlist requires these three items to modify the trivial item for the s node:

```
s id t.
```

Below are the results in succession, along with the mod rule that produces the result.

```
s 1 see(X,Y)                        (Rule 1)
s 1 Y=mary&see(X,Y)                 (Rule 3)
s 1 each(man(X),Y=mary&see(X,Y))   (Rule 6)
```

Recall that analyze actually interprets a tree with an extra node (labeled top:nil) at the top. This causes an extra use of mod in which the result just obtained modifies the trivial item sem(top:nil,id,t). (For this sentence, this makes no difference in the final outcome.) Rule (1) applies, giving

```
top 1 each(man(X),Y=mary&see(X,Y)).
```

Finally, lfsimplify takes the logical form component of this and produces the result:

```
each(man(X),see(X,mary)).
```

The operators dealt with so far in the mod rules are not sufficient for handling adverbial focalizers (like "only" and "often"). As indicated in Section 5.4.1, "Verb Phrases, Complements, and Adjuncts," the logical terminal for an adverb like "only" will be

```
(B<F) - only(B,F).
```

The idea of the operator B<F is roughly that the base B of "only" lies to the left of "only" and the focus F lies to the right. We will look at an example to see how this operator can be handled by suitable mod rules. We will introduce the new mod rules as we go. Let us take the sentence

```
John sees only Mary.
```

The syntactic structure is

```
s
    np
        1-(X=john)
    1-see(X,Y)
    avp
        (B<F)-only(B,F)
    np
        1-(Y=mary)
```

For the s node, `synsem` gets the following list of augmented semantic items as interpretations of the daughter list.

```
np 1 X=john
terminal 1 see(X,Y)
avp B<F only(B,F)
np 1 Y=mary
```

In this example, reshaping does not change the order at all. (In general, the idea is to get the adverbial focalizer, followed by its focus, to the end of the clause; but for this sentence this is already the case.)

Thus, `modlist` will require this list of items to modify the trivial item

```
s id t.
```

Again, no raising will apply, so it is a question of using `mod` successively.

The first step is to modify the trivial s item by the "Mary" item. Rule (1) above for `mod` applies, giving

```
s 1 Y=mary.
```

Next, this item must be modified by the "only" item. We will use the following `mod` rule, introducing a new operator:

```
mod((B<F)-P,Op-F,focal(B,P,Op)-t).
```

From this, we see that the resulting augmented semantic item will be

```
s focal(B,only(B,Y=mary),1) t.
```

In the operator `focal(B,P,Op)` appearing in the new `mod` rule, information has been "saved" — namely, the focalizer's logical form P (with its focus already instantiated), along with its base B (initially uninstantiated) and the operator Op associated with the focus F. This information will be stored in the operator while we build up the base of the focalizer. The base will be built by further modification of the logical form associated with the `focal` operator, which now is just t. Eventually, the logical form for the base will be unified with B.

The next step is to modify our latest result

```
s focal(B,only(B,Y=mary),1) t
```

by

```
terminal 1 see(X,Y).
```

Rule (3) would apply, but we need another `mod` rule that takes precedence over rule (3):

```
mod(Op-P,focal(B,Q,Op1)-P1,focal(B,Q,Op2)-P2) <-
    mod(Op-P,Op1-P1,Op2-P2).
```

(We will later indicate the ordering of the total list of `mod` rules.) For the recursive call to `mod`, rule (3) applies, and our latest result is then

```
s focal(B,only(B,Y=mary),1) see(X,Y).
```

Next, this result must be modified by the "John" item. The same two mod rules as for the preceding step apply, and we get

```
s focal(B,only(B,Y=mary),1) X=john&see(X,Y).
```

(Note that we are building up the base of only in the logical form component.)

What we have obtained so far is the final augmented semantic item for the s node; but recall that analyze adds on the extra top node with label top:nil, so the result for the s node should modify the item

```
top id t.
```

For this, we need another mod rule

```
mod(focal(B,P,Op)-B,Sem1,Sem2) <-
   mod(Op-P,Sem1,Sem2).
```

The main effect of this is to unify the base B of only with

```
X=john&see(X,Y).
```

In the recursive call to mod, rule (1) applies, and our final augmented semantic item is

```
top 1 only(X=john&see(X,Y),Y=mary).
```

The "cleaning up" procedure lfsimplify takes the logical form of this and produces the analysis for the sentence

```
only(see(john,Y),Y=mary).
```

In doing this interpretation, we have introduced three new mod rules. We actually need still other mod rules involving focal, in order to cover other interactions. Here is a more complete list, integrated with the earlier mod rules.

```
mod(focal(B,P,Op)-B,Sem1,Sem2) <- /&
   mod(Op-P,Sem1,Sem2).                              (1)
mod(Sem,id-*,Sem) <- /.                              (2)
mod((B1<F1)-P1,focal(P1,P2,Op)-F1,
               focal(B1,P2,Op)-t) <-/.               (3)
mod(((B:E)<F)-P,@E-F,focal(B,P,1)-t) <-/.            (4)
mod((B<F)-P,Op-F,focal(B,P,Op)-t) <-/.               (5)
mod(@P-Q,focal(B,P,Op)-B,Op-Q) <- /.                 (6)
mod(Op-P,focal(B,Q,Op1)-P1,
         focal(B,Q,Op2)-P2) <- /&
   mod(Op-P,Op1-P1,Op2-P2).                          (7)
mod(id-P,Sem,Sem).                                   (8)
mod(1-P,Op-Q,Op-R) <- and(P,Q,R).                    (9)
mod(r-P,Op-Q,Op-R) <- and(Q,P,R).                    (10)
mod(P/Q-R,Op-Q,@P-R).                                (11)
```

```
mod(@P-Q,Op-P,Op-Q).                                    (12)
mod(subst(P)-t,Op-P,1-t).                               (13)
```

The `focal` rules not yet illustrated are (3), (4), and (6). Rule (6) comes up for the sentence

```
Each man sees only Mary.
```

The list of augmented semantic items resulting from interpretation of the daughters of the s node will be

```
np @P each(man(X),P)
terminal 1 see(X,Y)
avp B<F only(B,F)
np 1 Y=mary
```

Again, reshaping does not change the order of items. When the last three items have modified the trivial s item, the result will be (just as in the case of the previous sentence)

```
s focal(B,only(B,Y=mary),1) see(X,Y).
```

This must then be modified by the "each" item, and rule (6) applies, giving

```
s 1 each(man(X),only(see(X,Y),Y=mary)).
```

Thus the final logical form is

```
each(man(X),only(see(X,Y),Y=mary)).
```

Rule (4) is needed when the focus of an adverbial focalizer is a quantified phrase, as in

```
John sees only some men.
```

The list of interpreted daughters of the s node is

```
np 1 X=john
terminal 1 see(X,Y)
avp B<F only(B,F)
np @Q some(man(Y),Q)
```

The "only" item will modify the item

```
s @Q some(man(Y),Q).
```

For this, rule (4) will apply, giving

```
s focal(B,only(B:E,some(man(Y),E)),1) t
```

Then we proceed just as in the case of "John sees only Mary" illustrated above, and we get the logical form

```
only(see(john,Y):E, some(man(Y,E)).
```

Rule (3) is applicable when there are two adverb focalizers in the same sentence, and we leave it as an exercise to trace the working of such an example.

The focalizers `yesno(B,F)` and `dcl(B,F)`, produced by the `topic` rule on page 353, have an operator of the form B<<F in their logical terminals. These focalizers behave slightly differently from the adverb focalizers (with the operator B<F). It is left as an exercise for the reader to investigate what the differences should be and to capture them in `mod` rules. (Alternatively, the reader can write the grammar so that `dcl` is omitted and `yesno` is treated more simply as a one-place predicate that has widest scope.) A hint in dealing with B<<F is that the rule analogous to rule (5) above is

```
mod((B<<F)-P,Op-F1,focal(B,F,P,Op,F1)-t) <- /.
```

Thus, instead of unifying F and F1, we save them both in the new `focal` operator. This is necessary for dealing with the rule analogous to rule (6) above, which will be used in getting the analysis

```
Does each man love Mary?
yesno(each(man(X),E), love(X,mary):E).
```

(We assume here that the base (topic) of the `yesno` focalizer is "each man".)

5.5.3 Reshaping

Reshaping handles scoping of modifiers by moving their semantic items into positions suitable for the straightforward process of modification to take place. There are two kinds of movement in reshaping.

- *Raising* promotes daughters of a node to be left sisters of the node. This is handled by the procedure `raise`, called by `modify` (see page 369).

- *Reordering* rearranges modifiers within a given level, and is handled by `reorder`, called by `synsem`, page 368.

Let us look first at a case where raising is needed, and then see how we can handle it.

First consider the sentence

```
John knows the teacher of each boy.
```

We want the logical form

```
each(boy(Z),the(teacher(Y,Z),know(john,Y)))
```

so the "each boy" item must be raised to be a left sister of the "the teacher" item.

The syntactic structure is

```
s
   np
       1-(X=john)
       1-know(X,Y)
   np
       det
           (P<Q)-the(Q,P)
       1-teacher(Y,Z)
       np
           det
               (R<S)-each(S,R)
           1-boy(Z)
```

Let us look at what synsem does in getting the interpretation of the np node for "the teacher of each boy". There are three daughters, and there are no surprises in what synsemlist produces for their interpretations:

```
det P<Q the(Q,P)
terminal 1 teacher(Y,Z)
np @R each(boy(Z),R)
```

Reordering (as we will see below) rearranges this list into the list

```
det P<Q the(Q,P)
np @R each(boy(Z),R)
terminal 1 teacher(Y,Z)
```

Now it is time for synsem (see the definition on page 368) to call modlist on this list of daughters, so that they can modify (using the procedure modify) the trivial np item. In this process, modify can call raise or mod, and will choose raise if it can apply.

When we try to modify the trivial np item by the "teacher" item, raise will not apply, and we just get a result

```
np 1 teacher(Y,Z)
```

toward the interpretation of our np node.

Next, we want to modify this item by the "each boy" item, and modify will call raise:

```
raise(sem(np:*,@R,each(boy(Z),R)),
      sem(np:*,1,teacher(Y,Z)),
      Sem2).
```

Here we have not shown the full labels for the augmented semantic items appearing in the first two (input) arguments for raise, because the rules we will give for raise below do not use them. As we will see, raise does succeed in this call (we raise the "each boy" item above the "teacher" item). The output argument Sem2 is to represent the form of the raised item, which sometimes could be changed by the raising, but in this case, Sem2 will just be bound to the first argument of `raise`. Note that `modify` (page 369) puts the raised item into the difference list of left sisters of our `np` node, and the current interpretation of the node itself still stands at

    np 1 teacher(Y,Z).

Next, this item needs to be modified by

    det P<Q the(Q,P).

Raising will not apply, and we use `mod` (rule 11, page 374), getting the interpretation

    np @P the(teacher(Y,Z),P)

for the `np` node we have been looking at.

Now let us pop up to the list of interpretations for the daughters of the `s` node. Because of the results just obtained for the object `np` node, this list will be

    np 1 X=john
    terminal 1 know(X,Y)
    np @R each(boy(Z),R)
    np @P the(teacher(Y,Z),P)

Reordering converts this to the list

    np 1 X=john
    np @R each(boy(Z),R)
    np @P the(teacher(Y,Z),P)
    terminal 1 know(X,Y)

In modifying the trivial `s` item by these items, no raising occurs. The use of `mod` is straightforward, and we get the desired logical form

    each(boy(Z),the(teacher(Y,Z),know(john,Y)))

for the sentence.

To handle the above sort of raising, we can use the following rules

    raise(Sem,Sem1,Sem) <-
        label(Sem,L) & label(Sem1,L1) &
        (L=np & (L1=np | L1=pp) |
        ¬L=terminal & L1=verbph).

    label(sem(L:*,*,*),L).

Thus, raising can depend just on the phrasal categories of the two items in question. In particular, these rules will raise any `np` modifier of an `np`. It should be noted, however, that these rules are only approximate. In a sentence like "John handles every application for a new account", raising should not occur. In writing the rules for `raise`, we are free to look at any parts of the augmented semantic items that are given as input. In particular, looking at more of the labels could help. (This is done for `reorder` below.) It is left as an exercise to write `raise` rules making finer distinctions.

Let us look at another example of raising, one in which the raised item changes form.

```
John knows each boy's teacher.
```

The syntactic structure is

```
s
    np
        1-(X=john)
    1-know(X,Y)
    np
        np
            det
                (R<S)-each(S,R)
            1-boy(Z)
            1-poss
        1-teacher(Y,Z)
```

First let us look at the interpretation of the np node for the possessive noun phrase "each boy's". The list of items representing daughters is

```
det R<S each(S,R)
terminal 1 boy(Z)
terminal 1 poss
```

Reordering has no effect. So the first step is to modify the trivial np item by the `poss` item. Here we want raising to occur, and we call upon a special `raise` rule that changes the form of the `poss` item:

```
raise(sem(Label,1,poss),
      sem(np:*,*,*),
      sem(Label,P/Q,the(Q,P))).
```

Thus we will get an item

```
terminal P/Q the(Q,P)
```

as a left sister of our possessive np node. The other two items remaining combine (through mod) to form the item

```
np @R each(boy(Z),R)
```

Thus the list of items obtained for the higher np node (for "each boy's teacher") will be

```
terminal P/Q the(Q,P)
np @R each(boy(Z),R)
terminal 1 teacher(Y,Z)
```

Reordering rearranges this as

```
np @R each(boy(Z),R)
terminal P/Q the(Q,P)
terminal 1 teacher(Y,Z)
```

Note that this is rather similar to the list of daughter items for the np "the teacher of each boy", discussed above. The items for "the" and "teacher" will be combined with mod to form the item

```
np @P the(teacher(Y,Z),P).
```

As before, the "each" item will get promoted by raise, so that the list of daughter interpretations for the s node will be

```
np 1 X=john
terminal 1 know(X,Y)
np @R each(boy(Z),R)
np @P the(teacher(Y,Z),P)
```

This is exactly the same situation as for the preceding example, so we will get the same final result:

```
each(boy(Z),the(teacher(Y,Z),know(john,Y))).
```

Now let us turn to reordering. The examples of reordering that we have seen so far have involved only the movement of terminal items to the end of the modifier list (although this was not done in all of the examples). Let us examine the need for more "serious" reordering.

We will look first at reordering of interpreted modifiers, such as quantified noun phrases under a clausal node, independently of the problem of adverbial focalizers. Things would be simplest if the scoping of such modifiers respected left-to-right order, with the leftmost modifier having the widest scope. This is the convention in mathematical English, and it is generally the case that greater clarity is obtained when sentences are constructed so that intended scoping follows left-to-right order.

However, this convention is not always followed, even in standard written English. Left-to-right order has an influence on the interpretation of scoping, but the particular modifiers and the other lexical material in their sister modifiers often matter more. For example, a noun phrase beginning with "a certain" always has wide scope, as in

All the clients saw a certain representative in sales.

The function of "certain" is just to indicate wide scope.

Noun phrases that are universally quantified (especially with "each" and "any") tend to scope higher than existentially quantified noun phrases (especially those with indefinite article or plural noun phrases without determiner), as in

A company representative has visited each site.
Company representatives have visited every site.

For some pairs of quantifiers, the decision about their relative scoping depends less on their relative positions than on the particular verb and the nouns involved, together with real-world knowledge about what is the most reasonable intent.

The procedure `reorder` is free to look at any of the information in the augmented semantic items it is dealing with, including logical forms or semantic types. In a completely adequate system, it would probably be necessary to look at logical forms and do inference with them. However, a method that works fairly well is to assign *precedence numbers* to augmented semantic items (by a scheme to be described), and then just to sort the modifiers by precedence (where modifiers with higher precedence move to the left). We have seen that certain quantifiers (like "a certain") tend to have wider scope, independently of the other lexical material. For modifiers that get assigned the same precedence, `reorder` will not disturb their original relative order, so for them we can rely on the left-to-right convention.

Let us assume that there is a procedure

```
prec(Sem,N)
```

which associates a precedence number `N` (a nonnegative integer) with any semantic item `Sem`. Then we can write `reorder` as a sorting procedure, as follows. (The definition is independent of the notion of semantic items, and depends only on the existence of the ranking procedure `prec`.)

```
reorder(X.L,R1) <- reorder(L,R) & insert(X,R,R1).
reorder(nil,nil).

insert(X,Y.L,Y.L1) <-
  prec(X,PX) & prec(Y,PY) & gt(PY,PX) &/&
  insert(X,L,L1).
insert(X,L,X.L).
```

Now let us look at a definition of `prec` for augmented semantic items.

```
prec(Sem,N) <- dtype(Sem,DT) & dtprec(DT,N) &/.
prec(Sem,1).
```

We are factoring the definition through a predicate `dtype` which extends the notion of *determiner type* for noun phrases.

```
dtype(sem(np:*:*:DT,*,*), DT) <- /.
dtype(sem(det:*:*:DT,*,*), DT) <- /.
dtype(sem(*,*,t), t) <- /.
dtype(sem(*,*,dcl(*,*)), dcl) <- /.
dtype(sem(*,*,yesno(*,*)), yesno) <- /.
dtype(sem(Cat:*,*,*), Cat).
```

Then we can define `dtprec`, working on these `dtype` categories, by rules like the following.

```
dtprec(t,10).
dtprec(wh,10).
dtprec(ex1,8).
dtprec(dc1,6).
dtprec(yesno,6).
dtprec(def,6).
dtprec(all1,6).
dtprec(all2,4).
dtprec(ex2,4).
dtprec(terminal,2).
```

Here we could assign "each" and "any" the determiner type all1, but assign "all" the type all2. The determiners "a certain" and "a particular" (viewed as units) would be assigned ex1, but "a" would be assigned ex2. Note that terminals have a low precedence, so they tend to move to the end, as we have seen in examples above.

Now let us look at the requirements for reordering made by adverb focalizers (like "only" and "always"). In the example

```
John sees only Mary.
```

given on page 372 to illustrate the operation of mod for such focalizers, the focus of "only" immediately follows it, and the pair focalizer/focus is situated so that no reordering is needed. However, we can also write

```
John only sees Mary.
```

with the same meaning, or underline

```
John only sees Mary.
```

or stress in speech to make this meaning clearer. In such a case, we still want reorder to get the same ordering as before

```
np 1 X=john
terminal 1 see(X,Y)
avp B<F only(B,F)
np 1 Y=mary
```

in order for mod to do its work. For both of the sentences

```
Only John sees Mary.
John only sees Mary.
```

the focus on "only" is "John" and we want reorder to produce

```
terminal 1 see(X,Y)
np 1 Y=mary
avp B<F only(B,F)
np 1 X=john
```

so that the logical form produced by mod will be

```
only(see(X,mary),X=john).
```

The focus can consist of more than a single connected phrase in the sentence, as in

```
John only sees Mary.
```

(This could be an answer to the question "Who sees whom?") For this sentence, `reorder` should produce

```
terminal 1 see(X,Y)
avp B<F only(B,F)
np 1 X=john
np 1 Y=mary
```

and the logical form would then be

```
only(see(X,Y),X=john&Y=mary).
```

There can be more than one adverb focalizer in the sentence. We could have

```
Only John sees only Mary.
```

For this, `reorder` should produce

```
terminal 1 see(X,Y)
avp B1<F1 only(B1,F1)
np 1 Y=mary
avp B2<F2 only(B2,F2)
np 1 X=john
```

and then `mod` will produce

```
only(only(see(X,Y),Y=mary),X=john).
```

The augmentation of `reorder` to handle focus is basically left as an exercise, but with the following discussion and suggestions.

First, there is the question of recognition of foci. If an adverb focalizer immediately precedes a noun phrase, as in

```
Only John sees Mary.
```

then we can assume that its focus is that noun phrase. In certain cases, we can just take the focus to be everything after the adverb (after precedence reordering), as in

```
Crocodiles often seem lethargic.
```

But in general, when a focalizer adverb immediately precedes the verb, the focus can be in many different places. In spoken language, stress is often a good indicator of focus, although things get complicated when more than one focalizer is involved. In written language, underlining or italics are sometimes used as an indicator of focus (as in the examples above), although this is not done very often. Ultimately, one would need to take account of the preceding discourse and world knowledge to determine the focus. However, for the purposes of the exercise let us just assume that focus can be determined in three ways: (1) by explicit use of an underline (2) by taking the following noun phrase if the adverb immediately precedes the noun phrase, and otherwise (3) by just allowing the adverb to participate in precedence reordering and letting the focus be whatever comes out in the operation of modification.

For handling the underlines technically, the following two things can be done: (a) Decide on a representation (such as an underbar following an "underlined" word) and modify the tokenizer so that a special `stress` token is put in the token list. (b) Modify the grammar so that stresses are allowed (say, just for nouns), and, when present, produce a determiner type which is marked as stressed.

In writing the augmented version of `reorder`, it is useful to think of adverb focalizers *capturing* their foci. The focus elements will be positioned after the focalizer, and then the whole group focalizer/focus will be lumped into one data structure (say, into a list), so that the group behaves as a unit (almost like a phrase with the focalizer as head). The focal group moves as a unit during precedence reordering.

The new version of `reorder` can be written with three stages:

```
reorder(Sems1,Sems4) <-
    reorder1(Sems1,Sems2) &
    reorder2(Sems2,Sems3) &
    flatten(Sems3,Sems4).
```

Here `reorder1` is like the previous version of `reorder` (doing precedence reordering), but it also allows focalizer adverbs that immediately precede noun phrases to capture those noun phrases. The second step, `reorder2`, sees to the capturing of stressed foci by focalizers. The simplest way to do this is see to it that stressed items are moved all the way to the right by precedence reordering (they can be given precedence number 0), and then the rightmost focalizer that did not capture anything in step 1 can capture them. The third step, `flatten`, unbundles the focalizer/focus groups, so that `Sems4` is simply a list of augmented semantic items.

5.5.4 A One-Pass Approach

The MLG system for syntax and semantics, as we have described it so far, is a two-pass system. Given a sentence, the first pass uses the syntactic component and produces a syntactic analysis tree for the sentence. The second pass takes this tree and uses the semantic interpretation procedures to produce a logical form analysis. It is interesting that MLG analysis can also be done with a one-pass system. In this subsection, this alternative method will be described very briefly.

In the one-pass version of an MLG system, the very same syntactic component can be used as in the two-pass version. Also, the semantic component is essentially the same as the one that has been described in the current section. All of the same issues of scoping are dealt with. The difference is that the rule compiler is altered so that the structures built during parsing are logical forms (actually, augmented semantic items) instead of syntactic analysis trees. Calls to the semantic component are automatically compiled in, so that the construction of logical forms is interleaved with parsing. The system is still modular, because the same (modular) syntactic component and semantic interpretation component are used.

In more detail, the rule compiler adds a call to semantics at the end of every strong rule. Also, a shift generates a call to semantics. The extra arguments added to nonterminals are used to manipulate augmented semantic items rather than syntactic structures. The calls to semantics are to a single procedure, `semant`, which also works with augmented semantic items.

We can give the definition of `semant` easily, but for doing so, it is best to recall the definition of `synsem` from page 368:

```
synsem(syn(Label,Mods), Sems2,Sems3) <-
    synsemlist(Mods,Sems) &
    reorder(Sems,Sems1) &
    modlist(Sems1,sem(Label,id,t), Sem,Sems2,Sem.Sems3).
```

(The reader should review the context of `synsem` and the nature of the structures it works with.) Basically, `semant` just does what is done in `synsem` in its calls to `reorder` and `modlist`. We define it as follows

```
semant(Label,Sems, Sems2,Sems3) <-
    reorder(Sems,Sems1) &
    modlist(Sems1,sem(Label,id,t), Sem,Sems2,Sem.Sems3).
```

In fact, with this definition, `synsem` can be redefined simply as

```
synsem(syn(Label,Mods), Sems2,Sems3) <-
    synsemlist(Mods,Sems) &
    semant(Label,Sems, Sems2,Sems3).
```

Thus, `semant` is like `synsem`, but without the call to `synsemlist`, which goes down in the syntax tree, recursively interpreting nodes. With the one-pass system, we do not have to go down because results are passed up at every level through the interleaved calls to `semant`.

Note that the one-pass system and the two-pass system share most of the semantic interpretation component, since `synsem`, the top level of semantic interpretation for the two-pass system, is defined in terms of `synsemlist` (which is short) and `semant`, which is the top level of semantic interpretation for the one-pass system.

In rough detail, the rule compiler for the one-pass system adds structure-building arguments to nonterminals in the following way. For strong nonterminals, *two* such arguments are added (instead of one in the two-pass system), representing the difference list of augmented semantic items for the interpretation of the phrase being built. (Recall that a *list* of items is needed because of raising.) For weak nonterminals, four arguments are added. One pair represents the difference list of augmented semantic items analyzing the phrase spanned by the nonterminal. The other pair represents the changing conjecture for the interpreted daughter list for the next higher strong nonterminal.

As for efficiency, there does not seem to be a significant difference between the one-pass system and the two-pass system. In the one-pass system, interpretations are built up "on the fly" during parsing, but when there is a lot of backtracking, useless work is done.

Advantages of the two-pass system, which motivated the emphasis on it in this chapter, are the following. (1) The two-pass rule compiler is slightly simpler, and can be understood independently of semantic interpretation. (2) Syntactic structures are useful to have in understanding the workings of the grammar and in debugging it. (3) They are also useful in some applications.

A possible advantage of the one-pass system would be to exercise semantic constraints during parsing by working with the partial logical forms built up by `semant`. Although type-checking is probably adequate for applications with limited or specialized vocabularies, it is probably not adequate in general. It might be appropriate to employ some sort of combination of semantic type-checking with more powerful constraints involving inference with logical forms. Of course it would also be possible to exercise such constraints with the logical forms produced by the two-pass system, with backtracking into the parse when logical analyses are blocked.

[Note: The methods of semantic interpretation of this section are also discussed in (McCord 1985a). They have evolved from previous work in (McCord 1982a, 1981, 1984).]

5.6 APPLICATION TO QUESTION ANSWERING

In this section we illustrate the techniques of this chapter in a question answering system for databases. The database used in the illustration deals with university records involving courses, classes, students, faculty, departments, etc. The database can be viewed as a relational database, because its entries are just unit clauses in Prolog, although there are ancillary predicates for the domain, defined by conditional clauses.

The scheme is to take an English question about the database, get its logical form by use of the MLG syntax/semantics system described in the preceding sections, and then use the logical form to answer the question. The logical form will be an LFL expression whose predicates are senses of words that are natural for the database domain, like *taking* a course, *getting* a grade, being a *major* in a certain *subject*, being a *member* of a *department*, etc. It is possible to give Prolog definitions of all these predicates (in terms of the basic database predicates), so that the LFL analysis of a question is directly executable for getting an answer. However, it is more efficient to take an extra analysis step in which the original LFL form is translated into a form whose predicates are closer to those of the database. This translated analysis will then be executed to answer the question.

5.6.1 A Sample Database

The basic relations in our sample university database are as follows.

```
dept(Subject,Name,Chairman)
fac(Faculty_Member,Name,Subject,Rank)
stdnt(Student,Name,Year,Major)
crs(Course,Subject,Number,Credits)
cls(Class,Course,Instructor,Season,Yr,Days,Hr,Bldg,Rm)
enrl(Student,Class,Grade)
grade(Grade,Numeric_Value)
bldg(Building,Name)
season(Season)
days(Days)
```

The meanings of these relations should be clear from the identifiers used. All of the relations are keyed solely by their first arguments, except enrl ("enrolled"), that is keyed by its first two arguments. The keys are atomic symbols; for example, students' ID numbers can be used for students. The arguments called Name are full names, represented as lists of atoms. There could of course be duplications of names.

Sample entries for all the relations are the following unit clauses.

```
dept(cs,computer.science.nil,f301).
fac(f301,charles.a.coleman.nil,cs,prof).
stdnt(s19206,bill.w.baker.nil,4,cs).
crs(cs420,cs,420,3).
cls(c20581,cs420,f301,spring,1985,mwf,11,wh,214).
enrl(s19206,c20581,b).
grade(b,3).
bldg(wh,whitney.hall.nil).
season(spring).
days(mwf).
```

From these, the following are sample sentences that we want to be parsable by the grammar, with logical forms that are true.

```
Bill W. Baker took Computer Science 420
    from Charles A. Coleman in Spring 1985.
Coleman is chairman of the
    Computer Science Department.
Coleman taught CS 420 in Whitney Hall in Spring 1985.
Baker was given a B by Coleman
    in Computer Science 420.
Baker is a computer science major.
```

A great amount of control of parsing can be exercised by use of semantic types, as described in Section 5.3.4, "Semantic Types," and it is easy to set them up in a domain as limited as the present one. It is convenient to make the type hierarchy rather flat and specific, as follows.

```
entity <=> prsn | dept | sbj | crs |
           time | session | year | days | hour |
           place | bldg.
prsn   <=> stdnt | fac.
```

Thus, the type expression for a student will be

```
entity(prsn(stdnt)).
```

Since there is no cross-classification of entities, it is convenient just to omit the use of `entity(*)` in types, so that we will write the student type simply as

```
prsn(stdnt).
```

In the database, we distinguish between *classes*, given by the relation `cls`, and *courses*, given by the relation `crs`. *Classes* are events that occupy a certain location in space-time, and *courses* are more abstract entities, which can be instantiated as classes at various space-time locations. In English questions about the database, there is not a very clear distinction between classes and courses, as in

```
Which courses did Baker get an A in?
Which classes did Baker get an A in?
```

In fact, we normally can refer to a specific class only by naming a certain course (like Computer Science 420), tied down uniquely by a time, place, or perhaps instructor. Because of this, we use the same semantic type `crs` for both courses and classes.

The space-time location of a class is given by the last six arguments of the `cls` relation. It is convenient to group these six specifications into a single data structure, a `con` (context), of the form

```
con(time(session(Season,Year),Days,Hour),
    place(Building,Room)).
```

We define an auxiliary relation

```
cls1(Class,Course,Instructor,Context)
```

by the rule

```
cls1(Class,Course,Instructor,
    con(time(session(Season,Yr),Days,Hr),
        place(Bldg,Rm))) <-
  cls(Class,Course,Instructor,
      Season,Yr,Days,Hr,Bldg,Rm).
```

5.6.2 Setting up the Lexicon

Now that we have discussed the basic entities and basic relations of the domain, let us turn to the vocabulary and construction of the lexicon.

Proper noun entries should be created automatically from the database itself, which is the source of them. For each of the relations

```
dept, fac, stdnt, crs, grade, bldg, season, days,
```

there is a key (like cs) in the first argument of each entry which should become a proper noun. In addition, for the relations

```
dept, fac, stdnt, crs, bldg,
```

there are fuller names (like Computer Science) that should become proper nouns. (For course names, like Computer Science 420, one needs to use both crs and dept to create the full name.)

To handle proper nouns that consist of more than one token, we can modify the propernoun rule given on page 357 as follows.

```
propernoun(X:Type,Num) ==>
  +Noun: propern(Noun,Noun0,Num,Type):
  1-(X=Noun0).
```

Here, propern is now a nonterminal, which, given the *initial* element Noun of a compound proper noun, will read the *remaining* elements of the compound. The argument Noun0 will be the unique identifier associated with the compound. Thus, given the stdnt entry in the database:

```
stdnt(s19206,bill.w.baker.nil,4,cs).
```

we should get a proper noun rule

```
propern(bill,s19206,sing,stdnt) ==> +w: +baker.
```

For making s19206 a proper noun, we would want the rule

```
propern(s19206,s19206,sing,stdnt) ==> nil.
```

And if we want "Baker" to refer to student s19206, we could also add the rule

```
propern(baker,s19206,sing,stdnt) ==> nil.
```

Since the creation of these propern rules has to be done for several different types of entities, it is worth having a general procedure to do it. We can define

```
addproper(Noun,ID,Type,List) <-
  maketerminals(List,Terms) &
  gtrans((propern(Noun,ID,sing,Type)==>Terms),Axiom) &
  addax(Axiom).
```

Here `maketerminals` converts a list like `w.baker.nil` into the expression `+w: +baker`. (Writing this is left as an exercise.) Thus, we will want to execute goals like

```
stdnt(ID,FirstName.Rest,*,*) &
addproper(FirstName,ID,stdnt,Rest) &
addproper(ID,ID,stdnt,nil) &
fail.
```

We leave it as an exercise to write all appropriate goals of this type.

If there is a problem of storage space for all of these `propern` clauses because the database is large, then a possibility is to put them in secondary storage and retrieve them as appropriate for the actual words in the user's queries, using the techniques of Section 5.3.5, "Lexical Look-up."

Now let us look at verbs for this domain. The reader should be familiar with the material from the sections above on *Inflections* and *Slot frames*. Consider "take", as in

```
Has Baker taken Computer Science 420?
Which mathematics courses
     did Baker take in Spring 1985?
```

For the morphology of "take", we can enter the clause

```
v(take,takes,took,taken,taking).
```

For the sense of "take" just indicated, we can write the `verb` clause

```
verb(take,take1(X,Y),E,X:prsn(stdnt),(obj:Y:crs).nil).
```

We do not need to specify the verb type `E` (but see below, in the treatment of adverbial prepositional phrases). We will deal with the meaning of `take1(X,Y)` in terms of the database when we come to the translation step below.

We can distinguish two senses of "teach", as in

```
Coleman taught CS 420.
teach1(f301,cs420).

Coleman taught Baker in CS 420.
teach2(f301,s19206,cs420).
```

(We ignore tense here.) For these, we can use the two `verb` entries

```
verb(teach,teach1(X,Y),E,
     X:prsn(fac),(obj:Y:crs).nil).
verb(teach,teach2(X,Y,Z),E,
     X:prsn(fac),
     (obj:Y:prsn(stdnt)).(pobj(in):Z:crs).nil).
```

[Note: It is debatable whether the `crs` modifier for `teach2` should be considered a complement of `teach2`, but it is convenient to treat it as such.] The slot `pobj(*)` can be declared optional so that we can also have

```
Coleman taught Baker.
teach2(f301,s19206,*).
```

We leave it as an exercise to write the `v` and `verb` entries for the verbs underlined in the following sample sentences. All of the modifiers given should be taken as complements, except for the postmodifier of "met".

```
Coleman had Baker in CS 420.  (have1)
Baker had Coleman for CS 420.  (have2)
Baker made a B in CS 420.  (make1)
Baker got a B from Coleman in CS 420.  (get1)
Coleman gave Baker a B in CS 420.  (give1)
CS 420 met in Whitney Hall.  (meet1)
Baker majored in computer science.  (major1)
Baker is a CS major.  (be1)
Baker was given a B by Coleman.  (be_passive)
Baker has taken CS 420.  (have_perf)
```

Now let us look at the lexicon for common nouns. There are two senses of the noun "major", as in

```
Baker is a computer science major.  (major1)
How many majors in mathematics are there?  (major1)

Baker's major is computer science.  (major2)
What is the major of Bill W. Baker?  (major2)
```

We can therefore have two `noun` entries

```
noun(major,major1(X,Y),X:prsn(stdnt),
     (pobj(in):Y:sbj).nil).
noun(major,major2(X,Y),X:sbj,
     (pobj(of):Y:prsn(stdnt)).nil).
```

For morphology, we should also have

```
n(major,majors).
```

Writing of `n` and `noun` entries for the following underlined nouns is left as an exercise. The number of arguments of each noun is given in parentheses.

```
Coleman is in the CS department. (2)
Coleman is chairman of the CS department. (2)
Coleman is a professor of computer science. (2)
Coleman was the instructor of Baker in CS 420. (3)
Coleman is a member of the CS department. (2)
What is Coleman's rank? (2)
Baker took a course in CS. (2)
Baker is a student in computer science. (2)
Baker is an undergraduate. (1)
Smith is a graduate. (1)
What was Baker's grade in CS 420? (3)
In which semesters was CS 420 taught? (1)
In which building did CS 420 meet
      in Spring 1985? (1)
In which room did CS 420 meet in Spring 1985? (1)
```

We can view most adjectives for this domain as one-place predicates that modify nouns by right-conjoining. Thus we would get the analysis

```
Baker took a graduate course in computer science.
ex(course1(X,cs)&graduate1(X), take1(s19206,X)).
```

```
How many graduate students in mathematics
      did Coleman have in CS 420?
howmany(X, student1(X,ma) & graduate2(X) &
      have1(s301,X,cs420)).
```

It was left as an exercise in Section 5.4.3, "Noun Phrases" to modify the noun phrase rules so as to handle adjective premodifiers. Using whatever format for adjective entries was set up in that exercise, the reader should write entries for the two senses of "graduate" just indicated, for corresponding senses of "undergraduate", and the adjectives in

```
assistant professor,
associate professor,
full professor.
```

On page 350, the rule for prepositional phrase modifiers of verbs was given. This rule makes a call to prep like

```
prep(for,for_time(T,P),T:time,P:event).
```

In our application domain, the following prep entries are useful. For each of them a sample sentence, with logical form, is given.

```
prep(in,insession(X,P),X:session,P:event).
Coleman taught CS 420 in Spring 1985.
insession(session(spring,1985), teach1(f301,cs420)).
```

```
prep(on,ondays(X,P),X:days,P:event).
Baker took CS 420 on MWF.
ondays(mwf,take1(s19206,cs420)).
```

```
prep(at,athour(X,P),X:hour,P:event).
Baker took CS 420 at 11.
athour(11,take1(s19206,cs420)).
```

```
prep(in,inbldg(X,P),X:bldg,P:event).
Computer Science 420 met in Whitney Hall.
inbldg(wh,meet1(cs420)).
```

```
prep(in,inplace(X,P),X:place,P:event).
Computer Science 420 met in
    Whitney Hall 214.
inplace(place(wh,214),meet1(cs420)).
```

When there are several pp modifiers, the logical forms just pile up:

```
CS 420 met in Whitney Hall on MWF at 11.
inbldg(wh,ondays(mwf,athour(11,meet1(cs420)))).
```

Although intensional forms for preposition senses are necessary in general because of scoping possibilities (see Section 5.1.8, "Prepositions"), scoping order does not matter in our domain (for the prepositions given above). In fact, in the translations given below, we will unwind these nested forms to conjunctive forms where the prepositions predicate on contexts (con forms).

On page 359, rules were given for postmodification of noun phrases by prepositional phrases. As a sample entry for such a preposition, we have

```
prep(in,indept(X,Y),X:sbj,Y:prsn(fac)).
```

Determiners and pronouns are essentially "general-purpose" words that should not require special treatment in an application domain. On the whole, what has already been said about them is sufficient for our application, although the reader should fill out the vocabulary for these types of words (not trying to deal with definite pronouns). Indefinite pronouns (like "who" and "everybody") that were marked human above should be marked prsn(*). This type can be unified with either prsn(stdnt) or prsn(fac), depending on other lexical items. For instance, in

```
Who took Computer Science 420 in Spring 1985?
```

the "who" item would get type prsn(stdnt).

It is useful to consider some strings like *how many* and *at least N* as multiword determiners. A sample analysis using howmany was given above. An example with *at least 10* is

```
At least 10 Computer Science majors
     took Mathematics 414.
atleast(10, X, major1(X,cs)&take1(X,ma414)).
```

As an exercise, the reader should extend the definition of det (on page 358) so as to cover multiword determiners (compare with the treatment of proper nouns above). Other multiword determiners of interest are *at most N, exactly N, fewer than N, more than N, a certain,* and *a particular.*

Adverbs are not of great importance for this domain. What has been said above about general-purpose adverbs like the adverbs of quantification is sufficient.

5.6.3 Translation to Executable Form

Now let us turn to the problem of getting answers to queries. As indicated at the beginning of this section, it would be possible to give direct definitions of all the predicates appearing in the LFL analyses we have been looking at. However, for this domain it is more efficient to translate the LFL analyses into forms that are closer to the database. It is also satisfactory as a simplifying device to ignore certain features of the LFL analyses, such as tense and presuppositions. For example, we will just convert a form yesno(B,F) (which shows a presupposed topic B and a comment F) into the form yesno(B&F), where yesno(P) simply executes P and writes "yes" or "no" according as P succeeds or not. It is also satisfactory to convert the(B,F) into BF, making the assumption that the user has no false presuppositions about existence and uniqueness of B.

The procedure we will use for translation to the simplified form is

```
qtrans(P,C,Q),
```

which translates form P into form Q, assuming a context C for P (where *contexts* are the space-time con structures discussed above). The definition of qtrans is as follows

```
qtrans(P,C,P) <- var(P) & /.
qtrans(P,C,Q) <- qt(P,C,Q) & /.
qtrans(P:P1,C,t) <- / & qtrans(P,C,P1).
qtrans(P,*,Q) <-
  cons(Pred.Args,P) &
  qtranslist(Args,Args1) &
  cons(Pred.Args1,Q).

qtranslist(P.L,Q.M) <-
    qtrans(P,*,Q) & qtranslist(L,M).
qtranslist(nil,nil).
```

The first clause just says that a variable translates into itself. The second clause defers to the auxiliary translation procedure qt, that is really the heart of translation, and has many specialized clauses that we will get to. The third clause deals with forms involving the indexing operator, as in

```
Did every student take CS 420?
yesno(all(student1(X),E), take1(X,cs420):E),
```

binding E to the translation of take1(X,cs420). The last clause for qtran, together with qtranslist, defines a kind of default translation, where a form is just translated by translating its arguments and keeping the same principal functor.

Now let us look at qt, the heart of translation, first for verbs. A very useful predicate to use in translations of verbs is take0, defined by

```
take0(Stdnt,Crs,Fac,Grade,Context) <-
    enr1(Stdnt,Cls,Grade) &
    cls1(Cls,Crs,Fac,Context).
```

Thus, we can define our vocabulary items take1, teach1 and teach2 by the qt clauses:

```
qt(take1(X,Y),C,take0(X,Y,*,*,C)).
qt(teach1(X,Y),C,cls1(*,Y,X,C)).
qt(teach2(X,Y,Z),C,take0(Y,Z,X,*,C)).
```

Then the LFL analysis

```
teach2(f301,s19206,cs420)
```

will translate into

```
take0(s19206,cs420,f301,*,*),
```

which is executable against the database.

The auxiliary verbs be1, be_passive, and have_perf can (in this domain) get trivial translations:

```
qt(be1(X,X),C,t).
qt(be_passive(X,P),C,Q) <- qtrans(P,C,Q).
qt(have_perf(X,P),C,Q) <- qtrans(P,C,Q).
```

Thus, we will get the analyses

```
Coleman has taught Baker in CS 420.
have_perf(f310,teach2(f301,s19206,cs420)).
take0(s19206,cs420,f301,*,*),
```

Writing the definitions of the other verb translations is left as an exercise.
Sample noun definitions are

```
qt(major1(X,Y),C,stdnt(X,*,*,Y)).
qt(major2(X,Y),C,stdnt(Y,*,*,X)).
qt(course1(X,Y),C,crs(X,Y,*,*)).
qt(professor1(X,Y),C,fac(X,*,Y,*)).
```

The noun predicate `graduate2` can just translate into itself (by the default `qtrans` rule), and can be defined for execution by

```
graduate2(X) <- stdnt(X,*,Year,*) & gt(Year,4).
```

It is left as an exercise to define the translations of the other nouns in the vocabulary, and the adjectives.

The translation of prepositions, involving contexts, is interesting. Given the analysis

```
Coleman taught CS 420 in Spring 1985.
insession(session(spring,1985), teach1(f301,cs420))
```

we want to get the translation

```
cls1(*,cs420,f301,C) &
    session1(C,session(spring,1985)).
```

Here, `session1` is a selector procedure for contexts, defined by

```
session1(con(time(S,*,*),*),S).
```

To accomplish this translation, we can write a general `qt` rule

```
qt(PP,C,Q1) <-
   pform(PP,P,C,PP1) &/&
   qtrans(P,C,Q) &
   appand(Q,PP1,Q1).
```

where `pform` is defined for various prepositions by clauses like

```
pform(insession(X,P),P,C,session1(C,X)).
pform(ondays(X,P),P,C,days1(C,X)).
pform(athour(X,P),P,C,hour1(C,X)).
pform(inbldg(X,P),P,C,bldg1(C,X)).
pform(inplace(X,P),P,C,place1(C,X)).
pform(attime(X,P),P,C,time1(C,X)).
```

The procedure `appand` is defined by

```
appand(t,P,P) <- /.
appand(P&Q,R,P&S) <- /& appand(Q,R,S).
appand(P,Q,P&Q).
```

(Given the goal `appand(p&q&r,s,T)`, the result `T=p&q&r&s` is obtained.)

Thus, the preposition senses are reduced to right-conjoined applications of selector predicates (`session1`, `days1`, `hour1`, `bldg1`, `place1` and `time1`) for contexts (which the reader can supply). For the analysis

```
CS 420 met in Whitney Hall on MWF at 11.
inbldg(wh,ondays(mwf,athour(11,meet1(cs420)))).
```

we get the translation

```
cls1(*,cs420,*,C) & hour1(C,11) &
    days1(C,mwf) & bldg1(C,wh).
```

Note that this can actually be even closer to the database by

```
cls(*,cs420,*,*,*,mwf,11,wh,*).
```

The reader may want to investigate such optimization. However, it is important to use the data structures in contexts in some cases. For example, for a query like "Where have CS courses met?", we want a final analysis that picks out places, which are data structures involving both buildings and room numbers.

For translations of determiners, we can use the qt rules

```
qt(ex(P,Q),*,P1&Q1) <-
    qtrans(P,*,P1) & qtrans(Q,*,Q1).
qt(the(P,Q),*,P1&Q1) <-
    qtrans(P,*,P1) & qtrans(Q,*,Q1).
qt(no(P,Q),*,¬(P1&Q1)) <-
    qtrans(P,*,P1) & qtrans(Q,*,Q1).
```

For other determiner senses, like atleast(N,X,P) and wh(X,P) (for "which"), we can use the default qtrans rule. (They translate into themselves after translating their arguments).

The following clauses provide definitions of some of these determiners for query answering.

```
all(P,Q) <- ¬(P&¬Q).
wh(X,P) <- set_of(X,P,L) & writelist(L).
howmany(X,P) <- num(X,P,N) & write(N).
num(X,P,N) <- set_of(X,P,L) & length(L,N).
atleast(N,X,P) <- num(X,P,M) & ge(M,N).
```

As an example of a query with "which", consider

```
Which undergraduate CS majors took CS 420
    in Spring 1985?
```

The LFL analysis will be

```
wh(X,(major1(X,cs) & undergraduate2(X)) &
    insession(session(spring,1985),take1(X,cs420))).
```

The executable translation of this will be

```
wh(X,(stdnt(X,*,*,cs) & undergraduate2(X)) &
    take0(X,cs420,*,*,C) &
    session1(C,session(spring,1985))).
```

For yes-no questions, we can translate the two-place `yesno` form by the `qt` rule

```
qt(yesno(P,Q),*,yesno(P1&Q1)) <-
    qtrans(P,*,P1) & qtrans(Q,*,Q1).
```

and we can define the one-place `yesno` by

```
yesno(P) <- P & / & write("Yes").
yesno(P) <- write("No").
```

5.6.4 A Driver for Question Answering

Finally, let us look at the top-level procedures for receiving a user's queries, analyzing them, and getting answers. For the benefit of the person developing the system, it is useful to have some feedback on partial results and failures of the various stages of analysis.

```
go <- rd(Str) & process(Str).

process('quit.') <- / & write("Return to Prolog..").
process('stop.') <- / & stop.
process(Str) <- process1(Str) & go.
```

Here, we assume that `rd(X)` reads a sentence, which may span several lines and ends with a sentence terminator. The characters read are put into the character string X. The next step, with `process1`, is to do tokenizing, as in Section 5.3.1, "Tokenizing":

```
process1(Str) <-
    st_to_li(Str,Chars) &
    words(Words,Chars,nil) & / &
    process2(Words).
process1(*) <-
    write("Word separation failed").
```

Now with `process2` we are ready to do syntactic analysis

```
process2(Words) <-
    s(Syn,Words,nil) & / &
    display(Syn) &
    process3(Syn).
process2(*) <-
    write('Parse failed').
```

Here, `display` displays the syntax tree, as in the exercise given in Section 5.2.2, "Modular Logic Grammars." One could make the display optional, according to the setting of a flag. Now we are ready to do semantic interpretation

```
process3(Syn) <-
   synsem(syn(top:nil,Syn:nil),sem(*,*,LF0):nil,nil) &
   lfsimplify(LF0,LF) &/&
   write('Logical form..') &
   write(LF) &
   process4(LF).
process3(*) <-
   write('Semantic interpretation failed').
```

See the Section on *The top level* of semantic interpretation for the meaning of
synsem and lfsimplify. Next we do query translation, as in the previous
subsection

```
process4(LF) <-
   qtrans(LF,*,Q) &
   lfsimplify(Q,Query) &/&
   write('Query..') &
   write(Query) &
   write('Answer..') &
   Query.
process4(*) <-
   write('Query translation failed').
```

The extra call to lfsimplify is useful because of proper noun equations
X=Noun and occurrences of t ("true") that are unnecessary after query
translation.

Now let us look at the analysis of an example:

```
How many CS majors who took CS 420 in Spring 1985
     made A in CS 520?
```

The syntactic analysis tree is

```
s
   np
      det
          F1/B1-howmany(X,B1&F1)
      1-(Z=cs)
      1-major1(X,Z)
      relclause
          1-take1(X,Y)
          np
             1-(Y=cs420)
          pp
             @P-insession(S,P)
             np
                1-(S=session(spring,1985))
```

```
    1-make1(X,U,V)
np
    1-(U=a)
np
    1-(V=cs520)
```

The LFL analysis is

```
howmany(X,(major1(X,cs) &
            insession(session(spring,1985),
            take1(X,cs420))) &
        make1(X,a,cs520)).
```

Finally, the translated query is

```
howmany(X,(stdnt(X,*,*,cs) &
            take0(X,cs420,*,*,C) &
            session1(C,session(spring,1985))) &
        take0(X,cs520,*,a,*)).
```

As a grand finale exercise, the reader should pull things together in all the components of the system so that the following queries can be handled. Some of the sentences illustrate problems of scoping.

```
Who taught CS 670 in Spring 1985?
Have at least 10 students taken every computer science course?
Did Coleman give A only to graduate students in CS 520?
Has any computer science major taken every computer science course?
What is Mary Jones's CS 520 instructor's rank?
Which graduate students majoring in mathematics has Anderson
    had in an undergraduate computer science course?
How many students that got C from Dalton in CS 670
    have had Dalton for CS 520?
Which CS majors made A only in CS courses?
Which CS majors only made A in CS courses?
In which semesters has CS 670 been taught by Dalton?
Does every CS course meet in a certain building?
Who taught courses that John Smith made B in?
Is there any undergraduate CS course that no assistant professor
    has taught?
Did everybody in every department teach a graduate
    course in Spring 1985?
How many members of the CS department are there?
Are there any undergraduates taking CS 420 in Fall 1985
    who have not taken at least 6 undergraduate CS courses?
In which buildings were CS courses taught in Spring 1985?
Where did CS 670 meet in Spring 1985?
When has Anderson taught courses in Whitney Hall?
```

EXERCISES

The following exercises are keyed closely to the development of the text; a page reference is given in each exercise. The reader who works through the text and the exercises will build up a system capable of analyzing an interesting variety of English sentences and using the analyses in database queries.

1. Write `simplify(Clause1,Clause2)`, as described on page 323.

2. Modify the procedure `dcgtrans` (page 323) so as to handle disjunctions in the right hand sides of DCG rules.

3. Write a tree-printing procedure as specified on page 330.

4. Modify the `mlgtransb` (page 333) so as to handle disjunctions in the righthand sides of DCG rules.

5. Write a procedure `getsentence(S)` that reads lines of text from the terminal, stopping when a line ends with a sentence terminator (".", "?", or "!"), and binds `S` to the concatenation of all the lines read. (See page 333.)

6. Complete the definition of the tokenizer `words`. (See page 334).

7. Look up the treatment of English inflectional morphology in (Winograd 1972) and implement this in Prolog (see discussion on page 336).

8. Write the procedure `typetree(List,TypeTree)`, as described, with hints, on page 341.

9. Write a Prolog procedure that looks at a dictionary file LEXi, as described on page 342, and constructs the binary index tree BTREEi associated with LEXi.

10. Write the procedure `choose(Slot,Slots,Slots1)`, as described on page 347.

11. Write `satisfied(Slots)` (page 349).

12. Write rules for the nonterminal `qualifiers` (page 351).

13. Modify the grammar rules built up so far on page 354 so as to handle agreement in person (as well as number) between subject and finite verb.

14. Modify the noun phrase rules so as to handle adjective premodifiers of nouns (see page 360).

15. Modify the grammar so that extraposition out of noun phrases is handled (page 360).

16. Complete the modification of `mlgtransb` for treatment of the shift operator (page 364).

17. Write a small grammar using the shift operator that produces all possible bracketings of a sequence of nouns (page 366).

18. Write the procedure `lsimplify` as described on page 369.

19. By hand, trace the modification process for a sentence involving two adverb focalizers (page 376).

20. Investigate the improvement of the modification rules for handling focalizers like yesno and dcl (page 376).

21. Improve the rules for raise along the lines indicated on page 379.

22. Improve reorder so as to handle focus (see discussion on page 383).

23. Write maketerminals as described on page 390.

24. Write the goals that create proper noun entries, as indicated on page 390.

25. Write the v and verb clauses for the verbs underlined in the examples on page 391.

26. Write the n and noun clauses for the nouns underlined in the examples on page 391.

27. Write the lexical entries for the adjectives given on page 392.

28. Extend the definition of det so as to cover multiword determiners, as indicated on page 394.

29. Add the necessary qt rules (see page 395) for the remaining verbs in the database vocabulary.

30. Add the necessary qt rules (see page 396) for the remaining nouns and adjectives in the database vocabulary.

31. Grand finale: Pull together all the components of the system so that the queries on page 400 are handled.

6
Conclusions

Adrian Walker

> "The only way to rectify our reasonings is to make them as tangible as those of the mathematicians, so that we can find our error at a glance, and when there are disputes among persons, we can simply say: Let us calculate, without further ado, in order to see who is right."
>
> Gottfried Wilhelm Leibniz, *The Art of Discovery*.

This book is about artificial intelligence, logic, and programming. The methods we have described are based on computational logic, which acts as a bridge between the empirical aspects of knowledge systems and the formal foundations of reasoning in logic. We have looked at the ties between the theory and practice of Prolog in Chapter 1, and in Appendix B we suggest a clear basis for the term "declarative knowledge." Chapters 2 and 3 cover many important programming techniques in Prolog, particularly for artificial intelligence. Chapters 4 and 5 set out some of the uses for these techniques in expert system shells and in natural language processing. Appendix A goes into detail about how to use IBM Prolog in actual sessions at a terminal. In fact, logic programming, in the form of the Prolog language, has made it possible for us to talk in one book about a wide range of subjects, and to do so in the practical sense that we have shown how to program much of what we have discussed. Although this kind of coverage is unusual now, we hope it will be normal in the future, because logic programming naturally tends to bring together (we are tempted to say *unify*) concepts that used to be rather far apart. There are now efficient versions of Prolog that can take their place along with Lisp and the other established programming languages. As pointed out in Chapter 1, early attempts at computing with full classical logic were not efficient. Prolog corresponds to only a part of logic unless we metainterpret to extend its power, in which case we tend to lose some efficiency.

When we ask a question of a Prolog program, the answer is normally either "yes" (perhaps with some bindings of variables) or "nothing found." If the answer is "yes," then Prolog has shown that there is a proof that the answer follows from the program. Prolog is normally used with the convention that "nothing found" means "no." So, provided that the computation started by a question terminates, the answer is bound to be either "yes" or "no."

In full classical logic, a question can result in a proof of a "yes" answer, or in a proof of a "no" answer, or in a terminating computation indicating that the answer is unknown, based on the information given. One can also get a "yes" answer to an *indefinite* question such as "Is it true that Fred is at the office or that Fred is at home," i.e

```
at(fred,office) | at(fred,home).
```

In ordinary Prolog we cannot answer such a question unless we can prove one of the *definite* answers

```
at(fred,office).
at(fred,home).
```

The third case, when Fred is at one of the two but the program does not contain enough information to say which, cannot be handled directly in Prolog, but is quite natural in full logic.

So Prolog alone is normally geared to supplying a definite "yes" or "no" answer to a question where possible, and it can be very efficient when used to do this. The efficiency comes from the fact that if a question matches a rule, it does so in only one place, the head. In full logic, a question can potentially match any literal in a rule, so there is a choice. This choice is compounded with subchoices if a question leads (as it usually does) to subquestions.

In database-like uses of Prolog, definite answers are often quite satisfactory. In other situations, we sometimes need to reason with indefinite items, and one way of doing this is to metainterpret, but to do so just as little as is needed. In this way we can provide what is necessary, without all of the efficiency penalties of computing with full logic. In fact there are many kinds of reasoning that we can explore by writing metainterpreters in Prolog, keeping as close to Prolog as we can for efficiency. For example, for assumption-based reasoning we may wish to write a metainterpreter that assumes that Fred is in the office if it is 10 am on a weekday, *unless* there is a fact that would contradict this, e.g Fred is unwell and he stayed at home.

In general, it's not easy to make useful choices in setting up such reasoning methods unless we can try them out experimentally on a computer. Once a method is set up, it is not always easy to develop a correct theory for it. Here again, experimental programming can help. It can help in formulating a theory, by generating examples from which common features can be extracted, and it can help to find places where a prediction made by the theory is false, indicating that the theory must be revised.

Assumption-based reasoning often seems useful in our daily lives, yet it is elusive when we try to capture all of it as a theory. In this situation, it appears to be a good idea to try a combined empirical and formal approach. We can broaden our subject of study to include the ways in which we use English to do assumption-based and other kinds of reasoning. For example the sentence

    Is the cat that Bill owns Siamese?

contains the presupposition that Bill does own a cat, and a natural language understanding program for this kind of sentence must be able to reason about such presuppositions. When our study is English, rather than a particular reasoning method, it seems even more important to use a combined empirical and formal approach. A Prolog program that translates English sentences into a logical form can be viewed in two ways: empirically and formally. Empirically, we can use the program to translate a sentence into a logical goal, and we can "run" the goal on a knowledge base to get an answer. Formally, the program is a specification of a logical meaning for each of the sentences it can handle. If the program is in pure Prolog, we can in principle study it, together with a knowledge base, using the formal apparatus of mathematical logic. Viewed in this way, the meaning of a Prolog program that translates from English to logic is independent of the fact that it can be run as a Prolog program.

Some of the more ambitious reasoning methods are not efficient as Prolog metainterpreters, but are useful as research tools. However, there are several reasons for supposing that today's research tools will also be directly useful before too long:

- Some metainterpreters can usefully be "compiled down" to Prolog.

- Recent Prolog implementations contain efficient support for metainterpretation.

- Prolog interpreter/compilers are getting faster on conventional machines, and a speed limit does not yet seem to have been reached.

- Parallel machines designed specially for fast execution of Prolog are starting to appear.

Because artificial intelligence is a relatively young subject, there is a considerable amount of heart-searching about how scientific its methods are. There are people working empirically on knowledge systems who feel that attempts at formalization are premature at best—that the subject is inherently empirical and is likely to remain so, perhaps for ever. People who work empirically will often justify their method along the following lines: The human brain appears, after all, to be constructed ad hoc rather than according to some mathematically pleasing design, so why should our knowledge systems be any different? In any case, how can we tell what to formalize until we have lots of practical experience about what is important and what is not?

On the other hand, there are those who point to relatively weak structure in the knowledge system literature. It does not seem to build up formally, to the extent that say physics does, by repeatable experiment and extension of previous work. Reasoning methods were studied in logic long before the first computer. People who work formally tend to argue along the lines: Logic is a product of that ad hoc thing, the human brain, but it is mathematically elegant. Perhaps what we should do is to formalize first, by writing theories of reasoning, then begin to put these theories to the practical test in knowledge systems.

Our point of view in this book is that we are now starting to combine the best of the empirical and formal worlds. Although knowledge bases are typically larger than physical theories, writing knowledge bases in logic simplifies them enough so that we can isolate some succinct theory questions. These questions guide us in the kind of theory we develop. Occasionally, some theory that already exists answers the questions. Sometimes (as with negation as absence of proof versus proof of a negation) empirical information points us toward modification of an existing theory, which then allows us to answer our practical questions. We can summarize the promise of this approach by saying that

The significance of theory + practice

is much greater than

the significance of theory + the significance of practice.

Logic programming, we think, makes it useful to follow this advice in our work in artificial intelligence. We hope that this book is a step in this direction, and that the outcome is knowledge systems that are progressively more useful, reliable, and friendly.

A

How to Use IBM Prolog

Adrian Walker
and Walter G. Wilson

The purpose of this section is to show how to actually run a program in IBM Prolog. IBM Prolog runs under the VM operating system (VM/Prolog), and also under the MVS operating system (MVS/Prolog). The pure core of the language is the same for both operating systems; however the details about how to use it depend on whether one is using VM or MVS. We shall describe in detail how to use VM/Prolog. Then in Section A.9, "MVS/Prolog" we outline some of the main differences in using MVS/Prolog. First we shall show how to run a simple example taken from page 28. Then, since we have emphasized the importance of metainterpreters we shall take one as an example and we shall go through the steps needed to set it up and run it. In doing this, we shall cover:

- getting a program to be metainterpreted from a file,
- setting goals for the metainterpreter from the terminal,
- selective tracing, and
- swapping between VM/Prolog and an editor.

We also discuss in detail how the various parts of the metainterpreter work, and how some of the built-in predicates of VM/Prolog are used.

This section can be used to get a feeling for how VM/Prolog is used. Readers who would like to run the simple example or the metainterpreter on a computer will need the following:

- VM/Prolog installed on an IBM computer using the VM operating system,
- *VM/Programming in Logic*, IBM document SH20-6541, popularly known as "the VM Prolog manual," and
- *System Product Editor User's Guide*, IBM document SC24-5220-2, popularly known as "the Xedit manual."

Readers using MVS/Prolog will need a copy of *MVS/Programming in Logic*, IBM document SH40-0030, popularly known as "the MVS Prolog manual."

We shall show how to use the basic VM/Prolog facilities for swapping between Prolog and the Xedit editor, and for selective tracing. We have found that some people work in the style we shall show, while others prefer to use the same basic facilities to build more sophisticated program development tools, which they then use instead. A word of caution here—since Prolog is different from other languages, the kinds of tools that turn out to be useful are often different too.

A.1 A SIMPLE EXAMPLE

On page 28 we looked at a simple Prolog program about children and their parents, part of which follows.

```
child(antigone,iokaste).    child(antigone,oidipous).
child(eteokles,iokaste).    child(eteokles,oidipous).

male(oidipous).    male(eteokles).
female(iokaste).    female(antigone).

mother(M,C) <- child(C,M) & female(M).
```

Suppose we have used the Xedit editor to type this program into a file called `family prolog`. (The Xedit manual describes how to do this.) For convenience, we shall also place in the file the rule

```
e <- edconsult(family).
```

We can now run the program. To start VM/Prolog, one can either type in "vmprolog new ws mixed" or one can use an exec that defines the details so that it is only necessary to type "vmprolog." What follows is a transcript of a session at the terminal. In the transcript we use three typefaces:

■   What we type in on the keyboard is in this typeface,

■   `What the computer puts on the screen is in this typeface`, and

■   *Some comments that we have added afterwards are in italics.*

vmprolog
Start VM/Prolog
consult(family).
`4MS SUCCESS`
 `<- consult(family) .`
mother(M,C).
`OMS SUCCESS`
 `<- mother(iokaste,antigone) .`

We type in a semicolon to
;   *ask Prolog to backtrack*
OMS SUCCESS
 <- mother(iokaste,eteokles) .
;   *ask Prolog to backtrack*
OMS FAIL
     next we turn on some tracing
trace(mother(*,*)) & trace(child(*,*)) & trace(female(*)).
1MS SUCCESS
 <- trace(mother(V1,V2)) & trace(child(V3,V4)) &
    trace(female(V5)) .
     We ask a question
mother(M,C).
 1 : call ==> mother(V1,V2) .
  2 : call ==> child(V1,V2) .
  2 : exit ==> child(antigone,iokaste) .
  2 : call ==> female(iokaste) .
  2 : exit ==> female(iokaste) .
 1 : exit ==> mother(iokaste,antigone) .
2MS SUCCESS
 <- mother(iokaste,antigone) .
;   *ask Prolog to backtrack*
 1 : redo ==> mother(iokaste,antigone) .
  2 : redo ==> female(iokaste) .
  2 : fail ==> female(iokaste) .
  2 : redo ==> child(antigone,iokaste) .
  2 : exit ==> child(antigone,oidipous) .
  2 : call ==> female(oidipous) .
  2 : fail ==> female(oidipous) .
  2 : redo ==> child(antigone,oidipous) .
  2 : exit ==> child(eteokles,iokaste) .
  2 : call ==> female(iokaste) .
  2 : exit ==> female(iokaste) .
 1 : exit ==> mother(iokaste,eteokles) .
4MS SUCCESS
 <- mother(iokaste,eteokles) .
     now we turn off the tracing
trace(mother(*,*),off) & trace(child(*,*),off) &
trace(female(*),off).
OMS SUCCESS
 <- trace(mother(V1,V2),off) &
trace(child(V3,V4),off) & trace(female(V5),off) .
     now we switch to the editor
e.

*while in the editor, we add the following clauses
to the file "family prolog":*

   father(F,C) <- child(C,F) & male(F).

<- father(F,C) & write(F:C) & fail.

the second clause is a goal. As soon as we leave the
editor, both clauses appear in the Prolog workspace,
and the goal is executed, yielding the answer:

```
oidipous : antigone .
oidipous : eteokles .
24MS SUCCESS
 <- e() .
```
The goal "e" of "edconsulting" the current program
has now succeeded. To leave VM/Prolog we type
fin.

The "e." goal switched us to the editor. While we were "in" the editor, we added
a rule and a goal to the `family prolog` file. When we left the editor, the file
was automatically reconsulted which caused the changes we made to appear in
the Prolog workspace. The first change was to add a rule for `father`. The
second change was to add a goal to the file. When a goal appears in a file like
this, it is launched as soon as the file is consulted. So, immediately after leaving
the editor, the goal was executed, and it showed the two children of `ouidipous`.

Strictly speaking, we would be closer to Prolog's roots in logic if we also set
goals from the terminal by typing `<-goal..` However, typing the "`<-`" every
time is awkward, so the normal convention for IBM Prolog is:

A goal is set from the terminal simply by typing it

for example "goal."

A goal is set from a file by prefixing it with an arrow

for example "<-goal."

The convention that allows us to type a goal without an arrow means that we
cannot type in a fact to the terminal "as is," since it would be understood as a
goal. To make the distinction, a fact or a rule typed in at the terminal should be
prefixed with a "`.`", as in

.male(laios).

.parent(P,C) <- child(C,P).

This treatment of goals and facts is the normal one for IBM Prolog.
However, as with many pragmatic matters concerning the language, the

treatment can be changed using a predicate called `pragma`. (See the IBM Prolog manuals for details—this pragma is called `allgoal`.) We note in passing that pragmas should not be changed lightly, since a change in a pragma setting may make it necessary to check all of the relevant programs to see if they are affected. Also, the use of non-standard pragma settings can make it difficult to swap programs between computers. So it is often worthwhile to use the normal pragma setting rather than to follow one's own preferences freely.

A.2 DETAILED PROGRAMMING OF A METAINTERPETER

Our main example program is the backchain iteration metainterpreter described in Section 4.2.3, "Inside the Syllog Shell." That section discussed the top levels of the interpreter, and the purpose of the main predicates `demo`, `backchain`, and `iterate`. We now look at the whole program, in six sections:

(A) The top level, which defines how the interpreter works, starting with `demo`.

(B) High level predicates supporting the top level, such as `frontier`.

(C) Lower level predicates, such as `builtin`.

(D) Opening and closing a file.

(E) Tracing, and swapping between Prolog and Xedit.

(F) Loading the program to be metainterpreted, and control of the metainterpreter from the terminal.

Although we are looking at the program in six sections, we have actually typed it into a single file called `backit   prolog`, using the Xedit editor. Here is section A.

Backit   Section A

```
demo(Question,Answer) <-
    backchain(Question,Rules) &
    write(rules=Rules) &
    iterate(Question.Rules,nil,Lemmas) &
    set_of(Question,member(Question,Lemmas),Answer).
```

```
backchain(Question,Rules) <-
    backchain1(Question.nil,nil,Rules).

backchain1(Questions,Rules,NewRules) <-
    set_of(A<-Bs,
            member(A,Questions) & rule(A<-Bs) &
            ¬in_gen(A<-Bs,Rules),
           Rs) &
    Rs=/nil & append(Rs,Rules,IntRules) &
    frontier(Rs,Qs) &
    backchain1(Qs,IntRules,NewRules).
backchain1(Questions,Rules,NewRules) <-
    most_gen(Rules,NewRules).

iterate(Rules,Lemmas1,Lemmas3) <-
    execute(Rules,Lemmas1,Lemmas2) &
    Lemmas1=/Lemmas2 &
    iterate(Rules,Lemmas2,Lemmas3).
iterate(Rules,Lemmas,Lemmas).

execute(Rule.Rules,Lemmas1,Lemmas3) <-
    execute1(Rule,Lemmas1,Lemmas2) &
    execute(Rules,Lemmas2,Lemmas3).
execute(nil,Lemmas,Lemmas).

execute1(A<-Bs,Lemmas1,Lemmas3) <- / &
    set_of(A,
            execute2(Bs,Lemmas1) | fact(A),
            Lemmas2) &
    union(Lemmas1,Lemmas2,Lemmas3).
execute1(A,Lemmas1,Lemmas3) <- / &
    set_of(A,fact(A),Lemmas2) &
    union(Lemmas1,Lemmas2,Lemmas3).

execute2(B&Bs,Lemmas) <- / &
    execute2(B,Lemmas) & execute2(Bs,Lemmas).
execute2(¬B,*) <- builtin(B) & / & ¬B.
execute2(¬B,*) <-
    demo(B,Answer) & / & ¬member(B,Answer).
execute2(B,*) <- builtin(B) & / & B.
execute2(B,*) <- fact(B).
execute2(B,Lemmas) <- member(B,Lemmas).
```

The working of the rules in section A is described in detail in Section 4.2.3, "Inside the Syllog Shell." We are looking at the program "top down," in

the sense that the predicates in section A rely on additional predicates such as
set_of, rule, and in_gen in the later sections. Section B is shown below.

Backit   Section B

```
frontier(Rs,Qs) <-
    set_of(B,
            member(A<-Bs,Rs) & and_list(Bs,L) &
                        member(B,L) & pos(B)),Qs).

set_of(X,PX,S) <- compute(set,X,PX,nil,S) & /.
set_of(X,PX,nil).

in_gen(X,Y.Ys) <- (X=*=Y | mg(Y,X)) & /.
in_gen(X,Y.Ys) <- in_gen(X,Ys).

union(nil,L,L).
union(X.Xs,Ys,Zs) <-
    member_check(X,Ys) & / & union(Xs,Ys,Zs).
union(X.Xs,Ys,X.Zs) <- / & union(Xs,Ys,Zs).

most_gen(Rs,Gs) <-
    qsort(Rs,Ss) & most_gen1(Ss,Gs) & /.

most_gen1(nil,nil).
most_gen1(R.Rs,Gs) <-
    member(G,Rs) & mg(G,R) & / & most_gen1(Rs,Gs).
most_gen1(R.Rs,R.Gs) <- most_gen1(Rs,Gs).

mg(U,V) <- ¬¬(U=V) & copy(U,UU) & copy(V,VV) &
    UU=VV & V=*=VV & ¬(U=*=UU).

qsort(A,B) <- qsort1(A,nil,B).

qsort1(nil,R,R).
qsort1(X.L,R0,R) <-
    partition(L,X,L1,L2) &
    qsort1(L2,R0,R1) & qsort1(L1,X.R1,R).

partition(nil,*,nil,nil).
partition(X.L,Y,L1,X.L2) <-
    mg(X,Y) & / & partition(L,Y,L1,L2).
partition(X.L,Y,X.L1,L2) <- partition(L,Y,L1,L2).
```

Here frontier(Rs,Qs) collects positive (non-negated) predicates from the
bodies of the rules in Rs and places them as a list of questions in Qs. The
predicate frontier uses set_of, which collects the set of literals B such that

B is in the right side of a rule and B is positive, into the result Qs. To do this, each right hand side Bs of a rule is converted from a conjunct to a list, then its predicates are extracted one by one using member(B,L). Each such B is tested to make sure it is not negated by pos(B). The predicate set_of is itself defined in terms of compute, which is a built-in utility provided by IBM Prolog. The predicate in_gen(X,Ys) is used to check whether an item X, or an item more general than X, is in the list Ys. The item X is defined to be in the list Ys if it is the same, up to some renaming of variables, as an item in Ys, for example

> in_gen(p(U),q(X).p(Y).nil)

succeeds. This kind of equality is tested by IBM Prolog's =*= operator. As another example,

> in_gen(p(1,2),q(U).p(1,X).nil)

succeeds, because p(1,X) is more general than p(1,2), in a sense defined by the predicate mg(General,Specific). The rule for mg(U,V) is defined so as not to alter the bindings of U and V. The first test in the body of the rule is equivalent to U=V, except that by writing it ¬¬(U=V) we prevent binding. We then use VM/Prolog's built-in predicate copy to make fresh copies UU and VV of U and V. This allows us to unify UU=VV without altering U and V. (Note that the preliminary test ¬¬(U=V) is not needed logically; it is there for efficiency, to filter out hopeless cases quickly.) Finally, we test to see if the unification UU=VV left V and VV the same (up to renaming of variables), and caused U and UU to differ.

The predicate union(Xs,Ys,Zs) essentially appends the list Xs to the list Ys, giving the result Zs. The only difference from the standard append is that duplicates are eliminated from Zs, using a predicate member_check defined in section C.

At the end of the backchain phase of the interpreter, a list Rs of rules is produced, and only the most general rules in the list are retained, as another list Gs. This is done by the predicate most_gen(Rs,Gs). The first step is to use a quicksort predicate qsort (see page 92) to sort Rs into another list Ss in which the more general items are at the end. Then the predicate most_gen1(Ss,Gs) makes a single pass along Ss to filter out just the most general elements into Gs.

The next section is:

Backit   Section C

```
pos(¬*)<- / & fail.
pos(*)
```

```
and_list(B&Bs,B.L) <- / & and_list(Bs,L).
and_list(B,B.nil) <- B =/ (* & *).

append(nil,L,L).
append(H.T,L,H.U) <- append(T,L,U).

rule(R) <- ax(*,R,rule).
fact(F) <- ax(F,F,fact).

builtin(A) <- (A =.. (P.*)) &
    member_check(P,
    var.'='ᵀ.gt.lt.ge.le.sum.diff.prod.quot.nil) & /.

member(X,X.*).
member(X,*.Y) <- member(X,Y).

member_check(X,X.*) <- /.
member_check(X,*.Y) <- member_check(X,Y).
```

The predicate pos checks that a literal is positive; for example pos(p(X)) succeeds, while pos(¬p(X)) fails. The rule and fact predicates are used by the metainterpreter to reach the rules and the facts of the program being interpreted. These are placed in named VM/Prolog spaces at the start of a run, so that they can be found by ax(*,R,rule) and ax(F,F,fact), which are calls to a VM/Prolog built-in predicate. (Actually, it would be more efficient to place these calls directly in the main metainterpreter, rather than going via rule(R) <- ax(*,R,rule) and fact(F) <- ax(F,F,fact) .) The named VM/Prolog spaces are useful in several ways here. Firstly, they prevent the metainterpreter from trying to interpret its own rules! The metainterpreter is also present, but in a space labeled backit, while the program being interpreted in is in the rule and fact spaces. Secondly, when we want to interpret a different program, we get rid of the old program by deleting everything in the rule and fact spaces. Otherwise, we would risk loading two programs to be metainterpreted at once. Thirdly, although we do not do this here, it is sometimes convenient for a metainterpreter to hand over part of its task to Prolog—say a call to a predicate that can only make use of non-recursive rules, and is therefore safe. Since the rules and facts are actually in the Prolog workspace too, they are equally accessible for direct execution.

Still in section C, the predicate builtin(A) checks whether A is a call to a VM/Prolog built-in such as sum(X,Y,Z). To do this, the name sum is isolated using VM/Prolog's =.. operator, which has the effect of producing from sum(X,Y,Z) the list sum.X.Y.Z.nil. The predicate member_check is like the list membership predicate member, except that while member(X,L) will yield successive members X of the list L on backtrack, member_check(X,L) is designed for use with X instantiated. It is more efficient, but less general than member(X,L).

The next section allows us to open a file containing a program to be interpreted, so that we can load it into the `rule` and `fact` spaces, and then to close the file again.

Backit   Section D

```
open(File,input) <-
    dcio(File,input,file,File,prolog,a,v,80).

close(File) <- dcio(File,close).
```

The predicate `dcio` is a VM/Prolog built-in for dealing with files, and it is described further on page 422 and in the VM/Prolog manual.

The next section deals with tracing, and with swapping between VM/Prolog and the Xedit editor.

Backit   Section E

```
op(traceon,prefix,20).
op(traceoff,prefix,20).

traceon P <- ax(PX,*) & (PX =.. P.X) & trace(PX).
traceoff P <-
    ax(PX,*) & (PX =.. P.X) & trace(PX,off).

edit <- edconsult(backit).
```

The first four lines define a simple way of turning tracing on or off for a specific predicate. For example, if we say

```
traceon demo.
```

then VM/Prolog's built-in `ax` will find out that there is a rule starting with `demo(Q,A)`. The built-in predicate `trace` then sets a trace point on `demo`. (We leave it as an exercise to extend this simple idea so that if a predicate name is used with different numbers of arguments, e.g `ax`, then `traceon` can specify the name and the number of arguments. In addition, this can be made more efficient.) The last line allows us to call on VM/Prolog's `edconsult` built-in predicate to swap from Prolog to the Xedit editor, make changes in `backit` if we wish, then return to Prolog. Any changes we make then appear in Prolog.

The last section of our backchain iteration program deals with loading a program to be metainterpreted, and with control of the metainterpreter from the terminal. The goal `go` makes the program ask for the file name of the program to be metainterpreted, binds the file name to the variable `F`, clears any previous program from the `rule` and `fact` spaces, opens `F`, reads it in, closes it, then calls `attend`. The predicate `attend` forms the main loop of a small

command processor, which allows us to control the metainterpreter from the
terminal.

Backit   Section F

```
go <- nl &
   writex("name of program to be metainterpreted: ") &
      nl & read(F) & nl &
      clear & open(F,input) & read_in(F) &
      close(F) & nl & attend.

attend <- nl & writex(">>") & nl & read1(G) &
   ( G=edit & edit |
     G=stop & fin |
     G=(traceon P) & (traceon P) & attend |
     G=(traceoff P) & (traceoff P) & attend |
     G=prolog |
     demo(G,A) & write(answer=A) & attend ).

read_in(F) <-
     read(C,F,3) & add(C) & write(C) & fail.
read_in(*).

add(A<-B) <- addax(A<-B,rule) & /.
add(A) <- addax(A,fact) & /.

clear <- bloc_delete(fact) & bloc_delete(rule).

read1(X) <- read(X) & /.

<- go.
```

The predicate nl is a VM/Prolog built-in that writes a new line to the terminal.
The predicate clear uses a VM/Prolog built-in called bloc_delete to
remove any previous program from the rule and fact spaces.   In
read_in(F), the predicate read(C,F,3) reads a rule or a fact from the file
F, and will read further items on backtrack, while add places these in the rule
or fact spaces as appropriate, using the built-in predicate addax.

The attend loop starts by writing a prompt >> on the screen of the
terminal, reads a goal G that we type in, and then processes it:

- If G is edit, the built-in predicate edconsult allows us to edit the
  backchain iteration interpreter. When we leave the editor, any changes we
  have made appear in the next Prolog run.

- If G is stop, we leave VM/Prolog and return to the VM operating system.

- If G is traceon P, we call traceon to set a trace, and then attend to
  another command; likewise for traceoff.

- If G is prolog, we leave the attend loop so that we can type instructions directly to VM/Prolog. For example, we can then type attend to get back to where we were.

- Finally, the main point! If G is none of the above, then we call demo(G,A) to get an answer A, then return to attend.

This completes our description of the metainterpreter, and we are almost ready to test it.

A.3 TESTING THE METAINTERPRETER AT THE TERMINAL

To run the metainterpreter, we shall need a program for it to interpret. In fact, we shall show it working on two programs. The first is called test1, and we have typed it into a file called test1 prolog, using the Xedit editor. Here is test1:

```
a(X,Y) <- b(X,Y).
a(X,Z) <- a(X,Y) & b(Y,Z).

b(1,2).  b(2,3).  b(3,4).  b(4,5).
```

The second program is called test2:

```
t(X,Z) <- r(X,Z) & ¬s(X,Z).

s(X,Z) <- s(X,Y) & s(Y,Z).

r(1,5).  r(5,1).

s(1,2).  s(2,3).  s(3,4).  s(4,5).
```

It is used to demonstrate double recursion, and the way in which the backchain iteration interpreter calls itself recursively to deal with negation. Now we are ready. We start VM/Prolog by typing the word "vmprolog." What follows is a transcript of a session at the terminal. In the transcript we use three typefaces:

- What we type in on the keyboard is in this typeface,
- What the computer puts on the screen is in this typeface, and
- *Some comments that we have added afterwards are in italics.*

vmprolog
   Start VM/Prolog
consult(backit).
   Load in the metainterpreter

```
name of program to be metainterpreted:
test1.
```
the name of a program
to be interpreted

```
a(V1,V2) <- b(V1,V2) .
a(V1,V2) <- a(V1,V3) & b(V3,V2) .
b(1,2) .
b(2,3) .
b(3,4) .
b(4,5) .
```
the test1 program is shown on the screen

```
>>
```
the metainterpreter asks for a goal,
this is the goal we set:

```
a(1,*).
rules = ((a(1,V1) <- b(1,V1)) .
    (a(1,V2) <- a(1,V3) & b(V3,V2)) . nil) .
answer = (a(1,2) . a(1,3) .
    a(1,4) . a(1,5) . nil) .
```

```
>>
traceon most__gen.
```
set a trace on most__gen(Rs,Gs)

```
>>
a(1,*).
```
we set the same goal as above
```
  1 : call ==>
  most_gen((a(1,V1) <- a(1,V2) & b(V2,V1)) .
       (a(1,V3) <- b(1,V3)) . nil,V4) .
  1 : exit ==>
  most_gen((a(1,V1) <- a(1,V2) & b(V2,V1)) .
       (a(1,V3) <- b(1,V3)) . nil,
       (a(1,V3) <- b(1,V3)) .
       (a(1,V1) <- a(1,V2) & b(V2,V1)) . nil) .
rules = ((a(1,V1) <- b(1,V1)) .
    (a(1,V2) <- a(1,V3) & b(V3,V2)) . nil) .
answer = (a(1,2) . a(1,3) . a(1,4) . a(1,5) . nil) .
```

```
>>
```
the metainterpreter asks for a goal
```
traceoff most__gen.
```
we turn off the trace of most__gen(Rs,Gs)

```
>>
a(1,9).
```
we set a goal
```
rules = ((a(1,V1) <- b(1,V1)) .
    (a(1,V2) <- a(1,V3) & b(V3,V2)) . nil) .
answer = nil .

>>
prolog.
```
we leave the metainterpreter and drop into Prolog

```
ax(A,A,fact).
```
ask prolog for a fact belonging to test1
```
1MS SUCCESS
 <- ax(b(1,2),b(1,2),fact) .
```
here is one such fact
```
;
```
we type a semicolon to ask for another
fact from test1
```
OMS SUCCESS
 <- ax(b(2,3),b(2,3),fact) .
```
here is the next fact
```
ax(A,A<-B,rule).
```
ask prolog for a rule belonging to test1
```
2MS SUCCESS
 <- ax(a(V1,V2),a(V1,V2) <- b(V1,V2),rule) .
```
here is a rule
```
attend.
```
go back to the metainterpreter's
command loop

```
>>
```
the metainterpreter asks for a goal
```
edit.
```
we say we want to look at backit using Xedit

(editing session not shown here)

when we leave the editor, test1 is cleared out

```
name of program to be metainterpreted:
test2.
```
this time test2 is to be metainterpreted

```
t(V1,V2) <- r(V1,V2) &  ¬s(V1,V2) .
s(V1,V2) <- s(V1,V3) & s(V3,V2) .
```

```
r(1,5) .
r(5,1) .
s(1,2) .
s(2,3) .
s(3,4) .
s(4,5) .
```
the test2 program is shown on the screen

>>

the metainterpreter asks for a goal
```
t(5,*).
```
we set this goal
```
rules = ((t(5,V1) <- r(5,V1) &  ¬s(5,V1)) . nil) .
answer = (t(5,1) . nil) .
```

the demo predicate was used more than once.
let's use traceon to look at this

>>
```
traceon demo.
```

>>
```
t(5,*).
```
now set the same goal as above
```
 1 : call ==> demo(t(5,V1),V2) .
rules = ((t(5,V1) <- r(5,V1) &  ¬s(5,V1)) . nil) .
 2 : call ==> demo(s(5,1),V1) .
 2 : exit ==> demo(s(5,1),nil) .
 2 : call ==> demo(s(5,1),V1) .
 2 : exit ==> demo(s(5,1),nil) .
 1 : exit ==> demo(t(5,V1),t(5,1) . nil) .
answer = (t(5,1) . nil) .
```

indeed demo was re-used because of the
negation sign in the test2 program

>>
```
stop.
```
leave the metainterpreter and VM/Prolog,
and return to the VM operating system

This completes our session at the terminal. The programs we used were:

- the VM/Prolog interepreter,

- a metainterpreter, in a file called backit prolog,

- two programs that we metainterpreted; these were in files called test1 prolog and test2 prolog, and

- the Xedit editor, which we used to look at `backit` without leaving VM/Prolog.

It's worth noting that IBM Prolog has several ways of working closely with the operating system on which it runs (VM or MVS). In particular, it can work with a database management system—SQL/DS on the VM operating system, and DB2 on the MVS operating system. If a Prolog program has a large number of facts, then it can be more efficient to store the facts in a database. The Syllog shell described in Chapter 4 can be set up to use a database in this way.

There is one more practical matter about running a program at the terminal. When we run a program containing recursions, we may occasionally get into a loop. When that happens, the program may exhaust stack space and come rapidly to a halt with an error. However, it may also just keep running, particularly if the loop is subject to tail recursion optimization—hence similar to a loop in a conventional language such as Pascal. When this happens, we can stop VM/Prolog by typing sp (for stop Prolog). This leaves us in Prolog. Or we can type hx (for halt execution), which returns us to the VM operating system

In the next two sections, we outline some of the ways in which VM/Prolog can work with the VM operating system. More details are to be found in the VM/Prolog and MVS/Prolog manuals.

A.4 VM/PROLOG INPUT AND OUTPUT

VM/Prolog input and output uses *Logical File Names*, abbreviated LFNs. An LFN is used as the name of an input source or output target. Possible sources are files or the terminal, and possible targets are files, the terminal or the VM/CMS *console stack*. VM/Prolog is usually started by an exec called, appropriately, "vmprolog." When started it begins reading goals from its primary input source, usually the terminal. (We discussed the form of a goal typed at the terminal versus a goal in a file on page 410.) VM/Prolog uses a predefined logical file name `stdin` for this purpose. After it reads a goal, it executes it. The goal succeeds or fails, and VM/Prolog writes the results to its primary output. This is normally the terminal, also. The logical file name `stdout` is used for this purpose.

The `dcio` built-in predicate, which we used on page 416, is used to tell VM/Prolog to which source or target an LFN refers. To declare the LFN `pgm_in` to refer to the input file `file1 data a`, we execute the goal

```
dcio(pgm_in,input,file,file1,data,a)
```

This says "pgm_in is the LFN for the input file `file1 data a`." To have `pgm_out` refer to the output file `file2 data a` we execute

```
dcio(pgm_out,output,file,file2,data,a).
```

If the output file does not already exist, record format and blocksize must be specified. To make the output file be fixed block 80, we say

```
dcio(pgm_out,output,file,file2,data,a,f,80).
```

To direct output to the screen and input from the terminal, console should be specified instead of file in the dcio. Record format is not an option, but record length can be specified. dcio(pgm_in,input,console,80) can be used for input, and dcio(pgm_out,output,console,80) can be used for output.

The CMS console stack is automatically available for input when console is specified in dcio. To direct output to the stack use

```
dcio(pgm_stk_out,output,stack,80)
```

An optional fifth argument can specify lifo or fifo for the stack, as in

```
dcio(pgm_stk_out,output,stack,80,lifo)
```

In addition to input, and output, we can use dcio with next to specify the record number at which input or output is to begin, and with close, which resets the current record number of a file. This can be used to explicitly manage secondary storage.

If all of the arguments of dcio are specified, then the specified LFN is established. The dcio predicate can be used to retrieve information about an LFN. If one or more of the arguments is an unbound variable, then the dcio will try to bind the variables to an existing LFN specification. For example, assume the previous LFN examples are in effect. Then

```
dcio(pgm_stk_out,output,stack,Size)
```

will succeed, binding Size to 80. Also,

```
dcio(IN,MODE,file,file1,data,a)
```

will bind IN to pgm_in and will bind MODE to input. This can be used to find out whether an LFN already exists for a given file with the proper mode (input or output), what the buffer size is for a console stack LFN, and so on.

VM/Prolog provides a variety of read options. Once an LFN has been established for input, then it is possible to read general Prolog terms, atoms, single characters, and entire lines using, respectively, read(U,LFN), readat(V,LFN), readch(W,LFN) and readli(X,LFN). If a read has only one argument, then the LFN defaults to the standard console input LFN.

When input is from a file, VM/Prolog must be told what to do in case a read is attempted and an end-of-file is found. VM/Prolog gives two options. One is to simply fail the read request. That is the most usual case. The other option, which is not often used, is to cause an error which purges the goal stack and returns control to the top level. Whether to fail or abort to top level is specified by the third argument of read(Term,LFN,N). If N is an *even* integer, then an error occurs. If N is *odd*, then a fail occurs.

We can also specify what happens when backtracking returns control to a read. There are again two possibilities. The read can be treated as deterministic and backtracking can continue on past the read, or the read can

succeed again with the next term from the file or console. Which should happen
is determined also by the third argument to `read`. If the second least significant
bit in the binary representation of `N` is 0, then the `read` is deterministic.
Otherwise it is non-deterministic.

Which value of `N` to specify for which combination can be found in the
following table.

	eof error	eof fail
backtrack deterministic	0	1
backtrack nondeterministic	2	3

If `N` is not specified, its value is assumed to be 0.

VM/Prolog has buffered input and output. For each LFN, there is a
corresponding input or output buffer. A read request from an LFN reads the
next term from the buffer. If the buffer becomes empty before the term is
completed, then the buffer is loaded with the next record from the I/O source for
the LFN. The buffer size can be specified in the `dcio` that establishes the LFN.

A complete term could be read without exhausting the buffer. In that case
the remainder of the buffer is kept and used to satisfy the next `read` request.
The built-in predicate `readempty(LFN)` can be used to determine if the buffer
for the specified `LFN` is currently empty. If so, then the next `read` request for
that `LFN` will cause a physical read from the input source (e.g a disk) into the
buffer.

The buffer is handled in the same way whether the `read` request is for a
term, a character, an atom, or a line. The call `readli(String,LFN)` (here
`readli` stands for "read line") binds `String` to the entire remaining contents
of a non-empty buffer as a Prolog string. If the buffer is empty, then `readli`
forces the buffer to be refreshed from the input source. The result of `readli` in
that case is the entire record. Similarly, `readch` (for "read character") reads
the next character from the buffer, and `readat` (for "read atom") reads the
next atom.

There are various forms of output. The predicate `write(T)` appends the
term `T`, followed by a period, to the end of the output buffer. The buffer is then
printed, and a new line is created. Subsequent output to the same LFN will
begin in this new line. The predicates `writes` and `writex` do not terminate
the term with a period, and the buffer is not written unless it has become full. A

write request may have more characters than will fit in the remaining buffer. In that case the buffer is filled, written, and emptied, then the remaining characters start filling the now empty buffer. The built-in predicate `nl(LFN)` forces the buffer to be written and initiates a new line.

The predicate `prst(Expression,LFN)` evaluates `Expression` to a string. The resulting string is then written to the output buffer for the `LFN`. String delimiters are *not* written, nor is a new line forced. This predicate can be used to create output in any desired format.

A.5 VM/PROLOG AND THE VM OPERATING SYSTEM

There are several ways of getting VM/Prolog and the VM/CMS operating system to work together on a task. We can use a built-in predicate called `system` to call any of the operating system services; we can set and test variables in operating system "exec" programs; and we can `suspend` VM/Prolog, compute using the operating system, then return to the Prolog computation where we left off.

The `system(ST,AD,RC)` predicate can be used to invoke execs and other CMS functions. `ST` is a VM/Prolog computable expression which evaluates to some CMS command. `AD` is "CMS" or the name of a function to be specified for the CMS program interface SVC 202. `RC` is the return code generated by the called function.

As mentioned VM/Prolog is usually invoked by an exec program written in the Rexx language. (This language is described in the manual "System Product Interpreter User's Guide," IBM document SC24-5238-2.) During Prolog execution, the environment established by the exec is available to the Prolog program. In particular, we can pass information between Rexx and Prolog using the built-in predicate `rexvar(Var,Val)`. Before doing this one must set `pragma(rexvar,1)`. We can also use the `suspend()` built-in predicate along with `rexvar(Var,Val)` to coroutine between an exec and Prolog. Once in the Rexx exec, any operating system service can be used.

VM/Prolog loads itself as a CMS nucleus extension, which means that it can be suspended, other interactive work can take place, and then Prolog execution can be resumed from the point of suspension. The built-in predicate `suspend()` accomplishes this. In the goal

    ...p(X) & suspend() & q(X) ...

p(X) executes, perhaps binding X, then `suspend()` executes. Control is returned to CMS or the Exec that invoked Prolog. Whenever the `Prolog` command is issued, execution of the Prolog program resumes after the `suspend()` at q(X). There is a similar Prolog built-in `fin` that causes Prolog execution to be terminated. The Prolog state is maintained in terms of `addaxed` clauses and optional switch settings, but the execution stack is flushed. When Prolog is resumed, there are no outstanding goals.

A.6 TAILORING VM/PROLOG

VM/Prolog can be tailored so that its appearance and use change considerably. The main ways of doing this are:

- Setting up different sizes for the stacks used by VM/Prolog. (This is usually done in a vmprolog exec.)

- Choosing either the standard or the mixed Prolog workspace. (Throughout this book we have used "mixed." Programs for the standard workspace use upper case letters only.)

- Using `op` to make new operators known to Prolog. For example `op(is_a,rl,100)`.

- Using `pragma` to change the Prolog environment. For example, putting `<-pragma(lcomment,1)` at the head of a program allows comments in the program to span more than one line.

- Using `scan` to change Prolog's use of certain symbols. For example to make `@` the *and* operator instead of `&`.

When VM/Prolog is called, it allocates space for four different purposes. There are parameters which allow one to specify how much space is to be allocated. The four areas are the *local stack*, the *global stack*, the *trail*, and the *rule stack*. Program clauses are stored in the rule stack. This limits the size of a program one can load. The other three areas are used by the interpreter to manage procedure calls, and to create terms. In setting the sizes of the four spaces, it is useful to know that deterministic programs tend to use less local stack space and more global stack space than do programs that depend on non-determinism.

When VM/Prolog senses that it is about to run out of space in one of these areas, it calls a *garbage collector* which tries to reclaim unused space. If it cannot reclaim enough space, then the currently executing Prolog program is terminated, and VM/Prolog reverts to its top level.

There are pragma settings which specify when to start garbage collection, and the minimum amounts that must be reclaimed in order to continue. These are

```
freeblocs
gsmin          gsminp          gsgained
trailmin       trailgained
seqrulemin
```

See the IBM Prolog manuals for details on how these operate.

VM/Prolog comes with two possible formats, the so-called *Standard* and the *Mixed*. You may select whichever format you wish by specifying the workspace parameter when invoking VM/Prolog. This book consistently uses the mixed format. In this format upper and lower case letters are allowed, and variables start with a capital letter. Thus `abc` is an atom, whereas `ABC` is a variable. The asterisk is used to signify anonymous variables. The "standard" workspace translates all input into upper case, and variables must begin with an asterisk.

The language in which error messages appear may also be selected when VM/Prolog is started. You have the choice of English or French.

The `op(Symbol,Fix,Precedence)` declaration is used to tell the interpreter's parsing routines how to treat specific words. It is `addaxed` and treated like any other clause. The `op` declaration was discussed in Chapters 2 and 3.

The Prolog environment settings can be changed by using the `pragma` and `scan` built-in predicates. These are executable, and they cause side effects that change the nature of a session. The `scan(Char,Option)` predicate can be used to change VM/Prolog's use of certain symbols. For example `&` is the normal *and* operator, but this can be changed by a suitable call of `scan`.

The environment settings for such things as garbage collection can be changed using `pragma`. The `pragma(Option,Value)` predicate, when executed with its arguments instantiated, causes a side effect. For example, executing the goal `pragma(freeblocks,10000)` will have the side effect of causing the interpreter to initiate garbage collection whenever there are 10,000 free bytes left in the heap. The complete set of possible `pragma` and `scan` settings is described in the VM/Prolog manual. Some of the more interesting ones are:

- `allgoal` determines whether top level goals must be prefixed by `<-`.
- `clauseprint` controls whether rules newly added to the workspace are immediately redisplayed.
- `lcomment` determines whether comments may span more than one line.
- `list` is used to allow the list `(a.b.c.nil)` to be read and written as `[a,b,c]`.
- `long` determines whether character strings and atoms may span more than one line.
- `norule` determines whether calling a goal for which no clause at all exists causes an error message.
- `rexvar` which we set to 1 to allow Prolog to test and set the value of a Rexx variable using the built-in predicate `rexvar(VarName,Value)`.
- `uppervar` determines whether an identifier beginning with an uppercase letter is a variable. One can specify that variables are to begin with a capital letter, or that a special character shall begin variables, but not both.

The syntax of Prolog terms is controlled by the `op` and `scan` predicates. VM/Prolog has the notion of a *connector*. The meaning of a connector is built into the language. Connectors make up the abstract structure of the Prolog language. In "pure" Prolog, the connectors are `<-` for "if", `&` for "and", and `|` for "or". VM/Prolog has added many more. The complete list can be displayed by setting the goal

```
op(X,Y,Z) & write(op(X,Y,Z)) & fail
```

and it is described in detail in the VM/Prolog manual.

The most commonly used operators are:

- /, cut the cut operators,
- label for defining labels,
- ¬ for defining "not,"
- A->B;C for "If A then B else C,"
- ; for top level backtrack request,
- '' for delimiting atoms,
- ' for delimiting strings,
- [...] for delimiting lists, and
- * for anonymous variables.

Each of these characters or atoms can be changed arbitrarily. Thus a syntax identical to Edinburgh Prolog (Pereira et al. 1980) can be created, with the important exception that the comma cannot be used as a constructor. It cannot replace & to mean "and", for example.

Another difference from Edinburgh syntax is the handling of operator precedence declarations. In VM/Prolog, the higher the precedence value, the tighter the operator binds. Given op(''%'',rl,50) and op(''#'',rl,45) then the term a % b # c is the same as (a % b) # c. This is exactly the opposite of the Edinburgh Prolog convention. Some further differences are:

- The Edinburgh operators xfy associate right-to-left, corresponding to VM/Prolog rl operators,
- yfx is lr,
- yf is suffix,
- fy is prefix.

A.7 CLAUSE NAMES AND MODULES

VM/Prolog has two very powerful mechanisms for building systems to manage Prolog clauses. These are *clause names* and *predicate prefixes*. Each clause that is added to the Prolog workspace by addax has a *name* associated with it. Clauses can be retrieved by name. The ax(Head,Clause,Name) predicate can be used to retrieve axioms with a certain name. This is useful for adding and deleting clauses in groups. The bloc_delete(N) predicate specifically deletes all clauses with clause name N. The library predicates consult and reconsult use a clause name to record which file each clause came from. The clause name normally has no function during the execution of a pure Prolog program. It is only visible to predicates such as ax, axn, addax, delax, and bloc_delete.

Each predicate has a *prefix*. Unlike the clause name, the prefix *can* affect program execution. The best way to understand how a prefix is used is to think of each predicate name as having two parts. What one normally thinks of as the

predicate name is the *short predicate name*: The short predicate name of p(X)
is p. In VM/Prolog, each predicate also has a *prefix*. A colon is used to
separate the prefix from the short name. The prefix of b:p(X) is b and p is its
short predicate name.

Using the `pragma` options defpref0 and defpref1, defaults can be
specified for the prefix to be used by the interpreter when only the short
predicate name is specified for a goal. There are actually two defaults available.
The defpref0 prefix is normally used. Its initial value is nil. The clause
a(X) <- b(X) is actually kept by the system as nil:a(X) <- nil:b(X).
The second prefix defpref1 is selected if the short predicate name begins with
a colon, but is without prefix. If pragma(defpref1,abc) is in effect, then
:a(X) <- :b(X) becomes abc:a(X) <- abc:b(X). By "becomes," we
mean that addax inserts the current default prefix as required. Goals executed
from the terminal also have the current default prefix applied. If the one in
effect at the time of the addax is not the same one in effect when the goal is
executed, then the interpreter will not find a matching clause for the goal.

The prefix mechanism can be used to write *modules* in VM/Prolog. By
changing the default prefix at the beginning of a file, the predicate names used in
the file can be "hidden." The following example shows how to define a module
called moda which only has the predicate a(X) usable by clauses not in the file.

```
a(X) <- moda:a(X).

<-pragma(defpref0,Oldvalue) &
    /* find current default */
  addax(moda:saveprefix(Oldvalue),1) &
    /* save it */
  pragma(defpref0,moda).
    /*change it */

/* the following now have prefix "moda"  */
a(X) <- b(X).
b(1). b(2).
  . . .

<-moda:saveprefix(Oldvalue) &
    /* find saved default */
  delax(moda:saveprefix(*)) &
    /* erase note */
  pragma(defpref0, Oldvalue).
    /* restore old default */
```

The clause a(X) <- moda:a(X) essentially says that the name a is known
outside the "module." Other programs may call the goal a(Y) and have the
default prefix used. Assuming the default is nil, then the definition is
equivalent to nil:a(X) <- moda:a(X). In the course of executing some

other program from some other module, a(123) is actually nil:a(123), which by virtue of this rule invokes moda:a(123).

The definition for moda:a(X)   <-   moda:b(X) is used to invoke moda:b(123). So other programs may use clauses for b(X) without any interference from moda:b(X). Of course, name conflicts are not completely eliminated. One must still watch out for duplicate prefixes!

There is one further detail. The built-in predicate pprio(Pred,N) can be used to override application of the default prefix for predicates with the short predicate name Pred. Instead, the prefix built is used. This feature makes some predicates globally available regardless of current prefix defaults.

A.8 TYPES, EXPRESSIONS, AND SETS

In IBM Prolog, as in most Prologs, variables are not typed a priori. This means that a variable X can be bound to a number, later to string, still later to a list, and so on. Curiously, much of the power of Prolog is lost if we insist on strong typing of variables—for example it becomes quite difficult to write a metainterpreter. In IBM Prolog constants such as atoms, strings, numbers and predicates are of different types. There are several built-in type conversion predicates. For example, st_to_at(S,A) converts the string S to the atom A, and vice versa. Some care is needed, for if the string consists only of numerical digits, we get a number, not an atom. The atom "123" does not unify with the integer 123. Also, it is necessary to distinguish between the atom p and the nullary predicate p(). In IBM Prolog p and p() do not unify. For example, since ax(Head,Clause) succeeds when the head of Clause unifies with Head, one would expect the following clause always to succeed:

    add_it(P) <- addax(P) & ax(*,P).

However, add_it(p()) succeeds whereas add_it(p) fails. The addax(p) appropriately converts p to p(), but ax(*,p) does not. So some care is needed when using addax and ax directly.

As noted in Chapters 2 and 3, Prolog is mainly a relational language. If it were purely relational then we would have to write an arithmetic expression such as Y = (2+3)*X as

    sum(2,3,Temp) & prod(Temp,X,Y)

This is not very convenient, so IBM Prolog provides a several predicates which evaluate their arguments. Y   :=   X evaluates the expression bound to X and binds the result to Y. Similarly, the predicates

    prst   system   rexvar   sql

evaluate their first argument, which is normally a string expression. (The predicate sql is for accessing a SQL/DS or DB2 database.)

The mathematical functions allowed in computable expressions are

    -, +, *, /, max, min, abs, sin, cos, pi, exp, log

The string functions allowed are

```
||, len, strip, upper, lower, substring
```

In this book, we have often used the notion of the set S of all items X such that a predicate p(X) holds. The set S is normally represented as a list, without repeated elements. We have used the notation set_of(X,p(X),S). It is sometimes thought that it is not possible to define set_of in Prolog without using side effects. Actually it *is* possible, but the known programs are not efficient. IBM Prolog has a built-in predicate called compute that can produce both the set of all X such that p(X) (a list without repeats), and the corresponding "bag" of all such X (a list that may contain repeats).

We have defined set_of like this

```
set_of(X,PX,S) <- compute(set,X,PX,nil,S) & /.
set_of(X,PX,nil).
```

and bag_of like this

```
bag_of(X,PX,S) <- compute(list,X,PX,nil,S) & /.
bag_of(X,PX,nil).
```

The general form of compute is

```
compute(Type,Term,Goal,Vars,Answer)
```

where Answer is a list of all terms Term for each possible solution to Goal. Type can be either list or set. If duplicates are not desired, then set is specified. In this case the resulting list is sorted. We discussed the Vars argument of compute on page 300.

A.9 MVS/PROLOG

So far in this Appendix we have talked about how to use VM/Prolog, i.e IBM Prolog on the VM operating system. IBM Prolog is also available for the MVS operating system, as MVS/Prolog. Pure Prolog programs written for VM/Prolog are very similar to those for MVS/Prolog. However, there are some differences, concerning matters such as input from files. In this section we outline some of the differences between VM/Prolog and MVS/Prolog, and we show how to run a simple program in MVS/Prolog. The program uses a built-in predicate called dasd that deals with the available disk storage.

VM/Prolog and MVS/Prolog have essentially the same syntax and functions with the following exceptions. In MVS/Prolog:

- Square brackets around lists are replaced by braces, as in {a,b,c}. The dot notation, a.b.c.nil, is common to both Prologs.

- The dcio predicate has a slightly different syntax that allows for handling both sequential and partitioned data sets. The consult predicates have similar changes.

- There is no `lisp` predicate.

- The `consult` predicate gives messages and maintains a table about the source of its information.

- `rexvar` is replaced by `ispfvar`.

- MVS/Prolog has some extra operators, including > and <.

Otherwise, the two Prologs are similar, and they have essentially the same syntax and the same built-in predicates. They differ in the way in which each runs under its operating system: VM/Prolog is a nucleus extension, MVS/Prolog is an ISPF subtask.

MVS/Prolog and VM/Prolog execute goals and rules in the same manner. In fact, most programs that execute properly in VM/Prolog will also execute properly in MVS/Prolog, provided one takes into account the differences between the underlying operating systems. This means, for example, that since MVS has a different way of handling files ("data sets"), the `dcio` predicates are specified somewhat differently. This is also true of any predicate (such as `consult`) that has as one of its arguments the name of a file.

One can start MVS/Prolog either directly from the TSO command line, or alternatively from an ISPF panel. In both cases, MVS/Prolog is run as a subtask of ISPF. But when MVS/Prolog is started from the TSO command line, no panels are displayed. Instead the Prolog interpreter is made ready for input from the terminal.

If you select MVS/Prolog on an ISPF panel two interpreter interfaces are available: a line mode interface such as VM/Prolog has, and a full-screen interface. The full-screen interface allows you to enter Prolog statements on a command line and view the results in a scrollable window. The full-screen interface also has an ISPF command line and a field for activating an MVS/Prolog console log.

An advantage of running MVS/Prolog as an ISPF subtask is that the PDF editor is available for use by the `edconsult` and `ed` predicates. However you must always make sure that the data sets you want to edit have already been allocated. MVS/Prolog does not allocate new data sets for use by the editing predicates. When you are using the `dcio` predicate to create new output data sets, this restriction does not apply and MVS/Prolog performs the allocation for you using the information you specify as arguments to the `dcio` predicate.

To use MVS/Prolog, log on to your TSO system to an ID that has been set up to run MVS/Prolog. By "set up" we mean that the person who installed MVS/Prolog has both given you access permission to the MVS/Prolog data sets and established PrologON as your TSO logon procedure. Once you are logged on and TSO has displayed the `Ready` message, type the command: "PROGO." This calls a CLIST (Command List) that calls ISPF to set up MVS/Prolog. After a few seconds, you will see an ISPF panel with the name "MVS/Prolog Primary Option Menu."

If this is the first time you have used MVS/Prolog you should follow the instructions for first time users as outlined in the installation chapter of the

"MVS/Prolog Product Description and Operations Manual." Once you have done this, or if this is not the first time you have used MVS/Prolog, select option 2, "Execute" to start the Prolog interpreter.

Since we are using the default options to load the MVS/Prolog interpreter, you should now be presented with a screen containing a command line on the top, an input and display area in the middle, and an input line on the bottom. This is full-screen mode. The command line on the top is for ISPF and the input line on the bottom is for Prolog.

One of the first things we need to do is to allocate a sequential data set called (say) `testds.prolog`. We can do this by typing "pdf" on the upper command line and using PDF services. Although we can make the data set any format and size we wish, we suggest a variable record size with logical record length of 80 bytes and a block size of 400 bytes. Once we are finished doing this, we exit PDF in the normal way.

With our data set allocated, we are ready to run a test. This is shown in the transcript that follows:

    edconsult(testds.prolog).

    this says we want to edit testds.prolog
    while in the editor, type in the rules:

list__size(nil,Length,Length).
list__size(notvar $ (Head.Tail),X,Length) <-
    Y := X + 1 & list__size(Tail,Y,Length).

    when we leave the editor, after having saved the data set
    we see the following:

```
CONSULTING:  walker.testds.prolog
260MS SUCCESS
  <- edconsult(testds.prolog) .
```

ext__pred(dasd(*,*,*),exam,4).
```
OMS SUCCESS
  <- ext_pred(dasd(V1,V2,V3),exam,4) .
```

    this predicate is a sample external predicate found in
    the standard MVS/Prolog installation. Its arguments
    return information about the Direct Access Storage Devices
    connected to your MVS system.

dasd(*,*,*).
```
4MS SUCCESS
  <- dasd('MS5020','0860','3350') .
```

*these values (which will be different on your system)
represent a volume serial number, a unit address, and
a device type. What we want to know is what types of
dasd we have.*

```
compute(set,Type,dasd(*,*,Type),nil,Result).
29MS SUCCESS
 <- compute(set,V1,dasd(V2,V3,V1),nil,
              '3330' . '3350' . '3380' . nil) .
```

*now we would like to know how many there are of each type.
to make things interesting, let's use a compute inside a
compute. The inner compute gets all the address for a given
device type and counts the addresses. The outer compute
gets this for all device types.*

```
compute(list,pair(Type,Number),
     compute(list,Addr,dasd(*,Addr,Type),
                  Type.nil,R) &
      list__size(R,0,Number),nil,Result).
```

*notice that we've indented the goal to help make sense of the
query. When the query finishes, it returns a list, bound to
Result, that, for our system, is:*

```
pair('3330',88) . pair('3350',48) .
     pair('3380',416) . nil
```

```
fin.
```

*stops the interpreter and returns to
the Primary Option Menu.*

In MVS/Prolog, we can do data set I/O in either sequential or partitioned
data sets. MVS/Prolog also manages workspaces and clauses stored via
`bloc_save` in workspace and predicate libraries.

B
Logical Basis
for Prolog and Syllog

Adrian Walker

B.1 MODEL THEORY PROVIDES THE DECLARATIVE VIEW

Throughout this book we have spoken about the declarative and procedural ways of looking at a Prolog program. We have said that, declaratively, a Prolog program without side effects is viewed as a collection of facts and if-then rules that happen to be true about some subject, such as sorting a list. Procedurally, on the other hand, we can figure out step by step how the Prolog interpreter uses the program to sort a list. Both views turn out to be useful. The declarative view can be used to tell us, independently of any particular Prolog interpreter or compiler, exactly what it should be possible to deduce from a program; but the declarative view tells us nothing about how to make these deductions efficiently. As we shall see, in its purest form the declarative view does not even tell us how to make deductions; it just tells us how to *test* whether a statement about a program is true, and is silent about how to find the statement to be tested. On the other hand, the procedural view allows us to reason about efficiency—for example we can use it to find out that generate-and-test is much slower than quicksort—but it is difficult to use the procedural view to say what it should be possible to deduce from a program. There seems to be little rational basis for preferring one person's favorite interpretation procedure over another.

This section describes some of the ideas behind the rather elegant logical basis that is emerging for Prolog. The basis uses *model theory*, in which the idea is that a *model* of a program P is a set M of items such that each relevant instance of each rule and fact of P evaluates to *true* in M. This means that each fact in the program is in the model, and if an instance of the body of a rule is in the model, then so is the corresponding instance of the head of the rule. For example, if P is

```
a <- b.
b.
c <- d.
```

then {a, b} is a model of P but {b} and {a} are not. The set

    {a, b, c, d}

is also a model of P, but it is not a *minimal* model, since it has proper subsets
that are also models. For pure Prolog programs without negation the model
theory has been clear for a number of years. However a model theory for
programs with negation is only just appearing, after a period of considerable
doubt that one could be found at all. Readers may use this section as an
introduction to some of the general results in the research literature. The book
by Lloyd (1984) is a good reference for the model theory of programs without
negation, while some more recent theory for programs with negation is described
by Apt et al. (1986).

    To keep things simple, we shall look only at database-like programs, that is,
at programs without function symbols. So for example we deal with programs
such as

```
a(X,Z) <- a(X,Y) & b(Y,Z).
a(X,Y) <- b(X,Y).

b(1,2).        b(2,1).
```

but not with programs such as

```
tree(t(Left,Node,Right)) <-
    tree(Left) & tree(Right).
tree(empty).
```

or

```
append(nil,L,L).
append(H.T,L,H.U) <- append(T,L,U).
```

(In the append example, the dot is an infix function symbol.)

    If a program has no function symbols, and no built-in predicates, then we
can in principle decide whether or not any item is a consequence of the program.
On the other hand, if there are function symbols present, then it is not in general
possible to make this decision, since this ability would amount to a "solution" to
the famous, and unsolvable, *halting problem*, see e.g Rogers (1967).

    The idea then is to use the declarative view, based on model theory, as an
abstract standard for correctness, and to see how well various procedural
methods (such as a simple Prolog interpreter or a Syllog-like inference engine)
achieve the twin goals of computing exactly what the declarative meaning says
they should and of computing efficiently. Because there are no function symbols
or built-in predicates, it is also reasonable to ask that our inference engines
always stop, rather than sometimes getting into a loop and running forever.

The next section describes the model theory of Prolog programs without negation. Then we look at a model theory for programs with negation. The following section defines a simplified Prolog-like interpreter that can be shown to behave as required by the model theory. However, in keeping the interpreter simple, we have given up some opportunities to make it efficient. A more realistic interpreter is described in the last section.

B.2 LOGICAL BASIS FOR PROLOG WITHOUT NEGATION

As we mentioned, we use model theory as the logical basis for Prolog. Since Prolog without negation (or side effects) can be viewed as a part of mathematical logic, the model theory of Prolog is similar to that of logic. However, because Prolog is only a part of logic, its model theory is particularly simple. We say that a Prolog program without negation (i.e, not containing the symbol ¬) is a *positive program*

Suppose P is a positive program with no function symbols or built-in predicates. The *Herbrand Base* of P is the set

```
H(P) = {q(c1, ..., cn) |
              q is a predicate symbol in P, and
              c1, ..., cn are constants in P     }
```

For example if P is the program

```
a(X,Z) <- a(X,Y) & b(Y,Z).
a(X,Y) <- b(X,Y).

b(1,2).        b(2,3).
```

then

```
H(P) = { a(1,1), a(1,2), a(1,3),
         a(2,1), a(2,2), a(2,3),
         a(3,1), a(3,2), a(3,3),
         b(1,1), b(1,2), b(1,3),
         b(2,1), b(2,2), b(2,3),
         b(3,1), b(3,2), b(3,3) }
```

In general, the Herbrand Base is a very large set (and is infinite if there are function symbols), so we do not use it to compute anything about a program. Rather, it serves as a basis for thinking about the declarative meaning of a program. Intuitively, we shall be looking for a subset of the Herbrand Base that contains all of the facts in a program, and that is as small as possible while maintaining the condition that if it contains the premise of a rule, then it also contains the conclusion.

This can be made more precise by distinguishing between rules that contain variables, and rule instances that only contain constants. The items in the Herbrand base are said to be *ground*, because they do not contain variables.

Likewise, an instance of a rule is ground if it contains no variables. We now need to be able to say when a fact or a rule is *true* in a subset S of the Herbrand base. We define *true* like this.

Suppose S is a subset of H(P).

- A ground literal, such as b(1,2), is *true* in S if it is actually in S.
- A conjunct of literals, such as a(1,2) & b(2,3), is *true* in S if each of its literals is *true* (i.e present) in S.
- A ground instance of a rule, such as

    a(1,3) <- a(1,2) & b(2,3)

    is *true* in S if either the head of the rule is in S, or if the body of the rule is not true in S.
- A rule, such as

    a(X,Z) <- a(X,Y) & b(Y,Z)

    is *true* in S if each of its ground instances is true in S.

Now we can say what it means for something to be a model of a program. A subset M of the Herbrand Base of P is a *model* of P if

- each fact in P is true in M, and
- each rule in P is true in M.

Looking back at our example, it's clear that the Herbrand Base H(P) is a model of P. However, it's not a very satisfactory one, because it contains facts such as a(1,1) that can be removed to form a smaller model. What we want is a *minimal* model, that is a model such that if we remove anything, the result is no longer a model.

It turns out that the models of a positive program have two rather interesting properties:

- the intersection of any two models of a program is also a model of the program, and
- there is just one minimal model of a program, and it is the intersection of all of the models.

To return for a moment to our example, the minimal model of the program above is

$$\{ \ a(1,2), \ a(2,3), \ a(1,3),$$
$$b(1,2), \ b(2,3) \qquad \ \}$$

Although the program has this simple minimal model, corresponding to its declarative meaning, Prolog does not compute the model since it loops on the left recursion in the first rule. In Section B.4, " Further Techniques for Interpreting Knowledge" we shall show that no strictly top down, left-to-right interpreter can compute the models for programs like this, even if provided with a means of terminating loops. However, interpreters that use bottom up information can do so with ease.

B.3   LOGICAL BASIS FOR PROLOG WITH NEGATION

As we have mentioned, Prolog's normal method of arriving at a negation is different from that of mathematical logic. For example, if we say

    p <= ~p

(that is, p is implied by ~p) in ordinary logic, then this is just another way of writing   p or p, which is simply p. In Prolog, if we say

    p <- ¬p

then we are saying that

> p is proved if we cannot prove p,

which is something of a contradiction!

So, since Prolog's way of showing negation is difficult to study, why bother with it? Because Prolog with its strong way of obtaining negation is much more efficient than any known theorem prover for ordinary logic. Also, this strong negation is often a rather simple and useful notation for knowledge.

So let's look again at the problematic program

    p <- ¬p

Let us say that ¬p is true in a set S if p is *absent* from S. Then our model theory chooses the single model {p}, which is satisfactory, although as we mentioned it is difficult to explain why p follows from such a rule.

Let's see how the approach works on another example, namely

    p <- ¬q

The models are {p}, {q}, and {p, q}. The model {p, q} is not minimal, so we are left with the first two. Now we have a problem. We want our model theory to tell us what an interpreter should compute, but here the model theory is ambiguous—it gives us two minimal models. So we can note that there is no fact q, and no rule with q on the left, and use this as a reason for choosing the minimal model {p}.

Now how about the following program?

    p <- ¬q
    q <- ¬p

It has the same minimal models as before, but now there is no asymmetry to help us to choose between them. Worse, when read procedurally it seems to say that

> p can be proved by showing that we cannot prove that we cannot prove p

which is dubious at best.

The interesting thing about this last example is that it has a recursion that goes "through" a negation, from p back to p again. It seems to be difficult to define a meaning for such programs, even when there is only one negation. For example, the program

```
p <- ¬q
q <- p
```

has models {p, q} and {q}. Since {q} is minimal, it is the model we choose, but it is unusual in that the body p of the rule with head q is not in the model. That is, q has no visible means of support in the program!

In practice it is rare to find Prolog programs, or Syllog knowledge bases that contain a recursion through negation. Usually, a predicate that is negated in a higher level of a program is first computed by a lower level, as in

```
t(X,Z) <- r(X,Z) & ¬s(X,Z).

s(X,Z) <- f(X,Y) & s(Y,Z).
s(X,Y) <- f(X,Y).
```

Such a program is stratified into layers, and the lower layers are used as the subject of negation in a higher layer. It turns out that, for these kinds of programs, we can essentially use something like the model theory of positive programs—but we use it one layer at a time. To do this, we need to be able to say more precisely what it means for a program to be stratified, and what it means for a subset of the Herbrand base to be a model of a program containing negation.

It's convenient to speak of the *definition* of an m-place predicate q in a program P as the collection of rules in P with $q(t1, \ldots, tm)$ on the left, where the ti's may be any constants or variables. (For simplicity assume that no predicate has different arities in the same program, although this is actually allowed in Prolog.) Then we can say that a program P is *stratified* if it can be partitioned into layers P1, P2,..., Pn so that

- if a predicate p appears without negation in Pi, then its definition is contained in P1, P2, ..., Pi, and

- if a predicate ¬p appears in Pi, then its definition is contained in P1, P2, ..., Pi-1.

For example, the program

```
t(X,Z) <- r(X,Z) & ¬s(X,Z).

s(X,Z) <- f(X,Y) & s(Y,Z).
s(X,Y) <- f(X,Y).
```

is stratified as P1, P2, where P1 is

```
s(X,Z) <- f(X,Y) & s(Y,Z).
s(X,Y) <- f(X,Y).
```

and P2 is

```
t(X,Z) <- r(X,Z) & ¬s(X,Z).
```

Because of the way stratification is defined, the bottom layer of a program never contains the negation symbol. So we can use our model theory of positive programs directly on the bottom layer. However, for the higher layers, we need to be able to say what it means for a rule with negation to be true in a subset S of the Herbrand base. The idea is that a ground item, such as ¬s(a,b) is true in S if s(a,b) is *absent* from S.

Now we can proceed like this. We want to be able to talk about the items that are relevant to each layer of the program. Obviously, the Herbrand base of a layer is relevant, but that's not all. As a simple example the program

```
a <- ¬b
```

has an empty layer P1, and a layer P2 consisting of the rule a <- ¬b. In a sense, the value of b is defined by (its absence from) P1. So in general we want the base of a layer to consist of its Herbrand base *plus* the Herbrand base of the items that appear negated in the next higher layer. Let us call this augmented base Bi. Then in our simple example, B1 is {b} and B2 is {a}.

Now we can define our model for a program P that is stratified into layers P1, P2, ..., Pn. This is done in stages, by defining the model M(P1) of P1, then the model M(P1,P2) of P1 plus P2, and so on.

- M(P1) is the intersection of the models of P1 (remember, P1 is a positive program).

- M(P1, ..., Pi) is the intersection of the models of P1, ..., Pi, each such model having the property that its intersection with Bi-1 is M(P1, ..., Pi-1), that is the model of the layers below.

Then the model of P is just the model M(P1, ..., Pn) of all of the layers of P.

As an example, the program

```
t(X,Z) <- r(X,Z) & ¬s(X,Z).

s(X,Z) <- f(X,Y) & s(Y,Z).
s(X,Y) <- f(X,Y).

f(a,b). f(b,c). r(a,c). r(c,a).
```

can be stratified into the layers P1

```
s(X,Z) <- f(X,Y) & s(Y,Z).
s(X,Y) <- f(X,Y).

f(a,b). f(b,c). r(a,c). r(c,a).
```

and P2

```
t(X,Z) <- r(X,Z) & ¬s(X,Z).
```

For the first layer P1, the model M(P1) is

```
{f(a,b), f(b,c), r(a,c), r(c,a),
 s(a,b), s(b,c), s(a,c)            }
```

and for the second layer P2, M(P1, P2) is

```
{f(a,b), f(b,c), r(a,c), r(c,a),
 s(a,b), s(b,c), s(a,c), t(c,a) }
```

that is, M(P1) plus t(c,a).

So now we know how to assign a model to a stratified program. If the program has no function symbols, and uses no built-in predicates, then the model is a finite set that describes exactly the conclusions we would like to be able to draw. However the process for constructing a model goes via the Herbrand base, which is in general a very large set, so this process is not actually of practical use for making deductions. Rather, the model tells us what we would like our more efficient methods to compute. If an interpreter computes everything in the model of any program, then it said to be *complete*; if it computes only items in the model, then it is said to be *sound*. Often, as in the case of Prolog, we are content to sacrifice some completeness to gain efficiency. In the next section, we look at some techniques for regaining some completeness (i.e, for executing more programs correctly) while keeping as much efficiency as we can.

B.4   FURTHER TECHNIQUES FOR INTERPRETING KNOWLEDGE

In the past two sections, we looked at a model theory that says what a program (possibly including negation) should compute. For simplicity, we are just looking at programs that are *database-like*, in the sense that they contain no function symbols, and no built-in predicates. By excluding function symbols, we avoid the possibility that a program can make arbitrarily large data structures. By excluding built-in predicates, we avoid infinite domains, such as the integers that can be generated by calling sum(X,Y,Z) in a recursive loop. Clearly these restrictions can be relaxed a bit while maintaining finite domains, but they serve to simplify the discussion. As mentioned above, an interpreter is *complete* if it produces all of the items in the model of a each program. Prolog is efficient for many database-like programs, but it is not complete on all of them. For example, the program

```
a(X,Z) <- a(X,Y) & b(Y,Z).
a(X,Y) <- b(X,Y).

b(1,2).        b(2,1).
```

has the model

```
{ a(1,1), a(1,2), a(2,1),
    a(2,2), b(1,2), b(2,1) }
```

but from Prolog we can only get the b consequences. Any goal of the form

```
a(X,Y)
```

sends the system into a loop, so no answer is given (usually just an error message).

We can change the program to another one

```
a(X,Y) <- b(X,Y).
a(X,Z) <- b(X,Y) & a(Y,Z).

b(1,2).        b(2,1).
```

that has the same model. Now things are better. If we ask about each of the items in the model, each is confirmed by Prolog. But we are not out of the woods yet. If we ask a(1,3), then the Prolog interpreter loops, whereas we would like it to terminate with a failure to indicate that the answer is "no." More generally, we would like to be able to ask for the set of pairs (X,Y) such that a(X,Y) holds, and have the system stop and return just the four answers in the model of the program.

For both of the above programs, the problem is caused by the fact that in evaluating some goal Prolog reaches the same goal again. Once this happens, the system is in a loop. So our first approach for getting the behavior we want is to see if we can "trap" such loops by looking to see if the current goal has itself as an ancestor. Sometimes this is a useful thing to do in specific Prolog programs. However, it turns out that no method that relies only on looking upward at the partial proof tree developed by Prolog can ever be complete, even for our database-like programs.

To see this, we can think about a family of programs Pn of the form:

```
a(X,Z) <- a(X,Y) & b(Y,Z).
a(X,Y) <- b(X,Y).

b(1,2).    b(2,3).    .... b(n,n+1).
```

The idea here is that P2 has just the facts b(1,2) and b(2,3); P3 has in addition b(3,4), and so on. Declaratively, the program says that a is the transitive closure of b; for example a(1,3) is in the minimal model of P2. Now suppose we are executing some Pn top down, left to right, to find some X and Z such that a(X,Z). We start with the goal

```
a(X,Z)
```

Applying the first rule replaces the goal with the new goal

```
a(X,Y1) & b(Y1,Z)
```

Applying the first rule again gives us

```
a(X,Y2) & b(Y2,Y1) & b(Y1,Z)
```

After m steps we shall have

```
a(X,Ym) & b(Ym,Ym-1) & ... & b(Y2,Y1) & b(Y1,Z)
```

Now suppose we stop applying the first rule, based on some properties of the top down process we have been using. (We must stop sometime, else we are in a loop.) Then we can apply the second rule to get

```
b(X,Ym) & b(Ym,Ym-1) & ... & b(Y2,Y1) & b(Y1,Z)
```

This allows us to conclude a(1,m+2), but not a(1,m+3). So, for large enough n, *any* loop trapping mechanism that uses information only about the rules in Pn must miss some of the answers in the minimal model. That is, any purely top down loop trapping technique is incomplete. For a more formal version of this argument, see Brough and Walker (1984).

So it seems that if we want to compute the minimal model of a program (even of just a positive database like program), and we want to do so in a Prolog style, then we cannot do so in a way that uses only information about the rules. Somehow we must use information about the facts too. We can start with a Prolog-like interpreter, such as this one.

```
demo(G) <- set_of(G, d(G), As) & write(As).

d(A & B) <- / & d(A) & d(B).
d(¬A) <- / & ¬d(A).
d(A) <- ax(A,A,fact).
d(A) <- ax(A,A<-B,rule) &
        d(B).
```

When run with a goal such as demo(a(X,Z)), this interpreter tries to compute all of the pairs (X,Z) for which a(X,Z) is true. However, it will loop on programs such as P2. To stop it looping, we can have it keep track of the goals it has tried, and we can prevent it from trying a goal repeatedly:

```
demo(G) <- set_of(G, d(G, nil), As) & write(As).

d(A & B, S) <- / & d(A, S) & d(B, S).
d(¬A, S) <- / & ¬d(A, S).
d(A, *) <- ax(A, A, fact).
d(A, S) <- ax(A, A<-B, rule) &
            ¬stack_member_check(A, S) &
            d(B, A.S).
```

This is like the last interpreter, except that d now has a second argument that works as a *goal stack*, in which it keeps a record of the goals leading to the current goal. We could define stack_member_check in several ways, for example

```
stack_member_check(X, Y.*) <- X==Y & /.
stack_member_check(X, *.Y) <-
    stack_member_check(X, Y).
```

which uses the IBM Prolog predicate == that tests whether two goals are literally the same. Unfortunately, this will still loop on P2, since the goals a(X,Y1), a(X,Y2) and so on never repeat! On the other hand, replacing == by IBM Prolog's =, which tests whether the goals are unifiable, is too strong. In fact, as we have argued, there is no test (however elaborate) that will serve our purposes here—we must somehow make use of the facts, and we must try to do so efficiently.

Since we cannot decide correctly whether two uninstantiated goals are the same (for purposes of loop trapping), our next step is to instantiate the goals, using constants from the facts:

```
demo(G) <- set_of(G, d(G, nil), As) & write(As).

d(A & B, S) <- / & d(A, S) & d(B, S).
d(¬A, S) <- / & ¬d(A, S).
d(A, *) <- ax(A, A, fact).
d(A, S) <- ax(A, A<-B, rule) &
            ground(A<-B) &
            ¬stack_member_check(A, S) &
            d(B, A.S).
```

This interpreter is like the last one, but we have added the predicate ground. The effect of ground(A<-B) is to bind any variables in the rule A<-B to constants in the facts in the program. (Actually it is only necessary to ground the variables in A.) This binding is done nondeterministically. Effectively we are saying that instead of computing with the rules as given, we shall compute with ground instances of the rules.

Now we are using information from the facts as well as the rules. It can be shown that this approach is correct for database like programs with negation allowed, that is, the set of items that can be established using demo is the model of the program being interpreted. Apt et al. (1986) give a formal proof of this. However although the interpreter is correct, and runs well on examples with just a few facts, it is not efficient enough to be of practical interest in general. Its main interest lies in the fact that it is simple enough that we can actually prove that it is correct.

We have looked at a very simple technique for making sure that the information needed to terminate a computation reached the rules from the facts—namely, we just use ground instances of the rules. This has the virtue that it is relatively easily to formalize such an interpreter so that it can be proved to be complete and sound, that is to say correct. However, the interpreter, which we shall call the ABW interpreter, is not efficient enough to be of general practical interest. Our next step is a slightly more complicated interpreter that also has the virtue of being more efficient, though still not efficient enough for general use on large Prolog programs. We shall call it the EPW interpreter, for it is based on a parsing algorithm by Earley (1968) adapted by Pereira and Warren (1983) to form an interpreter.

In the ABW interpreter, we made each rule ground before using it. In the EPW approach, the idea is to keep a collection of partly grounded rules called the `state` of the interpreter. In fact we also keep *fragments* of partly grounded rules in the state, as we shall see in a moment. Intuitively, the ABW approach is backchaining, while the EPW method interleaves backchaining and forward chaining. EPW is rather different from the Backchain Iteration method, which we described in Section 4.2.3, "Inside the Syllog Shell."

There are two basic steps in EPW, called *instantiation* (which we can think of as backchaining) and *reduction* (which we can think of as forward chaining).

- Instantiation: if `A <- B & Bs` is in the state, `C <- Ds` is a rule in the program being interpreted, and B and C can be unified (made the same) by a substitution `f`, then add `f(C <- D)` to the state.

- Reduction: if `A <- B & Bs` is in the state, C is a fact either in the program being interpreted or in the state, and B and C can be unified (made the same) by a substitution `f`, then add `f(A <- Bs)` to the state.

In

    A <- B & Bs

B is the first goal in the body of the rule, and Bs are the remaining goals. For convenience we shall write `true` in place of Bs when there are no remaining goals. EPW stops when neither instantiation nor reduction can add anything to the state.

Both instantiation and reduction add an item to the state. In fact, it is not necessary to add the item if it is already in the state, or if it is a special case of an item in the state.

To get an idea of how EPW works, we can try it on a simple program:

    a(X,Z) <- a(X,Y) & b(Y,Z).
    a(X,Y) <- b(X,Y).

    b(1,2).   b(2,3).

To simplify what comes next we can rewrite the two rules as

    a(X,Z) <- a(X,Y) & b(Y,Z) & true()
    a(X,Y) <- b(X,Y) & true()

Now suppose our goal is to find all of the (X,Y) pairs such that a(X,Y). Then we can start with the state containing just one "dummy" rule

    a(X,Y) <- a(X,Y) & true() .

that starts the EPW process. In the first round of instantiation, the dummy rule causes the two rules of the program (above) to be added. Then reduction of

```
a(X,Y) <- b(X,Y) & true()
```

using the two facts adds

```
a(1,2) <- true()
a(2,3) <- true()
```

The state is now

```
a(1,2) <- true() .
a(2,3) <- true() .

a(X,Z) <- a(X,Y) & b(Y,Z) & true() .
a(X,Y) <- b(X,Y) & true() .

a(X,Y) <- a(X,Y) & true() .
```

In the next round, there are no instantiations, but the rule `a(X,Z)  <- a(X,Y) & b(Y,Z) & true()` reduces with `a(1,2) <- true()`, adding `a(1,V1) <- b(2,V1) & true()` to the state. In the final round, this is reduced by the fact `b(2,3)` to `a(1,3) <- true()`. The final state is

```
a(1,3) <- true() .

a(1,X) <- b(2,X) & true() .
a(2,X) <- b(3,X) & true() .

a(1,2) <- true() .
a(2,3) <- true() .

a(X,Z) <- a(X,Y) & b(Y,Z) & true() .
a(X,Y) <- b(X,Y) & true() .

a(X,Y) <- a(X,Y) & true() .
```

The answer consists of the three items in the state with `true()` on the right, namely `a(1,2)`, `a(2,3)`, and `a(1,3)`.

In our outline of the two basic steps in EPW interpretation, *instantiation* and *reduction*, we did not say how to choose which step to do next. In fact, the basic EPW idea can be programmed in many different ways, some of them more efficient than others. Here we shall just look at a simple EPW interpreter that does as many instantiations as it can, then as many reductions as it can, then repeats the whole process as long as new items are being added to the state.

To find all of the answers to a question Q, our EPW interpreter first sets up a state consisting of `(Q<-Q&true()).nil`, then applies instantiation and reduction repeatedly until they produce no change in the state. The answer is then those instances of Q such that `Q<-true()` is in the final state:

```
demo(Q) <-
    epw((Q<-Q&true()).nil, S) &
    set_of(Q, member(Q<-true(), S), Ans) &
    write(answer=Ans).

epw(S1, S4) <-
    instantiate(S1, S2) & reduce(S2, S3) &
    S1=/S3 & epw(S3, S4).
epw(S, S).

instantiate(S1, S2) <-
    set_of(B<-C, member(A<-B&Bs, S1) &
                 ax(B, B<-C, rule) &
                 ¬mem(B<-C, S1),
                         Is) &
    append(Is, S1, S2).

reduce(S1, S2) <-
    set_of(A<-Bs, member(A<-B&Bs, S1) &
                  (member(B<-true(), S1) |
                   ax(B, B<-true(), fact)) &
                  ¬mem(A<-Bs, S1),
                          Rs) &
    append(Rs, S1, S2).
```

In the instantiation and reduction steps, we used a predicate mem to check whether something we are about to add to the state is already there. In fact, mem is defined to also say that an item is in the state if something more general is in the state—for example it will say that p(b)<-q(b,X) is already in a state containing p(Y)<-q(Y,X). The definition of mem is

```
mem(X, Y.Ys) <- mg(Y, X) | X=*=Y.
mem(X, *.Ys) <- mem(X, Ys).
```

It uses a predicate mg(U,V) that decides whether U is more general than V.

```
mg(U,V) <- copy(U,UU) & copy(V,VV) & UU=VV &
    V=*=VV & ¬(U=*=UU).
```

It's interesting note that although we talk about adding items to the state of the EPW interpreter, there is no use of addax to modify the program. We are following the good Prolog programming practice of carrying information in the arguments of predicates where feasible. Thus the predicate epw changes state S1 to S2 using instantiate, then to S3 using reduce. If S3 is different from S1, then epw calls itself recursively to produce another state S4. Otherwise, the second rule for epw is used to terminate the interpretation and return the final state.

Bibliography

1. Aho, A. V. & J. D. Ullman (1979) "Universality of data retrieval languages," *Proceedings 6th Annual Symposium on Princinciples of Programming Languages*, Association for Computing Machinery, New York, 110-119.

2. Apt, K. R., H. Blair & A. Walker (1986) *Towards a Theory of Declarative Knowledge*, report RC 11681, IBM T. J. Watson Research Center, New York.

3. Apt, K. R. & M. H. van Emden (1982) "Contributions to the theory of logic programming," *Journal of the Association for Computing Machinery*, Vol. 29, No. 3, 841-862.

4. Bancilhon, F. & R. Ramakrishnan (1986) *An amateur's introduction to recursive query processing strategies*, unpublished manuscript.

5. Barwise, J. & J. Perry (1983) *Situations and Attitudes*, MIT Press, Cambridge, Massachusetts.

6. Bloch, C. (1984) *Source-to-Source Transformations of Logic Programs*, report, Department of Applied Mathematics, Weizmann Institute of Science, Rehovot, Israel.

7. Bowen, D., L. Byrd, F. Pereira, L. Pereira & D. H. D. Warren (1982) *DECsystem-10 Prolog User's Manual*, University of Edinburgh, Department of Artificial Intelligence.

8. Bowen K. A. & R. A. Kowalski (1982) "Amalgamating language and metalanguage in logic programming" In: *Logic Programming*, K. L. Clark & S. A. Tarnlund eds., Academic Press, New York, 153-172.

9. Brough, D. & A. Walker (1984) "Some practical properties of logic programming interpreters," *Proceedings Japan FGCS84 Conference*, Institute for New Generation Computer Technology, Tokyo, 149-156.

10. Brownston, L., R. Farrell, E. Kant & N. Martin (1985) *Programming Expert Systems in OPS5: An Introduction to Rule-based Programming*, Addison-Wesley, Reading, Massachusetts.

11. Buchanan, B. & R. Duda (1982) *Principles of Rule-Based Expert Systems*, report STAN-CS-82-926, Department of Computer Science, Stanford University, Stanford, California.

12. Buchanan, B. & E. Feigenbaum (1978) "Dendral and Meta-Dendral: their applications dimension," *Artificial Intelligence*, Vol. 11, 5-24.

13. Buchanan, B. & E. Shortliffe (1984) *Rule-Based Expert Systems*, Addison-Wesley, Reading, Massachusetts.

14. Bundy, A., L. Byrd & C. S. Mellish (1982) "Special-purpose, but domain-independent, inference mechanisms" In: *Progress in Artificial Intelligence*, L. Steels & J. Campbell eds. Ellis Horwood, 1985.

15. Bundy, A. & B. Welham (1981) "Using meta-level inference for selective application of multiple rewrite rules in algebraic manipulation," *Artificial Intelligence*, Vol. 16, 189-212.

16. Chang, C. L. & A. Walker (1986) "Prosql: A Prolog programming interface with SQL/DS" In: *Expert Database Systems*, L. Kerschberg ed., Benjamin/Cummins, Menlo Park, California, 233-246.

17. Clark, K. (1978) "Negation as failure" In: *Logic and Databases*, H. Gallaire & J. Minker eds., Plenum, New York, 293-322.

18. Clocksin W. F. & C. S. Mellish (1981) *Programming in Prolog*, Springer-Verlag, New York.

19. Codd E. F. (1971) "Relational completeness of data base sublanguages" In: *Courant Computer Science Symposium 6: Data Base Systems*, Prentice-Hall, Englewood Cliffs, New Jersey, 65-98.

20. Coelho H., J. C. Cotta & L. M. Pereira (1980) *How to Solve it with Prolog*, University of Lisbon, Lisbon, Portugal.

21. Colmerauer, A. (1975) *Les Grammaires de Metamorphose*, internal report, Groupe d'Intelligence Artificielle, Univ. d'Aix-Marseille, Luminy, France.

22. Colmerauer, A. (1978) "Metamorphosis grammars" In: *Natural Language Communication with Computers*, Lecture Notes in Computer Science, L. Bolc ed., Springer-Verlag, New York, 133-189.

23. Colmerauer, A. (1979) "Un sous-ensemble interessant du francais," *RAIRO Informatique Theorique*, Vol. 13, 309-336.

24. Colmerauer, A. (1982) "An interesting subset of natural language" In: *Logic Programming*, K. L. Clark & S.-A. Tärnlund eds., Academic Press, London.

25. Colmerauer, A., H. Kanoui, R. Pasero & P. Roussel (1972) *Une Systeme de Communication en Francais*, internal report, Groupe d'Intelligence Artificielle, Univ. d'Aix-Marseille, Luminy, France.

26. Dahl, V. (1977) *Un Systeme Deductif d'Interrogation de Banques de Donnees en Espagnol*, Doctoral Thesis, Univ. d'Aix-Marseille, Luminy, France.

27. Dahl, V. & M. C. McCord (1983) "Treating coordination in logic grammars," *American Journal of Computational Linguistics*, Vol. 9, 69-91.

28. Date C. J. (1977) *An Introduction to Database Systems*, Addison-Wesley, Reading, Massachusetts.

29. Davis, R. (1984) "Interactive transfer of expertise" In: *Rule-Based Expert Systems*, B. Buchanan & E. Shortliffe eds., Addison-Wesley, Reading, Massachusetts, 171-205.

30. de Callatay, A. M. (1985) *Intelligent Processor Systems Compared to the Human Brain*, Elsevier, Amsterdam.

31. Duda, R., J. Gaschnig & P. Hart (1979) "Model design in the prospector consultant system for mineral exploration" In: *Expert Systems for the Microelectronic Age*, D. Michie ed., Edinburgh Press, 153-167.

32. Dwork, C., P. Kanellakis & J. Mitchel (1984) "On the sequential nature of unification," *The Journal of Logic Programming*, Vol. 1, No. 1, 35-50.

33. Earley, J. (1968) *An Efficient Context-Free Parsing Algorithm*, Ph.D. Thesis, Carnegie-Mellon University, Pittsburgh. Also see *Communications of the Association for Computing Machinery*, Vol. 13, No. 2, 1970, 94-102.

34. Emde, W., C. U. Habel & C.-R. Rollinger (1983) "The discovery of the equator, or concept driven learning," *Proceedings of the International Joint Conference on Artificial Intelligence, Karlsruhe, W. Germany*, William Kaufmann, Los Altos, California, 455-458.

35. Fagin, R., G. M. Kuper, J. D. Ullman & M. Y. Vardi (1986) "Updating logical databases" In: *Advances in Computing Research*, Vol. 3, Paris C. Kanellakis ed., JAI Press Inc., Greenwich Connecticut, 1-18.

36. Feigenbaum, E. A. & P. McCorduck (1983) *The Fifth Generation*, Addison-Wesley, Reading, Massachusetts.

37. Fellenstein, C., C. O. Green, L. M. Palmer, A. Walker & D. J. Wyler (1985) "A prototype manufacturing knowledge base in Syllog," *IBM Journal of Research and Development*, Vol. 29, No. 4, 413-421.

38. Fikes, R. & T. Kehler (1985) "The role of frame-based representation in reasoning," *Communications of the Association for Computing Machinery*, Vol. 28, No. 9, 904-920.

39. Forgy, C. L. (1981) *OPS5 User's Manual*, report CMU-CS-81-135, Department of Computer Science, Carnegie-Mellon University, Pittsburgh.

40. Furukawa, K., R. Nakajima & A. Yonezawa (1983) *Modularization and Abstraction in Logic Programming*, technical report TR-022, ICOT, Institute for New Generation Computer Technology, Tokyo, Japan.

41. Goldberg, A. & D. Robson (1983) *Smalltalk-80: The Language and its Implementation*, Addison-Wesley, Reading, Massachusetts.

42. Green, C. (1969) "Application of theorem proving to problem solving," *Proceedings of the First International Joint Conference on Artificial Intelligence*, 219-239.

43. Griesmer, J. H., S. J. Hong, M. Karnaugh, J. K. Kastner, M. I. Schor, R. L. Ennis, D. A. Klein, K. R. Milliken & H. M. VanWoerkom (1984) "YES/MVS: A continuous real time expert system," *Proceedings of the National Conference on Artificial Intelligence, Austin, Texas*, William Kaufmann, Los Altos, California, 130-136.

44. Hayes, B. (1984) "On the ups and downs of Hailstone numbers," *Scientific American*, Vol. 250, No. 1, 10-16.

45. Hewitt, C. (1977) "Viewing control structures as patterns of passing messages," *Artificial Intelligence*, Vol. 8.

46. Hirsch, P., M. Meier, S. Snyder & R. Stillman (1985) "PRISM: Prototype inference system," *AFIPS Conference Proceedings 54*, 121-124.

47. Hirsch, P., M. Meier, S. Snyder & R. Stillman (1986) "Interfaces for knowledge builders' control knowledge and application-specific procedures," *IBM Journal of Research and Development*, Vol. 30, No. 1, 29-38.

48. Hoare, C. A. R. (1962) "Quicksort," *Computer Journal*, Vol. 5, No. 1, 10-15

49. Hobbs, J. (1978) "Resolving pronoun references," *Lingua*, Vol. 44, 311-338.

50. IBM (1985) *VM/Programming in Logic*, IBM document SH20-6541.

51. IBM (1986) *MVS/Programming in Logic*, IBM document SH40-0030.

52. ICOT (1981) *Proceedings of the International Conference on Fifth Generation Computer Systems*, Institute for New Generation Computer Technology, Tokyo, Japan.

53. ICOT (1984) *Proceedings of the International Conference on Fifth Generation Computer Systems*, Institute for New Generation Computer Technology, Tokyo, Japan.

54. Jaffar, J., J. -L. Lassez & J. Lloyd (1983) "Completeness of the negation as failure rule," *Proceedings of the International Joint Conference on Artificial Intelligence, Karlsruhe, W. Germany*, William Kaufmann, Los Altos, California, 500-506.

55. Kitakami, H., S. Kunifuji, T. Miyachi & K. Furukawa (1984) "A methodology for implementation of a knowledge acquisition system," *Proceedings of the International Symposium on Logic Programming*, Atlantic City NJ, 131-142.

56. Knuth, D. (1973) *The Art of Computer Programming, Vol. 3, Sorting and Searching*, Addison-Wesley, Reading, Massachusetts.

57. Knuth, D. & L. Moore. (1975) "Analysis of alpha-beta pruning," *Artificial Intelligence*, Vol. 6, No. 1, 293-326

58. Komorowski, H.J. (1981) *A Specification of an Abstract Prolog Machine and its Application to Partial Evaluation*, Dissertation No. 69, Software Systems Research Center, Linkoping University, Sweden.

59. Kowalski, R. A. (1974) "Predicate logic as a programming language" In: *Proceedings IFIP 74*, North Holland Publishing Co., Amsterdam, 569-574.

60. Kowalski, R. A. (1975) *Journal of the Association for Computing Machinery*, Vol. 22, No. 4, 572-595.

61. Kowalski, R. A. (1979) *Logic for Problem Solving*, North-Holland.

62. Kowalski R. A. & M. Sergot. (1985) *A Logic-based Calculus of Events*, report, Department of Computing, Imperial College, London.

63. Lassez, J.-L. & M. Maher (1983) "The denotational semantics of Horn clauses as a production system," *Proceedings of AAAI Conference Washington D.C.*, William Kaufmann, Los Altos, California, 229-231.

64. Lenat, D. B. (1983) "The role of heuristics in learning by discovery: three case studies" In: *Machine Learning*, R. S. Michalski, J. G. Carbonell & T. M. Mitchell eds., Tioga Publishing Co., Palo Alto, California, 243-306.

65. Lewis, D. (1975). "Adverbs of quantification" In: E.L. Keenan ed., *Formal Semantics of Natural Language*, Cambridge University Press.

66. Lloyd, J. W. (1984) *Foundations of Logic Programming*, Springer-Verlag, New York.

67. Matsumoto, Y., H. Tanaka & M. Kiyono (1986) "BUP: A bottom-up parsing system for natural languages" In: *Logic Programming and its Applications*, M. van Caneghem & D. H. D. Warren eds., Ablex, Norwood, New Jersey, 262-275.

68. McCarthy, J. (1980) "Circumscription—a form of non-monotonic reasoning," *Artificial Intelligence*, Vol. 13, 27-39.

69. McCarthy, J., P. W. Abrahams, D. J. Edwards, T. P. Hart & M. I. Levin (1962) *Lisp 1.5 Programmer's Manual*, MIT Press, Cambridge, Massachusetts.

70. McCord, M. C. (1981) *Focalizers, the Scoping Problem, and Semantic Interpretation Rules in Logic Grammars*, technical report, University of Kentucky, Lexington. Appeared in: *Logic Programming and its Applications*, M. van Caneghem & D. H. D. Warren eds., Ablex, Norwood, New Jersey, 1986.

71. McCord, M. C. (1982a) "Using slots and modifiers in logic grammars for natural language," *Artificial Intelligence*, Vol. 18, 327-367.

72. McCord, M. C. (1982b) *LP: A Prolog Interpreter Written in LISP*, technical report 85-82, Computer Sciences Department, University of Kentucky, Lexington.

73. McCord, M. C. (1984) "Semantic interpretation for the EPISTLE system," *Proceedings of the Second International Logic Programming Conference*, Uppsala, Sweden, 65-76.

74. McCord, M. C. (1985a) "Modular Logic Grammars," *Proceedings 23rd Annual Meeting of the Association for Computational Linguistics*, Chicago, 104-117.

75. McCord, M. C. (1985b) "Semantics of natural language: LFL," Presentation at IBM Europe Institute, Oberlech, Austria, July 1985.

76. McCord, M. C. (1985c) "LMT: A Prolog-based machine translation system" (extended abstract), In: Nirenburg, S. ed., *Proceedings of the Conference on Theoretical and Methodological Issues in Machine Translation of Natural Languages*, Colgate University, Hamilton, 179-182.

77. McCord, M. C. (1986) "Design of a Prolog-based machine translation system," *Proceedings of the Third International Logic Programming Conference*, London, July 1986.

78. McDermott, J. (1982) "R1: a rule-based configurer of computer systems," *Artificial Intelligence*, Vol. 19, 39-88.

79. Michalski, R. S. & R. L. Chilausky (1980) "Learning by being told and learning from examples: an experimental comparison of the two methods of knowledge acquisition in the context of developing an expert system for soybean disease diagnosis," *Policy Analysis and Information Systems*, Vol. 4, No. 2.

80. Michie, D. (1982) "Game playing programs and the conceptual interface," *Association for Computing Machinery Sigart Newsletter*, No. 80, 64-70.

81. Minsky, M. (1975) "A framework for representing knowledge" In: P. H. Winston ed., *The Psychology of Computer Vision*, McGraw-Hill, New York.

82. Mitchell, T. M. (1978) *Version Spaces: an Approach to Concept Learning*, Doctoral Thesis, Department of Computer Science, Stanford University, Stanford, California.

83. Mitchell, T. M., P. Utgoff & R. Banerji (1983) "Learning by experimentation: acquiring and refining problem-solving heuristics" In: *Machine Learning*, R. S. Michalski, J. G. Carbonell & T. M. Mitchell eds., Tioga Publishing Co., Palo Alto, California, 163-190.

84. Moore, R. C. (1975) *Reasoning from Incomplete Knowledge in a Procedural Deduction System*, Master's Thesis, MIT, Cambridge, Massachusetts.

85. Neumann, G. (1986) *Meta-Interpreter Directed Compilation of Logic Programs into Prolog*, report RC 12113, IBM T. J. Watson Research Center, New York.

86. Newell, A., J. C. Shaw & H. A. Simon (1963) "Empirical explorations with the logic theory machine: a case study in heuristics" In: *Computers and Thought*, E. A. Feigenbaum & J. Feldman eds., McGraw-Hill, New York, 109-133.

87. Newell, A. & H. A. Simon (1963) "GPS, a program that simulates human thought" In: *Computers and Thought*, E. A. Feigenbaum and J. Feldman eds., McGraw-Hill, New York, 279-293.

88. Newell, A. & H. A. Simon (1972) *Human Problem Solving*, Prentice-Hall, Englewood Cliffs, NJ.

89. Nilsson, N. (1980) *Principles of Artificial Intelligence*, Tioga Publishing Co., Palo Alto, California.

90. Pearl, J. (1984) *Heuristics, Intelligent Search Strategies for Computer Problem Solving*, Addison-Wesley, Reading, Massachusetts.

91. Pereira, F. (1981) "Extraposition grammars," *American Journal of Computational Linguistics*, Vol. 7, 243-256.

92. Pereira, F. (1983) *Logic for Natural Language Analysis*, technical note 275, SRI International, Menlo Park, California.

93. Pereira, F. & Warren, D. H. D. (1980) "Definite clause grammars for language analysis - a survey of the formalism and a comparison with transition networks," *Artificial Intelligence*, Vol. 13, 231-278.

94. Pereira, F. & Warren, D. H. D. (1983) "Parsing as deduction," *Proceedings 21st Annual Meeting of the Association for Computational Linguistics*, Cambridge, Massachusetts, 137-144.

95. Pereira, L. M., F. C. M. Pereira & D. H. D. Warren (1978) *User's Guide to Decsystem-10 Prolog*, occasional paper No. 15, Department of Artificial Intelligence, University of Edinburgh.

96. Quinlan, J. R. (1983) "Learning efficient classification procedures and their application to chess end games" In: *Machine Learning*, R. S. Michalski, J. G. Carbonell & T. M. Mitchell eds., Tioga Publishing Co., Palo Alto, California, 463-482.

97. Raphael, B. (1976) *The Thinking Computer*, Freeman, San Francisco.

98. Reinhart, T. (1985) *Anaphora and Semantic Interpretation*, University of Chicago Press.

99. Robinson, J. A. (1979) *Logic: Form and Function*, North Holland, New York.

100. Robinson, J. A. (1965) "A machine oriented logic based on the resolution principle," *Journal of the Association for Computing Machinery*, Vol. 12, 23-41.

101. Rogers H. (1967) *Theory of Recursive Functions and Effective Computability*, McGraw-Hill, New York.

102. Roussel, P. (1975) *Prolog: Manuel de Reference et d'Utilisation*, Groupe d'Intelligence Artificiel, Universite d'Aix-Marseille, Luminy, France.

103. Saint-Dizier, P. (1986) "An approach to natural language semantics in logic programming," *Journal of Logic Programming*, in press.

104. Schank, R. C. & C. K. Riesbeck (1981) *Inside Computer Understanding*, Lawrence Erlbaum, New Jersey.

105. Sergot, M. (1982) *A Query-the-user Facility for Logic Programming*, report, Department of Computing, Imperial College, London.

106. Shapiro, E. (1983) *Agorithmic Program Debugging*, MIT Press, Cambridge, Massachusetts.

107. Shapiro, E. & A. Takeuchi (1983) "Object oriented programming in concurrent Prolog," *New Generation Computing*, Vol. 1, No. 1, 25-48.

108. Simon, H. A. (1983) "Why should machines learn?" In: *Machine Learning*, R. S. Michalski, J. G. Carbonell & T. M. Mitchell eds., Tioga Publishing Co., Palo Alto, California, 25-37.

109. Sowa, J. (1984) *Conceptual Structures: Information Processing in Mind and Machine*, Addison-Wesley, Reading, Massachusetts.

110. Stefik, M., D. G. Bobrow, S. Mittal & L. Conway (1983) "Knowledge programming in loops: report on an experimental course," *The Artificial Intelligence Magazine*, Fall issue, 3-13.

111. Suwa, M., A. C. Scott & E. H. Shortliffe (1984) "Completeness and consistency in a rule-based system" In: *Rule-Based Expert Systems*, B. Buchanan & E. Shortliffe eds. Addison-Wesley, Reading, Massachusetts, 159-170.

112. Takeuchi, A. & K. Furukawa (1985) *Partial Evaluation of Prolog Programs and its Application to Meta-Programming*, technical report TR-126, ICOT, Institute for New Generation Computer Technology, Tokyo, Japan.

113. Ullman, J. D. (1980) *Principles of Database Systems*, Computer Science Press, Potomac, Maryland.

114. van Emden, M. H. (1979) "Relational programming illustrated by a program for the game of Mastermind," *Computer Languages and Computational Linguistics*, October 1979.

115. van Emden, M. H. & R. A. Kowalski (1976) "The semantics of predicate logic as a programming language," *Journal of the Association for Computing Machinery*, Vol. 23, No. 4, 733-742.

116. Walker, A. (1977) *On the induction of a decision making system from a database*, report CBM-TR-80, Department of Computer Science, Rutgers University, New Brunswick, New Jersey.

117. Walker, A. (1980) "On Retrieval from a small version of a large data base," *Proceedings Sixth International Conference on Very Large Data Bases*, Montreal, Canada, 47-54.

118. Walker, A. (1981) *Syllog: a Knowledge Based Data Management System*, report No. 34, Department of Computer Science, New York University, New York.

119. Walker, A. (1982) *Automatic Generation of Explanations of Results from Knowledge Bases*, report RJ 3481, IBM Research Laboratory, San Jose, California.

120. Walker, A. (1983) "Prolog/Ex1, an inference engine which explains both yes and no answers," *Proceedings of the International Joint Conference on Artificial Intelligence, Karlsruhe, W. Germany*, William Kaufmann, Los Altos, California, 526-528.

121. Walker, A. (1984) "Data bases, expert systems, and Prolog" In: *Artificial Intelligence Applications for Business*, Ablex, Norwood, New Jersey, 87-109.

122. Walker, A. (1986) "Syllog: an approach to Prolog for non-programmers" In: *Logic Programming and its Applications*, M. van Caneghem & D. H. D. Warren eds., Ablex, Norwood, New Jersey, 32-49.

123. Walker, A. & A. Porto. (1983) *KBO1: A knowledge based garden store assistant*, report RJ 3928, IBM Research Laboratory, San Jose, California.

124. Walker, A. & S. Salveter (1981) *Automatic Modification of Transactions to Preserve Database Integrity without Undoing Updates*, technical report 81/026, Department of Computer Science, State University of New York at Stony Brook, New York.

125. Warren, D. H. D. (1981) "Efficient processing of interactive relational database queries expressed in logic," *Proceedings International Conference on Very Large Data Bases*, 272-281.

126. Warren, D. S. (1984) *Database Updates in Pure Prolog*, technical report 84/073, Department of Computer Science, State University of New York at Stony Brook, New York.

127. Weizenbaum J. (1966) "ELIZA—A computer program for the study of natural language communication between men and machines," *Communications of the Association for Computing Machinery*, Vol. 9, 36-45.

128. Weizenbaum J. (1976) *Computer Power and Human Reason*, Freeman, San Francisco.

129. Winograd, T. (1972) *Understanding Natural Language*, Academic Press, New York.

Author Index

Subject Index